'Inclusive education, in my opinion, is in an intellectual rut, with little new that pushes the field forward. A book like this has the potential to shift the conversation in significant ways and to introduce novel ideas into the field. The international reach of the book is good, offering perspectives from the Global North and South. This is an ambitious volume and the editors correctly identify the need for new voices and fresh perspectives in inclusive education. The distinctive features include the international reach of the book, the inclusion of perspectives of emerging and established scholars in the field, topics that expands the purview of inclusive education, and engaging with wider issues of equity. This book could be a key marker in the development of inclusive education internationally, and could contribute to much needed shifts in focus and approach.'

Elizabeth Walton, *University of Nottingham, UK*

'The proliferation of UN policies and documents has impacted nations far and wide, and inclusion itself has taken on a wide variety of meanings depending on the location. Scholars are now very engaged in this kind of international investigation. This book fits squarely within this growing area of interest. I can see this as a primary text in courses on inclusive education policy and practice. I also think it will be a primary text in courses on international or comparative education. What impresses me most is the breadth. This volume extends to virtually all corners of the world.'

Scot Danforth, *Chapman University, USA*

'The book puts forward a truly inclusive idea of inclusive education that does not equate the field with special education. It includes chapters examining the relationship of language policy to education, the cultural rights of indigenous people, and others who are likely to face barriers or feel invisible in education systems. The major strength of this volume is the way that it builds a conversation between different parts of the education field, bringing together academic researchers and professionals who advocate and implement policy in education. It is also one of the few books where scholars who have advocated for inclusive education are engaging in reflection to problematize the practical interpretation of inclusion as another form of deficit thinking.'

Kate Lapham, *Education Program, Open Society Foundations*

GLOBAL DIRECTIONS IN INCLUSIVE EDUCATION

Global Directions in Inclusive Education pushes the conceptual boundaries of 'inclusive education' and explores new ways to research and envision inclusion and diversity in education for all children. This pioneering book problematizes 'inclusive education' as a global currency, as another form of deficit-thinking, and as a universal application.

The expert team of international contributors argue that much of the field of inclusive education needs a reinvigoration of new ideas, critical introspection, and ways of knowing that can overcome the well-worn deficit paths of inclusive education study, namely: 'barriers' to inclusion, teacher attitudes, policy-practice gaps, lack of resources, and lack of teacher training. Seeking diverse ways forward that represent new visions and innovations from around the world, this text features voices and ideas from both early career and established scholars, to enliven debate and promote a more positive and productive dialogue.

Global Directions in Inclusive Education is ideal for students, researchers, and scholars of inclusive education; development practitioners seeking new ideas; and practitioners seeking to gain a deeper and more global understanding of inclusive education both in theory and in practice.

Matthew J. Schuelka is a researcher at the Institute on Community Integration and lecturer in the College of Education and Human Development at the University of Minnesota, USA. He is also the founder and CEO of Fora Education.

Suzanne Carrington is a Professor in The Centre for Inclusive Education (C4IE) and a member of the Faculty of Creative Industries, Education and Social Justice, Queensland University of Technology, Australia.

GLOBAL DIRECTIONS IN INCLUSIVE EDUCATION

Conceptualizations, Practices, and Methodologies for the 21st Century

Edited by Matthew J. Schuelka and Suzanne Carrington

LONDON AND NEW YORK

Cover image: © Getty Images

First published 2022
by Routledge
2 Park Square, Milton Park, Abingdon, Oxon OX14 4RN

and by Routledge
605 Third Avenue, New York, NY 10158

Routledge is an imprint of the Taylor & Francis Group, an informa business

© 2022 selection and editorial matter, Matthew J. Schuelka and Suzanne Carrington; individual chapters, the contributors

The right of Matthew J. Schuelka and Suzanne Carrington to be identified as the authors of the editorial material, and of the authors for their individual chapters, has been asserted in accordance with sections 77 and 78 of the Copyright, Designs and Patents Act 1988.

All rights reserved. No part of this book may be reprinted or reproduced or utilised in any form or by any electronic, mechanical, or other means, now known or hereafter invented, including photocopying and recording, or in any information storage or retrieval system, without permission in writing from the publishers.

Trademark notice: Product or corporate names may be trademarks or registered trademarks, and are used only for identification and explanation without intent to infringe.

British Library Cataloguing-in-Publication Data
A catalogue record for this book is available from the British Library

Library of Congress Cataloging-in-Publication Data
Names: Schuelka, Matthew J., editor. | Carrington, Suzanne, editor.
Title: Global directions in inclusive education : conceptualizations, practices, and methodologies for the 21st century / edited by Matthew J. Schuelka and Suzanne Carrington.
Description: Abingdon, Oxon ; New York, NY : Routledge, 2022. | Includes bibliographical references and index.
Identifiers: LCCN 2021030212 (print) | LCCN 2021030213 (ebook) | ISBN 9780367550950 (hardback) | ISBN 9780367550936 (paperback) | ISBN 9781003091950 (ebook)
Subjects: LCSH: Inclusive education--Cross-cultural studies.
Classification: LCC LC1200 .G56 2022 (print) | LCC LC1200 (ebook) | DDC 371.9/046--dc23
LC record available at https://lccn.loc.gov/2021030212
LC ebook record available at https://lccn.loc.gov/2021030213

ISBN: 978-0-367-55095-0 (hbk)
ISBN: 978-0-367-55093-6 (pbk)
ISBN: 978-1-003-09195-0 (ebk)

DOI: 10.4324/9781003091950

Typeset in Bembo
by SPi Technologies India Pvt Ltd (Straive)

CONTENTS

Contributors   x

1 Innovative and global directions for inclusive education in the 21st century   1
Matthew J. Schuelka and Suzanne Carrington

PART I
Conceptual innovation   27

2 International perspectives on inclusive education in rural contexts: Finding (un)common ground   29
Julie Dillon-Wallace

3 Beginning with language: Inclusive education strategies with sign languages in Rwanda, Singapore, United States, and Việt Nam   45
Audrey Cooper, Sonia Holzman, Maegan Shanks, and Phoebe Tay

4 Affects and materiality in Santiago de Chile's schools: The importance of relationality in the co-enactment of inclusion   66
Rosario Palacios

5 Conceptualising inclusion within Indonesian contexts   81
Nur Azizah, Elga Andriana, and David Evans

6 Is inclusive education enough for Australian Aboriginal students?: Making the case for belonging education to disrupt the normalised agenda of assimilation 99
Sheelagh Daniels-Mayes, Gary Fry, and Karen Sinclair

PART II
Pragmatic innovation 117

7 Visibly rewarding learners for academic achievement: The guise of excellence 119
Shakira Akabor

8 Diagnosis, integration, and inclusion: The experiences of schools and families in Cambodian policy and practice 135
Anne E. Crylen

9 Talking about self: Exploring the potential of teacher's talk in professional learning communities for inclusive pedagogy 151
Wacango Kimani

10 Localizing a universal claim: Applying universal design strategies to support inclusion in Armenia 169
Armenuhi Avagyan, Christopher Johnstone, Ofelia Asatryan, Lilia Khachatryan, and Aleksandr Shagafyan

11 Critical reflexivity as a pedagogy for inclusivity in teacher education 183
Levan Lim and Thana Thaver

12 Re-turning insights on belonging: An international collaboration between Flanders and New Zealand 200
Hanne Vandenbussche, Elisabeth De Schauwer, Evelyn Christina, Missy Morton, and Geert Van Hove

PART III
Methodological innovation 215

13 Being seen and heard: Using photovoice methodology in inclusive education research 217
Alisha M. B. Braun

14 Collaborative B-learning as a tool to studying and preparing
    for inclusion in a culturally diverse environment   231
    Silvia Romero-Contreras, Ismael García-Cedillo, and
    Gabriela Silva-Maceda

15 Into the mesa: A case study of Jordanian inclusion policy   255
    Sarah K. Benson

16 Becoming an activist: A story of parental advocacy for
    inclusive education   276
    Glenys Mann and the Queensland Collective for Inclusive Education

17 Exploring the congruence between Bhutanese teachers'
    views about inclusion, Gross National Happiness, and Buddhism   293
    Dawa Dukpa, Suzanne Carrington, Sofia Mavropoulou,
    and Matthew J. Schuelka

Index   *312*

CONTRIBUTORS

Shakira Akabor is currently a postdoctoral fellow in the Department of Inclusive Education at UNISA, South Africa. Her PhD is entitled, *The intention and impact of visibly rewarding learners in two Gauteng high schools*, which she completed at the University of the Witwatersrand, Johannesburg. Shakira has taught in a mainstream classroom since 2003, and is especially passionate about reducing competitiveness in classrooms and increasing opportunities for all learners to develop and learn to their full potential.

Elga Andriana is currently the head of the Center for Life Span Development and lecturer at the Faculty of Psychology, Universitas Gadjah Mada, Indonesia. She has experience as a teacher and school principal and now is working with students and teachers from various schools to implement inclusive education in Yogyakarta, Indonesia. Her research interest is in inclusive education, children's voice, children as researchers, and Universal Design for Learning.

Ofelia Asatryan is a secondary school History and Citizenship teacher at a public school in Yerevan, Armenia. She has ten years of practice in working in an inclusive school.

Armenuhi Avagyan has holistic experience in various projects and activities aimed at the implementation of inclusive education in Armenia. Armenuhi is the founder of ARMAV Continuous Education Center, focused on professional interventions and research in the field of inclusive education. Recently, she completed her post-doctoral research on Peer-Mediated Augmentative and Alternative Communication Intervention for Non/Minimally Verbal Preschoolers as a Fulbright scholar at Appalachian State University. She was a team member of a two-year partnership between the University of Minnesota and Armenia State Pedagogical University, which produced the book *Inclusive Education Strategies: A Textbook*, available in English and Armenian. She is the professional editor of the Armenian translation of the textbook.

Nur Azizah currently teaches at the Special Education Department, Universitas Negeri Yogyakarta (UNY), Indonesia. Prior to UNY, she was a special education teacher in a primary school and worked with students with disabilities from different backgrounds. Her research includes inclusive education and transition education.

Sarah K. Benson is a lecturer at the University of Birmingham, Dubai campus. In addition, she is the program lead for Inclusion and Special Educational Needs at both the United Kingdom and Dubai campuses. Her research has taken her from public schools in Jordan to private schools in the United Arab Emirates. Currently she is engaged in research projects spanning inclusion in home-learning during the pandemic, awareness-raising campaigns in Jordan, and the use of service animals on academic and social well-being of students experiencing SEN. Sarah has ongoing research interests at all levels of inclusive education with policy makers and schools throughout the Middle East.

Alisha M. B. Braun is an assistant professor of social foundations in the Department of Educational and Psychological Studies at the University of South Florida, United States. Her research interests include educational policies and practices related to access to quality education for marginalized children, especially those in developing contexts. Her current research focuses on the inclusive education of students with disabilities in sub-Saharan Africa. She completed her PhD in Educational Policy from Michigan State University with graduate specializations in International Development and African Studies.

Suzanne Carrington is a professor in The Centre for Inclusive Education (C4IE) and a member of the Faculty of Creative Industries, Education and Social Justice at the Queensland University of Technology, Australia. Suzanne's areas of expertise are in inclusive education, ethical leadership for inclusive schools, disability, and teacher preparation for inclusive schools. She has engaged in research to inform policy and practice in Australian and international education contexts including Bhutan.

Evelyn Christina is a doctoral candidate at the University of Auckland, New Zealand. Her research focuses on the entanglements of school, diversity, and children's peer relationships. She works closely with families, schools, and local organisations to build inclusive communities where all members can belong.

Audrey Cooper is an associate professor and Program Director for the MA Program in International Development at Gallaudet University, United States. A linguistic and public anthropologist, her research focuses on sign language social action, education, and disaster leadership, deaf transnational development-oriented contact, and deaf-led disability inclusive initiatives. From 2012–14 she was also a technical consultant/trainer for the World Bank–sponsored *Intergenerational Deaf Education Outreach—Vietnam*.

Anne E. Crylen is a Fulbright Fellow and global educational leader with a traumatic brain injury. Her work has taken her to lead an international school in Shanghai, China; fieldwork on autism in Cambodia; and many years in the Chicago public schools. Anne has published her research on school re-entry and the return-to-learn process for students following traumatic brain injuries. As a champion for students with disabilities, she continues her work on education equity through inquiry-based learning and teaching emphasizing student voice and ownership. She currently works in Grand Rapids public schools, growing the International Baccalaureate in Michigan, United States.

Sheelagh Daniels-Mayes is a Kamilaroi woman who lost her eyesight as a child. Sheelagh is the coordinator of the Sydney Indigenous Research Network at the University of Sydney, Australia. Her work focuses on higher education's responsibilities in achieving equity and social justice. Sheelagh uses Critical Race Theory, cultural responsiveness, and Critical Access Studies to problematize and disrupt normalised social constructions. Sheelagh has studied in the areas of education, sociology, psychology, and criminology.

Elisabeth De Schauwer is working as guest professor in the field of disability studies at Ghent University, Belgium. Her PhD was around the inclusion processes of children with severe communicative difficulties. Her research now focuses on intra-actions with difference in (pedagogical) relations. She works closely together with children, parents, and schools in the praxis of inclusive education. For her, activism, research, and teaching go hand in hand.

Julie Dillon-Wallace is a senior lecturer in the School of Early Childhood and Inclusive Education, Queensland University of Technology, Australia. She lectures to pre-service and post-graduate teachers in relation to inclusive practice, applied research methods, and child development. Julie has a particular interest in using both quantitative and qualitative research methods to explore issues and pedagogies associated with inclusive practice.

Dawa Dukpa is a PhD candidate in the Faculty of Creative Industries, Education and Social Justice at the Queensland University of Technology, Australia, and an Associate Fellow of the UK Higher Education Academy. He has led research projects and development of a postgraduate course/programme in Inclusive Education at Paro College of Education, Bhutan, prior to undertaking his PhD. He has published on inclusive education and disability in Bhutan and his current research interest is in autism, inclusion, and teacher education.

David Evans is professor of Special and Inclusive Education in the Sydney School of Education and Social Work at the University of Sydney, Australia. He teaches and researches in the area of special and inclusive education with special focus on curriculum design and inclusive pedagogies. He has undertaken extensive research and professional learning across the Indonesian archipelago over the past five years.

Gary Fry is a Dagoman man from the Katherine region in the Northern Territory, and currently works as Assistant Dean Indigenous Education in the College of Education, Charles Darwin University, Australia. Gary has been a classroom teacher; senior executive school principal in remote Aboriginal schools and urban schools; director of the Northern Territory Centre for School Leadership; and education consultant. He completed his PhD research at the University of Sydney in 2019, which focused on improving the NT remote Aboriginal education policy environment.

Ismael García-Cedillo is a full professor in the Graduate School of Psychology at Autonomous University of San Luis Potosí, México, and National Researcher Level II in the area of humanities and social sciences. He directed the National Project for Educational Integration in México and the International Inclusive Education Teacher Training Graduate Program. His research interests focus on national and comparative studies on special and inclusive education policy and teacher preparation. He is the first author of three national courses and one certificate on inclusive education for Mexican teachers.

Sonia Holzman is a program specialist and outreach liaison for the MA Program in International Development at Gallaudet University, United States, promoting partnerships and career pathways to expand inclusive development. Sonia holds an MA in International Development and BS in Child Development. She has worked with deaf students and students with disabilities in the US, Uganda, and Rwanda and conducted research on sign languages in education.

Christopher Johnstone is an associate professor of comparative education at the University of Minnesota, United States. His research focuses on inclusive education and internationalization of higher education. Johnstone's chapter in this book reflects ongoing collaborations with colleagues in Armenia, which have been supported by UNICEF and US Embassy Alumni Engagement Innovation Funds.

Lilia Khachatryan has been teaching in both secondary and higher education since 2006. She has more than ten years experience in educational resource development in frames of various local and international projects to make citizenship education more inclusive and accessible for learners. She is also a core contributor to the Armenian Center for Democratic Education-CIVITAS, NGO as a content and resource developer and teacher trainer. Lilia has participated in several trainings and professional development programs: she is an alumna of the Teaching Excellence and Achievement program of the US State Department and IREX. She has published articles in philosophy, ethics, and cultural memory studies.

Wacango Kimani is a PhD candidate at the University of the Witwatersrand. Her research is on professional learning for inclusive pedagogy, and she has previously conducted voice research with young schooling mothers. She manages a social enterprise – *Sayari Vision* – which runs adult programmes that promote lifelong learning. She holds post-graduate qualifications in inclusive education and library science.

Levan Lim is an associate professor at the Psychology and Child & Human Development Academic Group at the National Institute of Education (NIE), Nanyang Technological University, Singapore. He obtained his PhD in special education from Lehigh University (Pennsylvania, USA) and previously worked at Charles Sturt University and the University of Queensland. He was Head of the Early Childhood & Special Needs Education Academic Group from 2009 to 2018, which was the department at NIE responsible for teacher education in special needs at the pre-service, in-service, and graduate levels. His research and teaching commitments and interests are focused on the inclusion of persons with disabilities, teacher development for inclusion, and interventions for teaching and supporting individuals with disabilities.

Glenys Mann is a co-program leader in The Centre for Inclusive Education (C4IE) and lecturer in Inclusive Education at the Queensland University of Technology, Australia. Her research supports the development of inclusive culture and practice in schools through giving voice to parents of students with disabilities and contributing to better parent-teacher partnerships. She believes that parents are experts in the lives of their children, key witnesses to the performance of education systems, and critical partners in inclusive education reform.

Sofia Mavropoulou is a senior lecturer at the School of Early Childhood & Inclusive Education and study area coordinator for the area of Inclusive Education (Master of Education) in the Faculty of Creative Industries, Education and Social Justice at the Queensland University of Technology, Australia. Sofia has extensive experience teaching in pre-service, in-service, and post-graduate teacher training courses in universities located in Europe and Australia. Sofia has participated (as chief investigator and associate researcher) in educational research for students on the autism spectrum, with funding from the Greek government and the European Union. Sofia is very passionate about creating autism-friendly environments to accommodate the strengths and preferences of persons with autism to promote their inclusion, independence, and well-being.

Missy Morton is professor of Disability Studies and Inclusive Education in the School of Critical Studies in Education at the University of Auckland, New Zealand. Her work focuses on the intersecting discourses of curriculum, pedagogy, assessment and difference, and how these support or impede belonging in early childhood, school and tertiary communities.

Rosario Palacios is an associate researcher at Centro de Justicia Educacional, Universidad Católica de Chile, Chile. Her research interests relate to the intersections of culture, space, and inequality. She received her PhD at the London School of Economics and her MSc in Urban Planning at Columbia University, New York.

The Queensland Collective for Inclusive Education is a group of families who promote inclusive lives for children with disability and work together to make inclusive schools a reality for all. All members work in a voluntary capacity to advocate for children's rights to inclusive education. The goal of the organisation is that all children learn, grow, and play together at their mainstream school – every Queensland child is welcomed and attending their regular school with same-age peers, and actively participating in all aspects of school life.

Silvia Romero-Contreras is a full professor in the Graduate School of Psychology at the Autonomous University of San Luis Potosí, México, and National Researcher Level II in the area of humanities and social sciences. She was an advisor to the National Project for Educational Integration in México and Academic Coordinator for the International Inclusive Education Teacher Training Graduate Program. Her research interests focus on culturally appropriate language and literacy educational practices and special and inclusive education practice, policy, and teacher preparation. She is the author of various books for parents and teachers in the area of language and literacy. Currently, she is Principal Investigator of the Word Generation project for Mexico in coordination with Harvard University and the SERP Institute.

Matthew J. Schuelka is founder and CEO of Fora Education, a non-profit consultancy firm dedicated to inclusion and sustainability in education around the world. He is also a lecturer in the College of Education and Human Development at the University of Minnesota, USA; and is a researcher at the University of Minnesota's Institute on Community Integration. Formerly, Matt was assistant professor of Inclusive Education at the University of Birmingham (UK and Dubai campuses), assistant professor at the University of Nottingham-Malaysia Campus, and lecturer at the Royal Thimphu College in Bhutan. He is an active researcher, writer, teacher evaluator, and has been hired as an education consultant for organizations such as USAID, UKAID, UNICEF, and the World Bank.

Aleksandr Shagafyan has been engaged in public education in Armenia since 2002 in various capacities. He is a co-founder and former Executive Director of Armenian Center for Democratic Education-CIVITAS, NGO. As a civic educator, Aleksandr has more than ten years of teaching, teacher training, and educational resource development experience.

Maegan Shanks is faculty and program assistant for the MA Program in International Development at Gallaudet University, United States, training students in project design and implementation for social change. Maegan is also a PhD student in the School of International Service at American University, exploring transnational education policymaking and implementation angled around disability and development, language justice, and intersectionality within the International Relations and International Development field.

Gabriela Silva-Maceda is a full professor at the Graduate School of Psychology at Autonomous University of San Luis Potosí, México, and a candidate to National Researcher in the area of Humanities and Social Sciences. Her research is focused on literacy development and differentiated instruction for disadvantaged populations, as well as evidence-based teaching practices and programs at various educational levels.

Karen Sinclair is a Ngarrindjeri teacher educator who is currently the Program Director of Aboriginal Studies in Justice and Society at the University of South Australia. Karen has been a junior primary teacher and Aboriginal education coordinator. Her research interests focus on Aboriginal knowledges in curriculum; Aboriginal research methodologies; and transformative pedagogies.

Phoebe Tay is a PhD student (IGP-Global Asia) in the College of Humanities, Arts and Social Sciences at Nanyang Technological University, Singapore. Phoebe holds dual MAs in International Development and Linguistics from Gallaudet University. Her research interests include linguistic typology, linguistic anthropology, sociolinguistics, and historical linguistics. She is particularly interested in exploring language ideologies, multilingualism, language shift, and constructions of identity and variation in the context of the Singapore Deaf Community.

Thana Thaver is a senior lecturer with the Psychology and Child & Human Development Academic Group, National Institute of Education, Nanyang Technological University, Singapore. She teaches a range of courses from general pedagogies in teaching and learning to educational psychology to inclusive education. She is currently Assistant Dean, Professional & Leadership Development at the Office of Graduate Studies and Professional Learning, NIE. Prior to joining NIE, she was with Singapore's Ministry of Education where she was involved in curriculum development and coaching teachers in the Gifted Education Programme.

Hanne Vandenbussche is a PhD student connected to the field of disability studies at Ghent University, Belgium. She has specific interest in the relationship between disability studies and philosophy. In her research she focuses on belonging and inclusive citizenship; she cooperates with parents, children, and young adults following inclusive trajectories.

Geert Van Hove is full professor at the Department of Special Needs Education, University of Ghent, Belgium. His field of research is 'Disability Studies and Inclusive Education.' Most of his research projects are focused on narratives of disabled persons and their families.

1
INNOVATIVE AND GLOBAL DIRECTIONS FOR INCLUSIVE EDUCATION IN THE 21ST CENTURY

Matthew J. Schuelka and Suzanne Carrington

Introduction

With a history of thousands of years of varied formal education systems and institutions around the world, the notion that going to school and receiving a quality education as a right for *everyone* is actually a very recent phenomenon. While there were growing movements for formalized mass education – particularly in Europe and North America – beginning in the 18th and 19th centuries (Ramirez & Boli, 1987), it was not until the late 20th century that nation-states and national education systems began policies and initiatives to expand access to schooling for all children. The focus of these 'inclusive' policies and initiatives was particularly targeted towards students with 'disabilities,' as well as students with other socially marginalized characteristics. That there needed to be significant and somewhat radical educational reforms just to allow marginalized and disabled students to even access *any* form of schooling points to the fact that, for thousands of years, formal education was an elite societal institution that served a sliver of the general population. In most ways, we continue to grapple with this historical legacy as we shift our imperatives towards education systems for all children.

The proliferation of national and global policies supporting inclusive education – a somewhat abstract and contentious term, but at its core meaning a right to an education for all children at their local school – began perhaps most significantly with the Salamanca Statement and Framework for Action on Special Needs Education in 1994. The Salamanca Statement was a result of the World Conference on Special Needs Education and was signed by over one hundred countries and international organizations. However, now with over 25 years of hindsight, the Salamanca Statement may not have been enough to truly challenge the entrenched elitism and exclusivity that education systems are built upon. It also maintained a 'special' conceptualization of marginalized and disabled children in the name of 'inclusive' education. The Salamanca Statement and the neoliberal education discourse of the late 20th century have placed the burden of inclusive education reform on schools rather than on national institutions, policies, and structures (Anderson & Boyle, 2019). In other words, Salamanca fostered a global discourse on inclusive education, but placed the onus of reform on local level practices rather than critically examine institutional, systemic, and conceptual issues at national and international levels.

Since Salamanca in 1994, there has been a progression of global initiatives that promote at least equal access to education for all children such as Education for All (EFA), the Millennium Development Goals (MDGs), the Convention on the Rights of Persons with Disabilities (CRPD), and now the Sustainable Development Goals (SDGs). We will discuss these further in the next section. However, in many ways, the same challenges remain for inclusive education as they did in 1994, despite a steady progression of inclusive education discourse, aspirational statements, and research. It is true that if you look at any available global education longitudinal statistic, the overall trends have been positive in terms of educational participation and access (Roser & Ortiz-Ospina, 2016). However, these general statistical trends only tell part of the story. Explore inside these statistics and there remain significant disparities between and within countries, and there are significant challenges in school progression, drop-out, and outcomes. In other words, more children are being given access to education, but educational quality and educational socio-economic utility still continue to mitigate positive trends. There has been a significant focus on the inequality of educational access, without proper attention to the inequality of educational outcomes, and, indeed, the inequality of quality in education. The 2015 Global Education Monitoring Report acknowledged this in suggesting that the push for the right to educational access has overshadowed the right to a quality education once access has been gained (UNESCO, 2015). This can be read in two ways. First, one could view this as a natural progression: now that we have asserted the right to education for all, we can begin the work of making the education system better for all. Second, however, is that one could view this as a failure: pushing more children into schools without accompanying reforms – quality, increase in resources, rethinking how teachers are prepared, and innovations in how schooling can be structured – has led to an increase in marginalization and disparity in educational outcomes. Indeed, the second scenario has become more prevalent and inclusive education has experienced more resistance. For example, the number of children in special schools in England has been exponentially rising since 2006 (Black, 2019), whereas once England was an early model of inclusive education. Mary Warnock (2005), a famous early proponent of inclusive education in England, backed away from her earlier assertions against segregated schooling. There is a similar trend occurring in Ireland as well, in which 'inclusive education' merely replaced 'special' and segregated education policy, without much consideration as to what reforms and resources are needed to truly be inclusive (Shevlin & Banks, 2021). Imray and Colley boldly declared *Inclusion Is Dead, Long Live Inclusion* (2017), to which Slee wrote his rebuttal *Inclusive Education Isn't Dead, It Just Smells Funny* (2018).

We agree with Slee that the notion of inclusive education itself is not over or flawed in its root directive to provide all children with a quality education alongside their peers. Indeed, as Slee (2018) avers, inclusive education is the cornerstone of the modern democratic state. Therefore, we challenge all researchers, practitioners, education professionals, and policymakers to move inclusive education to the center of the meaning of education in society itself. This is the argument made by Schuelka, Johnstone, Thomas, and Artiles (2019) to move beyond the term 'inclusive education' – and the unhelpful discourse of trying to define and redefine it – and embrace the notion of inclusion and diversity *in* education. They argue:

> Children in classrooms around the world want to experience a positive sense of belonging, identity, safety, learning, and societal contribution and … could not care less what adults call it. Many scholars of inclusive education frame these desires within a framework of inclusion dilemmas, but to us it is very simple: We advocate moving beyond the term 'inclusive education', as well as beyond the terms 'special education', 'special needs', and 'integration'. Rather, what we seek is an expanded definition of what we simply refer to as quality education.
>
> (p. xxxvi)

One of the reasons that we argue for a similar conceptual shift towards inclusion and diversity in education is that too often 'inclusive education' has been a palimpsest for 'special education' and has lost its critical and radical intent for rethinking entire educational systems (Armstrong, Armstrong & Spandagou, 2010). In this regard, 'inclusive education' is often conceptualized entirely as pertaining to students with 'disabilities,' and semantically this implies that 'disability' exists outside of the conceptualization of what and who education is for. It is the paradox of inclusion – or sometimes framed as a 'dilemma of difference' (Minow, 1990; Norwich, 2008) – in that education systems must first define who it is for, before deciding who it is *not* for but should be included anyway. Imagine sitting in a park and a stranger walks up to you and congratulates you for being 'included.' This is a surprise to you. Part of you may be happy to be affirmed, but there will always be another part of you wondering whether you could be *un*-included at any moment; in what manner your inclusion in the park is conditional; and by whose rules you are deemed to be included or excluded. All of the sudden, the park has become reconceptualized as a place where it cannot be assumed that you belong.

Often it is the school as a cultural institution that defines inclusion and exclusion, which has implications for the type of society it reflexively produces. In Schuelka's ethnographic work on inclusion and schooling in Bhutan, he found that the culture and institution of formal schooling itself produced and constructed disabilities (Schuelka, 2018). This was happening not just in Bhutan, of course, and is observed in other contexts as well. McDermott's (1993) pioneering work in the United States laid bare the socio-cultural institutions of schooling ready to predeterminately marginalize and sort children by ability. In Bhutan, it was evident that the socio-cultural structures of schooling were not conducive to including a heterogenous student population – knowledge was fixed, the curriculum was rigid, pedagogy was authoritative, and failure and drop-out was prevalent. This was easily observed in Bhutan because the entire formal school system itself was so new, as was the idea of 'inclusive education.' Students go to school in Bhutan primarily for human capital socio-economic advancement in a newly formed market economy. Thus, a modern formal education system in Bhutan serves as a novel social institution that sorts the population into those that 'can' and those that 'cannot' through the construction of educational achievement as a measure of overall ability. The Bhutan case is illustrative and resonates because it affirms the historical purpose of schooling as "providing access *and* advantage, promoting equality *and* inequality" (Labaree, 2010, p. 3). Bhutan is not being singled out here, but rather demonstrates that educational systems around the world have not done nearly enough to move past their elitist roots, nor critically examined the historical legacies of the educational systems from which they are referencing and borrowing, nor re-imagining themselves as socially embedded institutions for the common good of all. Education for children labelled with a disability began as a charitable and 'extra' – or, of course, 'special' – feature of education systems (Richardson & Powell, 2011). This begs the question; how much has really changed with the emphasis today on inclusive education? An educational system that features failure, expulsion, age and ability grouping, and a one-size-fits-all curricular and pedagogical structure, was never designed to educate all children.

In this introductory chapter, and throughout the edited book, we will return to this context, history, and paradox of inclusion and how this can be turned towards the notion of 'inclusion and diversity *in* education.' The chapter authors in this book were given these considerations as well. We argue that as we move firmly into the 21st century, it is increasingly apparent that our understanding about inclusivity and access to education needs to be refreshed and reconsidered in light of shifting social and economic situations and new evidence. We also argue that research should move beyond the work of school access and into new spaces of educational quality, utility, and social opportunity. This book considers international perspectives on schooling, culture, systems, teacher preparation and practice, school leadership, and policy incentives. In many ways, we push on the conceptual boundaries of 'inclusive education' and explore new ways to research and conceptualize inclusion and diversity in education for all children. The aim of this book is to problematize 'inclusive education': as a global currency, as another form of deficit-thinking, and as a universal application. However, in this book we also seek new and diverse ways forward that represent new visions and innovations from around the world.

This book acknowledges that 'inclusion' does not only refer to students with disabilities, but also to race, ethnicity, religion, socio-economic status, and many other factors. In other words, we explore how we can better create educational spaces that are designed and meant for all to use. This necessitates some radical thinking in terms of questioning and understanding how schooling is currently structured.

For example, what is the purpose of grades and marks and failure? Why should classrooms be organized by age? Why should children be in classrooms at all? We wanted to approach this book with an openness to new ideas and a blank slate in terms of our assumptions of the way things are or should be. That being said, some of the chapters are more specific to a disability-inclusion perspective but are sufficiently broad enough to discuss 'inclusion' from a more systemic perspective. For example, the chapter by Cooper and colleagues discusses specifically the deaf and hard of hearing community within the inclusive education agenda, which serves as a reminder of the dilemmas of language and communication in trying to create educational spaces that are inclusive to all. The chapter written by Avagyan and colleagues critically examines assumptions within global inclusive education discourse, such as the universality of universal design for learning.

This book, and the remainder of the introductory chapter, are divided into three broad themes: conceptual innovation, pragmatic innovation, and methodological innovation. Conceptual innovation refers to a critical exploration of inclusive education conventional wisdom and practice; and rethinking how we understand culture(s), structures, systems, and policies. Pragmatic innovation refers to a critical exploration of current inclusive education models, practices, policies, and new ways of knowing and understanding 'inclusion' in education. Methodological innovation refers to new ways of researching, understanding, and studying 'inclusion' in education.

As the reader can already detect, there is a general mixing of terminology in the book – referring to 'inclusion,' 'inclusive education,' and 'inclusion and diversity in education' in equal measure. While we do argue that 'inclusive education' as a term has become a mere replacement of 'special education' in many ways – particularly in policy – the authors in this book use 'inclusive education' to mean creating educational spaces that are equal and equitable for all children. In a sense, we are attempting to reclaim 'inclusive education' as a term and return it to its original intentions, while also bringing 'inclusion and diversity in education' into the same orbit. At the end of the 20th century, Giangreco (1997) clearly articulated this vision for inclusive education:

1. *All* students are welcomed in general education classes in their local schools. "Inclusion for some" is a contradiction in terms.
2. Students are educated in classes where the number of those with and without disabilities is proportional to the local population.
3. Students are educated with peers in the same age groupings available to those without disability labels.
4. Students with varying characteristics and abilities participate in shared educational experiences while pursuing individually appropriate learning outcomes with necessary supports and accommodations.
5. Shared educational experiences take place in settings predominantly frequented by people without disabilities (e.g., general education classroom, community work sites).

6. Educational experiences are designed to enhance individually determined valued life outcomes for students and therefore seek an individualized balance between the academic/functional and social/personal aspects of schooling.
7. Inclusive education exists when each of the previously listed characteristics occurs on an ongoing daily basis. (Giangreco, 1997, p. 194)

The chapters in this book do not represent a complete or summative stance on the directions that inclusive education will, or could, take in the 21st century. Rather, the chapters in this book are examples of just a few different directions that have been taken. These are exemplary chapters, to be certain, but we – the editors and the chapter authors – fully acknowledge that there is excellent and innovative work happening in inclusive education that cannot be fully captured in only one book.

Conceptual innovation

Around the world, education systems are attempting to move towards a more inclusive model of education that has a focus on education for all, including students with disabilities. Despite persistent challenges, and the next-order issues of educational quality and utility that were mentioned previously and throughout this chapter, the overall trend has been that more students have access to schooling than ever before (UNESCO, 2020). This does not mean that the challenge of inclusive education has been solved, of course. According to the 2020 Global Education Monitoring Report, 17% of children are still out of school globally, and these approximately 258 million children are disproportionately located in low- and middle-income countries. Many children that are in school receive a poor-quality educational experience in exclusive and marginalized settings (UNESCO, 2020).

An inclusive approach to education is a universal human right and focuses on all children learning and socializing together at the local school, acknowledges our shared humanity, and respects the diversities that exist in ability, culture, gender, language, class, and ethnicity (Carrington et al., 2012; UNESCO, 2017). Inclusive education is a goal in the 2030 Agenda for Sustainable Development and the Sustainable Development Goals (SDGs), and the 2030 Agenda describes a plan of action for people, our planet, our shared prosperity, and seeks to strengthen universal peace by supporting collaborative partnerships. There are seventeen SDGs that build on the Millennium Development Goals that lasted from 2000–2015 (United Nations, 2015). The SDGs build on decades of work by the United Nations and emphasize a human rights approach with a particular focus on gender and equity. Education for all is a key priority. SDG #4 states that we must 'Ensure inclusive and equitable quality education and promote lifelong learning opportunities for all' (United Nations, 2015). This goal focuses on ensuring governments provide equal access to all levels of education, including students with disabilities, and supports the provision of inclusive and safe education facilities that are child, disability, and gender sensitive; and provide effective learning environments for all students.

In 2006, the UN Convention on the Rights of Persons with Disabilities (United Nations, 2006) was published and has been ratified by 181 countries. Article 24, General Comment 4, which followed in 2016, established what we see as the authoritative operational definition of what inclusion in education is, and what it is not:

> Inclusion involves a process of systemic reform embodying changes and modifications in content, teaching methods, approaches, structures, and strategies in education to overcome barriers with a vision serving to provide all students of the relevant age range with an equitable and participatory learning experience and environment that best corresponds to their requirements and preferences. Placing students with disabilities within mainstream classes without accompanying structural changes to, for example, organisation, curriculum and teaching and learning strategies, does not constitute inclusion. Furthermore, integration does not automatically guarantee the transition from segregation to inclusion.
>
> (United Nations, 2016, p. 4)

Historically, education for students categorized as having a 'disability' – or other socially marginalized characteristic – has taken place in segregated 'special' settings with attention focused on the child and his or her supposed mental and physical inadequacy (Carrier, 1986; Richardson & Powell, 2011). For many years this has been done due to the assumption that children with a disability are better served in special education settings, but there is no evidence to support this belief (Hehir et al., 2016). Evidence instead demonstrates that placement in segregated special settings for children with disabilities has resulted in a marginalized population that has been institutionalized, undereducated, socially rejected, and excluded from society (ACIE, 2020; Biklen, 1988). Segregating children with a disability also deflected attention away from mainstream educational practices and the broader social and cultural forces which shape them (Carrier, 1986).

One of the dominant influences that shaped professional definitions and practices in special education around the world has been the medical model of disability. This model emphasized *in*ability, a deficit approach, and contributed to a dependency model of disability. Labels such as 'invalid,' 'handicapped,' 'retarded,' and 'slow learner' sanctioned individual pathology and negative views of disability. In educational organizations across the world, there is an ongoing tendency to reinforce an individual deficit view of special educational needs and disabilities. Personal beliefs and attitudes about difference are crucial because they legitimate certain assumptions about disability and associated discriminatory practices (Barton, 1996). In an inclusive approach, drawing on the social model of disability (Oliver, 2009), difference is not viewed as a problem. The focus rather is on valuing and respecting all people with consideration to social justice and equity principles.

While the medical model of disability assumes that 'disability' is a universal condition that all persons experience in similar ways according to their diagnosis, the social model of disability frames 'disability' more in relational terms. A disabled person is such because of attitudes, structures, policies, and systems and not necessarily because of any specific innate characteristic. The social model has been advanced further by exploring how 'disabilities' are socially constructed and shaped by historical and socio-cultural structures (e.g. Groce, 1985; Ingstad & Whyte, 2007; Jenkins & Barrett, 2004; Schuelka, 2018). In other words, the construction of 'difference' has significant implications as to how inclusion and diversity in education is conceptualized.

We strongly believe that context is important in shaping inclusive education conceptualization, policies, plans, and practices. When we consider context, we need to acknowledge such factors such as geography, history, economy, society, culture, and religion to name just a few. We must also consider issues of power, intersectionality, and post-coloniality. Nguyen argues, "Inclusion could be seen as an imperialist project which produces forms of subjugation on bodies and nations" (2019, p. 29). A number of authors in this book highlight contextual factors that impact on how inclusive education is conceptualized and practiced in various countries. For example, Azizah and colleagues share the perspectives of teachers, parents, and students from various geographical areas of Indonesia that highlight some confusion about understanding what inclusive education means within the context of Indonesia where there have been historical and cultural beliefs about persons with disabilities. These beliefs contribute to the ongoing disparity of opportunities and outcomes for students from different backgrounds. Chapters in this book support an improved global understanding of inclusive education by sharing the challenges of moving from a deficit paradigm that commonly influences health providers' interactions with families, to a social model of disability that informs inclusive education. These challenges are evident in the chapter by Crylen where she discusses how service providers and schools in Cambodia work independently with conflicting models of disability that create gaps in services and confusion for families. An understanding of culture and context can inform our thinking and work with education systems, governments, school leaders, teachers, parents, and students in the context of schools. This is evident in the chapter by Dawa Dukpa and colleagues in highlighting socio-cultural factors with a focus on how the cultural model of disability impacts school staff and community understanding of disability, as well as the policy and practical incentives that shape inclusive education conceptualization by Bhutanese teachers. They argue that these factors should be considered beyond reductive studies on teacher 'attitudes.' Dillon-Wallace, in her chapter, considers the context of rurality and the impact on teaching students, particularly students with complex learning profiles. She focuses on how inclusive education is implemented in rural contexts and considers the challenges in professional learning, staffing of schools, and access to resources.

Just as context shapes the conceptualization of inclusive education, so too does the individual experience of students in schools. Palacios, in her chapter, deftly explores *affects* – emotions, sensations, tones, ambiences – in relation to *materiality*. This chapter highlights the importance of the student experience of belonging, and how this is shaped through their affective interaction with a school's materiality and space. This innovative approach towards understanding and conceptualizing inclusive education builds upon other work that has moved in this direction, for example, the focus on a student's experience of 'belongingness' (Braun, 2019), the subjective experience of inclusion within different community groupings (Engsig, 2019), the experience of 'otherness' in constructing identity (Welply, 2020), and 'embodied space' and socio-spatial inclusion (Rattray, 2013). Many chapters in this book, including Vandenbussche and colleagues and Daniels-Mayes and colleagues, explore the experience and notion of 'belonging' in their conceptualization of inclusive education.

One conceptual model that attempts to account for both context and subjective experience in inclusive education is Complex Educational Systems Analysis (CESA) (Schuelka & Engsig, 2020). This framework advances the notion that education systems are complex social institutions and must be understood in complex ways, acknowledging the openness, interdependence, unpredictability, and interactional nature of education systems. Complete reforms in complex systems such as education can be very difficult – if not impossible – because of the unpredictable and misaligned elements in a system. There is also considerable involution occurring (borrowing from Geertz, 1963), in which there is increasing complexity and intensification in education systems, but not necessarily leading to change and evolution. The CESA[3] model can be seen in Figure 1.1.

The CESA[3] shows the multiple communities that can be considered in analyzing the experience of inclusion and belongingness, but also considers other dimensions. In conceptualizing inclusion and diversity in education, the attributes of access, quality, and utility must be considered. As has already been argued in this chapter, the notion of 'access' is only one attribute that contributes to inclusivity in an

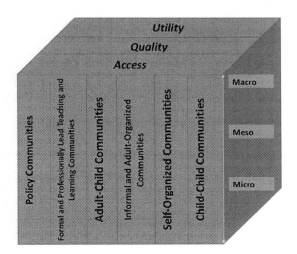

FIGURE 1.1 The complex educational systems analysis cube (CESA[3]). Source: Author, published in Schuelka and Engsig (2020, p. 6).

educational system. Access is dependent on the quality of the education that is being provided, just as quality of education is dependent on access and participation. Crucially, educational utility – the purpose and outcome of schooling – affects all dimensions in that it dictates the reasons, incentives, and justifications for inclusion within all community groupings and at all levels from the individual to the global.

Authors in this book, while not explicitly using the CESA framework, nonetheless reflect the qualities of this conceptualization of inclusive education within a complex system. For example, Benson argues, and demonstrates in her case study on Jordan, that research on inclusive education policy needs to go beyond discourse analysis and into a complex understanding of policymakers, political incentives, and institutional cultures in shaping inclusive education practices. In another example, Dillon-Wallace explores the construction of 'rurality' at various levels and the meaning of 'place' amongst various community groups and its influence on attributes such as access, quality, and utility.

In terms of where we would like to see conceptual innovation in the field of inclusive education in the 21st century, given the discussion in this section and throughout the book, we advocate for 'inclusive education' to transcend its historical roots in 'special education' and to take on the mantle of restructuring education to authentically be designed for all children. As we argued, schools historically were not designed for all learners and existed to promote a select – or, often preselected – few. As Schuelka et al. (2019) argue, instead of 'inclusive education,' we should instead reconceptualize it as 'inclusion and diversity *in* education.' The inevitable presence of difference among students means that schools need to become more comfortable with building inclusive communities that value diversity (Carrington, 1999). The United Nations (2016) definition of 'inclusion,' given earlier, generally fits this innovation in advocating for structural and systemic changes. Reconceptualizing 'inclusive education' suggests that we move beyond a fixation on individual student deficits and onto work that focuses on structural and systemic deficits in including individual students. This also means that schools may not – and probably will not – look the same as they did in the 20th century. The practical implications of this will be addressed in the next section.

Pragmatic innovation

Schooling in the traditional sense, that is not described as inclusive, can reproduce inequalities and perpetuate hierarchies in society. It can do this by making assumptions about how schooling should look, how children learn, which children should learn, and what knowledge should be valued. In contrast, inclusive education has the power to expand opportunities and outcomes and address social inequities by expanding the practices of teaching and learning and who benefits from them.

Inclusive education has developed from a long history of educational innovation and represents school improvement on many levels for all students (Skrtic, Sailor & Gee, 1996). Theories dealing with democratic community (Dewey, 1916; Danforth, 2019) provide opportunities to rethink how we can improve acceptance of difference and create communities inclusive of all members of society (Turner & Louis, 1996). For example, an inclusive learning community should foster collaboration, problem solving, personalized learning, and critical discourse (Skrtic et al., 1996). Separation or stereotyping differences creates divisions and status systems that detract from the democratic nature of the community and the dignity of the individuals. Communities in inclusive schools cooperate and collaborate for the common good of all (Apple & Beane, 1995).

There is ample evidence that inclusion and diversity in education equates to a quality education for all. In a large-scale global literature study, the European Agency for Special Needs and Inclusive Education (EASNIE, 2018) evidences that inclusive education increases social inclusion, academic performance, the likelihood for continued education after secondary level, and the likelihood for employment for *both* youth with and without identified disabilities. There has been extensive research on how individual and collective beliefs, knowledge, and values contribute to the practice of inclusive education on topics such as social justice and equity issues, understanding of disability and learning, barriers to inclusive schooling, pedagogical approaches, the goals of education, organization of students and management of student behavior, the nature and implementation of curriculum, leadership within the school, the professional learning needs of teachers, and the individual needs of students (Carrington, 2000). In this section of the book, and the introductory chapter, we will transition from a theoretical and conceptual look at inclusion and move towards how this can be realized in practice.

Teachers: Training and professional practice

Teachers are a fundamental element to education systems. Across the world, teachers report a lack of confidence about their knowledge and skills in working with diverse learners (Mayer et al., 2017). McCrimmon (2015) notes that one of the most frequently cited barriers to achieving the goals of inclusive education is inadequate teacher education. However, teachers do not act within a vacuum. There has been entirely too much blame placed on teachers when education systems are perceived to be 'failing' (e.g. Goldstein, 2015) but, despite a few exceptions, teachers can only rise to the professional expectations and training that is afforded to them by the complex educational systems in which they are embedded. Teachers perceived as 'high-quality' can only be so if they are surrounded by a high-quality system that produces them (Darling-Hammond et al., 2007). Chapters in this book that focus specifically on teachers also draw attention to the ecosystem that surrounds their practices – be it policy, socio-cultural norms, training, professional incentives, or the like.

The first opportunity in inclusive education pragmatic innovation is in how we prepare *all* teachers, and not just those designated as 'special' or 'inclusive' educators. Over the last decade there has been much discussion about the particular skills and knowledge that are needed for teachers to be inclusive (Forlin & Chambers, 2011). Teacher preparation for inclusion and diversity must move beyond the weekly focus on a different category of disability or difference, because this perpetuates a special education model of categorization and intervention that assumes that young people with disabilities need to 'be fixed.' Focusing on categories of medical disability diagnosis and so-called 'best practices' for each category universalizes disability and difference – which, as we have already argued, runs counter to 'disability' as a constructed, relational, contextually defined, and social experience. This kind of teacher training prepares teachers not to look at the child in front of them, but rather to only look at the disability or difference. Further to this problem is that some so-called inclusion subjects are described as Inclusion *and* Special Educational Needs, which clearly indicates a lack of understanding of the underlying differences in theory and assumptions of these two approaches to education. To quote Slee (2013, p. 13), this confusion of terms serves to "tap a bifurcated conception of the nature of the student population and the purpose of schools and this bifurcation reflects a preordained hierarchy." In an inclusive education model, disability can be viewed as just one form of socially constructed difference. It is the cultural and social constructions of difference and school success and failure that are represented in beliefs, attitudes, and values that shape how teachers and educators interact with students (Carrington, 1999).

We argue for a new approach to coursework that systematically develops pre-service teachers' conceptual and contextual understandings of inclusion and diversity in education, and for greater links between coursework and fieldwork within a conceptual framework. All teachers should be trained and prepared to inhabit a professional role that includes heterogeneous and diverse classrooms. Walton and Rusznyak (2020) discuss research about initial teacher education and how coursework and fieldwork prepares or does not prepare teachers to teach in inclusive ways. They describe a range of topics that are included in coursework such as knowledge about various disabilities and categories of diversity, models of disability, policy and legal frameworks, instructional adjustments and approaches, and models of collaboration between colleagues and stakeholders. There has also been a range of research that identifies the need to consider positive beliefs and attitudes as being equally important to knowledge and skills (Forlin & Chambers, 2011). We propose that inclusion and diversity in education should be infused in all aspects of teacher preparation courses rather than as separate units of study. This would require consideration of curriculum, pedagogy, assessment, pastoral care, and promoting a school culture where all students and families are respected and belong; underpinned by the values of inclusion and equity. Opportunities for more in-depth elective study in various specialist areas could still be encouraged, as we acknowledge that there continues to be a need for specialist knowledge and skills to provide the personalized support required for some learners.

A number of chapters in this book describe innovative ways of supporting teacher preparation for inclusive schooling with a focus on understanding and value for diversity drawing on a socio-cultural approach. Lim and Thaver describe a critical reflexive model that influences how teachers can critically consider beliefs and assumptions that inform culture, policy, and practice in education contexts. Critical reflexivity involves the act of interrogating one's situatedness in society, history, and culture to arrive at an understanding about how we construct our knowledge from our experiences and interactions as well as our own agency in rethinking. The authors share pragmatic and innovative ideas that can be used to challenge the tradition of deficit and medical models of disability where educators perceive that failing at school is a problem that resides in the child rather than considering cultural and social influences that impact on school academic and social outcomes. It is exciting to consider a critical reflexive approach as a new way of preparing teachers for inclusive education that supports meaningful learning for all students, and as a means to move beyond a traditional and categorical approach of learning about a new disability each week. It is necessary to support teachers to examine issues, biases, prejudices, and assumptions that they carry into schools and how these inform and influence teaching and curriculum. A critical reflexive approach supports a need to constantly engage in a process of examining and critiquing our own thoughts and perspective.

In her chapter, Kimani argues that preparing teachers for inclusive education should not just focus on knowledge and skills but also on teacher identity and agency. This chapter reports on a project about teacher's interactions in a professional learning community in an inclusive school in South Africa. Professional learning can be facilitated in collaborative ways that highlight teacher professional identity and agency, acknowledges where they are at with their thinking and practice, and supports their development and commitment to be an inclusive education teacher.

Cooper and colleagues turn our attention to professional learning for educators with a focus on education programs for deaf and hard of hearing (DHH) learners and consider how innovative approaches can be used to support quality and equitable language learning. The authors present four cases of community-led efforts to promote and preserve sign languages in education that value culture, language of instruction, teacher instructional proficiency in those languages, and deaf community engagement in providing DHH cultural and linguistic resources. Authors such as Azizah and colleagues describe how local communities in Indonesia have worked together to ensure that education is more accessible for all students. The practical ideas of exploring inclusion and belonging in the local community are innovative ideas that have impact on understanding and practice.

Education leadership for inclusive education

Education leadership, and school leadership in particular, requires more attention in our collective work of promoting inclusion and diversity in schools. If education systems around the world expect school leaders to lead socially just change for greater equity in schools, there is a need for consideration of the knowledge, values, and skills needed to mobilize equity in schools. Addressing equity in education is a challenge when "exclusion resides deep in the bones of education" (Slee, 2018, p. 11) and can perpetuate divisions in social class due to race, ethnicity, gender, geography, sexuality, ability and disability, and religion. School leaders are often tasked with working 'between' spaces and negotiating state and/or national education policies with the everyday micro-practices of schools. Many inclusive education leaders see their role as an 'agent of change' while also being restricted within a larger bureaucratic system (Dobson & Douglas, 2020). That being said, this is exactly why the role of school leadership is so fundamentally important to positive change in inclusive school practices.

Moving forward to a global focus on inclusive education will require more attention to researching and developing a critical and transformative approach to school leadership (Carrington, in press). Education and school leaders need to build relationships and work in partnership with students, parents, and educators to initiate transformative reform and support equity in education. This will take time due to the need for critical reflection, dialogue, and commitment to shared values of equity and inclusion to support long-term actions for the greater good for all in schools.

Moving towards inclusive school cultures

School communities involve students, teachers, school leaders, specialist teachers, parents, and the wider community. The beliefs, values, and assumed ways of doing things among the school community contribute to the culture of the school (Carrington, 2007). The pressures and perverse incentives faced by educators in a school can impact a school culture and create barriers to inclusion. In many countries there is an increased focus on standardization, testing, and accountability. These international trends have led to increased, rather than decreased, disparities in education quality and opportunity between advantaged and marginalized groups because it may be perceived that supporting students who need additional help, such as students with disabilities, poses a threat to success in the competitive school market. For example, in Malaysia schools are ranked and evaluated based on an aggregate of all student achievement scores, and so most schools are disincentivized to include children with disabilities at all because school leadership perceive that they will lower their scores and lessen their reputation (Schuelka, fieldnotes, 2018). This practice of school 'accountability' through aggregate student achievement test scores is common in many countries, including the United States (Vanderwood et al. 1998; Schneider, 2017), although countries like the United States have separate laws that require students with disabilities to be included in mainstream educational settings and in national standardized achievement testing – for better or worse (Schuelka, 2013). In a country like Malaysia where schools have a choice as to which students they include, children with disabilities are often the first to be excluded because of their perceived 'threat' to school quality (Jelas & Ali, 2014).

In her chapter, Akabor highlights how rewards for academic achievement influence a culture of competitiveness in South African schools. The disparity between the meritocratic environment and the ideals of inclusion for all students is evident in the data from the mixed-method study in this chapter. This discussion poses some challenges in how we continue to focus on improving academic achievement while supporting collaboration, cooperation, and progress towards inclusive and equitable schools.

When students are included at school, they feel a sense of belonging (Carrington et al., in press). Daniels-Mayes and colleagues argue that there needs to be a greater focus on ensuring schools become places of belonging for Aboriginal children in Australia. They suggest that the concept of inclusive education is actually a damaging concept because it hides, in their view, the damaging purpose of assimilation and absorption into the mainstream. These three Indigenous teacher educators make a strong case for Belonging Education which would require educators to understand and emphasize ways of knowing, being, and doing in learning and to see Aboriginality as an asset for learning. The focus, they say, should be on creating culturally safe school communities for Aboriginal students, their families, and communities. Vandenbussche and colleagues describe how a sense of belonging is evident in the documentary film *Inclusief* [*Inclusive*]. Their analysis provides evidence of 'belonging' through how students are noticed, recognized, and given time and space to participate in daily educational practices. They remind us of the complexity and multilayeredness of belonging, not as procedures but as a powerful becoming-process in schools that entails deep relationality.

Flexibility: Rethinking what school looks like

The Covid-19 pandemic challenged what we think of when we think of 'school' and 'learning,' and demonstrated that providing flexibility into educational systems has more benefits than drawbacks. That being said, the Covid-19 pandemic also exposed and exacerbated the persistent underlying challenges of schooling around the world, in the form of social inequality (Bayrakdar & Guveli, 2020). Many children around the world were excluded from formal learning because of issues around technology access and unsupportive home learning environments, not to mention the negative effects the pandemic had on the mental health and well-being of most children (e.g. Mbazzi et al. 2021). Education systems themselves cannot solve social inequality alone, but the Covid-19 pandemic has shown that education systems can be nimble, innovative, flexible, and provide alternative modes of school and learning when forced through circumstance. We believe that the Covid-19 pandemic has exposed the resistance to educational reform, innovation, and flexibility as merely bureaucratic inertia that lacked the will and incentives to change. Despite the constant discourse of educational 'crises' historically and transnationally (Takayama, 2007), education systems around the world have not radically reformed educational practices (Cuban, 2013), particularly in schools that serve marginalized student populations (Payne, 2008). It is complex to be sure, but now we can see clearly that change is possible in education systems.

Avagyan and colleagues report on how Universal Design for Learning (UDL) was implemented in a school in Armenia. The flexible adaptation of the approach in a particular context highlights social and cultural factors that need to be considered when implementing what is understood to be the 'universality' of universal design. The authors emphasize that educators in various contexts need to adapt teaching approaches so that they have meaning and impact for their students. Global research on the implementation of the UDL guidelines will support understanding of how the approach can be more flexible and adapted in various social and cultural contexts. In another chapter of this book, Romero-Contreras and colleagues highlight innovative and flexible learning in Latin America, with an emphasis on collaboration and partnership with teachers through a blended learning approach.

In terms of where we would like to see pragmatic innovation in the field of inclusive education in the 21st century, as we have argued throughout this section and are supported by the chapters in this book, there needs to be greater attention paid towards how teachers are prepared, supported, and incentivized; but more than that there needs to be an acknowledgment that teachers operate in a complex educational system and are not the only element in creating inclusive education. School leadership is especially important in setting the tone for an inclusive culture within schools, as well as how teachers are heard and supported. Curriculum and pedagogy must also adapt and become more flexible in order to nimbly respond to the demands of inclusion and diversity in education. Pragmatic innovation requires work in multiple dimensions and levels and across communities, just as the CESA[3] indicates from the previous section. The three sections – conceptual, pragmatic, and methodological – are interdependent and linked. How inclusive education is conceptualized, and how it is practiced, also has major implications for how it is studied.

Methodological innovation

There have been differing opinions over ideology, politics, theories, research methods, policies, and practices in inclusive education which makes this field of research powerful and progressive (Allan & Slee, 2008). The body of research acknowledges the history of how societies respond to difference and highlights the social and cultural norms and values that dominate education. The chapters in this book extend not only an understanding of innovative methodologies, but also the underlying ideologies and epistemologies that inform research in inclusive education.

As we have argued, we believe that inclusive education needs to move beyond a myopic focus on access, as well as a singular focus on teachers in the process of inclusion, and into a more complex view of inclusion within a larger system informed by historical, socio-cultural, and economic contexts. This has significant implications in terms of methodological approaches to inclusive education as well. To be specific, what we mean here is to reduce the primacy of easily obtained quantitative statistics. For example, while the SDGs provide a more progressive approach to inclusion by focusing on the pluralization of rights and the relational aspects of inclusion, nonetheless the indicators associated with SDG #4 are driven by counting students that are physically 'there,' but do not do nearly enough to understand the quality of education nor the students' feeling of belonging (Johnstone et al. 2020). The SDG indicators also need to be further localized and relevant (Sprunt et al., 2017). We would like to see quantitative 'access' statistics become more nuanced and acknowledge that learning and belonging are complex and relational processes. Measuring quality in education comes with its own sets of conceptual challenges, but there are good examples such as the UNESCO's (2017) *Guide for Ensuring Inclusion and Equity in Education* and EASNIE's (2011) *Key Principles for Promoting Quality in Inclusive Education*. Notice that we believe that quality education and inclusive education share the same conceptual space and indicators.

We are also particularly inspired by Save the Children's work in Laos and their development of a set of indicators for quality and inclusion in education (Grimes, 2010). There are seventeen broad indicators that include the following:

1. All pupils feel welcome in the school
2. All students support each other in their learning
3. All students are well supported by school staff
4. Teachers and parents cooperate well
5. All students are treated equally as valued members of the school
6. All students feel that their opinions and views are valued
7. All students can access learning in all lessons
8. All students can access all parts of the school building
9. All students attend school every day
10. All students enjoy lessons
11. All students are engaged in all lesson activities
12. All students achieve their learning in all subjects according to their individual ability
13. All students learn together
14. All students have access to appropriate health services as necessary
15. School ensures that all students enter the school
16. All vulnerable children are successful in their learning
17. School creates a school environment which supports all students' learning

Note that some of the questions pertain to access, but a fair amount of them attempt to get at something more. There is a preference for the student experience, as well as understanding the ecosystem that surrounds the child, the classroom, and the school. As Schuelka and Engsig (2020) argue, these indicators complement the conceptualization of education as a complex system. The data for these indicators are collected through a variety of means, including questionnaires, school reviews and observations, interviews, participatory discussion groups, community focus groups, and reviews of school documentation. A plethora of data collection methods is entirely appropriate, and preferred, to understand any educational phenomenon.

We also believe that research such as teacher attitude surveys on disability and inclusion should be retired. These are relatively and methodologically simple research projects to undertake, and often seen in master's and doctoral theses because of their proclivity towards online questionnaire sampling, but they do nothing to advance inclusive education practice or even theoretical conceptualization. Oliver (2009) takes a more critical stance on disability attitude research and argues that it perpetuates a disability deficit and pathologized mindset. In general, the main takeaways from teacher attitude survey research is that there is not enough training, resources, materials, and adequate class sizes for teachers to effectively include students (summarized in Avramidis & Norwich, 2002). Further, teachers in these surveys indicate that they are more likely to have positive attitudes towards disabilities and inclusive education if they are inclusive and special education teachers (Avramidis & Kalyva, 2007). We are not deliberately singling out any particular study, but merely making the point that there is not much more to be gained from this type of research. Avramidis and Norwich (2002) argue for better research methodology themselves, citing the poor quality of most attitude questionnaires. More useful research in the 21st century might look at the factors that go beyond attitude and into other factors that inform and shape these attitudes to being with. Through research, more emphasis needs to be placed on the reasons why the material and structural supports for inclusive education are not being provided for teachers, and more emphasis needs to be placed on how inclusive education fundamentally reshapes our conception of the values and goals of going to school. This is not to say that research looking into teachers' worldviews and professional identity is not relevant to inclusion education innovation. Rather, we believe that this should only be part of how teaching practice is viewed. A good example from research is the Supporting Effective Teaching (SET) project (Jordan et al., 2009), which connects all of the elements of school cultures and norms, teacher beliefs and attitudes, teacher efficacy, classroom practices, and the outcomes of students. It is this kind of research work that is necessary to connect the dots and avoid being reductive, myopic, or exhibit fundamental attribution error. In this book, chapters such as Lim and Thaver, Akabor, Kimani, Avagyan and colleagues, and Dawa Dukpa and colleagues present innovative and more complex approaches to researching teachers.

While how we research and understand teachers in an educational system is of vital importance, so too must we expand how we research and understand the relationship between various layers of contexts and actors. Research and development on inclusive education and disability has been identified and criticized as having a Global North-to-Global South knowledge transfer (Grech, 2015; Le Fanu, 2013; Nguyen, 2019) rather than a mutually beneficial exchange. There is a tendency of Global North researchers and development agencies to transplant a universalistic idea of 'inclusive education' directly into foreign soil without an understanding that inclusive education is rooted in specific historical and socio-cultural educational contexts. Global inclusive education research and development practices must be critically examined for their seemingly one-way direction of knowledge transfer, and pushed towards "radical inclusion rooted in local cultural knowledge as the new norm" (Phasha et al. 2017, p. 5). This has historically not been the case, as "inclusive education has largely ignored the complex histories and socio-cultural conditions of developed and developing nations that shape how inclusive agendas are defined and implemented" (Kozleski et al. 2011, pp. 4–5). We argue for research in and on inclusive education to be reflective and self-aware of its history. We also argue for greater agency for researchers from so-called 'developing' countries, who are often receiving international aid support, to further their policies and practice grounded in local contexts. An international human rights agenda, such as within the CRPD or the SDGs, may promote inclusion with the best of intentions. However, as we have argued many times throughout this chapter, inclusion is entirely relational and context specific. Researchers cannot go into contexts with a set of assumptions as to 'who is disabled' and a deploy universal toolbox of 'solutions.' Schuelka (2019) terms this a 'macro-universalistic' approach. While a 'micro-phenomenological' approach might indeed provide a rich account of lived experiences and the production of the self in relation to a person's structural surroundings that disable them, this too has its shortcomings. The truth is that 'inclusive education' cuts across both the global and local at the same time. This is reflected in the CESA[3] model (Schuelka & Engsig, 2020) introduced earlier in this chapter. As Artiles and Dyson (2005, p. 37) argue:

> The question of whether inclusive education is best understood as a global or a local phenomenon cannot, we suggest, be separated from the location of that phenomenon at a particular historical moment. If inclusive education is global, that is because it has emerged in a period that is characterized by globalization in many aspects of human activity. And if the global nature of inclusive education cannot quite obscure its local flavours, that is because of the ambiguous nature of globalization itself.

The chapter by Benson in this book argues that a multilayered analytical approach is important to understand inclusive education policy, since policy is not only made at one level but enacted and interpreted by all actors at all levels (Massouti, 2018). Benson specifically makes an argument that more attention should be paid to the 'mesa' level of educational policy – that is those that perhaps do not craft the policy itself but are the administrators and overseers of educational policies. The worldviews and lived experiences of mesa-level actors is an important consideration to make when analyzing inclusive education implementation, enactment, and outcomes.

Another important consideration for inclusive education research is the intersectionality of marginalizing characteristics such as gender, race, poverty, class, and disability alongside a cultural-historical analytical perspective (Artiles, Dorn & Bal, 2016). It is well documented that children of racially and ethnically marginalized backgrounds are disproportionately represented in special education around the world (Gillborn, 2015; Graham, 2012; Harry & Klingner, 2014). There is also significant overlap between children receiving 'special education' services and otherwise marginalized from schooling who do not speak the dominant language of instruction as their first language (Artiles et al., 2005; Valdiviezo & O'Donnell, 2019). This evidence points to the fact that inclusive education often seeks first to marginalize and create difference based on multiple 'disabling' characteristics – the paradox of inclusion, as discussed earlier in this chapter. Research in and on inclusive education must pay more attention to intersectionality and the multiple constructions of difference. In their chapter, Daniels-Mayes and colleagues present a compelling case on the construction of 'Aboriginality' as a category of difference in Australian schools, and as inclusive education as an attempt to assimilate these differences. They approach their argument through multiple research methods, with each one preferencing the worldviews and lived experiences of local actors from teachers to policymakers.

Like many of the chapters in this book, we argue that inclusive education research must preference the voices of those it proposes to study: teachers, parents, and – above all – children with disabilities or other socially marginalized characteristics. Messiou (2017) rightly argues that inclusive education research has not traditionally been very collaborative with its subjects, nor transformative, nor has it included a broad definition of participants. Inclusive education research often does not pay enough attention to power, and power differentials between the researcher and participant (Stone & Priestley, 1996). In the same way that critical discourse analysis can expose and examine notions of power in inclusive education policy (i.e. Liasidou, 2011), so too must researchers critically examine their own role and the purposes of their research. There are promising ideas already out there in the world of research, such as 'inclusive research' (Nind, 2014) and 'universal design of research' (Williams & Moore, 2011). In this book, Braun's chapter on photovoice methodology demonstrates an innovative and collaborative approach to inclusive research. She partnered with children and researchers in Ghana to present a visual representation of lived experience directly from the children themselves. Likewise, Romero-Contreras and colleagues present a collaborative project in partnership with local actors and teachers. In her chapter, Mann, along with members of the Queensland Collective for Inclusive Education, presents the critical voices of parent-advocates in research, as well as her own auto-ethnography as a parent and privileged researcher. Additionally, Mann's chapter is effective in its presentation of research in narrative and storytelling form.

In terms of where we would like to see methodological innovation in the field of inclusive education in the 21st century, we advocate for inclusive education research to construct, rather than deconstruct. We believe that innovative inclusive education research should move beyond a 'challenges and barriers' to inclusive education deficit approach and seek out positive and empowering conceptualizations and practices. This does not mean that the purpose of such research is to 'scale-up' and universalize 'best practices.' Transformative research in inclusive education recognizes the specific contexts in which policies and practices are enacted, while focusing on deep and equitable change and enabling local factors and existing community assets. As we have argued, this means rethinking the narrow focus on the quantitative counting of 'access'; acknowledging teachers as having agency but still working within institutional, political, and socio-cultural structures; recognizing the multiple discursive layers that inform inclusive education from the micro to the macro; paying attention to intersectionality and the historical factors that have constructed societal difference and used difference as a cultural cudgel; and acknowledging researcher positionality and privilege by encouraging participant collaboration and keeping participant voices and experiences in the foreground of research.

Conclusion

There is still much work to do to advance inclusion and diversity in education, and the chapters in this book barely scratch the surface of the interesting and innovative work that is already being done in the 21st century. Throughout this introductory chapter, we have argued that the most important and significant innovation for inclusive education in the 21st century is to break free of its historical roots in elitism, exclusion, and constructions of difference and to embrace a future that reimagines the place of the school in society and what that school looks like. Education systems need to be reimagined as a place for all students, which is a break from its past conceptualization as a place for only the elite few. In order to realize this, there must be innovations in practice – from how teachers are prepared and inhabit their professional roles, to educational leadership that sets the tone of inclusive school cultures, to a flexibility in rethinking curriculum and pedagogical practices. Similarly, there must be innovations in inclusive education research that is transformative and does not perpetuate a deficit and neocolonial mindset.

Before learning happens, children must feel that they belong and have value. As Kunc (1992, pp. 38–39) writes,

> When inclusive education is fully embraced, we abandon the idea that children have to become "normal" in order to contribute to the world…We begin to look beyond typical ways of becoming valued members of the community, and in doing so, begin to realize the achievable goal of providing all children with an authentic sense of belonging.

This must be the primary objective of any work on inclusive education – beyond learning, beyond academic achievement, beyond credentials and employment – that schools can provide children with an 'authentic sense of belonging,' and teach that all humans have value in their communities. This is the innovative and global direction to which we must aspire in the 21st century.

References

ACIE [Australian Coalition for Inclusive Education] (2020). Driving change: A roadmap for achieving inclusive education in Australia. Retrieved from https://acie105204494.files.wordpress.com/2020/04/acie-roadmap-final_july-2020.pdf

Allan, J. & Slee, R. (2008). *Doing inclusive education research*. Rotterdam: Sense Publishers.

Anderson, J. & Boyle, C. (2019). Looking in the mirror: Reflecting on 25 years of inclusive education in Australia. *International Journal of Inclusive Education*, 23(7–8), 796–810. https://doi.org/10.1080/13603116.2019.1622802

Apple, M.W. & Beane, J.A. (1995). *Democratic schools*. Alexandria, VA: Association for supervision and curriculum development.

Armstrong, C.A., Armstrong, D. & Spandagou, I. (2010). *Inclusive education: International policy and practice*. London: SAGE.

Artiles, A.J., Dorn, S., & Bal, A. (2016). Objects of protection, enduring nodes of difference: Disability intersections with "other" differences, 1916 to 2016. *Review of Research in Education*, 40(1), 777–820. https://doi.org/10.3102/0091732X16680606

Artiles, A.J. & Dyson, A. (2005). Inclusive education in the globalization age: The promise of a comparative cultural-historical analysis. In D. Mitchell (Ed.), *Contextualizing inclusive education: Evaluating old and new international perspectives* (pp. 37–62). London: Routledge.

Artiles, A.J., Rueda, R., Salazar, J.J. & Higareda, I. (2005). Within-group diversity in minority disproportionate representation: English language learners in urban school districts. *Exceptional Children*, 71(3), 283–300. https://doi.org/10.1177/001440290507100305

Avramidis, E. & Kalyva, E. (2007). The influence of teaching experience and professional development on Greek teachers' attitudes towards inclusion. *European Journal of Special Needs Education*, 22(4), 367–389.

Avramidis, E. & Norwich, B. (2002). Teachers' attitudes towards integration/inclusion: A review of the literature. *European Journal of Special Needs Education*, 20(2), 129–147.

Barton, L. (1996). Sociology and disability: Some emerging issues. In L. Barton (Ed.), *Disability and society: Emerging issues and insights* (pp. 3–17). New York: Addison Wesley Longman.

Bayrakdar, S. & Guveli, A. (2020). *Inequalities in home learning and schools' provision of distance teaching during school closure of COVID-19 lockdown in the UK*. ISER Working Paper Series, No. 2020-09. Colchester: University of Essex, Institute for Social and Economic Research.

Biklen, D. (1988). The myth of clinical judgment. *Journal of Social Issues*, 44(1), 127–140.

Black, A. (2019). A picture of special educational needs in England: An overview. *Frontiers in Education*, 4(79). Published online: https://doi.org/10.3389/feduc.2019.00079

Braun, A.M.B. (2019). Psychological inclusion: Considering students' feelings of belongingness and the benefits for academic achievement. In M.J. Schuelka, C.J. Johnstone, G. Thomas & A.J. Artiles (Eds.), *The SAGE handbook on inclusive and diversity in education* (pp. 66–75). London: SAGE.

Carrier, J. (1986). *Learning disability: Social class and the construction of inequality in American education*. Connecticut: Greenwood Press.

Carrington, S. (1999). Inclusion needs a different school culture. *International Journal of Inclusive Education*, 3(3), 257–268. https://doi.org/10.1080/136031199285039

Carrington, S. (2000). *Accommodating the needs of diverse learners; The impact of teachers' beliefs on classroom practice*. PhD Thesis, The University of Queensland.

Carrington, S. (2007). Developing an inclusive school culture. In M. Keeffe & S. Carrington (Eds.), *Schools and diversity* (2nd ed.) (pp. 31–45). Sydney: Pearson Education Australia.

Carrington, S. (in press). Leadership for equity. In R. Tierney, F. Rizvi, K. Ercikan and G. Smith (Eds). *International encyclopedia of education*. Fourth volume. Elsevier.

Carrington, S., MacArthur, J., Kearney, A., Kimber, M., Mercer, L., Morton, M., & Rutherford, G. (2012). Towards an inclusive education for all. In S. Carrington & J. MacArthur (Eds), *Teaching in inclusive school communities* (pp. 3–38). Milton: John Wiley & Sons Australia.

Carrington, S., Saggers, B., Shochet, I., Wurfl, A., Orr, J. (in press). Researching a whole school approach to school connectedness. *International Journal of Inclusive Education*. https://doi.org/10.1080/13603116.2021.1878298

Cuban, L. (2013). *Inside the black box of classroom practice: Change without reform in American education*. Cambridge, MA: Harvard University Press.

Danforth, S. (2019). Dewey and the philosophy of inclusion. In M.J. Schuelka, C.J. Johnstone, G. Thomas & A.J. Artiles (Eds.), *The SAGE handbook on inclusive and diversity in education* (pp. 41–50). London: SAGE.

Darling-Hammond, L., Burns, D., Campbell, C., Goodwin, A.L., Hammerness, K., Low, E.L., McIntyre, A., Sato, M. & Zeichner, K. (2007). *Empowered educators: How high-performance systems shape teaching quality around the world*. San Francisco, CA: Jossey-Bass.

Dewey, J. (1916). *Democracy and education*. New York: Macmillan.

Dobson, G. & Douglas, G. (2020). Who would do that role? Understanding why teachers become SENCos through an ecological systems theory. *Educational Review*, 72(3), 298–318. https://doi.org/10.1080/00131911.2018.1556206

EASNIE (2018). *Evidence of the link between inclusive education and social inclusion: A review of the literature*. (S. Symeonidou, Ed.) Odense, Denmark: EASNIE.

EASNIE [European Agency for Special Needs and Inclusive Education] (2011). *Key principles for promoting quality in inclusive education: Recommendations for practice*. Odense, DK: EASNIE. https://www.european-agency.org/sites/default/files/Key-Principles-2011-EN.pdf

Engsig, T.T. (2019). The experience of inclusion in Danish schools: Between politicization and pedagogical ideals. In M.J. Schuelka, C.J. Johnstone, G. Thomas & A.J. Artiles (Eds.), *The SAGE handbook on inclusive and diversity in education* (pp. 380–391). London: SAGE.

Forlin, C. & Chambers, D. (2011). Teacher preparation for inclusive education: Increasing knowledge but raising concerns. *Asia-Pacific Journal of Teacher Education*, 39(1), 17–32. https://doi.org/10.1080/1359866X.2010.540850

Geertz, C. (1963). *Agricultural involution: The process of ecological change in Indonesia*. Berkeley, CA: University of California Press.

Giangreco, M.F. (1997). Key lessons learned about inclusive education: Summary of the 1996 Schonell Memorial Lecture. *International Journal of Disability, Development and Education*, 44(3), 193–206. https://doi.org/10.1080/0156655970440302

Gillborn, D. (2015). Intersectionality, critical race theory, and the primacy of racism: Race, class, gender, and disability in Education. *Qualitative Inquiry*, 21(3), 227–287.

Goldstein, D. (2015). *The teacher wars: A history of America's most embattled profession*. New York: Anchor Books.

Graham, L.J. (2012). Disproportionate over-representation of Indigenous students in New South Wales Government Special Schools. *Cambridge Journal of Education*, 41(4), 163–176.

Grech, S. (2015). *Disability and poverty in the global south: Renegotiating development in Guatemala*. London: Palgrave Macmillan.

Grimes, P. (2010). *A quality education for all. A history of the Lao PDR Inclusive Education Project, 1993–2009*. Report written for Save the Children Norway. Retrieved from: https://www.eenet.org.uk/resources/docs/A_Quality_Education_For_All_LaoPDR.pdf

Groce, N. (1985). *Everyone here spoke sign language: Hereditary deafness on Martha's Vineyard*. Cambridge, MA: Harvard University Press.

Harry, B. & Klingner, J. K. (2014). *Why are so many minority students in special education?* New York, NY: Teachers College Press.

Hehir, T., Grindal, T., Freeman, B., Lamoreau, R., Borquaye, Y., & Burke, S. (2016). *A summary of the evidence on inclusive education*. São Paulo: Alana Institute.

Imray, P. & Colley, A. (2017). *Inclusion is dead: Long live inclusion*. London: Routledge.

Ingstad, B. & Whyte, S.R. (Eds.) (2007). *Disability in local and global worlds*. Berkeley, CA: University of California Press.

Jelas, Z.M. & Ali, M.M. (2014). Inclusive education in Malaysia: Policy and practice. *International Journal of Inclusive Education*, 18(10), 991–1003. https://doi.org/10.1080/13603116.2012.693398

Jenkins, J.H. & Barrett, R.J. (Eds.) (2004). *Schizophrenia, culture, and subjectivity: The edge of experience*. Cambridge, UK: Cambridge University Press.

Johnstone, C., Schuelka, M.J., & Swadek, G. (2020). Quality education for all? The promises and limitations of the SDG framework for inclusive education and students with disabilities. In A. Wulff (Ed.), *Grading goal four: Tensions, threats, and opportunities in the sustainable development goal on quality education* (pp. 96–115). Leiden: Brill | Sense.

Jordan, A., Schwartz, E. & McGhie-Richmond, D. (2009). Preparing teachers for inclusive classrooms. *Teaching and Teacher Education*, 25, 535–542. https://doi.org/10.1016/j.tate.2009.02.010

Kozleski, E.B., Artiles, A.J. & Waitoller, F.R. (2011). Equity in inclusive education: Historical trajectories and theoretical commitments. In A.J. Artiles, E.B. Kozleski & F.R. Waitoller (Eds.), *Inclusive education: Examining equity on five continents* (pp. 1–14). Cambridge, MA: Harvard University Press.

Kunc, N. (1992). The need to belong: Rediscovering Maslow's hierarchy of needs. In R.A. Villa, J.S. Thousand, W. Stainback, & S. Stainback (Eds.), *Restructuring for caring and effective education: An administrative guide to creating heterogeneous schools* (pp. 25–39). Baltimore: Paul H. Brookes Publishing.

Labaree, D.F. (2010). *Someone has to fail: The zero-sum game of public schooling*. Cambridge, MA: Harvard University Press.

Le Fanu, G. (2013). The inclusion of inclusive education in international development: Lessons from Papua New Guinea. *International Journal of Educational Development*, 33, 139–148. http://dx.doi.org/10.1016/j.ijedudev.2012.03.006

Liasidou, A. (2011). Unequal power relations and inclusive education policy making: A discursive analytic approach. *Education Policy*, 25(6), 887–907. https://doi.org/10.1177/0895904810386587

Massouti, A. (2018). (Re)thinking the adoption of inclusive education policy in Ontario schools. *Canadian Journal of Educational Administration and Policy*, 185, 32–44.

Mayer, D., Dixon, M., Kline, J., Kostogriz, A., Moss, J., Rowan, L., Walker-Gibbs, B. & White, S. (2017). *Studying the effectiveness of teacher education: Early career teachers in diverse settings*. Singapore: Springer.

Mbazzi, F.B., Nalugya, R., Kawesa, E., Nimusiima, C., King, R., van Hove, G. & Seeley, J. (2021) The impact of COVID-19 measures on children with disabilities and their families in Uganda. *Disability & Society*, published online. https://doi.org/10.1080/09687599.2020.1867075

McCrimmon, A.W. (2015). Inclusive Education in Canada: Issues in Teacher Preparation. *Intervention in School and Clinic*, 50(4), pp. 234–237. https://doi.org/10.1177/1053451214546402.

McDermott, R. (1993). The acquisition of a child by a learning disability. In S. Chaiklin & J. Lave (Eds.), *Understanding practice: Perspectives on activity and context* (pp. 269–305). Cambridge, UK: Cambridge University Press.

Messiou, K. (2017). Research in the field of inclusive education: Time for a rethink? *International Journal of Inclusive Education*, 21(2), 146–159. https://doi.org/10.1080/13603116.2016.1223184

Minow, M. (1990). *Making all the difference: Inclusion, exclusion, and American law*. Cornell, NY: Cornell University Press.

Nguyen, X.T. (2019). Unsettling 'inclusion' in the Global South: A post-colonial and intersectional approach to disability, gender, and education. In M.J. Schuelka, C.J. Johnstone, G. Thomas & A.J. Artiles (Eds.), *The SAGE handbook on inclusive and diversity in education* (pp. 28–40). London: SAGE.

Nind, M. (2014). *What is inclusive research?* London: Bloomsbury.

Norwich, B. (2008). *Dilemmas of difference, inclusion, and disability: International perspectives and future directions*. London: Routledge.

Oliver, M. (2009). *Understanding disability: From theory to practice*, 2nd ed. London: Palgrave Macmillan.

Payne, C.M. (2008). *So much reform, so little change: The persistence of failure in urban schools*. Cambridge, MA: Harvard University Press.

Phasha, N., Mahlo, D. & Dei, G.J.S. (2017). Inclusive schooling and education in African contexts. In N. Phasha, D. Mahlo & G.J.S. Dei (Eds.), *Inclusive education in African contexts: A critical reader* (pp. 1–18). Rotterdam: Sense.

Ramirez, F.O. & Boli, J. (1987). The political construction of mass schooling: European origins and worldwide institutionalization." *Sociology of Education*, 60(1), 2–17. https://doi.org/10.2307/2112615.

Rattray, N.A. (2013). Contesting urban space in disability in highland Ecuador. *City & Society*, 25(1), 25–46. https://doi.org/10.1111/ciso.12008.

Richardson, J.G., & Powell, J.J.W. (2011). *Comparing special education: Origins to contemporary paradoxes*. Stanford, CA: Stanford University Press.

Roser, M. & Ortiz-Ospina, E. (2016) Global Education. Published online at OurWorldInData.org. Retrieved from: https://ourworldindata.org/global-education.

Schneider, J. (2017). *Beyond test scores: A better way to measure school quality*. Cambridge, MA: Harvard University Press.

Schuelka, M.J. (2013). Excluding students with disabilities from the culture of achievement: The case of the TIMSS, PIRLS and PISA. *Journal of Education Policy*, 28(2), 216–230.

Schuelka, M.J. (2018). The cultural production of the 'disabled' person: Constructing difference in Bhutanese schools. *Anthropology & Education Quarterly*, 49(2), 183–200. https://doi.org/10.1111/aeq.12244

Schuelka, M.J. (2019). Advancing a comparative case study approach towards education and disability research: An example from Bhutan. In N. Singal, P. Lynch, and S. Johansson (Eds.), *Education and disability in the global south: New perspectives from Asia and Africa* (pp. 89–106). London: Bloomsbury.

Schuelka, M.J. & Engsig, T.T. (2020). On the question of educational purpose: Complex educational systems analysis for inclusion. *International Journal of Inclusive Education*. Published online: https://doi.org/10.1080/13603116.2019.1698062.

Schuelka, M.J., Johnstone, C.J., Thomas, G. & Artiles, A.J. (Eds.) (2019). *The SAGE Handbook of inclusion and diversity in education*. London: SAGE.

Shevlin, M. & Banks, J. (2021). Inclusion at a crossroads: Dismantling Ireland's system of special education. *Education Sciences*, 11(4), 161. https://doi.org/10.3390/educsci11040161

Skrtic, T. M., Sailor, W. & Gee, K. (1996). Voice, collaboration, and inclusion. *Remedial and Special Education*, 17(3), 142–157.

Slee, R. (2013). Meeting some challenges of inclusive education in an age of exclusion. *Asian Journal of Inclusive Education*, 1(2), 3–17.

Slee, R. (2018). *Inclusive education isn't dead, it just smells funny*. London: Routledge.

Sprunt, B., Deppeler, J., Ravulo, K., Tinaivunivalu, S., & Sharma, U. (2017). Entering the SDG era: What do Fijians prioritise as indicators of disability-inclusive education? *Disability and the Global South*, 4(1), 1065–1087.

Stone, E. & Priestley, M. (1996) Parasites, pawns and partners: disability research and the role of non-disabled researchers. *British Journal of Sociology*, 47(4), 699–716.

Takayama, K. (2007). *A Nation at Risk* crosses the Pacific: Transnational borrowing of the U.S. crisis discourse in the debate on education reform in Japan. *Comparative Education Review*, 51(4), 423–446. http://www.jstor.org/stable/10.1086/520864

Turner, C.S.V. & Louis, K.S. (1996). Society's response to differences. A sociological perspective. *Remedial and Special Education*, 17(3), 134–141.

UNESCO (2015). *Education for all 2000–2015: Achievements and challenges. Global Education Monitoring Report*. Paris: UNESCO.

UNESCO (2017). *A guide for ensuring inclusion and equity in education*. Paris: UNESCO. https://unesdoc.unesco.org/ark:/48223/pf0000248254

UNESCO (2020). *Inclusion and education: All means all.* Global Education Monitoring Report. Paris: UNESCO.

United Nations (2006). *Convention on the rights of persons with disabilities.* New York: United Nations.

United Nations (2015). *The Millennium Development Goals report.* New York: United Nations.

United Nations (2016). *Convention on the rights of persons with disabilities: General comment no. 4. Article 24: Right to inclusive education.* Geneva: United Nations.

Valdiviezo, L.A. & O'Donnell, J.L. (2019). 'To educate for them in different ways': Defining inclusion in popular and intercultural education in Argentina and Peru. In M.J. Schuelka, C.J. Johnstone, G. Thomas & A.J. Artiles (Eds.), *The SAGE handbook on inclusive and diversity in education* (pp. 468–480). London: SAGE.

Vanderwood, M., McGrew, K.S., & Ysseldyke, J.E. (1998). Why we can't say much about students with disabilities during education reform. *Exceptional Children, 64*(3), 359–370. https://doi.org/10.1177/001440299806400305

Walton, E. & Rusznyak, L. (2020). Cumulative knowledge-building for inclusive education in initial teacher education. *European Journal of Teacher Education,* 43 (1), pp. 18–37. https://doi.org/10.1080/02619768.2019.1686480

Warnock, M. (2005). *Special educational needs: A new look.* London: Philosophy of Education Society of Great Britain Publications.

Welply, O. (2020). Inclusion across borders: Young immigrants in France and England. *Forum for International Research in Education,* 6(1), 40–63.

Williams, A.S. & Moore, S.M. (2011). Universal design of research: inclusion of persons with disabilities in mainstream biomedical studies. *Science Translational Medicine,* 3(82), 82cm12. https://doi.org/10.1126/scitranslmed.3002133

PART I
Conceptual innovation

2
INTERNATIONAL PERSPECTIVES ON INCLUSIVE EDUCATION IN RURAL CONTEXTS

Finding (un)common ground

Julie Dillon-Wallace

Children with complex learning profiles

A challenge for *all* schools is ensuring that *all* students have equal and equitable access to schooling (Stenman & Pettersson, 2020). This chapter draws upon a dearth of literature that discusses the enduring need to provide an inclusive education for all children with complex learning profiles in rural contexts, in developing and developed countries, and attempts to find commonalities on (un)common ground.

Equal, equitable and inclusive education is brought about by the acknowledgement and actioning of strategies that recognize the rights of children who may have differing learning paths to high-quality education, within a community of learners (Ainscow, 2000). Historically, the education of children with complex learning profiles has shown to be a long and difficult road. Certainly in the past, they were not provided with any meaningful education (Rogers, 2013). Inclusive education *per se* has involved, and still continues to fight, a radical change to education systems that extends past class size and specialist support to challenging prejudices and norms that discriminate against learners within this cohort (Giangreco, 2010).

For the purposes of this discussion, the term "children with complex learning profiles" has been adopted. This broad definition allows for the embodiment of inclusive education as a fundamental human right, which extends far beyond disability. Human rights models present many challenges and hurdles, are visionary in nature, and certainly the multidimensional processes they present cannot be implemented overnight (Degener, 2016). However, human rights are acquired qua birth and are universal; where "social status, nor identity category, nor national origin or any other status", can prevent a person from accessing their fundamental human rights (Degener, 2016, p 4). To illustrate, children with complex learning profiles have been defined as:

> … having a combination of impairments affecting behaviour, cognition, communication, emotional regulation, communication, emotional regulation, mobility and/or sensory processing. Students in this group can also include those who have experienced childhood complex trauma arising from abuse, neglect and exclusion for education. Significant barriers may exist for students with complex learning profiles.
>
> (Graham, 2020, p. xx)

On the basis of this definition, children may require substantial and/or extensive adjustments to the learning environment, including the curriculum, pedagogical practices and/or assessment, in order to be included in a meaningful, respectful, and age-appropriate environment (Graham, 2020). In addition, teachers who work with children with complex learning profiles would be required to work in collaborative and transdisciplinary and multidisciplinary teams with the student, families, school community, and other relevant professionals to best support progress (Tait & Hussain, 2017).

This definition aligns with other countries that are moving beyond disability to include children from diverse groups such as minority ethnic and linguistically diverse backgrounds, socio-economically under-resourced sectors and/or disaster and climatic affected areas (Begum et al., 2019). It also encompasses newly emerging definitions of inclusive education that includes girls, child trafficking and sexual abuse, poverty, HIV/AIDS, child lepers, and child labourers (Khanal, 2015). In some of the most poorly resourced communities, such as rural areas, implementing inclusive programs can be complicated when there is a high reliance on external funding from aid agencies such as UNICEF, where there is less involvement and input from parents, teachers and communities (Edwards, 2011). This raises yet another debate: that the localisation of aid, and how the aid model is structured and delivered by western, developed countries and international agencies, is not conducted in partnership with local people and communities, and more importantly, not by those who live in the communities and understand the needs best.

The absence of a universally agreed definition of inclusive education has added to continued uncertainties, disputes and contractions in understanding the rights of children with complex learning profiles (Ainscow & Miles, 2008). Internationally, emergent rights have been foregrounded with the adoption of the Universal Declaration of Human Rights (UDHR – 1948) (Article 26) and the International Convention on Economic, Social and Cultural Rights (ICESCR – 1966) Articles 13 & 14. Whilst the UDHR is not a legally binding instrument/treaty, it is recognised as having very influential status in international human rights law. Similarly, the ICESCR (although a legally binding treaty on those countries that have signed up to it) contains what are known as aspirational, progressive or positive human rights, which are to be implemented by States for their populations when they have the means (and conditions) to do so, or alternatively, when feasible.

Furthermore, the United Nations Convention on the Rights of the Child (UNCRC) by the UN General Assembly in 1989, and the 1994 Salamanca Statement, asserted the rights of students with Special Education Needs to access mainstream schools and an adapted curriculum, individualizing their learning needs (Franck & Joshi, 2017). Despite more recent global initiatives such as the UNESCO Education for All (EFA) agenda, and international treaties, most notably the 2006 UN Convention on the Rights of Persons with Disabilities (Article 24), which mandates that people with disabilities should have the same rights to education as all learners (Franck & Joshi, 2017), significant challenges remain in opportunities for an equitable and accessible education for children with complex learning profiles. Regardless of an absence of consensus in conceptualizing inclusive education, the central intent of such international treaties is that all children have the right to a free and equitable education that is free from discrimination based on "caste, ethnicity, religion, economic status, refugee status, language, gender or disability" (UNESCO, 2005, p. 12). Regardless, implementing inclusive practice in affluent Western countries still presents many of the same challenges as developing countries around staffing, education and training of teachers, scarcity of resources, and access to all learners (Barrio, 2017; Panizzon & Pegg, 2007).

Many of the arguments for inclusive education for children in mainstream schools is from the viewpoint that relative mandates have been largely accepted nationally and internationally by policy makers, and therefore increasingly implemented in school systems (Miles, Westbrook, & Croft, 2018). According to UNESCO's 2020 Global Monitoring Report addressing full inclusion in education, less than 10% of countries have laws that ensure the availability of inclusive education for all learners. In spite of inclusive practice being promoted to a global level, many of the policies and laws are based on Western political and contextual norms (Miles & Singal, 2010). As a result, a phenomenon that prevents the implementation of human rights treaties is that of "regionalism" or "cultural relativism", which has a very different view of human rights. These phenomena reject the concept of "universality" of human rights, even if a country may have signed/ratified an international human rights treaty.

Defining rurality

Defining rurality and remoteness has promoted debate through inconsistent usage in the research, both locally and internationally (Arnold et al., 2005; Stelmach, 2011). As a consequence, this often means that "rurality" is defined for what it is not rather than what it is, adding to deficit perceptions (Miller, 2012). In Australia, several national classifications for measuring remoteness exist. The Australian Institute of Health and Welfare (AIHW) states that the term "rural and remote" includes all areas outside Australia's major cities. The five categories provided by Australian Statistical Geography Standard (ASGS) are shown as: major cities, inner regional, outer region, remote, and very remote Australia. Remoteness is calculated using an algorithm (ARIA+) that assigns values along a continuum of 0 to 12, relative to remoteness per square kilometre. The lower the value, the closer the region to major cities.

In the United States, the U.S. Census Bureau defines every state as including a rural element. This broad-brush term is measured by calculating population density and land usage metrics. This falls painfully short in articulating the socioecological landscape and what it means to live and work in these contexts (Sindelar et al., 2018). More recently, terminology has been adopted by the National Center for Education Statistics (NCES) to describe rural locales: rural fringe, rural distant and rural remote. Though these descriptors contribute to an understanding of locale, they fail to provide an understanding of the nuances of living and working in these environments, both between and within states (Sindelar et al., 2018).

In developing countries with very low socioeconomic status, rurality is often defined by the geographic makeup of the region. This can be diverse not only in landscape but also the cultural biases and discrimination that the specific locations bring, such as lack of parental support, caste-based practices, and the early marriage culture for girls (Begum et al., 2019). These challenges are compounded exponentially by regions classified as indigenous, flood affected, border area, and/or displaced nationals, as examples. In these areas, services are prioritised to very limited resources such as transport infrastructure, clean drinking water, health services and education for mainstream learners, rather than providing an inclusive education for children with complex learning profiles. In these communities, the farther away from an urban city, the scarcer resources become. Considering the compounded costs for educating children with complex learning profiles, making these children a priority is difficult, especially when social stigmas and superstitions around children with complex learning profiles still exist (Adams Hill & Sukbunpant, 2013; Obeng, 2007).

Evidently, the meaning of rural has been couched from differing parameters: land use, geographic boundaries, population density and/or behavioural qualities (Stelmach, 2011). As a result of the evasive nature of rurality, the way the term is used in relation to inclusive rural education becomes complex. The real risk is that local policy and practices are interpreted and enacted in different ways, which will not always meet the needs of the children who live there. If inclusive teaching practice in rural environments is to be more fully understood, consensus vis-à-vis what equal and inclusive education means in rural contexts, both nationally and internationally (Stenman & Pettersson, 2020), needs to be addressed. In this way, learning programs can be developed to enable equal, inclusive and high-quality education with some common foundation (Stenman & Pettersson, 2020).

Inclusivity in rural contexts

Ordinarily, educating children with complex learning profiles presents many challenges. The diverse profile of students who may be present in any mainstream classroom may consist of students from many subgroups of disability and learning, Indigenous populations, cultural heritage, and gender identities; to name but a few.

Specifically, the availability of diverse learning opportunities for children with complex learning profiles is seen as problematic, especially in rural contexts (Panizzon & Pegg, 2007; Tait & Hussain, 2017). In rural contexts, the challenges faced in providing education for students with complex learning profiles is magnified (Franck & Joshi, 2017). In many instances, rural schools state that they are disadvantaged in terms of educational provision, especially with regards to access to professional development and materials and supplies, which directly affect students' learning and outcomes (Barrio, 2017; Downes & Roberts, 2017; Tait & Hussain, 2017). Staffing schools with high-quality teachers, and retaining those teachers, poses challenges in providing all students with equitable learning environments within the school community, especially when compared to their metropolitan counterparts. These challenges for rural schools have shown to be a global phenomenon (Arnold, Newman, Gaddy, & Dean, 2005).

Teaching in rural contexts

Much of the rural discourse discusses, or is framed within, deficit understandings of rural settings (Green et al., 2013; Wallace & Boylan, 2009). Teaching in rural and remote settings has been portrayed as placing extra demands on teachers (Stenman & Pettersson, 2020). Reports of negative experiences of early career teachers by way of procuring affordable housing and limited professional development and isolation contributes to negative perceptions of rural postings, which deters teachers to consider teaching positions in these areas (Green et al., 2013; Roberts, 2013). Such reports further marginalise rural populations and enforces existing rural-deficit models (Ankrah-Dove, 1982). This "social othering" (Hughes, 2010) is further exacerbated by a second layer of deficit, or for want of a better term, a double deficit.

This existing "rural lens" calls for a reversal of thinking, not only outwards (and inwards) from the teaching profession, but to a position where the strengths that children with complex learning profiles bring to rural schools are highlighted and valued, especially where cultural biases can be deep seated (Adams Hill & Sukbunpant, 2013). Children with complex learning profiles are often viewed from a medical model, to address and identify issues surrounding complex learning pathways (Manago, Davis, & Goar, 2017). Though a medical model is compulsory for understanding the tenets around conditions that fall outside normative parameters, a social model from a strengths-based approach provides an important perspective of the lived experiences of those living with complex learning profiles in rural environments (Manago et al., 2017). This shift in thinking can be demonstrated by schools in Canada that have adopted a strengths-based approach to rural education as a strategy to sustain the social, cultural, and economic attributes of rural communities (Wallace & Boylan, 2009). This perspective strengthens the community capacity by way of building options through the provision of contextually relevant services, of which education and the staffing and support of rural and remote schools, is one cornerstone (Wallace & Boylan, 2009).

Social and human rights issues are largely parameters set by Western countries, and do not necessarily address or acknowledge the challenges faced by teaching in rural settings in developing countries (Miles et al., 2018). The paucity of research on teaching in these rural settings means that teachers who are responsible for implementing inclusive programs are provided with little guidance on best practice (Miles et al., 2018). Due to the myriad of rural classifications and multiplicity of special education 'categorizations', the numerous combinations and permutations make it challenging to research within and across contexts and countries. Compounding these challenges is that almost half of low-and middle-income countries do not collect enough education data about children with complex learning profiles. It is suspected that many more children with complex learning profiles are either not identified and/or do not attend rural schools (Blanks, 2014).

Nonetheless, the socioeconomic status of a country or region need not necessarily predicate the approach and support a community may employ when providing inclusive education for children with complex learning profiles. In some of the most socioeconomically disadvantaged countries, teachers carefully consider the tenets of inclusive education in rural settings by way of removing physical, attitudinal and structural barriers in order to support engagement and participation for children with complex learning profiles (Miles et al., 2018; Obeng, 2007). Core aspects of teachers' knowledge and pedagogical expertise in rural contexts are drawn upon to develop and implement inclusive programs for children in these places (Grech, 2014).

The notion of place

Place is not only a human conception, but also a social construction (Green et al., 2013). By definition, "it is the experiences, activities, routines and interactions (or ways of inhabiting a space) to which individuals or groups assign meaning" (Green et al., 2013, p. 96). Meaning making is a key attribute of a sense of Place. Wallace and Boylan (2009) specifically discuss Place in terms of an educational context that connects with the local tradition, culture and practice, with children learning contextually in their environment. The notion of Place is embodied when teachers are required to fully immerse themselves within the local culture and community and incorporate local values of education within relevant curriculum (Stelmach, 2011). However, Green et al. (2013) challenge this thinking by insightfully suggesting that Place isn't so much context *per se* but can be useful when challenging and repositioning preconceived ideas around inclusive practice in rural places, and when examining the lived experiences of the inhabitants.

Green et al. (2013), when drawing upon their various research methods and conceptual frameworks to inquire with families and teachers about the everyday life of living and working in remote locations in Australia, remained cognizant of what constituted a strong sense of Place. They paid attention to life within and outside classrooms, being aware of the significance of the resources, rules, routines, and available relationships that constituted school learning places. In this way, the complexity and dynamics of everyday life within the scope of place may be understood.

Families living with a child with a complex learning profile in a rural context face numerous (and complex) context-driven challenges and conditions that are constant and persistent, which magnifies the rural standpoint of Roberts (2014), "that rural people and communities *really* matter" (p.136).

Adopting notions of Place, instead of just context, reminds us of the human agency in Place making and incorporates the social structures and complex relationships that guide and respond to life experiences in rural and remote settings (Green et al., 2013). In order to understand the lived experiences of the inhabitants, it is important to let go of the stereotyped, negative aspects of rurality and teaching, in order to make sense of the complex sociocultural contexts and socioeconomic position specific to the context (Green et al., 2013). Miles et al. (2018) argue that inclusive education needs to come to terms with its identity as a social construct before taking into account wider structural inequalities in post-colonial contexts and global imbalances of power, which often occur in rural contexts.

To better understand these expanded views of rural education situated within Place, Helfenbein (as cited in Green et al. (2013)) states that there exists a reciprocal relationship between people and Places. His reasoning is that Place and its inhabitants simultaneously co-exist. Arnold (as cited in Panizzon & Pegg, 2007) supports this rationale by stating that schools are not isolated entities but are the epicentre of real communities. Corbett (2015) also adopts this expanded view when examining the factors that affect the notion of Place in rural settings. He states that while there is interest in place-based education as a research paradigm (Gruenewald, 2003; Gruenewald & Smith, 2008), there is little specificity of what the elements are *per se*, or how they affect Place.

Bronfenbrenner's socioecological theory supports this perspective, with its interconnected and reciprocal systems, and this model is particularly useful when examining inclusive practice (Dillon-Wallace, 2017; Summers, Behr, & Turnbull, 1988). This could be particularly important when researching rural Places, where some of the affordances and hindrances of inclusive opportunities for children with complex learning profiles are magnified by the very context in which they reside. In order to further illustrate, Bronfenbrenner's socioecological theory has been used to discuss the nexus between socio-cultural, political and economic factors that impact on school and community functioning (both positively and negatively) (Reid, 2017), and the multitude of factors that may need to be examined when theorizing and researching inclusive practices. This theoretical approach has been increasingly adopted, as there has been a paradigm shift in inclusive practice from fixing the individual (medical model) to modifying the environment (social model) (Turnbull, Turnbull, Shank & Smith, 2004).

Implementing inclusive education in rural contexts: A strengths-based approach

To ensure that children with complex learning profiles are provided an equal and inclusive education, it is paramount that the teaching and learning experiences are tailored to the context in which they live (Stenman & Pettersson, 2020). Barriers to implementing inclusive programmes in rural schools for children with complex learning profiles have been well documented across community, school contexts and teaching-related practices. Numerous studies (Berry & Gravelle, 2013; Miles, Westbrook, & Croft, 2018; Reid, 2017) have affirmed deficit models by explaining away poor academic achievement and attendance on the basis of race, gender, poverty, political forces, rural and remote status, and culture, to name but a few. Certainly rural schools face many challenges, such as a lack of opportunities and support, but this does not prevent many rural schools locally and internationally from using effective strategies and pedagogies that work towards inclusion (Telfer & Howley, 2014).

Research has shown that rural schools can and do provide the necessary education for children with complex learning profiles by implementing early interventions, differentiated practices, school teaching supports and universal design for learning, regardless of support factors (Telfer & Howley, 2014). Telfer and Howley also insist that although challenges in rural settings do exist, taking a strengths-based approach to overcome many of these challenges is within the possibilities for many rural contexts. Adopting a strengths-based approach, even in the most challenging locales, may provide insightful and resourceful ways of how to best support communities, schools, practitioners and families when implementing effective and well-planned inclusive programs for children with complex learning profiles.

As an example, in rural Bangladesh (Begum et al., 2019) positive education outcomes are evident for children with complex learning profiles due to an increased awareness of inclusive education by students, teachers, parents, and community members (though progress is reportedly slow). More assistive technology is being used to target specific learning needs, and outreach efforts to break down the culture of silence around inclusive education is creating safer educational environments, public spaces, and neighbourhoods of trust. More opportunities for children with complex learning profiles are being provided to participate in community activities, and they are encouraged to express themselves, enacting their voices.

Similarly, Franck and Joshi (2017) found when interviewing teachers in rural Ethiopia that combating stigmatization and discriminatory attitudes is a necessary starting point in working towards an inclusive education system. A multifaceted approach is required to build awareness, provide technical training, and resource competency in order to reinforce inclusive practice and gain support from parents, teachers and peers.

The remainder of this chapter will discuss the strengths-based approaches that have been implemented in differing contexts as examples of how best to support children with complex learning profiles, within and across community, schools, and teaching practice.

Community

Community-related factors can significantly contribute to the affordances or hindrances when implementing the educational provisions of children with complex learning profiles. Outmigration, poverty (Stelmach, 2011), discriminatory beliefs

(Blanks, 2014), diverse language, vast travel distances, caste-based practices, and gender inequality in the main (Begum et al., 2019; Khanal, 2015) constitute the larger challenges facing rural schools for both developed and developing countries. Changing deep-seated parenting practices and cultural beliefs is also a challenge (Blanks, 2014; Khanal, 2015; Obeng, 2007). These challenges are not restricted to developing countries (Stenman & Pettersson, 2020) and these problems are not ameliorated by simply providing access to inclusive education, as many of these issues intersect with social, cultural and political forces.

Teachers in rural schools such as those in the United States (Berry & Gravelle, 2013; Nagle, Hernandez, Embler, McLachlan, & Doh, 2006) and Malawi (Blanks, 2014) where effective inclusive education has been successfully implemented and embraced for children with complex learning profiles have reported a number of important characteristics. One of the enduring themes is the close ties between the school, parents and the community (Berry & Gravelle, 2013; McKittrick, Gill, Opalka, Tuchman, & Kothari, 2019; Nagle, Hernandez, Embler, McLachlan, & Doh, 2006). Telfer and Howley (2014) suggest that the desirable features of rural places (small size, cohesion, focussed direction, dedicated staff) can provide opportunities for addressing persistent achievement gaps for children with complex learning profiles, rather than focussing on supposed impediments that are associated with rural schools. Specifically, school programs have been shown to be more effective when a socioecological approach has been taken by communities to better understand the impact of poverty, especially when families are trying to support their child beyond the demands of the family unit (Begum et al., 2019). Initiatives to encourage parental engagement have been developed, such as meetings on Saturday mornings and open-door policies so that parents could spend time with their child at a manageable time (Nagle et al., 2006). In some rural schools, preference has been given to local teacher applicants because of the cultural capital and local understanding they bring to the context (Sindelar et al., 2018). Green et al. (2013) provides this provocation about preparing pre-service teachers and supporting rural and remote teaching:

> "What if, in preparing teachers for a profession which often requires moving to unfamiliar places (sometimes many times over the course of one's teaching career), there was a focus on teachers' awareness of, and capacities to develop, mutual relations with place through creating awareness of their connections to the places they inhabit – now, in the past, and in the (imagined) future?"
> (p. 111)

Schools adopting strengths-based paradigms have also reported that local community organizations such as churches and civic groups have worked in partnership with local schools to provide a rich source of support for families with fewer financial resources by supplying school resources, food and clothing for children with complex learning profiles. Where there are strong school–community partnerships, children with complex learning profiles are shown to have more positive outcomes (Berry & Gravelle, 2013; Hartman, Stotts, Ottley, & Miller, 2017).

Community support for students with complex learning profiles have required the creative use of resources, such as clustering and grouping students to make the most effective use of specialist staff. Members of the local community have volunteered to provide in-class learning support for struggling learners with complex learning profiles in rural schools in the United States (Nagle et al., 2006). In such schools, there is a high level of stability within the school community and a willingness for staff to work together (Berry & Gravelle, 2013). As a result, retaining teachers becomes less problematic.

School

School-related factors can also facilitate or hinder the implementation of inclusive programs for children with complex learning profiles. Small populations and higher living costs makes it untenable when maintaining an economy of scale for local schools (Witten, McCreanora, Kearns, & Runasubramanian, 2001). Ultimately, it becomes economically challenging to offer full-time positions to teaching staff who specialize in inclusive practices for any child who requires extensive educational support. Internationally, the limited resources available to rural schools has been a common theme for students with complex learning profiles (Blanks, 2014), making it challenging for students in this cohort to receive any individual attention or assistance (Berry & Gravelle, 2013; Blanks, 2014; Khanal, 2015).

Interestingly, financial incentives, such as bonus incentives for recruiting and retaining specialist teachers in rural schools, has been found to be ineffective, mainly because the monetary incentive was insufficient (as the bonuses aligned with their urban counterparts) and/or waned over time) (Sindelar et al., 2018). This is problematic for rural schools such as those in the U.S., as this can strain an already compromised school budget (Berry & Gravelle, 2013). Other tangible incentives such as lower cost of housing and/or rents proved to be more effective in reducing teacher turnover. For specialist teachers, other incentives were shown to be more important, such as the degree that they were appreciated and valued in the community and the degree to which the community were committed to supporting education for children with complex learning profiles (Sindelar et al., 2018).

Teachers in inclusive, rural schools report that they have high expectations for student performance and behaviour, and provide curriculum to students that is appropriate, accessible and relevant (Nagle et al., 2006; Telfer & Howley, 2014). Telfer and Howley (2014), in their examination of two Midwestern American schools (that were making strides in closing achievement gaps for children with complex learning profiles), identified a set of six shared practices that enabled them to be attentive to the overall strategy for making improvements to student outcomes. These included: using data well, establishing and maintaining focus, selecting and implementing shared instructional practices, implementing deeply, monitoring and providing feedback and support, and inquiring and learning. At this point, the importance of school leadership in facilitating positive and inclusive school cultures cannot be understated, as transformative leadership styles have shown to be central to supporting school change and creating opportunities for teachers to participate in ongoing professional development (Hoppey, 2016).

In Sweden, remoteness has been overcome by implementing new policies (2015) on remote teaching by way of using digital technologies (Stenman & Pettersson, 2020). In America, some rural and remote areas have subsidized installation of broadband, making distance technology increasingly available (Sindelar et al., 2018). Using digital technologies in remote areas has enabled specialist teachers to provide learning experiences to small classes of students who would otherwise be inaccessible (Hilli, 2018). Rural schools that have also leveraged technology to deliver mentoring and professional development to teachers in remote locations have witnessed promising results in retaining specialist teachers and supporting classroom teachers in providing inclusive programs (Sindelar et al., 2018). Ongoing collaborative efforts between universities and schools should include a culturally relevant model of professional development that is sensitive to the environmental constraints of the rural context, and understanding of Place (Blanks, 2014). However, this is not available to many remote schools, and without well-trained teachers in inclusive practices and educational reform, inclusive programs will not be effective and/or sustainable via this online delivery (Blanks, 2014).

Technology has also enabled more placements for pre-service teachers. Previously, these placements would have been costly and inefficient. Now, it is possible to provide mentoring, observation and professional development from university centres, including offerings for culturally and linguistically diverse cohorts (Sindelar et al., 2018). Programs such as these need to be developed to encourage pre-service teachers to take up rural placements in inclusive programs. Having said that, using digital technologies is dependent not only on the expertise of the teacher in designing and utilizing learning experiences and the supports and abilities for the student (Hilli, 2018), but the available physical resources and access in remote areas. This becomes particularly problematic in facilitating and ensuring the rights of education for children with complex learning profiles and providing an inclusive environment for learning in economically challenged communities and/or very remote contexts.

Teaching practices

From the literature, it has become apparent that it is not only the resources or availability of information that is solely responsible for the success or failure of inclusive practice in rural schools. Inclusion is about the willingness of staff to implement programs that meet the needs of children with complex learning profiles (Ainscow, 2000). There is a strong indication that the views of the staff working in rural schools have a significant effect on not only the students, but their colleagues, school and the communities in which they live (Blanks, 2014; Tait & Hussain, 2017). Some of these views include teachers' beliefs about difference, and the beliefs about their own abilities to work with children with complex learning profiles, often borne from a lack of available training (Blanks, 2014; Obeng, 2007). In some rural schools, problems are not associated with a lack of will to include all children in inclusive classrooms, but are based on scant knowledge and skills, which may be easily ameliorated with contextually responsive, professional development (Blanks, 2014).

Regardless, literature on inclusive classroom practice in rural contexts is scarce. There is a disproportionate focus on teacher attitudes rather than pedagogical practices in the classroom (Miles et al., 2018). It is argued that enquiries into the processes of inclusions (and exclusions) will have a greater impact on practice than will persistent monitoring of teacher's lives or other meta-surveillance measures. Green et al. (2013) calls for a stronger recognition of the ways teachers create and shape learning environments and how they affect children, their peers and others in the community, instead of focussing on a deficit approach of teachers' needs and inadequacies and the assumption that they are not going to stay long enough. Taking this strengths-based approach may provide teachers with an opportunity to develop a stronger sense of Place, and how that Place relates to them personally and professionally.

Berry and Gravelle (2013), through their survey of 55 rural districts in America, found that the nature of close knit-relations between school staff and a greater sense of familiarity with students and their families gave them the sense that they could individualize inclusive programs more effectively and improve student learning outcomes. In addition, the close-knit teaching community enabled specialist teachers to provide support and instruction to general education teachers, increasing their teacher knowledge and classroom efficacy.

Teacher knowledge rather than material resources is the cornerstone of professional development in Malawi. Malawi has one of the lowest socioeconomic statuses of any country in the world, yet Blanks (2014) found that in working with local rural schools, Malawi's education system may be far ahead of many developed nations by way of their practical and philosophical commitment to children with complex learning profiles. Malawi's professional development model is culturally relevant, co-constructed, and job-embedded, with improved student achievement the desired goal. Blank noted that when designing professional development for classroom teachers who teach children with complex learning profiles in Malawi, the focus was on what was possible for teachers to implement with the resources they had access to in their classrooms, avoiding traditional, charitable models for professional development where such Western materials quickly became forgotten clutter in the classroom.

Miles et al. (2018), in their study of 15 rural Tanzanian primary schools, concluded that the implementation of inclusive programs for children with complex learning profiles relies heavily upon the ingenuity, tenacity and resourcefulness of ordinary classroom teachers. Without diminishing these efforts, the authors argue that effective programs should not have to rely on this. They enforce that the expertise from teachers who work within the local context should be communicated and disseminated to school personnel as a matter of best practice. Effective inclusive pedagogies, supported with clearly written texts, imaginative explanation, appropriate use of assistive devices and classroom arrangements should become part of the everyday physical Place of the inclusive classroom (Miles et al., 2018). Here, as in many other under-resourced inclusive classrooms, the human rights debate as espoused in local and international policy/s is somewhat out of step with these nuanced challenges.

Conclusion

In many rural communities, ongoing and enduring exclusion for children with complex learning profiles is a part of daily life. These practices may be blatant or quite nuanced, but nonetheless the long-lasting effects are the same. Exclusionary practice and inequalities in both the developing and developed world have the same results: disadvantage, poverty and unemployment (Rogers, 2013). Slee (2011) warns that from the advantage of "home" it is too easy to position within a collective indifference", where the disadvantage and injustice is somehow otherworldly. We need to apply the same level of compassion and understanding to children with complex learning profiles in rural contexts that are not the same as our own, if there is truly a chance of change (Nussbaum, 2011).

It is imperative that we look beyond the rhetoric of inclusive practice that uses global surveillance measures formulated by western countries. Slee (2001) also said that inclusive education was an oxymoron, as not all schools were meant for everyone. Until specific attention is given to the sociocultural and economic factors of all rural Places, successful inclusion will not be able to be fully addressed and/or realised. A multidimensional and appropriately contextual approach is required if children with complex learning profiles are going to be able to access the type of education to which they are legally, morally and ethically entitled.

References

Adams Hill, D., & Sukbunpant, S. (2013). The comparison of special education between Thailand and the United States: Inclusion and support for children with autism spectrum disorder. *International Journal of Special Education*, 28(1), 120–134.

Ainscow, M. (2000). The next step for special education. *British Journal of Special Education*, 27, 76–80.

Ainscow, M., & Miles, S. (2008). Making education for all inclusive: Where next? *Prospects*, 38(1), 15–34.

Ankrah-Dove, L. (1982). The deployment and training of teachers for remote rural schools in less-developed countries. *International Review of Education*, 28(1), 3–27.

Arnold, M. L., Newman, J. H., Gaddy, B. B., & Dean, C. B. (2005). A look at the condition of rural education research: Setting a difference for future research. *Journal of Research in Rural Education*, 20(6), 1–14.

Barrio, B. L. (2017). Special education policy change: Addressing the disproportionality of English language learners in special education programs in rural communities. *Rural Special Education Quarterly*, 36(2), 64–72.

Begum, H. A., Perveen, R., Chakma, E., Dewan, L., Afroze, R. S., & Tangen, D. (2019). The challenges of geographical inclusive education in rural Bangladesh. *International Journal of Inclusive Education*, 23(1), 7–22.

Berry, A. B., & Gravelle, M. (2013). The benefits and challenges of special education positions in rural settings: Listening to the teachers. *The Rural Educator, 34*(2), 25–38.

Blanks, B. (2014). Culturally responsive professional development for inclusive education in rural Malawi. *The Journal of the International Association of Special Education, 15*(2), 4–10.

Corbett, M. (2015). Understanding Social Justice in Rural Education. *Journal of Research in Rural Education, 32*(1), 1.

Degener, T. (2016). Disability in a human rights context. *Laws, 5*(35), 1–24. https://doi.org/10.3390/law5030035.

Dillon-Wallace, J. (2017). Well-being of mothers and young children in contexts of special health care. In Li, L., Ridgeway, A. & Quinones, G. (Eds.). *Studying babies and toddlers: relationships in cultural contexts* (pp. 81–93). Springer: Singapore.

Downes, N., & Roberts, P. (2017). *Staffing rural, remote & isolated schools in Australia: A review of the research literature (2004–2016).* Retrieved from University of Canberra: http://www.canberra.edu.au/researchrepository/items/15bcde8b-9170-4468-a106-31ee81012d70/1/

Edwards, R. M. (2011). Disconnect and capture of education decentralisation reforms in Nepal: Implications for community involvement in schooling. *Globalisation, Societies and Education, 9*(1), 67–84.

Franck, B., & Joshi, D. K. (2017). Including students with disabilities in Education for All: Lessons from Ethiopia. *International Journal of Inclusive Education, 21*(4), 347–360. https://doi.org/10.1080/13603116.2016.1197320

Giangreco, M. F. (2010). Utilization of teacher assistance in inclusive schools: Is it the kind of help that helping is all about? *European Journal of Special Needs Education, 25*(4), 341–345.

Graham, L. J. (Ed.) (2020). *Inclusive education for the 21st Century: Theory, policy and practice.* Abingdon, Oxon: Routledge.

Grech, S. (2014). Disability, poverty and education: Perceived barriers and (dis)connection in rural Guatemala. *Disability in the Global South, 1*(1), 128–152.

Green, N., Noone, G., & Nolan, A. (2013). Contemporary paradigms of rural teaching: The significance of Place. *Australian and International Journal of Rural Education, 23*(1), 91–115.

Gruenewald, D.A. (2003). Foundations of Place: A multidisciplinary framework for Place-conscious education. *American Educational Research Journal, 40*(3), 619–654.

Gruenewald, D.A., & Smith, G.A. (2008). *Place-based education in the global age: Local diversity.* New York: Lawrence Erlbaum Associates.

Hartman, S. L., Stotts, J., Ottley, J. R., & Miller, R. (2017). School-community partnerships in rural settings: Facilitating positive outcomes for young children who experience maltreatment. *Early Childhood Education Journal, 45*(3), 403–410.

Hilli, C. (2018). Distance teaching in small rural primary school: A participatory action research project. *Educational Action Research, 28*(1). 38–52. https://doi.org/10.1080/09650792.2018.1526695

Hoppey, D. (2016). Developing educators for inclusive classrooms through a rural school-university partnership. *Rural Special Education Quarterly, 35*(1), 13–22. https://doi.org/10.1177/875687051603500103

Hughes, B. (2010). Bauman's Strangers: Impairment and the invalidation of disabled people in modern and post-modern cultures. *Disability & Society, 17*(5), 571–584.

International Covenant on Economic, Social and Cultural Rights, (1966). Retrieved from https://www.ohchr.org/en/professionalinterest/pages/cescr.aspx

Khanal, D. (2015). Children from the Dalit community in rural Nepal: A challenge to inclusive education. *Internal Journal of Inclusive Education, 19*(7), 710–720. https://doi.org/10.1080/13603116.2014.964568

Manago, B., Davis, J.L., & Goar, C. (2017). Discourse in action: Parents' use of medical and social models to resist disability stigma. *Social Science & Medicine.* 184, 169–177.

McKittrick, L., Gill, S., Opalka, A., Tuchman, S., & Kothari, S. (2019). A "can-do" attitude for students with disabilities: Special education in rural charter schools. *Journal of School Choice*, *13*(4), 537–554. https://doi.org/10.1080/15582159.2019.1683684

Miles, S., & Singal, N. (2010). The education for all and inclusive education debate: Conflict, contradiction or opportunity? *International Journal of Inclusive Education*, *14*(1), 1–15.

Miles, S., Westbrook, J., & Croft, A. (2018). Inclusions and exclusions in rural Tanzanian primary school: Material barriers, teacher agency and disability equality. *Social Inclusion*, *6*(1), 73–81. https://doi.org/10.176458si.v6i1.103

Miller, L. C. (2012). Situating the rural teacher labor market in the broader context: A descriptive analysis of the market dynamics in New York State. *Journal of Research in Rural Education (Online)*, *27*(13), 1.

Nagle, K. M., Hernandez, G., Embler, S., McLachlan, M. J., & Doh, F. (2006). Characteristics of effective rural elementary schools for students with disabilities. *Rural Special Education Quarterly*, *25*(3), 3–12.

Nussbaum, M. C. (2011). *Creating capabilities: The human development approach.* Cambridge, MA.: Harvard University Press.

Obeng, G. (2007). Teacher's views on the teaching of children with disabilities in Ghanaian classrooms. *International Journal of Special Education*, *22*(1), 96–102.

Panizzon, D., & Pegg, J. (2007). Chasms in student achievement: Exploring the rural-metropolitan divide. *Education in Rural Australia*, *17*(2), 3–20.

Reid, J. (2017). Rural education practice and policy in marginalised communities: Teaching and learning on the edge. *Australian an International Journal of Rural Education*, *27*(1), 88–103.

Roberts, P. (2013). The role of an authentic curriculum and pedagogy for rural schools and the professional satisfaction of rural teachers. *Australian and International Journal of Rural Education*, *23*(2), 89–99.

Roberts, P. (2014). Researching from the standpoint of the rural. In White, S., & Corbett, M. *Doing educational research in rural settings: Methodological issues, international perspectives and practical solutions.* (pp 135–147). New York, USA: Routledge.

Rogers, C. (2013). Inclusive education and intellectual disability: A sociological engagement with Martha Nussbaum. *Internal Journal of Inclusive Education*, *17*(9), 988–1002. https://doi.org/10.1080/13603116.2012.727476

Sindelar, P. T., Pua, D. J., Fisher, T., Peyton, D. J., Brownnell, M. T., & Mason-Williams, L. (2018). The demand for special education teachers in rural schools revisited: An update on progress. *Rural Special Education Quarterly*, *37*(1), 12–20.

Slee, R. (2001). Social justice and the changing direction in educational research: The case of inclusive education. *International Journal of Inclusive Education*, *5*(2/3), 167–177.

Slee, R. (2011). *The irregular school: Exclusion, schooling and inclusive education.* Oxon: Routledge.

Stelmach, B. L. (2011). A synthesis of international rural education issues and responses. *The Rural Educator*, *32*(2), 32–42.

Stenman, S., & Pettersson, F. (2020). Remote teaching for equal and inclusive education in rural area? An analysis of teachers' perspective on remote teaching. *The International Journal of Information and Learning Technology*, *37*(3), 87–98.

Summers, J.A., Behr, S.K., & Turnbull, A.P. (1988). Positive adaptation and coping strengths of families who have children with disabilities. In G.H.S. Singer & L.K. Irvin (Eds.). *Support for caregiving families: Enabling positive adaptation to disability* (pp. 27–40). Baltimore: Brookes.

Tait, K., & Hussain, R. (2017). Using Quality of Family Life Factors to explore parents' experience of educational provision for children with developmental disabilities in Rural Australia. *International Journal of Disability, Development and Education*, *64*(3), 328–344. https://doi.org/10.1080/1034912X.2016.1223280

Telfer, D., & Howley, A. (2014). Rural schools positioned to promote the high achievement of students with disabilities. *Rural Special Education Quarterly, 33*(4), 3–13. https://doi.org/10.1177/875687051403300402

Turnbull, R., Turnbull, A., Shank, M., & Smith, S.J. (2004). *Exceptional lives: Special education in today's schools.* Upper Saddle River, NJ: Pearson.

UNESCO. (2005). *Guidelines for inclusion: Ensuring access to education for all.* Retrieved from http://lst-iiep.iiep-unesco.org/cgi-bin/wwwi32.exe/[in=epidoc1.in]/?t2000=021573/(100)

UNESCO. (2020). *Global Education Monitoring Report. Inclusion and education: All means all.* Retrieved from https://en.unesco.org/gem-report/

Wallace, A. & Boylan, C. (2009). Reviewing the rural lens in education policy and practice. *Education in Rural Australia, 19*(2), 23–30.

Witten, K., McCreanora, T., Kearns, R., & Runasubramanian, L. (2001). "The impacts of a school closure on neighbourhood social cohesion: Narratives from Invercargill, New Zealand". *Health and Place,* 7(44), 307–317.

3
BEGINNING WITH LANGUAGE

Inclusive education strategies with sign languages in Rwanda, Singapore, United States, and Việt Nam

Audrey Cooper, Sonia Holzman, Maegan Shanks, and Phoebe Tay

Introduction

Global recognition of the educational exclusion of children with disabilities has made a case for worldwide reform to design education programming for diverse learners. Positive gains in access to education have reaped successes and created space to examine the practical elements that make education inclusive, and also the extent to which these are accessible and equitable. Evidence from educational, linguistic, and neurocognitive research underscores that education programming for deaf and hard of hearing (DHH)[1,2] learners is most effective when instructional languages are whole languages that are easily accessible, and curricula that reflect learners' diverse languages, cultures, and other intersectional backgrounds. The earliest international guidance on *Education For All* affirmed the importance of signed languages and underscored that access to education in national signed languages should be ensured for all deaf persons (UNESCO 1994 Salamanca Statement, Section A, Item 21). These principles have been reaffirmed in the Convention on the Rights of Persons with Disabilities (CRPD), and numerous human rights instruments. Holding consultative status with the United Nations, the World Federation of the Deaf further upholds that, "…inclusive education for children who are deaf is achieved through quality bilingual sign language schools and other educational settings teaching the national sign language(s) and national written language(s) (International Disability Alliance, 2020, p. 9). Despite these efforts, researchers note that DHH learners commonly lack access to language and culturally responsive environments in school settings (Komesaroff & McLean, 2006; Mathews, 2017; Snoddon & Murray, 2019). These circumstances have given rise to synergistic family, community, organizational, and school-based innovation to infuse sign language learning into everyday activities and educational practices.

In this chapter we start from the basis that there is a proliferation of inclusive education initiatives under way, yet presently little empirical evidence about how such

DOI: 10.4324/9781003091950-4

approaches ensure quality and equitable language settings for DHH learners. These circumstances enable us to explore seemingly disparate cases (e.g., settings with varying GDP, existing educational policies and programs, DHH community involvement) to examine the ways that local actors are innovating and promoting inclusive education access. The four cases presented in this chapter demonstrate how local actors advance ad hoc and/or longer-standing innovations to engage DHH learners in the most immediate and feasible ways. While seemingly limited in scope, we contend that they are powerful examples of community-led efforts to promote and preserve sign languages in education. Setting the context for these case examples, we open the chapter with discussion of sign language-centered inclusion in the context of insights on language development, the CRPD, and intersectional considerations. Ultimately, we show that effective forms of inclusive education programming for DHH learners is contingent upon coherent language policy and pedagogy founded on explicit recognition for all of the cultures and languages of instruction, teacher instructional proficiency in those languages, and deaf community engagement in providing DHH cultural and linguistic resources. We then close the chapter with a set of recommendations.

Insights from language development research

To promote language acquisition and overall human development, all children need early and ongoing access to the most easily accessible language input. Chen Pichler (2017) emphasizes that language acquisition is dependent on "quality input" from which children need to be exposed to early, via natural languages, and "optimized" for joint attention between child and adult, and child-directed signing. Quality input is, in turn, dependent on adult sign language proficiency which includes the ability to establish an object of mutual attention, turn-taking, and other natural features of interactions. Assistive listening devices may offer some DHH children additional resources for acquiring spoken languages; however, Dye & Emmorey argue that sign languages are the most "completely accessible natural languages [for DHH]" and do not require batteries, auditory processes, or therapists to provide input for meaningful communication to take place" (2017, p. 402).

For DHH children, a growing body of literature on language deprivation shows significant neurocognitive and social-psychological delays associated with lack of whole language input during the critical language development period of 0-5 years (Brown University, 2014; Hall, 2017; Glickman & Hall, 2019), with effects observed especially in the area of literacy (Humphries, et al., 2016). DHH children are also at risk for "chronic child cognitive fatigue" when they are expected to rely on auditory perception alone (Spellun & Kushalnagar, 2018, p. 1). Accordingly, quality and equitable education demands language policy and programming that reflect an "enrichment" approach to bilingual education that broadens "cultural pluralism and linguistic diversity" (Baker & Wright 2017, p. 198). Given that there are only an estimated 200 signed languages that have been documented thus far, and mostly for North Atlantic countries (Brentari, 2010), language research and policies regarding bilingual education with sign languages are desperately needed.

The CRPD & language-centered guidance

The CRPD contains multiple references to sign language access, most relevantly in Article 24 - Education. In the post-CRPD adoption era, guidance on language policy and planning has been a significant source of theoretical and practical innovation. Much of this work considers inclusive settings (e.g., schools, vocational training) and language modalities (signed, spoken, written, print, tactile), but does not fully address the juncture of language, culture, and sensory considerations for educational settings. To address this gap, Murray, De Meulder, & le Maire (2018, p. 39) argue that deaf people possess a "dual category" status with respect to sensory and language backgrounds that must be taken into consideration.

Examining the definition and interpretation of inclusion in CRPD Article 24, Murray, Snoddon, De Meulder, & Underwood (2018/2020) further argue that inclusion must "…take into account issues of linguistic rights and cultural identity" (Ibid.). Addressing such issues in post-ratification interpretations of the CRPD, General Comment No. 4, (adopted in 2016) states, "Students who are blind, deaf or deafblind must be provided with education delivered in the most appropriate languages and modes and means of communication…" (Section 34, item c). General Comment No. 6 (adopted in 2018) further states that DHH children must be provided access to deaf peers and deaf adult role models in sign language learning environments. When teachers possess proficiency in sign language, this contributes to the accessibility of the school environment, promoting inclusion and educational achievement. (section K, Article 24, item 65). In addition to language and sensory considerations, quality and equitable education takes into account the multiple intersecting identities and experiences of DHH learners–which are important factors in operationalizing education and promoting the rights of DHH people in broader society (Izsák-Ndiaye, 2017; UNDESA, 2019).

Operationalizing intersectionality

Current efforts to design education settings that affirm linguistic and sensory backgrounds build upon intersectional theorizing, first introduced in 1989 in the legal studies context by Kimberlé Crenshaw. Crenshaw recently described this as: "…a lens through which you can see where power comes and collides, where it interlocks and intersects.." (Crenshaw, n.d.). Intersectionality theory addresses linkages and interlocking inequities taking place at the juncture of cultural background, class, race and ethnicity, gender, socioeconomic and political status and representation, among other socially meaningful categories. As Walqui observes, "Education never takes place in a vacuum but is deeply embedded in a sociocultural milieu" (2006, p. 159). Policy, curricular, and pedagogical design that affirms DHH students' intersectional linguistic and sensory experiences, and the diversity of the broader sociocultural context, recognizes difference in an affirmative way.

Intersectionality theory also demonstrates the importance of macro-level analysis, given, as Collins (1990, p. 227) observes, "…the matrix of domination is structured on several levels; personal biography, group/community level of cultural context, and systemic level of social institutions". Intersectional analysis promotes education planning that recognizes the levels of systemic oppression, domination, and liberation that Collins describes. To transform conditions of dominance within education, investment and talent recruitment would benefit from engaging DHH people in professional training programs and hiring into core personnel positions and administration.

Introduction to country case examples

This section introduces four case examples exploring locally emergent education innovations that are responsive to DHH learners and to local resource availability. We arrived at this focus through conversations shared as International Development practitioners working in education and disability inclusion sectors, and via our mutual association with Gallaudet University's Master of Arts Program in International Development. The conversations that unfolded between us illuminated the prevailing misconceptions (including our own) about the types and availability of education resources for DHH learners for DHH learners, and prompted our attention to the ways that education settings reflected learners' intersectional backgrounds across the contexts in which we worked and conducted research. The resulting analysis identified creativity demonstrated in family, community, and education settings that promote and preserve signed languages in education.

The writing team comprises diverse personal and professional backgrounds. All four researchers share ASL and English as common languages. Two researchers identify as deaf (Shanks and Tay) and two as hearing (Cooper and Holzman). Four methodologies are used: Cooper (anthropological ethnography); Holzman (field-based autoethnography), Shanks (autoethnography), and Tay (sociolinguistic and autoethnographic). Each country case begins with a description of the broader education context in the respective country followed by discussion of educational innovation by local actors that affirm both the sensory and language backgrounds of DHH learners.

Case 1: Rwanda

Background on language in DHH education & inclusive education in Rwanda

Universal access to education and social unity are longstanding priorities for Rwanda's national development. These goals are reflected in the 98% primary school enrollment rates as of 2019 (UNICEF). The Rwandan government, international organizations, and local stakeholders have committed to inclusive education through legislation, public statements, and as early signatories to the CRPD. However, noted gaps remain in practice (Karangwa, Miles, Lewis, 2010). Children with disabilities face a range of barriers to education and are enrolled at a lower rate (70% compared to the national average). With limited disaggregated data, the rates of DHH children accessing school were as low as 3% in 2007 (Miles, Wapling,

Beart, 2011). The Special Needs and Inclusive Education Policy was revised in 2018 through a consultative process with a range of stakeholders, including the Rwanda National Union of the Deaf (RNUD) (Republic of Rwanda, 2018, 1). Faith based organizations and charitable causes have historically been the primary source of educational opportunities for DHH children and children with disabilities broadly. In more recent years, the Government has taken the initiative to look at education through an inclusion lens (Njelesani, Siegel, and Ullrich, 2018).

In 2014, the University of Rwanda College of Education established the School of Special Needs and Inclusive Education. Yet, at the time of this writing, there remains no specialization for teaching DHH learners and minimal exposure to Rwandan Sign Language (RSL). The Special Needs and Inclusive Education Policy was revised in 2018 through a consultative process with a range of stakeholders, including RNUD (Republic of Rwanda, 2018, 1). The revised policy now specifically references the promotion of "Deaf Culture", and critical assessment of education planning for DHH students that includes nationwide data collection to understand the linguistic diversity of deaf communities in Rwanda (Ministry of Education, 2018, 23). This policy additionally points to the need for research and training regarding signed languages in Rwanda, "…because Sign language as a Language of instruction for schools, is neither fully recognized by the Ministry of Education, nor integrated in teacher training programs." (Ministry of Education, 2018).

There are a total of 14 schools and centers providing education to DHH learners in Rwanda, with 5 schools for the deaf, and 9 schools that enroll smaller numbers of DHH students (Personal communication, 2020). Ntigulirwa states that as of 2019, deaf schools and centers for children with disabilities have been converted to enroll non-DHH students. This restructuring has not properly established sign language preservation plans and pedagogical approaches to teach in a bilingual setting (RSL and national languages) with learners newly exposed to RSL (Ntigulirwa, 2019). The need for language planning gained attention in 2008 when rapid policy change – altering the use of French, English, and Kinyarwanda in education – challenged schools to teach and learn in languages with limited proficiency (Williams, 2017). Within this context, RSL remains insufficiently researched and recognized in education and therefore poses challenges to actualizing inclusive education goals for DHH children.

Classroom settings and practical innovations in Rwanda

The following analysis is based on Holzman's volunteer work and autoethnographic research in Rwanda (January - June 2016) at the Ubumwe Community Center (UCC). UCC is a privately funded inclusive primary school and community center in Gisenyi, Rwanda. Holzman is from the US and began work with DHH communities in East Africa in 2013 as part of an education-based international development initiative. In 2016, UCC school served over 400 children with and without disabilities, including approximately 25 DHH students. The DHH students arrived at school with foundations of diverse language and education experiences. Some transferred from neighboring districts where a variant of RSL was used, others from families with DHH relatives, with the majority raised in homes with hearing families that did not know or use RSL.

Amidst limited resources and undefined standards of equitable access for the DHH students, innovative approaches were observed through the relationship between the school site and local deaf community members. The DHH students benefited immensely from the involvement of deaf adults and peers in both academic and social activities that occurred at UCC. Deaf adults served in a number of staff and volunteer roles, including grounds maintenance, a pre-primary teacher and two volunteers who provided direct support to DHH students. All students took an ongoing RSL class and the teachers participated in a range of RSL workshops over the years. RSL proficiency varied greatly, but a noticeable few students took a keen interest in RSL and developed language skills and close relationships with the cohorts of DHH students. The deaf teachers, fellow students and dedicated staff made each child feel welcome and supported, but the unmet aim of providing a sign language rich education was a stress shared by all.

One initiative was to invite DHH secondary school graduates to begin their teaching careers as volunteer interpreters and teaching assistants. Despite not possessing formal training, these volunteers had the language skills, secondary schooling, and shared DHH identity that created meaningful learning opportunities for many of the DHH students. The maintenance staff were also welcomed into the classrooms to clarify and discuss course content and took part in regular staff meetings and campus planning events. Beyond academics, a monthly "sign language day" was instituted by school administrators to promote RSL fluency across campus. This intentional shift in language use prompted teachers and students to communicate in RSL not as a means of accommodating their DHH classmates, but as a primary language on campus. The DHH students took pride in educating their peers and teachers and supporting others to navigate the visual environment of full RSL use. The ban on verbal communication was not applied to communication during academic courses due to a lack of teacher fluency to conduct courses fully in RSL. This heightened awareness of the need for more intensive and ongoing RSL training.

As a school and community center, UCC's inclusive practices did not stop at the end of the school day. Weekly deaf church services were hosted in classrooms and dance and theater programs encouraged full participation of DHH students and community members. This community level commitment supported the linguistic and identity development of DHH students and empowered them to continue their studies even when faced with barriers in the classroom. These approaches are innovative in that the school administration created mechanisms to engage with the broader deaf community in academic and social activities in the school-based setting. This case highlights the vital role of DHH adults' leadership in education and the need for training pathways for DHH teachers and community members to continue to advance inclusion in partnership with school administrators and staff. The mission of inclusive education at UCC expanded the campus walls and heightened awareness of disability rights, sign language and deaf culture within the surrounding community.

Case 2: Singapore

Background on language in DHH education & inclusive education in Singapore

Singapore's colonial history has influenced language ideologies which in turn has shaped language and education policies applied in the local education system and in deaf education (Kirkpatrick, 2016; Kadakara, 2015; Tay, 2018). In 1966, Singapore implemented an English-mother tongue bilingual policy requiring English to be adopted as the first language of instruction in schools, with other official languages – Mandarin, Malay, and Tamil – classed as second languages (Kirkpatrick, 2016). This led to the demotion of Chinese and Indian varieties in language policies (Leimgruber, 2013) and the exclusion of Singapore Sign Language (SgSL). There are currently three primary schools (2 special schools and 1 mainstream school) which enroll deaf children (Ministry of Education, 2020).

The Singapore Chinese Sign School was established in the early 1950s by Mr Peng Tsu Ying, a deaf man who moved to Singapore from Shanghai after World War II (Tay, 2018). Around the same period, Goulden, a British expatriate, started an oral class that had nine deaf children. This led to the establishment of the Singapore Oral School for the Deaf where English was adopted as the medium of instruction (Argila, 1976). The Singapore Chinese Sign School for the Deaf later merged with the Singapore Oral School for the Deaf in 1963 to become the Singapore School for the Deaf. The school closed in 2017 due to falling enrollment numbers and Mayflower Primary School was selected as the designated mainstream school to take in deaf students and provide access to SgSL from 2018 (Teng, 2017).

Although Signing Exact English (SEE), was used in the now defunct Singapore School for the Deaf –brought by Lim Chin Heng, a Singaporean graduate from Gallaudet College and Frances Parsons from the US in the 1970s--, its usage has caused division in the community; some believe in its effectiveness for teaching English while others perceive it as an improper language and advocate for SgSL as a legitimate language (Teng, 2017; Tay, 2018). Akbar (2020) found that although the use of SEE is supported by both deaf and hearing parents in their homes, "contradicting language practices" were observed; the deaf children are the "actual language managers of the family" instead of the parents having authority over the home language practices (p. 7). Deaf education has seen a shift from SEE to SgSL as DHH children appear to prefer using SgSL (Akbar, 2020). Despite positive attitudes toward SgSL, there are inaccurate understandings of the language and conflicting feelings using it due to limited support from the school and the government (Ibid.). These circumstances are a fertile soil for innovation because it illuminates the gaps, issues and lack of resources and knowledge in deaf education and linguistics.

Classroom settings & practical innovation in Singapore

Educational innovation in Singapore is visible in a few areas: from family and peer interactions, school instruction, upskilling for new and current educators of the deaf to groundbreaking research being done in the fields of deaf education and linguistics. The following analysis is based on a summer internship that Tay conducted in 2016 at the Singapore Association for the Deaf. Tay was assigned a research project on language and identity in the Singapore Deaf Community. She has been in and out of Singapore at regular intervals as Singapore is her home country. She has engaged with deaf and hearing individuals in the SgSL community. Tay's background in deaf education in Australia, along with her training in international development and linguistics positioned her to further develop her research skills and identify gaps in the local context. She conducted ethnographic research through interviews and participant observation of deaf individuals in various settings.

Between 2003 to 2006, there were 7 deaf teachers in Singapore (Yap & Lim, personal communication 2020). Currently (2020), there are 4 deaf teachers in Singapore. Despite observations of the differential treatment of deaf teachers compared to hearing teachers of the deaf, it has been found that the presence of deaf educators as role models in the classroom in inclusive education settings and classrooms in DHH settings still reaps benefits (Mei, personal communication, 2020). The deaf learners claimed they understood the deaf teacher's signing more easily than that of the hearing teacher. Chee (2020) found that although teachers in an oral school for the deaf were aware about advances in sign language research, they still believed that an oral program and learning to assimilate into the hearing world were more effective for the deaf children's success. Even those educators that seemed more positive toward sign language revealed ambivalent sentiments toward SgSL. However, none of the educators were overtly antagonistic toward sign language, indicating a slight positive shift in teachers' attitudes Chee (2020).

Teachers of DHH learners are required to possess a special education diploma; however, pedagogic courses focus on disabilities in general. In 2019, the Certificate in Teaching Students with Hearing Loss program was introduced to upskill current teachers of the deaf (Lee, personal communication, 2020). This is the first training program that offers specialized courses in deaf education. From 2021, there will also be the establishment of a mainstream kindergarten program at Mayflower Primary School. It will start offering access to SgSL as a language from 2022 to both the deaf and hearing students for the very first time in Singapore's history (Teng, 2020). In addition, access to external speech and language therapists and audiologists in school will be provided. This is a significant innovation and milestone in deaf education in Singapore on top of the introduction of the specialized training program in deaf education, because the best of both the deaf and hearing cultures are provided in this setting.

Case 3: United States

Background on language in DHH education & inclusive education in the US

The US initiated formal deaf education in 1817 and fostered a national network of deaf residential schools –now more than 78, though a number are at risk for closure (NAD, 2011). With the 1864 establishment of Gallaudet College (now University), the first higher education institution for DHH people, deaf education generated a pool of deaf professionals in various disciplines including education. While for nearly 100 years, Gallaudet resembled education in the general society in being racially segregated (until 1952), Gallaudet University modeled what accessible sign language-centered education meant for DHH learners. Recognizing that the university was also the site of controversies over the legitimacy of signs used by deaf people versus other approaches, e.g., oralism, fingerspelling without signs (Rochester Method), and invented communication systems such as Signed Exact English, Gallaudet University paved the way for DHH teachers to hone skills needed to expand educational opportunities to DHH learners.

Between 1960–1979, what came to be called American Sign Language (ASL) was analyzed to be a linguistic system; it created a space for ASL to be formally recognized as language and challenged the use of artificial sign communication systems in schools (Stokoe, 2005; Klima & Bellugi, 1979). Educators nevertheless believed that signing should follow English word order, promoting artificial sign communication systems in US schools and impacting education in other countries. The advent of formal special education teacher training prompted programs for DHH learners, which provided DHH learners with more opportunities to access formal education but yet neglected deaf cultures and sign languages. In the 1970s, key legislation ensured communication access for DHH people for the first time (Rehabilitation Act of 1973 (Section 504), followed by other key legislations such as Individuals with Disabilities Education Act of 1975. The Americans with Disabilities Act (ADA) is touted as the "strongest disability rights law in the world as it further protects the rights of people with disabilities to access public goods, yet it does not specify language or cultural protection for the Deaf community" (Holmes, 2019, p. 264). Legislation also overlooks Black ASL, which emerged in segregated schools for black DHH learners (McCaskill, et al., 2011), and first nations sign languages (Davis & McKay-Cody, 2010). However, the US currently has 50+ postsecondary Deaf Education Teacher Preparation Programs that also includes training of itinerant teachers, representing distinct DHH education philosophies and instructional languages. The availability and diversity of multiple programs expanded the opportunities for DHH learners to have qualified instructors providing more equitable access to education. The implications of not explicitly recognizing ASL as an instructional language for DHH learners contributes to marginalization of deaf teachers, as well as extensive use of interpreters in the classroom. Nevertheless, the aforementioned circumstances surrounding deaf education created a space for innovation to emerge (Maroney & Smith, 2010; Marchut, et al., 2019).

Classroom settings and practical innovations in the US

In conducting literature review on DHH education in the US, itinerant teaching emerged as an innovation that has received little critical attention despite its significance in bridging educational gaps for DHH learners, particularly in rural areas. The following analysis is based on this literature review, as well as retrospective ethnographic reflection on Shanks's own participation in itinerant teaching services from 1994 to 2007. Itinerant teachers are a significant resource for DHH learners as they provide direct one-on-one social interaction with DHH learners that may not be occurring in the mainstream classroom environment while simultaneously supporting their academic goals established by Individual Education Plans (IEPs). Such support for academic goals can include ensuring that DHH learners understand instructions provided by teachers on any subjects identified on the IEPs.

While itinerant teachers are a significant resource for DHH learners, they are working with limited language resources as itinerant teaching is not integrated into inclusive education classroom design and instruction as with bilingual education programs (one-on-one instruction rather than full immersion and interaction in a classroom setting). Shanks's experience in the mainstream education environment as a deaf black child involved leaving mainstream classrooms for about an hour twice a week to meet the itinerant teacher individually--which Shanks attributes to making a difference between getting lost and succeeding in the education system. The weekly meetings with itinerant teachers allowed Shanks to fully express herself using ASL and English to either review any confusion regarding assignments, to seek advice on how to advocate for self in the classroom, and to vent about being a deaf student in a mainstream classroom. Itinerant teaching emerged in response to massive shifts in DHH students' placements from deaf education to mainstream settings (as inclusive education is generally referred to in the US), accounting for more than 85% of DHH students (US GAO, 2011).

Itinerant teachers incorporate specialized training for working with DHH learners that travel to various schools in the assigned school district and provide "instruction and consultation for students" typically in a one-on-one format (Luckner & Ayantoye 2013, p. 409–410). However, this did not make up for miscommunications in the classrooms, condescending attitudes from students and teachers, and other difficult conditions within the classroom; moreover, all of Shanks's itinerant teachers were also hearing and white, except for one Latinx-identified teacher. If adapted to sign language-rich environments and students' intersectional backgrounds, itinerant teaching could be a sustainable innovation.

Itinerant teachers support DHH learners in mainstream environments, particularly those with multiple disabilities, and those living in areas with inadequate teaching resources (National Deaf Center on PostSecondary Outcomes 2019). Itinerant teaching assignments reflect goals in Individual Educational Plans determined by the school and the family. However, without deaf community involvement and in-class communication, students may not receive the language access that bilingual education programs (including deaf schools) with sign languages provide. Research on itinerant teaching finds that classroom teachers often may not have the qualifications or apply feedback to their classroom instruction, exacerbating learning and language barriers (Antia & Rivera, 2016; National Deaf Center on PostSecondary Outcomes, 2019).

Case 4: Việt Nam

Background on language in DHH education & inclusive education in Việt Nam

Việt Nam's sovereign nation is founded on the liberatory pursuit of literacy in the Vietnamese language, and achieved universal primary education in 2000 (EFA, 2015). Education is among Việt Nam's highest priority development sectors. Việt Nam was an early adopter of Education for All, and education planning and enrollment of learners with disabilities has increased substantially since the early 2000s; however, educational attainment for learners with disabilities is limited by a shortage of trained personnel and education resources, and also impacted by stigma among educators and the general public (CRPD Initial Report, 2018; Tran, 2014; Tran, et al., 2017). Moreover, only a fraction of DHH learners attend or complete school at any level (GSO, 2016). These circumstances have catalyzed significant innovation for DHH education and community action.

Việt Nam had one of the world's first schools for deaf students with instruction in sign language (Lái Thiêu School for the Mute-Deaf, est. 1886). After national reunification in 1975, the government instituted speech-based schooling in special school settings and discouraged use of sign language. By the late 1990s, DHH special schools were located throughout the country, and the government also promoted enrollment of DHH students in 'regular' schools (Nguyễn, et al., 2019). During this period, the government established bachelor's programs in special education, followed by masters and doctoral degree programs in "inclusive special education," established in 2011 and 2018 respectively (Ibid., p. 262).

Observing DHH learners' limited school enrollment and communication barriers between teachers and students, in 2000, Woodward (an American linguist) and Nguyễn (a former special-school teacher and administrator) established the *Center for Research and Promotion of Deaf Culture* (Trung tâm Nghiên cứu & Thúc đẩy Văn hoá Điếc), commonly referred to as the "Đồng Nai Deaf Education Project," to train deaf adults in the national curriculum and Hồ Chí Minh Sign Language analysis, teaching, and interpretation (Woodward & Nguyễn, 2012). Woodward and Nguyễn also established both a four-year and a university degree track in early deaf education. Still the only sign language bilingual education program in Việt Nam that trains students in the full national curriculum, 200+/- students have graduated with middle and upper secondary diplomas, and 20+/- students have earned university diplomas in Deaf Teacher Training.

DHH students in inclusive settings have fared less well. Researchers found that in six provinces studied, 29,382 DHH students were "in classrooms where spoken Vietnamese was the medium of instruction" and only "one child shared an effective communication channel with another person ["her devoted teacher"]" (Reilly & Nguyễn, 2004, p. 25). Conducting ethnographic research in southern special schools, Cooper (2017) found that teachers learned signs from students and felt the need to hide signing from school administrators. With the 2010 Law on Disability, use of Vietnamese sign languages is permitted and some teacher training programs offer sign language courses; however, such courses are not compulsory.

To meet the country's significant inclusive education needs, the government has supported numerous incubator and pilot projects, including those involving sign languages. Reflecting diverse education philosophies and approaches, these projects give constituencies an opportunity to test the various approaches. Although project outcomes are not observable for years, sometimes after the critical period for language development has passed (0–5 years of age), diverse projects enable educators, DHH community members, and families to interact, share ideas, support the initiatives they deem effective, and supplement available programming.

Classroom settings and practical innovations in Việt Nam

Educational innovation in Việt Nam is observable nearly everywhere and at multiple scales—from family, peer, and community instruction to large-scale national education projects—with education and training for learners with disabilities comprising increasing government attention. Whereas government training for key human resources professions has not been implemented yet (e.g., deaf teacher training; signed-spoken language interpretation; sign language instruction), deaf community members have led efforts to implement sign language training within schools and community settings. This section discusses three examples: two are drawn from ethnographic fieldwork that Cooper conducted in special schools and deaf community organizations in 2007–2009 and related training activities in 2012–2014, and the third spotlights deaf community training provided by the only deaf-founded and -led organization with official government recognition.

Demonstrating how language-centered planning introduced innovation to special school settings and beyond, the first two examples involve training of (hearing and non-signing) content-area instructors in Hồ Chí Minh Sign Language (HCMSL). Recognizing that content area teachers did not know HCMSL, the Đồng Nai Deaf Education Project trained deaf adult students to teach HCMSL (Woodward et al., 2003). This model proved effective for teaching the national curriculum; it also advanced affirmative language attitudes toward HCMSL and gave deaf instructors formal roles within education settings. Other education settings lack this deaf adult resource base, creating a dilemma for administrators interested in introducing HCMSL to their schools. Cooper (2017) describes special school principals who contravened speech-based education norms by inviting deaf community leaders to offer HCMSL classes, and by establishing school-based Deaf Clubs for deaf adults to interact with DHH learners and their families. Largely dependent on deaf people's voluntarism, some school personnel pooled small funds to support this work.

The third example involves the historic emergence of Việt Nam's first officially recognized deaf organization that promotes sign language education, training, and research for deaf people. The *Psycho-Education and Applied Research Center for the Deaf* (PARD) is dedicated to creating an inclusive society through education and advocacy initiatives, especially in rural settings. Established by Nguyễn Trần Thủy Tiên, a 2012 graduate of the Đồng Nai Deaf Education Project and also the first deaf person in Việt Nam to earn a master's degree (2017, Gallaudet University's Master of Arts Program in Sign Language Education), PARD's approach is extremely innovative in advancing training-of-trainers among deaf people for vital education and advocacy roles. Unlike many projects that train hearing community members with the expectation that they will train deaf people, PARD trains deaf community members in such areas as sign language development and teaching, rights awareness-raising (e.g., CRPD, national laws), and connects deaf trainers with communities and schools. PARD also engages government counterparts to offer input on inclusive education materials and programming.

In settings where the above innovations have been introduced, deaf community members and deaf students report pride in seeing their cultural and linguistic contributions reflected in education activities (Cooper 2017; Gallaudet IDMA, 2020). Both deaf and hearing community members also express a sense of interest and inspiration in having spaces to grow intercultural dialogue—which deaf community organizations lead through arranging "*giao lưu*" [cultural exchanges] (Cooper and Nguyễn, 2015; Cooper 2017). Sign language classes in the community and on TV are now increasingly vital to Việt Nam's wider education enterprise and are gaining broader support from the government, INGOs, and DPOs/OPDs.

Discussion & recommendations

The four country cases demonstrate country-specific circumstances of education, underscoring the contextually responsive nature of innovations designed for education with DHH learners. The cases also demonstrate a number of comparative commonalities, especially with respect to the significance of sign language recognition for DHH leadership, and the observed benefits to education quality when DHH adults are engaged in teaching, training, interpreting, mentoring, and support roles. In developing the four case studies, we identified prominent roles for i. advancing policy, and ii. advancing training and technical capacity building activities. Below we address each area and include a set of relevant recommendations.

Advancing policy

The case studies demonstrate that all four countries have laws or policies outlining quality and equitable education. Three of the countries also have disability specific laws (Rwanda, US, Việt Nam). None of the countries possesses national sign language bilingual education policy, such that instructional approaches and languages vary from setting to setting. Of the four countries, Rwanda is the only country to include reference to "Deaf Culture" in national policy (2018 Revised Special Needs and Inclusive Education Policy). Singapore and the United States are the only countries of the four that have Individual Educational Plans (or programs).

All of the country cases reflect government support for use of sign languages; however, all four countries also lack official sign language recognition, and have not provided specific content defining what a language is, how sign languages foster language development, and how they should be used to structure education activities. Language policy and guidance centered on the bilingual or multilingual use of the local sign, print, and spoken languages is a critical precursor to efficacious education approaches with DHH learners. The case examples show that sociocultural participation in the context of schools, the family, and the community can be meaningful—especially if developed and supported by DHH language communities. Advancement of signed languages within education settings requires the participation of DHH people in the life of schools, in all roles, including that of interpretation and translation. One of the most urgent needs, then, is to develop policy that ensures the rights of DHH adults to access to systems of higher education and policy that supports development of critical education and training infrastructures.

Policy Recommendations for Cultural and Language-Rich Education

- Create education legislation and regulations on national/regional sign language(s) as instructional language(s) (De Meulder et al. 2019)
- Seek guidance from sign language linguists and local DHH communities on inclusive education planning and questions pertaining to policy and inclusive education initiatives (Harris, et al. 2009; Hochgesang, 2015).
- Utilize research evidence and recommendations on language development for DHH learners to ensure early language development services are a key component of inclusive education policies and plans (Adoyo, 2017; Golos et al. 2018; Murray, Meulder, Maire, 2018).
- Limit the use of sign-spoken language interpreters in the classroom and increase the use of DHH educators, teaching assistants, and support staff in the classroom (De Meulder & Haualand, 2019; de Wit, 2011; Schick et al. 2006; Shantie & Hoffmeister 2000).
- Ensure that policy includes empirical evidence on the use of hearing aids, cochlear implants, and other technologies as additive elements of communication accessibility and not substitutes for language development and use of full languages (Glickman & Hall, 2019; Spellun & Kushalnagar, 2018).

Advancing training and technical capacities

Educational design and training infrastructures lag behind DHH learner enrollment in all four countries. Perhaps paradoxically, the absence of sign language(s) policy and related training infrastructures can be understood as a catalyst of innovation, particularly for people and groups that are directly engaged in the lives of DHH learners. Representing substantial leadership and creativity to implement education approaches for DHH learners, the four case studies demonstrate socioculturally-informed ways of mobilizing education innovation within resource-limited settings. For instance, in Rwanda, Singapore, and Việt Nam, DHH adults have recently been enabled to serve in voluntary or support staff roles, largely without education or training on their respective roles. Moreover, innovation by one organization in

Việt Nam (PARD) now trains DHH adults in language development and teaching offering a significant mechanism for ensuring quality language input for DHH learners in formal education settings as well as in the community.

Each of the four countries examined possess teacher training programs with varying structures and mandates related to teaching children with disabilities and/or inclusive education. These teacher training programs also tend to involve minimal exposure to the local/national sign language(s), including for the US, where some deaf education teacher credentialing programs offer specialized training in bilingual ASL-English pedagogy and others do not. Despite the limited availability of training in education services, and limited access to DHH adults, where schools engage DHH adults, they are relied upon to provide the cultural and linguistic grounding that is the foundation for effective education. To ensure teacher preparation to engage DHH learners in quality and equitable education experiences, teacher trainees require specialized language training and specialized training in bilingual pedagogy. The following recommendations highlight the actions that governments, education ministries, and DPOs/OPDs can undertake to bolster teacher preparation.

Partnership and Training Promoting Language-Rich Settings

- Promote training and hiring of DHH sign language teachers to develop curriculum and teach the local/national sign language as a school subject (McKee et al., 2014; Watkins et al., 1998).
- Partner with DHH educators to design training modules and ongoing assessments of sign language fluency for teachers studying inclusive education practices (Humphries & Allen, 2008; Rosen 2019)
- Provide training and compensation for DHH mentors to work with DHH children and their families in school-based and home settings (Cawthon et al., 2016; Golos et al., 2018)
- Invest in sign-spoken language interpreter training and provision to open up education, employment, civic leadership, and other social and human resource opportunities and opportunities for advancement (Houston, 2018).
- Seek and appoint DHH leaders and educators to serve as advisors and representatives in decision-making bodies leading education planning (Shantie & Hoffmeister, 2000).
- Encourage community based participatory research on language accessibility in education to strengthen evidence based inclusive education design and programming (Goico, 2019; De Clerck & Paul, 2016).

To devise language-rich and intersectionality-informed policy, training, and operational guidance, policy-makers and educational planners benefit from consultation with DHH community members in their local settings. With these points in mind, education designers could advance a principled stance to ensure a range of language development resources for all DHH learners delivered in accordance with bilingual education frameworks with signed languages.

Conclusion

The approaches described in this chapter entreat us to closely examine and support the local structures that contribute to language-rich education experiences for DHH learners. Language and education policy that affirms the intersectional backgrounds of DHH learners in their home communities, and training for DHH adults for technical capacities in education settings, is vital to inclusive education. Current education design and initiatives can benefit from applying the lessons learned from worldwide DHH communities, from definitions of inclusion developed from pedagogical innovations in bilingual education with sign languages, and from mobilizing human and technical resources used in local settings in new ways. In considering who is left behind, who has access to school, and what inclusion means in practical terms, leadership and innovation by local actors demonstrates that there are multiple pathways to language-rich quality education.

Acknowledgments

The authors are grateful to colleagues and communities that shared experiences and perspectives that contributed to our thinking on this chapter, including country delegates at the 2019 World Federation of the Deaf conference in Paris, France, and external reviewers Josh Josa, Kristin Snoddon, and Amanda Taylor who provided feedback at a critical juncture in our writing.

Notes

1 Throughout this paper we use lowercase 'd' as an inclusive term for all deaf people (and not "d/D"). The descriptor "d/D" was a convention developed by academics to differentiate non-culturally identified versus deaf cultural group members, which is now critiqued as promoting essentialism (Ruiz-Williams et al., 2015).
2 Several identities within deaf communities are not discussed, particularly deafblind and deafdisabled learners in education settings, who face similar challenges discussed, yet remain underrepresented in research. Further research is needed for a better understanding of deafblind and deafdisabled learners' experiences. (Kamenopoulou 2012).

References

Adoyo, P. O. (2017). Educating deaf children in an inclusive setting in Kenya: Challenges and considerations. *Electronic Journal for Inclusive Education*, 2(2), 1–13. https://corescholar.libraries.wright.edu/cgi/viewcontent.cgi?article=1087&context=ejie

Akbar, M. A. (2020). *Family language policies of families with deaf children in Singapore* (final year project). Nanyang Technological University, Singapore. Retrieved from https://hdl.handle.net/10356/138285

Antia, S. D., & Rivera, M. C. (2016). Instruction and service time decisions: Itinerant services to deaf and hard-of-hearing students. *Journal of Deaf Studies and Deaf Education*, 21(3), 293–302. https://doi.org/10.1093/deafed/enw032

Argila, C. A. (1976). Deaf around the world: singapore -- the tides of change. *The Deaf American*, pp. 3–5.

Baker, C. & Wright, W.E. (2017). *Foundations of bilingual education and bilingualism*. Bristol, UK: Multilingual Matters.

Brentari, D. (2010). *Sign languages*. Cambridge: Cambridge University Press.

Brown University. (2014). *Language deprivation syndrome lecture*. https://www.youtube.com/watch?v=8yy_K6VtHJw.

Cawthon, S. W., Johnson, P. M., Garberoglio, C. L., & Schoffstall, S. J. (2016). Role models as facilitators of social capital for deaf individuals: A research synthesis. *American Annals of the Deaf*, 161(2), 115–127. https://doi.org/10.1353/aad.2016.0021

Chee, C. W. (2020). *Teachers' perspectives on language policies for hard-of-hearing children: A case study on Canossian School (final year project)*. Nanyang Technological University, Singapore. Retrieved from https://hdl.handle.net/10356/138306

Chen Pichler, D. (2017). Language learning through eyes and ears. Webcast for the Laurent Clerc National Deaf Education Center. Gallaudet University, Washington, DC. Retrieved from https://clerccenteronline.ning.com/topic-interest-groups/language-learning-through-the-e

Collins, P. H. (1990). Black feminist thought in the matrix of domination. In C. Lemert (Ed.), *Black feminist thought knowledge, consciousness, and the politics of empowerment* (pp. 221–238). Boston: Unwin Hyman.

Cooper, A. C. (2017). *Deaf to the marrow: Deaf social organizing and active citizenship in Việt Nam*. Washington, DC: Gallaudet University Press.

Cooper, A. C., & Nguyễn, T. T. (2015). Signed language community-researcher collaboration in Việt Nam: Challenging language ideologies, creating social change. *Journal of Linguistic Anthropology*, 25(2), 105–127. https://doi.org/10.1111/jola.12081

Crenshaw, K. (n.d.). *Kimberlé Crenshaw on intersectionality, more than two decades later*. Retrieved January 09, 2021, from https://www.law.columbia.edu/news/archive/kimberle-crenshaw-intersectionality-more-two-decades-later

CRPD Initial Report. (2018). *Initial report submitted by Vietnam under Article 35 of the convention*. New York: United Nations.

Davis, J. & McKay-Cody, M. (2010). Signed languages of american Indian communities: considerations for interpreting work and research. In R.L. McKee & J. Davis (Eds.), *Interpreting in multilingual, multicultural contexts* (pp. 119–157). Washington, DC: Gallaudet University Press.

De Clerck, G.A.M. and Paul, P.V. (2016). *Sign language, sustainable development, and equal opportunities: Envisioning the future for deaf students*. Washington, DC: Gallaudet University Press.

De Meulder, M. & Haualand, H. (2019). Sign language interpreting services: A quick fix for inclusion? *Journal of the American Translation and Interpreting Studies Association*, 1–23. https://doi.org/10.1075/tis.18008.dem

De Meulder, M., Murray, J.J., & McKee, R. (2019). *The legal recognition of sign languages: advocacy and outcomes around the world*. Bristol, UK: Multilingual Matters.

Dye, M.W.G., & Emmorey, K. (2017). Special section on multimodal multilingual development of DHH learners. *Journal of Deaf studies and Deaf Education*, 22(4), 402–403. https://doi.org/10.1093/deafed/enx032

EFA. (2015). *Education for all 2015 national review report: Viet Nam*. Hà Nội, VN: Ministry of Education and Training.

Gallaudet IDMA. (2020). *Sign language research, teaching, & advocacy in 6 countries. International Day of Sign Languages Webinar*. https://www.youtube.com/watch?v=nvfLWOMAZQQ&list=PLH9wcxf2A0_4Rp1qdcrJ-M3A5MXx3Xsxi

Glickman, N. & and Hall, W.C. (2019). *Language deprivation and deaf mental health*. London: Routledge.

Goico, Sara A. (2019). The impact of "inclusive" education on the language of deaf youth in Iquitos, Peru. *Sign Language Studies*, *19*, 348–374. https://doi.org/10.1353/sls.2019.0001

Golos, D., Moses, A. M., Roemen, B. R., & Cregan, G. E. (2018). Cultural and linguistic role models: A survey of early childhood educators of the deaf. *Sign Language Studies*, *19*(1), 40–74. https://doi.org/10.1353/sls.2018.0025

GSO. (2016). *Việt Nam national survey on persons with disabilities*. Hà Nội: General Statistics Office.

Hall, W.C. (2017). What you don't know can hurt you: the risk of language deprivation by impairing sign language development in deaf children. *Journal of Maternal Child Health*, *21*(5): 961–965. https://doi.org/10.1007/s10995-017-2287-y

Harris, R., Holmes, H., & Mertens, D. (2009). Research ethics in sign language communities. *Sign Language Studies*, *9*(2), 104–131. Retrieved December 19, 2020, from http://www.jstor.org/stable/26190667

Hochgesang, J. (2015). Ethics of researching signed languages: the case of Kenyan sign language. In A. C. Cooper and K. K. Rashid (Eds.), *Citizenship, politics, difference: perspectives from sub-saharan signed language communities* (pp. 9–28). Washington, DC: Gallaudet University Press.

Holmes, T. (2019). Current laws related to the language development of deaf children and recommended advocacy strategies. In N.S. Glickman & W.C. Hall (Eds.), *Language deprivation and deaf mental health* (pp. 263–280). London: Routledge.

Houston, T.J. (2018). *Defining academia influences on mobility, identity, and culture of deaf scholars in higher education*. (doctoral dissertation). California State University Fresno. Retrieved from https://www-proquest-com.proxyga.wrlc.org/docview/2072338179?accountid=27346

Humphries, T., & Allen, B. (2008). Reorganizing teacher preparation in deaf education. *Sign Language Studies*, *8*(2), 160–180. Retrieved April 26, 2021, from http://www.jstor.org/stable/26190641

Humphries, T., Kushalnagar, P., Mathur, G., Napoli, D. J., Padden, C., Rathmann, C., & Smith, S. (2016). Language choices for deaf infants: Advice for parents regarding sign languages. *Clinical Pediatrics*, *55*(6), 513–517. https://doi.org/10.1177/0009922815616891

International Disability Alliance. (2020). *What an inclusive, equitable, quality education means to us*. Retrieved from https://www.internationaldisabilityalliance.org/ida-inclusive-education-2020

Izsák-Ndiaye, R. (2017). *Linguistic rights of linguistic minorities: A practical guide for implementation*. Geneva: UN Office of the High Commissioner for Human Rights.

Kadakara, S. (2015). Status of tamil language in Singapore: An analysis of family domain. *Education Research and Perspectives*, *42* (2015), 25–64. https://eric.ed.gov/?id=EJ1089175

Kamenopoulou, L. (2012). A study on the inclusion of deafblind young people in mainstream schools: Key findings and implications for research and practice. *British Journal of Special Education*, *39*(3), 137–145. https://doi.org/10.1111/j.1467-8578.2012.00546.x

Karangwa, E., Miles, S., & Lewis, I. (2010). Community-level responses to disability and education in Rwanda. *International Journal of Disability, Development and Education*, *57*(3), 267–278. https://doi.org/10.1080/1034912X.2010.501183

Kirkpatrick, R. (2016). *English language education policy in Asia*. Switzerland: Springer.

Klima, E.S. & Bellugi, U. (1979). *The signs of language*. Cambridge, MA: Harvard University Press.

Komesaroff, L.R. & McLean, M.A. (2006). Being there is not enough: Inclusion is both deaf and hearing. *Deafness and Education International*, *8*(2), 88–100. https://doi.org/10.1002/dei.192

Leimgruber, J.R.E. (2013). The management of multilingualism in a city-state: language policy in Singapore. In P. Siemund, I. Gogolin, M.E. Schulz, & J. Davydova (Eds.), *Multilingualism and language diversity in urban areas: Acquisition, identities, space, education* (pp. 227–255). Amsterdam: John Benjamins.

Luckner, J. L., & Ayantoye, C. (2013). Itinerant teachers of students who are deaf or hard of hearing: practices and preparation. *Journal of Deaf Studies and Deaf Education, 18*(3), 409–423. https://doi.org/10.1093/deafed/ent015

Marchut, A.E., Musyoka, M.M., & Clark, M.D. (2019). It's more than just interpreting: Educational interpreting interns' experiences in rural settings. *Psychology, 10*(7), 1003–1024. https://doi.org/10.4236/psych.2019.107066

Maroney, E. & Smith, A.R. (2010) Defining the Nature of the "gap" between interpreter education, certification and readiness-to-work: A research study of bachelor's degree graduates. *RID VIEWS, 27*(4), 35–37.

Mathews, E.S. (2017). *Language, power, and resistance: Mainstreaming deaf education*. Washington, DC: Gallaudet University Press.

McCaskill, C., Lucas, C., Bayley, R., Hill, J.C. (2011). *The hidden treasure of black ASL: Its history and structure*. Washington, DC: Gallaudet University Press.

McKee, D., Rosen, R. S., and McKee, R. (2014). *Teaching and learning sign languages: International perspectives and practices*. New York: Palgrave Macmillan.

Miles, S., Wapling, L., & Beart, J. (2011). Including deaf children in primary schools in Bushenyi, Uganda: a community-based initiative. *Third World Quarterly, 32*(8), 1515–1525. doi.org/10.1080/01436597.2011.604523

Ministry of Education. (2018). *Revised special needs and inclusive education policy*. Rwanda. Retrieved from https://www.mineduc.gov.rw/fileadmin/user_upload/pdf_files/SNE_Policy__4.10.2018.pdf

Ministry of Education. (2020). *Special educational needs*. Singapore. Retrieved from https://beta.moe.gov.sg/special-educational-needs/

Murray, J. J., De Meulder, M., & Le Maire, D. (2018). An education in sign language as a human right? The sensory exception in the legislative history and ongoing interpretation of article 24 of the UN convention on the rights of persons with disabilities. *Human Rights Quarterly, 40,* 37–60. Retrieved from http://josephjmurray.org/wp-content/uploads/2019/06/An-Education-in-Sign-Language-as-a-Human-Right.pdf

Murray, J.J., Snoddon, K., De Meulder, M., & Underwood, K. (2018/2020). Intersectional inclusion for deaf learners: Moving beyond general comment no. 4 on article 24 of the United Nations convention on the rights of persons with disabilities. *International Journal of Inclusive Education, 24*(7), 691–705. https://doi.org/10.1080/13603116.2018.1482013

NAD. (2011). NAD action alert: Preserve state schools for the deaf. Alexandria, VA: National Association of the Deaf. https://www.nad.org/2011/02/16/nad-action-alert-preserve-state-schools-for-the-deaf/

National Deaf Center on PostSecondary Outcomes. (2019). *Research brief: serving deaf individuals in rural communities*. Austin, TX: University of Texas at Austin.

Nguyễn X.H., Villa, R.A., Tac, L.V., Thousand, J.S., & Pham, M.M. (2019). Inclusion in Vietnam: More than a quarter century of implementation. *International Electronic Journal of Elementary Education, 12*(3), 257–264. https://doi.org/10.26822/iejee.2020358219

Njelesani, J., Siegel, J., & Ullrich, E. (2018). Realization of the rights of persons with disabilities in Rwanda. *PloS one, 13*(5), e0196347. https://doi.org/10.1371/journal.pone.0196347

Ntigulirwa, J. (2019, July 12). International spotlight: inclusive education and deaf children in Rwanda. *Raising and Educating Deaf Children: Foundations for Policy, Practice, and Outcomes*. http://www.raisingandeducatingdeafchildren.org/2016/09/26/about/

Reilly, C. and Nguyễn K.C. (2004). *Inclusive education for hearing-impaired and deaf children in Vietnam: final evaluation report*. Washington, DC: USAID.

Rosen, R.S. (2019). *Routledge handbook of sign language pedagogy*. New York: Routledge.

Ruiz-Williams, E., Burke, M., Chong, V.Y., and Chainarong, N. (2015). "My deaf is not your deaf": Realizing intersectional realities at Gallaudet University. In M. Friedner and A. Kusters (Eds.), *It's a small world: International deaf spaces and encounters* (pp. 262–273). Washington, DC: Gallaudet University Press.

Schick, B., Williams, K., & Kupermintz, H. (2006). Look who's being left behind: Educational interpreters and access to education for deaf and hard-of-hearing students. *Journal of Deaf Studies and Deaf Education, 11*(1), 3–20. https://doi.org/10.1093/deafed/enj007

Shantie, C., & Hoffmeister, R. J. (2000). Why schools for deaf children should hire deaf teachers: A preschool issue. *Journal of Education, 182*(3), 42–53. https://doi.org/10.1177/002205740018200304

Snoddon, K. & Murray, J.J. (2019). The salamanca statement and sign language education for deaf learners 25 Years on. *International Journal of Inclusive Education 23*(7–8), 740–753. https://doi.org/10.1080/13603116.2019.1622807

Spellun, A. & Kushalnagar, P. (2018). Sign language for deaf infants: An intervention for a developmental emergency. *Clinical Pediatrics, 57*(14), 1–3. https://doi.org/10.1177/0009922818778041

Stokoe W. C., Jr. (2005). Sign language structure: an outline of the visual communication systems of the american deaf. *Journal of Deaf studies and Deaf education, 10*(1), 3–37. https://doi.org/10.1093/deafed/eni001

Tay, P. (2018). Being d/Deaf in Singapore: A personal reflection of deaf culture and identity. *S/pores new directions in Singapore studies* Retrieved from http://s-pores.com/2018/11/being-d-deaf-in-singapore-a-personal-reflection-of-deaf-culture-and-identity-by-phoebe-tay/.

Teng, A. (2017, September 17). Singapore school for the deaf to close due to dwindling enrolment. *The Straits Times.* Retrieved from https://www.straitstimes.com/singapore/education/singapore-school-for-the-deaf-to-close-due-to-dwindling-enrolment

Teng, A. (2020, November 12). Children with hearing loss to get dedicated support at MOE kindergarten. *The Straits Times.* https://www.straitstimes.com/singapore/parenting-education/children-with-hearing-loss-to-get-dedicated-support-at-moe.

Tran K.V. (2014). Exploring the experience of children with disabilities at school settings in Vietnam context. *SpringerPlus, 3*(103). https://doi.org/10.1186/2193-1801-3-103

Tran T. B., Vu H.P., Vu P.T. (2017). *Ending stigma: Assessment from the perspectives of people with disabilities (Vietnam).* Hà Nội, VN: Knowledge Publishing House.

UNDESA. (2019). *Disability and development report.* New York: United Nations Department of Economic and Social Affairs.

UNESCO. (1994). *The salamanca statement and framework for action on special needs education.* Paris: UNESCO.

UNICEF. (2020). *Education.* Retrieeved from https://www.unicef.org/rwanda/education

US GAO. (2011). *Deaf and hard of hearing children: Federal support for developing language and literacy.* Washington, DC: U.S. Government Accountability Office. http://www.gao.gov/new.items/d11357.pdf.

Walqui, Á. (2006). Scaffolding instruction for English language learners: A conceptual framework. *International Journal of Bilingual Education and Bilingualism, 9*(2), 159–180. https://doi.org/10.1080/13670050608668639

Watkins, S., Pittman, P., & Walden, B. (1998). The deaf mentor experimental project for young children who are deaf and their families. *American Annals of the Deaf, 143*(1), 29–34. https://doi.org/10.1353/aad.2012.0098

Williams, T. P. (2017). The political economy of primary education: Lessons from Rwanda. *World Development, 96*, 550–561. https://doi.org/10.1016/j.worlddev.2017.03.037

de Wit, M. (2011). *A sign language interpreter in inclusive education: The view of deaf persons on their quality of life*. (MA Thesis). Retrieved from https://www.academia.edu/3520438/Wit_M_de_2011_A_Sign_Language_Interpreter_in_Inclusive_Education_The_View_of_Deaf_Persons_on_their_Quality_of_Life_MA_Thesis_Edinburgh_Heriot_Watt_University

Woodward, J.C. & Nguyễn T.H. (2012). Where sign language studies has led us in forty years: Opening high school and university education for deaf people in Viet Nam through sign language analysis, teaching, and interpretation. *Sign Language Studies*, *13*(1), 19–36. Retrieved April 26, 2021, from http://www.jstor.org/stable/26190723

Woodward, J.C., Nguyen T.H., & Nguyen T.T.T. (2003). Providing higher educational opportunities to deaf adults in Viet Nam through sign languages: 2000–2003. *Deaf Worlds*, *20*(3), 232–263. Retrieved from http://nippon.zaidan.info/seikabutsu/2005/00001/pdf/DeafWorldsPaper.pdf

World Federation of the Deaf. (2018). *Position paper on inclusive education*. Retrieved from https://wfdeaf.org/wp-content/uploads/2018/07/WFD-Position-Paper-on-Inclusive-Education-5-June-2018-FINAL-without-IS.pdf

World Federation of the Deaf. (2020). *The legal recognition of national sign languages*. Retrieved from https://wfdeaf.org/news/the-legal-recognition-of-national-sign-languages/

4
AFFECTS AND MATERIALITY IN SANTIAGO DE CHILE'S SCHOOLS

The importance of relationality in the co-enactment of inclusion

Rosario Palacios

Introduction

> I walk to Ovalle School from the bus stop through the main avenue with broken sidewalks packed with street vendors. Many of them are from Haiti; I hear creole, their language, mixed with Spanish. Cars are buzzing, people are arranging their stalls, babies are crying, among many other street noises. I don't want to miss the school I'm heading to, so I look for the signs in the street. Before I can recognise any, a big grey building appears in a corner. It is well maintained and contrasts with the rest of the built environment. It's a modern building made of concrete and wood. It has a neat entrance with a little window where you announce yourself to the porter. The inside is well-ordered too. The main courtyard is surrounded by the building in a way in which stairs and balconies connect different school spaces, and you do not feel watched but accompanied. There are some trees covered by colourful wool knitting, and some picnic-like tables outside the cafeteria, inviting you to have a sit.
>
> (Field notes, April 2018)

This very first impression of Ovalle School, which I visited for almost three months during my fieldwork, was a sensitive picture. I remember the autumn feeling in the atmosphere, the cold, the sound of recess, and the built space that I perceived as neat and harmonic. The materiality of the school and its environment affected me. Affects circulate among objects, sounds and temperatures. Affects also circulate among movements, social interactions and different practices in space. In this chapter, I reflect on the way affects and schools' materiality are implied in how students experience inclusion or exclusion in their everyday life at school. My aim is to identify affective processes as they are related to inclusion and diversity in education.

DOI: 10.4324/9781003091950-5

I have a special interest in looking at the way affects circulate among materiality and are experienced subjectively. The very different forms in which students' bodies are "affected" (Clough & Jean 2007; Massumi 2002; Thrift 2008) and how that experience is linked to their sense of being included or excluded is at the core of my exploration.

This chapter explores special educational needs (SEN) students' experiences in the context of regulations for inclusion in Chile, which mandate teaching all students in the same classroom, and focuses on their everyday practices in mainstream schools. Theoretical reflections on inclusion miss the link between its socially constructed understandings and students' everyday lives. In other words, inclusion on paper may mean assuring certain conditions in the classroom and school, but what appears in schools' guidelines or educational policies is not what happens in practice. In this vein, I present material and physical characteristics of classrooms, schoolyards and other places used by students and describe students' experiences in them. I present their experiences as intertwined with affects and materiality, in which spaces may act as scripts (O'Toole & Were 2008) for defining difference and order affecting SEN students' everyday.

The chapter is organised as follows: first, I situate my understanding of affects and explain how it is useful for the kind of research I am conducting. Then, I detail the research methodology situating it within affective methodologies literature. Then, I present my data as ordinary moments at school, stressing its affective content. I want my field notes to work as starting points for thinking in the many ways students are affected by the situations described, including the materiality of bodies and objects in them. I devote the main part of the chapter to offer these affective pictures, stressing the ambiguity of the affective in my data, and showing how affective meanings are uncatchable, particular and subjective. In the final section of the chapter, I reflect on the linkage among affects, materiality and inclusion, and analyse the affective content of what we have understood as inclusion within the educational context.

Affects and materiality at the centre of inclusion in education

The affective turn (Clough & Jean 2007; Gregg & Seigworth 2010; Massumi, 2002) has brought a rich perspective for analysis in social sciences and the field of education is not an exception. In this chapter I draw on some elements of that line of thinking that I find especially useful for making clear the importance of materiality in the way affects circulate in school environments and how they are related to students' experiences of inclusion and exclusion.

Sarah Ahmed's reflections on emotions (2004) may be an interesting starting point for delving into the idea of inclusion and schools' materiality. Ahmed presents emotions as belonging to social interactions rather than to individuals' experiences. Emotions appear attached to bodies. The recurrent association of a particular emotion to a particular body (human or non-human) sticks them together; thus, *sticky associations* appear. Emotions circulate in social interaction, and the unconscious drives the repetitive link between some of them and certain bodies. Ahmed stresses these sticky associations, arguing "emotions become attributes of bodies" (2004, 4). The whole notion of inclusion brought up by public policy resides in putting together students who are perceived as different in their ability to follow a defined standard. Particular emotions circulate between them, and after a while, stick to them. Teachers, classmates and other people in school feel about their bodies –marked through special educational needs and disability labels – in various different ways. Emotions also circulate among materiality at school and the iterative association of some of them to special rooms for SEN students, administrative forms, or special education teachers shapes those bodies. Materiality, within this perspective, does not refer to buildings and things only. It includes all kinds of educational technology brought in schools as public policy. Affects circulate among certain figures and categories such as "SEN" student, establishing associations, charging them with affective value and shaping the forms of objects, school corners, teachers, students and interactions.

My attention to affective elements in school follows Deleuze and Guattari (2004) and Spinoza's (1994) focus in the body and the way in which the nonverbal and unconscious dimensions are central to our embodied experience. Relationality is at the core of my approach to the affective dimension of students' experience. It emphasises the importance of observing and thinking experience as a whole without segregating different elements as belonging to separate ontologies. The affective works as a lens to understand inclusion (or exclusion and all the diversity of arrangements in between) as a way of "being in place" (Casey 1993), ultimately, as a way on inhabiting time-space (Massey 1996).

Ben Anderson's term "affective atmospheres" (2009) brings somehow the spatial and wrapping potential of affects. It helps to understand how the undefinable is at the core of what affects are and how materiality may relate to the way experiences, always affective, emerge in a relational manner. In this respect, affects transcend representational thinking and demand observing experience in a different way. In this chapter, I gather the non-spoken elements of experience using illustrations and descriptions, rather than explanatory quotes from informants. My aim is to present students' experiences as affective ones, linked to diverse situations in their everyday life at school. Instead of interpreting students' experiences as examples or inclusive or non-inclusive education, I want to break that dichotomy by describing "how emotions occur in everyday life, understood as the richly expressive/aesthetic feeling-cum-behaviour of continual becoming that is chiefly provided by bodily states and processes" (Thrift 2008: 175).

My special attention in materiality in this chapter is a way of understanding inclusion as a co-enactment that happens among human and non-human elements that belong to an affective world. The consequences of this argument for teaching practices are great (Watkins 2007). Educational policies should take into account the importance of emotional landscapes (Nairn & Higgins, 2011) and pay attention to the way affects circulate among the different ingredients present in their organisational forms and practices. Schools' buildings, courtyards, furniture, books and all sorts of objects happen with temperature, light, smell and students' density, among many other things. The way students perceive, and thus experience, their school (Merleau-Ponty 1962) is immersed in affects. Emotions are "a vital element of the body's apprehension of the world; emotions are a vital part of the body's anticipation of the moment." (Thrift 2008: 187).

In that vein, my interest in classroom spaces/materialities deals with what students do with them and the nature of the experience that emerges in the relationality between space/materiality and student practices. In Sarah Pink's words, how the "coming together and 'entanglement' of persons, things, trajectories, sensations, discourses, and more" (Pink 2009: 41) unfold. Place's materiality as an essential component of experience means that our material world is crucial in the process of constructing meaning (Miller 2005), and affects are at the centre of that process. What students may understand as inclusion or not emerges as a felt experience, not as a discursive one.

Methodology

This chapter is part of a broader study on inclusive public policies in Chilean schools. For the qualitative component, I approached the schools selected for our study, aiming to examine the implementation and the functioning of the 'School Integration Programme' ("Programa de Integración Escolar", or PIE per the Spanish acronym) policy. My main purpose was to understand how each school had enacted (Ball et al. 2012) the law mandating teaching SEN students in mainstream classrooms. Taking an ethnographic approach, I observed lessons, had informal conversations, conducted interviews and otherwise installed myself in each school over three months at least three days a week. I don't call it school ethnography because the time I spent in each school is less than what a regular ethnography involves, but I relate to that method in terms of the kind of interpretative analysis I do of my data and the emic perspective I take.

Data for this chapter comes from that inquiry. I conducted fieldwork in four schools in Santiago, Chile, selected using intentional sampling so state and private-subsidised schools located in poor neighbourhoods where PIE policy has been adopted were included. I observed one private-subsidised school and three very different state schools (one school for girls, one large school with primary and secondary levels, and one school with only primary levels). In each school I observed three different levels: two primary levels and one secondary level. Also, I interviewed the school principal, one pedagogic director, three SEN teachers and two SEN students. The principal gave me permission to conduct research through signed informed consent, as did every individual I interviewed and all teachers in charge of the classes I observed. I taped lengthy interviews, which I transcribed, and I took notes on informal conversations and lessons. In my observations, I paid special attention to place and materiality and the way in which they form part of classroom and playtime practices. For doing so, I made drawings of classrooms and schoolyards in order to avoid photography or video, which are more invasive forms of registering data. I worked with them as a means for both registering images and reflecting through the practice of making images (Bateson & Mead 1942 quoted in Banks & Morphy 1997).

Acknowledging the importance of visual methodologies, I used them not only as an illustration of what I am explaining verbally, but also as a way to reinforce my arguments related to how human and non-human bodies move within forms and behaviours that provide basic understandings. Also, drawings aim to be "data of a more embodied kind", they are field notes that "display the researcher" (Knudsen & Stage 2015: 12) in the process of collecting events. In this vein, I want to stress the importance of understanding the field as a whole, as a producer of knowledge, and the researcher as part of it. The analysis of data was made using open coding. In that process, the importance of affects and affective materiality arose and this chapter focuses on them.

Ordinary moments at school

Maitenes School reminds me of some scenes from movies about prisons where you could see the stairs and corridors surrounding the main courtyard. The image of the *Panopticon* comes to mind and the ideas of discipline and impersonality. Maitenes is a massive school of around 1000 students and 14 levels in total: two for preschool (PK and kindergarten), nine for primary education (year 1 to year 9), and three secondary levels. There are two classes for almost every level, and each class has around 40 students. Maitenes is a state school in a low-income residential area of Santiago, and its students get very low results on Chilean standardised tests. Among the many causes that have been identified in school performance studies, families' sociocultural level has been emphasised much more than conditions such as the number of students per classroom or the number of students at school in relation to the school's infrastructure.

My impression of massiveness did not change through my continuous visits to the school, but I discovered places where students relate to each other in a warmer and more personal way. The drawing of the structure of Maitenes School (Figure 4.1) shows its architectural programme: classrooms distributed along the perimeter of the school with doors facing the corridors surrounding the central courtyard. In terms of layout, I distinguished two modes of use of the exterior space during playtime: the first, fast and agile, is related to the ball games that happen in the court. Although it is a small space, and there are no goalposts but rather two pillars with basketball hoops, several simultaneous ball games occur during playtime in the quadrant. Different groups of students, mostly male, manage to play soccer or basketball. There are also some younger children who play other ball games. Each group is spatially overlapped with the others, and the games happen in an unorganised manner. Many times students are hit by balls as they cross the courtyard. The view of the scene is quite chaotic, and it looks like only students who feel strong and confident – and who have no problem with receiving the onslaught of balls, the shoves resulting from confusion, and the cries of their classmates – participate in these games. At the edge of the court, the first-floor corridors become a place for other practices, in which very different rhythms and interactions are displayed.

FIGURE 4.1 Maitenes School architectural plan and students' practices in it. Author's sketch.

In Figure 4.1, I try to outline how these corridors welcome students who do not want to be in the central courtyard. The corridors become an intermediate zone for those students who want to be outside during playtime in a safe manner. If a student spends playtime there, they can still participate in what is going on as an observer, and if something interesting comes up, they can actively join it. We find in the hallways a gradual multiplicity of ways to participate with others. Students choose the most comfortable spot within the range of possibilities that these kinds of hallways offer. Some corners are more hidden from the central courtyard than others, and along the corridors, there are different material objects that can be used for different games: steps, the low ceiling formed by the stairs, and some concrete benches attached to the wall. These last ones are an important part of the configuration of this space. The density of the movement during playtime made any game on the floor very difficult and risky, especially for those kids who want to be calmer and safe, so many students use them as tables to play with album stamps or cards, and others use them to rest, eat their food in peace, and watch what happens on the court.

Andrés

Andrés, a year five student, loves to play with marbles. He carries them in his pocket and looks after them carefully while he is playing, so he does not lose them. He plays in one of the corners of the corridor and is very proud of his proficiency playing marble games. He usually wins new marbles using just one of his own. In a conversation I had with him, he explained his tricks, showed me the different sizes and materials of the marbles and explained what you can do with each one. He got very specific: "I can beat all the balls with these two", he said, showing me two large marbles, and continued:

> With two …. One day with a little one, more or less like a nugget, but made of steel, so it was heavy, steel is heavy, my little steel marble weighed like, more or less, like a big marble, and I had a hard time holding it up because it went from one side to the other and I could not control my hand, then I threw it, and it was easier for me because my little ball was like … (he mimics the ball's speed) and my classmates' marbles are like that, so … I did it with a little steel marble, and I nudged it, and they can't nudge their marbles like I do because my little ball is like this (he gestures the ball's small size).
>
> (Conversation with Andrés, year five student, Maitenes School, June 2018)

The corner where Andrés plays with marbles is his space for displaying himself. It is a tile floor, and although it is very cold on winter mornings, it is smooth, and marbles roll well on it. Andrés concentrates on the game, interacts with his teammates and follows the agreed rules. When the bell rings to end playtime, the children pick up their balls and return to their classrooms. Andrés has been diagnosed with Attention-Deficit/Hyperactivity Disorder. The teacher assigned to him tells me later, in another conversation, that he has had problems at home and that some violence has occurred in his family. She suggests that Andrés's father has hit him and that she believes his behaviour also denotes some features of the autism spectrum. One day I went to observe a year five maths lesson, I was struck in noticing that Andrés was sitting in the last row of the room, far from the board and in a rear corner. The teacher explained to me that she had tried to have Andrés sit in the front so he could concentrate better, but she ultimately decided to send him to the back so he would not bother his classmates. I sat very close to him to observe the maths lesson. It was a winter day and the windows were closed. The air in the room was heavy with 40 people inside. The students' desks were arranged in rows in the room, and each one was very close to the next so they could fit in the space.

In Figure 4.2, I aim to show the high density of the classroom and the overwhelming feeling of being there. Maybe Andrés was overwhelmed too, as he did not show the same enthusiasm as during playtime. There, while talking about his marbles, he became very happy and self-confident. Here, he looked uninterested in what was happening. Suddenly, I saw him climbing the shelf located next to the window and sitting on the top of it so he could get some perspective of the classroom. Andrés was again looking for a way to be in place and be included. (Figure 4.2).

Andrés denies the given space, which his teacher shaped as the place for him, where he – the problematic student – will not bother his classmates. His teacher's feelings about him are not based on today's impression. Her contact with many

FIGURE 4.2 Maitenes School year five classroom setting. Author's sketch.

other SEN students through her history as a teacher shapes her actions. The front part of the classroom and the centre of the main courtyard are associated with hierarchy and ability. We could argue they are designed for behaviours considered normal in students: being attentive to the teacher, seated at your desk and in silence the entire 45-minute lesson, being good at sports, playing football or another ball game, exhibiting physical skills, having the personality to face others, and being part of a team. The classroom is programmed for the expectable student behaviour, discipline, schedules, work times and furniture use. Andrés escapes from this script; the materiality and affective features of the place move him towards another way of inhabiting that space. Affects circulate among materialities and forms, and the classroom's sounds, temperature, smell and layout affect him. On the other hand, in the courtyard's corners, Andrés is also affected and he acts as a concentrated student, attentive to the rules of the game and oriented towards an objective.

Special places

Sticky associations are challenged when we observe school spaces created especially for SEN students, such as special rooms. In most Chilean schools in which the School Integration Programme has been implemented, some teaching still happens in what is called the "special classroom", a room where students with special educational needs or disabilities go to learn specific content that is considered difficult to address in the mainstream classroom. In some schools, these spaces function as a recreation of the special school within the mainstream school, and SEN teachers choose to teach more in these rooms than in mainstream classrooms, even if public policy guidelines establish the contrary.

In Puelche School, the special classroom is on the second floor, far from regular classrooms, and does not belong to the original architectural plan, but was added

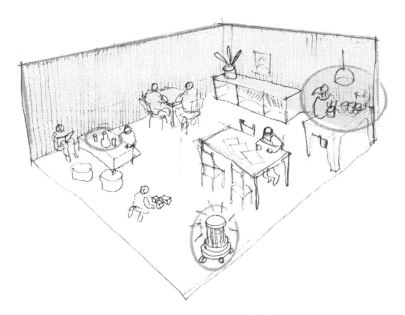

FIGURE 4.3 Puelche School special room. Author's sketch.

later. The first time I went in to look for a SEN teacher, the space reminded me of a club or treehouse. The wood walls gave the room a different atmosphere from the other classrooms, which have concrete walls. As I show in my croquis (Figure 4.3), there was a kerosene space heater on, expelling the typical smell of Chilean middle- and low-income houses in winter, and the work tables were not small, individual desks but large tables – there were four of them – in which the students sat in groups with the teacher. The materials were messy, but I did not perceive the disorder as a disaster, rather as part of a familiar, welcoming environment. Lina, the SEN teacher whom I met my first time there, offered me tea – they had an electric kettle and a small refrigerator in the room – and we sat down to talk around one of the work tables. During the time we were talking, many SEN students entered and left the room. They came to say hello, ask for some material or information, or just spend some time there.

The coming and going of students belonging to the School Integration Programme (those labelled as having special educational needs or disabilities) to the resource classroom happened every time I was there observing a lesson or talking with the teachers. Through my visits I could find out how the special room, although it is not the most well-maintained and physically attractive space at the school, operates as a place to feel comfortable, accompanied, heard and recognised. The flow of affects in the special room exceeds the programme's definition for students with special educational needs and the understanding of the room as a space for addressing learning difficulties. Students and teachers – through their daily practices of being together, sharing and counting on each other – transform the space into a meeting place, not focused on achievement or compassion, but on knowledge and affection for the others.

This space provides contrast for the two rigid possibilities that have driven the dynamics of inclusion and exclusion in Chilean educational policy. Inclusion programs understand inclusion as being inside the "normal" room and therefore in conditions to participate and be included, and exclusion as being in the special room and therefore without possibilities for participation. The transformation of space into something porous and movable, which can be used not only for special learning, shows the multiplicity of layers that exist concerning what has been understood as the inclusion of students with special educational needs. What we see is a continuum of practices and affects, rather than a dichotomy of inclusive and exclusive subjects and places. In this sense, school spaces are fluid; students transit along them no matter what is the spot's formal use. Special education teachers' caring and full recognition for their students, displace pity, difficulty, segregation and dullness, as emotions linked repeatedly to the special room. Instead, happiness, interest and belonging shape the place and their inhabitants. This experience opens the door to thinking about the importance of flexibility for school spaces; in other words, spaces that offer possibilities rather than closed uses. Also, it is central to comprehend the damage of consolidating exclusionary labels for students and materiality under a mistaken understanding of inclusion in education.

Vicente

All around the reception office of Maitenes School (Figure 4.4) are ordinary everyday things; mothers bringing forgotten school bags for their kids, teachers asking for office materials from receptionists, school visitors coming and going. As a connection zone between the outside and the inside, the space folds and unfolds in different directions, enveloping children and adults. There, I meet Vicente, a year three student. He wears orange plugs in his ears, like those used for swimming. He is skinny with brown hair, pale skin and brown eyes that look huge behind his glasses. It is recess, but he does not go to the playground. He prefers to play in the office area where there are three cubicles for interviewing parents.

As I try to show in my sketch (Figure 4.4), that corner looks like a bank, and Vicente pretends to be a bank teller.

> He sits behind the table, and spontaneously, I take the chair opposite him, pretending to be a customer.
>
> - What's your name? he asks me.
> - Rosario, I answer.
> - Who are you? Are you a teacher?

Vicente does not pay much attention to my answers and gets up and tries to use the phone that is on the desk. Apparently, it is disconnected because he

FIGURE 4.4 Maitenes School office and students' practices in it. Author's sketch.

hangs up, leaves the cubicle and goes to sit on the reception armchairs. He tries them one by one, reclining to stretch his body on them. The bell rings; it is a loud and prolonged sound. Upon hearing it, Vicente runs to the corner of the reception area, where there is a telephone on the wall. He picks it up, presses the buttons and asks out loud, "Who is speaking?" He keeps listening to the bell and asks again, "Who is it?" He looks curious, expecting an answer. The bell stops ringing and Vicente sits on a chair and balances. A man enters the room and Vicente says, "Stop the bell! It is unpleasant!"

A teacher appears and says to him, "Let's go to the classroom," but Vicente does not move, he keeps balancing on his chair.

(Field notes, Maitenes School, April 2018)

During my visits to Maitenes School, I often encountered Vicente in the reception office. Secretaries and teachers are used to seeing him there and, even though students are not supposed to go there during recess, Vicente's presence is not only accepted, but it completes the place. I imagine that for Vicente, noise must be very loud, and that he seeks refuge in the school reception area. Vicente is calmed there, wrapped in a playful atmosphere. The teacher does not force him to return to his classroom. She left without stressing him, recognising his place, understanding his rhythm. The space, departing from the fixed geometries of his being, opens out as a construct, to build a free plan in which he moves, invents concepts, unfolds drama (Rajchman 1997). Vicente can be himself at the reception office, he feels acknowledged by everyone there. It is a place for differences, where adults and students meet, parents from diverse backgrounds, men and women, all running errands at school.

Everyone takes advantage of the flexible style of the office in some way, where rules can be adapted in order to suit the needs of forgetful children, anxious mothers and laughing and loud staff. It is a place in school where things appear not to be "educational", because they lack the normativity and rationality often linked to education. As Kenway and Youdell note:

> Education is almost always positioned as rational – as a social and epistemological endeavour, as an abstract process, as a set of reasoned and logical practices, and as a series of formal spaces, the production and use of which is as 'uncontaminated' by emotion as possible.
>
> (2011)

Vicente's diagnosis is not what matters at the reception desk, he belongs there as much as anyone else, as a member of the community that comes and goes, he is not threatened by norms and takes his time doing what he wants to do. Teachers' approaches to Vicente at the reception desk take advantage of his act of transgression of being there instead of playing in the schoolyard or his classroom; they convert the office into an affective, in-between place with the potential to get Vicente to like school, feel comfortable and relaxed.

Final notes

By observing the way in which affective and material elements are entangled, I aim to move beyond the dualism between inclusion and exclusion. All students, not only SEN students, rely on materiality for deploying their social interactions, sense of belonging and well-being. However, an analysis of affects and materiality in relation to SEN students' experiences at school reveals possibilities for school design, curriculum and school community engagement. The experiences of some SEN students opens up possibilities to try out new alternatives for learning, friendship and participation. Conducting observations, including visual data and taking an ethnographic approach, allows us to think very practically about the consequences of affects and materiality in students' everyday life.

Within the context of the schools observed, we recognise features close to factory model education and social efficiency doctrine (Fallace & Fantozzi 2013), which do not take into account the affective dimension. School Integration Programmes are finally searching for standard students' outcomes, paying special attention to strategies oriented to diminish what they have identified as deficits in students' condition rather than to focus on students' diversity and their affective experiences at school. The way in which resources are invested tells us where the emphasis of School Integration Programmes' policy are; there is no money for initiatives related to the materiality of school. PIE's instructions for the use of its funding are very detailed and do not allow for spending on architecture and design projects at schools, which could contribute to SEN students' experience of being in place. Material investments are functional, such as ramps for students with mobility disabilities. The latest national strategic plan for school infrastructure takes access into consideration. It explicitly proposes standards for building new classrooms and focuses on bilingual signs, ramps, lifts and toilets for students with disabilities (MINEDUC 2016). Within this framework, school buildings and yards do not usually offer physical environments for inclusion and diversity. There is no attention to different sensibilities, ways of interaction, or diverse ways of learning.

However, to bring these elements to schools' design, policy resolutions are not enough. The understanding of what inclusion in education is should feed the decision to pay attention to space and materiality. In order to design spaces with no category, there should be no category for any student. Instead, school architecture could capture the free flow of abilities, preferences and rhythms present in students. Open spaces in the school, meaning spaces everybody may inhabit, are spaces for deploying difference and interchanging experiences. Schools should assure their spaces facilitate various appropriations, uses and meanings. Bernard Tschumi, writing about his project Parc de la Villette, emphasises that one of his aims was "to displace the traditional opposition between program and architecture", and to construct a complex architectural organisation without resorting to traditional rules of composition, hierarchy, and order" (Tschumi 1998: 198). In other words, the main purpose should be to offer alternatives, in the most open way possible so that students can complete the design in using their school.

The courtyard at Ovalle School provides an example of this possibility: instead of proposing a defined centrality, it opens itself to different use and occupation patterns. Figure 4.5 demonstrates how some basic concrete furniture acts as a transition

FIGURE 4.5 Ovalle School courtyard.

between the area closest to the building and the open courtyard. The design assumes that students inhabit both spaces with different rhythms, but it does not establish a strict distinction. Tranquillity and attention may prevail in one, while physical activity and disorder may predominate in the other. The form and materiality of the proposed furniture lend their potential to this malleable use. Figure 4.5 shows students' everyday scene sitting on something that is not a bench, but rather a multi-use structure. Their practices revolve around these simple structures: students sit and have lunch, rest, talk, wait for friends and play.

If we take that example to a classroom, we will be talking about a space where all students may look for their best way of being in it and learning. They could explore different sitting arrangements – there will not be fixed tables and chairs – and find alternative materials for completing their educational tasks. Interestingly enough, Universal Design for Learning (UDL) comes from architects' challenge to design buildings accessible for all, but UDL aims to go beyond mere accessibility and shape students' learning experiences. A focus on affect and materiality brings to inclusive education a perspective free from dichotomies and limits and centred in sensitive experiences about learning and encounter. What we know as inclusive education is rooted in difference and built through diagnosis, standards and ideas about what normality is. Recognising the work of emotions and the importance of materiality opens the door to a new understanding of inclusion in education, which celebrates the uniqueness of every student.

This chapter aims to open a discussion about how affects and materiality should be at the centre of our reflection while we are working for building inclusion and diversity in education. The ambiguity of affects help to move away from dichotomies such as inclusion/exclusion, ability/disability, schools' classrooms and courtyards for one use and not for others. The flow of affects refers to the diversity of experiences and the central role of senses in them. Within that context, affects are decisive in structuring what we understand as inclusion. Acknowledging affects circulate among schools' materiality, we may take the opportunity to set the scene for a more diverse and inclusive everyday experience for all students.

Acknowledgements

This research was funded by ANID PIA CIE160007. I would like to thank Rocío Berwart and Sofia Larrazabal for her work in the fieldwork for this research and their useful comments to this chapter.

References

Ahmed, S. (2004). *The cultural politics of emotion*. Edinburgh: Edinburgh University Press.
Anderson, B. (2009). Affective atmospheres. *Emotion, Space and Society*, 2, 77–81.
Ball, S., Maguire, M., & Braun, A. (2012). *How schools do policy: policy enactments in secondary schools*. New York: Routledge.
Banks, M. & H. Morphy. (1997). *Rethinking visual anthropology*. New Haven, London: Yale University Press.

Bateson, G., & Mead, M. (1942). *Balinese character; a photographic analysis*. New York: New York Academy of Sciences.
Casey, E. (1993) *Getting back into place*. Bloomington and Indianapolis: Indiana University Press.
Clough, P. & Jean, H. (Eds.) (2007). *The affective turn: Theorising the social*. New York: Duke University Press Books.
Deleuze, G. & Guattari, F. (2004). *A Thousand Plateaus*. London: Continuum.
Fallace & Fantozzi (2013). Was there really a social efficiency doctrine? The uses and abuses of an idea in educational history. *Educational Researcher* 42 (3), 142–150.
Gregg, M. & Seigworth, G. (Eds.) (2010). *The affect theory reader*. Durham: Duke University Press.
Kenway, J. & Youdell, D. (2011). The emotional geographies of education: Beginning a conversation. *Emotion, Space and Society* 4, 131–136.
Knudsen, B. & Stage, C. (Eds.) (2015). *Affective methodologies. Developing cultural research strategies for the study of affect*. New York: Palgrave, 12
Massey, D. (1996). *Space, place and gender*. London: Polity Press.
Massumi, B. (2002). *Parables for the virtual. Movement, affect, sensation*. Durham and London: Duke University Press
Merleau-Ponty, M. (1962). *Phenomenology of perception*. London: Routledge.
Miller, D. (2005). *Materiality*. Durham and London: Duke University Press.
Ministerio de Educación de Chile. (2016) *Transformando Espacios Educativos. Guía para Intervenciones de Conservación*. Santiago: MINEDUC.
Nairn, K. & Higgins, J. (2011). The emotional geographies of neoliberal school reforms: spaces of refuge and containment. *Emotion, Space and Society* 4 (3), 180–186.
O'Toole P. & Were P. (2008) Observing places: using space and material culture in qualitative research. *Qualitative Research* 8 (5), 616–634.
Pink, S. (2009) *Doing sensory ethnography*. London: Sage.
Rajchman, J. (1997) *Constructions*. Cambridge MA: MIT Press.
Spinoza, B. (1994) The ethics, trans E. Curley. In: Curley, E. (Ed.) *A Spinoza reader: The ethics and Other Works*. Princeton, NJ: Princeton University Press.
Thrift, N. (2008). *Non-representational theory. Space, politics, affect*. London: Routledge.
Tschumi, B. (1998) *Architecture and disjunction*. Cambridge MA, London: MIT Press.
Watkins, M, (2007) Disparate bodies: the role of the teacher in contemporary pedagogic practice. *British Journal of the Sociology of Education* 28 (6), 767–781.

5
CONCEPTUALISING INCLUSION WITHIN INDONESIAN CONTEXTS

Nur Azizah, Elga Andriana, and David Evans

International communities have responded to legislation, policy and conventions that highlight that all children and adolescents should have access to a quality, inclusive education. The delivery and enactment of quality inclusive education programs is central to achieving international commitments (e.g., United Nations Sustainability Development Goals 2030) and national and local strategic goals. Despite efforts over more than 30 years, there are still significant inequities in providing education for all (e.g., de Bruin, 2019; Gao & Postiglione, 2015; Singh & Mukherjee, 2018; Sullivan & Artiles, 2011).

Inclusive education is concerned with all students having access to a quality education in their local school alongside their peers without fear of discrimination (e.g., gender, religion, ability, cultural background). In acknowledging this wider interpretation of inclusive education, this chapter will focus on quality education for students with disabilities identified as a group marginalised by current policy, practices and attitudinal barriers across international boundaries (UNESCO, 2020a). Furthermore, this chapter will focus on students with disabilities in Indonesia where governments have developed policy, legislation and education reforms to promote and sustain inclusive education.

Inclusion is "a process that helps overcome barriers limiting the presence, participation and achievement of learners" (UNESCO, 2017; p. 13). The concept of inclusion in education emerged from the Salamanca Statement (UNESCO, 1994) and has become part of ensuing international conventions and statements. Signatories to the Convention on the Rights of Persons with Disabilities (CRPD) (United Nations, 2006), for example, have undertaken to uphold their legal obligations through a range of initiatives that address quality education for students with disabilities. These efforts have taken different forms and involved differing processes, with differing outcomes for students with disabilities.

DOI: 10.4324/9781003091950-6

Inclusion in education should ensure all children and adolescents have the "right to safe, quality education and learning throughout life" (UNESCO, 2018, p. 2). This should ensure that students with disabilities, for example, will not be marginalised either through exclusion from education, education in a separate context, access to a different and 'special' curriculum, or inappropriate, low-impact pedagogical practices. In the Indonesian context, however, only 18% of students with disabilities gain access to inclusive education, that is, education in the same context of their peers without disabilities (Maulipaksi, 2017). Additionally, about 24% of children with disabilities aged above five years old do not have access to education, and this is four times higher than non-disabled peers (Jayani, 2019).

Generally inclusive education in the Indonesian context is translated into the separation between 'regular' and 'special'. This includes schools implementing two different curricula, namely the national curriculum for regular students and a special curriculum for students with disabilities; attachment of a special needs teacher aiding one 'inclusive student'; and provision of facilities for a study room, practice rooms and consulting rooms dedicated only for students with disabilities (Andriana, 2018; Prasetiyo et al., 2020).

While there has been a clamour to achieve the intent of the principles of inclusion and to uphold quality inclusive education in schooling systems around the world, "profound challenges persist" (United Nations, 2016, p. 2). A key issue within this dilemma is the way the principles of inclusion have been interpreted and enacted. The Convention on the Rights of Persons with Disabilities (CRPD; United Nations, 2006), for example, stated in Article 24 that "States Parties shall ensure an inclusive education system at all levels and lifelong learning" (24.1). The idea of a 'system' in some cases appears to be interpreted as a range of different contexts made available for students to attend (e.g., neighbourhood schools, special classes, special schools). Education systems or sectors provide each of these options for students with disabilities. Segregated classes and schools, however, often prevent students from participating in learning alongside their peers without disabilities. This lost opportunity to benefit socially and academically is often the result of education systems failing to provide support to students and educators in the home classroom; this missed opportunity also perpetuates low expectations of students with disabilities (United Nations, 2016).

There is a growing concern that the principles of inclusion have been used as a veneer over existing, discriminatory practice and policy. Slee, Corcoran and Best (2019) argue that education authorities and researchers, in the rush to promote inclusion in education, have become "mixaphobic", with students with disabilities and their peers losing out (p. 4). The promises of inclusion and inclusive education appear to be "reproducing" the inequities that it was intended to overcome in a different form (Runswick-Cole & Goodley, 2015, p. 168). This is evident in different structures across the Indonesian contexts. In schools designated inclusion schools, inclusion is just another way of stating disabilities or special needs literally and in practice. Students with disabilities in regular school, for example, are often referred to as 'inclusion students', and their teachers are referred to as 'inclusion teachers'. Furthermore, teaching practice and pedagogical belief of these teachers predominantly focus on disabilities rather than inclusive pedagogy (Sheehy & Budiyanto, 2015). Various policies on the implementation of inclusive education also only focus on disabilities (e.g., Peraturan Menteri Pendidikan Nasional, No 70, 2009). Finally, the quota arrangement of the number of students with disabilities in regular schools also forces unfair selection where students who have more severe disabilities have a higher risk of being excluded. These practices strengthen discrimination rather than equality.

This chapter will examine the place of inclusive education within the Indonesian context. It will draw on different sources of fieldwork and ongoing professional learning within different geographical areas of Indonesia conducted by each of the authors to build a picture of the current place of inclusive education within the Indonesian context. The chapter will then reflect on this position through listening to the voices of key actors within Indonesia, in particular, Yogyakarta Province. Through reflecting on these voices regarding international statements, the future promises of inclusive education within Indonesia will be critically examined.

Background to inclusive education policy in Indonesia

The Indonesian education system for many decades has educated students with disabilities separately from their peers without disabilities. Widagdo (2016) reported that approximately 70% of students with disabilities were not accessing education in Indonesia. The Indonesian government has been committed over a period to ensuring all students with disabilities access an education. The current legal definition of disabilities in Indonesia states that people with disabilities are persons who have long term physical, intellectual, mental and/or sensory impairments that may lead to barriers to participation in all aspects of society on the same basis as persons without disabilities (Undang-Undang RI No 8, 2016). In the Indonesian education context, the terms of disabilities are often used interchangeably with special needs.

Although the Indonesian government committed to education for all by signing the Salamanca Statement in 1994, it was not until 2001 that focussed attention was given to developing and implementing inclusive practice within Indonesian schools. At this time, the Directorate of Special Education initiated a pilot project in Gunungkidul, Yogyakarta (Nasichin, 2001). Two years later, the Indonesia government published circular letter No 380/C.C6/MN/2003 (Directorate General of Primary and Secondary Education, 2003) persuading heads of the provincial office of the National Education Department to undertake pilot projects of inclusive education by enrolling students with disabilities at a range of schooling levels from primary school to secondary school. *Deklarasi Bandung* in 2004 and *Deklarasi Bukit Tinggi* in 2005 added further commitment to educating students with disabilities in regular schools. These early initiatives formed initial perspectives and understandings of inclusive education in the Indonesian context.

In 2009, the Indonesian government through the Ministry of National Education issued the first regulation on inclusive education titled *Inclusive Education for Children with Special Needs and Children with Talent and Giftedness* (No 70, 2009). This regulation supported schools across Indonesia to enrol students with special needs; these came to be known as Schools Providing Inclusive Education (SPIE). To be appointed as a SPIE, schools could apply through their provincial department of education. In other cases, the provincial department of education selected schools to be Schools Providing Inclusive Education. These schools were entitled to extra government funding and access for staff professional development provided by the Ministry and provincial department of education. At this point, however, other schools could still 'reject' or exclude students with disabilities simply for the reason that they were not designated as SPIE. Furthermore, the authorisation of SPIE status indicated an expertise in upholding the principles of inclusion, or in implementing inclusive practices at the school level (Purbani, 2013).

After Indonesia ratified the CRPD in 2011, a significant step in fulfilling this commitment towards equity and equality of individuals with disabilities was achieved through the enactment of the Disability Law in 2016. The Disability Law not only highlights the importance of educating students with disabilities with their non-disabled peers in regular schools but also mandates that teacher training universities provide pre-service teachers at least one unit of study in inclusive education.

Training programs for prospective teachers can enhance attitudes on inclusive education (Gokdere, 2012). Such training programs not only have a positive impact on pre-service teachers' attitudes but also significantly enhance their confidence in designing an inclusive classroom (Sharma, Ee & Desai 2003; Spandagou, Evans & Little, 2008). However, a study of pre-service teachers in Indonesia provided evidence that pre-service teacher self-efficacy in teaching students with disabilities in regular school was only 'fair' after a semester of study (Maulida, Atika & Kawai, 2020; Novembli & Azizah, 2020). This is different from studies from other countries where there are more established pre-service teacher education units of study (e.g., Finland — Savolainen, Engelbrecht, Nel & Malinen, 2011) that show greater value.

Strides towards building inclusive education programs through educating students with disabilities in regular schools has continued to be bolstered through a zone system of schooling enrolment (*Zonasi*). This latest national enrolment regulation states that school enrolment must be non-discriminatory, except for schools that specifically educate groups by gender and/or religion. According to this regulation, every school must accept students with disabilities, implying the concept of the SPIE is no longer used (i.e., all schools are now SPIE). Strengthening this development is *Peraturan Pemerintah* (Government Regulation, No 13, 2020) on reasonable accommodations for students with disabilities. This regulation covers four significant components such as: 1) provision on budgeting support and financial assistance, 2) provision on facilities and infrastructures, 3) provision on teachers' preparation and other school personnel, and 4) provision on curriculum.

However, the promise of SPIEs in breaking down barriers to education for students with disabilities has been difficult to achieve. The pioneering of the SPIE established attitudinal barriers that are not easy to remove. Educators and the community developed a mindset that promoted the idea that there were some schools that had expertise in educating students with disabilities, and others not. As a result, SPIEs ('inclusion schools', Andriana & Evans, 2017) enrolled a disproportionately high number of students with disabilities, placing even further stress on limited resources for supporting all students.

More recently, enrolment regulations have been interpreted differently by local education departments. Provincial education departments interpreted enrolment of students with disabilities in regular school by establishing a quota, and this varied among provinces ranging from 3%–10% of the total students enrolled in the schools. Explanations given for this indiscriminate use of proportions centred around securing places for students with disabilities at regular schools as well as preventing over-representation of students with disabilities in one school.

Families seeking to enrol their child with disabilities in a regular school are required to present a certificate of verification of their child's disability. This verification is typically provided by a doctor, paediatrician, psychiatrist, or personnel from a disability services unit. While schools believe this disability certificate might assist them to provide appropriate accommodations, evidence shows that often students with disabilities do not receive these accommodations (Purbani, 2013; Rudiyati, 2011) and that the diagnosis is of minimal assistance in supporting students educationally. This certification also creates a barrier to students who are already enrolled and may acquire a disability or may experience a more 'invisible' impairment (e.g., mental health condition). These students are not provided educational experiences and/or support to assist them access and participate in their education.

Many families cannot afford to consult a specialist to receive formal verification of their child's disability due to financial constraints, and hence another barrier to accessing education emerges (i.e., students cannot access appropriate support). This set of barriers to enrolment and participation has resulted in students failing to progress (i.e., they cannot meet minimum class standards to progress to the next class, or high school). In some instances, families may be asked to find another school for their child (e.g., inclusion school), or students drop out of education.

During these developments over the past two decades there have been substantial legislative and policy developments in the area of providing quality education for students with disabilities in Indonesia. One of the most recent, the Master Plan on National Development of Inclusive Education, builds on the 2016 legislation. This plan promises much, and has much to live up to, as recent data indicate that only 11% of schools provide access to an inclusive education (UNESCO, 2020b). One of the provinces leading the development of quality education for students with disabilities is Yogyakarta Province.

Inclusive education in Yogyakarta Province

Yogyakarta Province consists of five districts (i.e., Sleman, Bantul, Kulon Progo, Gunungkidul, and Yogyakarta). It is a geographical area of 3,133.15 square kilometres and is known as the 'city of education' in Indonesia. This recognition for education is primarily in regard to the high concentration of tertiary education institutions within the province. This concentration has also resulted in a focus on promoting research and community action in regard to the social inclusion of persons with disabilities.

Yogyakarta Province has a population of nearly four million people, with 1,073,754 students enrolled in 5,439 formal education institutions, ranging from kindergarten to higher Education (BAPPEDA, 2020). Finding the number of students with disabilities enrolled in regular education schools is difficult due to limited data collection. It is estimated that approximately 2,700 students with disabilities are educated in regular schools (i.e., less than .01% of students).

Yogyakarta has a strong connection in regard to inclusive education. It is the site where the Directorate of Special Education conducted their first project of inclusive education in Karangmojo Primary School in Gunungkidul in 2001. Since this initial project the commitment of Yogyakarta to implement inclusive education has grown stronger. The first regulation on implementation of inclusive education was the *Peraturan Walikota* (Mayor Regulation, No 47, 2008), one year ahead of national policy developments. In 2013, *Peraturan Gubernur* (Governor Regulation No. 21, 2013) was implemented, followed by *Peraturan Daerah* (District Regulation No. 4), which focussed on promotion, protection and fulfilment of the rights of persons with disabilities. The implementation of these latter regulations has been accompanied by ongoing and continuous improvement processes. This growing commitment at the political and policy level has been accompanied by supporting regulations. Regulation No 41/2013 was used to accelerate the implementation of inclusive education through the development and maintenance of inclusive education resources.

Today, the concept of inclusive education has been embedded in the future of Yogyakarta. The province has declared that by 2025 all schools in Yogyakarta will be 'inclusive' (i.e., all regular schools will enrol students with disabilities). Furthermore, a Disability Service Unit has been established by the Department of Education to support schools in achieving this vision. This unit plays an important role not only to serve students with disabilities, but also schools, parents and other relevant stakeholders. This is the first Disability Service Unit at the local or provincial level of education in Indonesia, with other units located within the many tertiary education providers in the province.

These developments within Yogyakarta Province are often held up as the benchmark for other provinces in Indonesia. Many provinces have followed Yogyakarta's example to enhance the implementation of inclusive education. The Global Education Monitoring Report acknowledged this development, stating: "The country [Indonesia] has strengthened the inclusiveness of its education system, decreasing the number of students in special schools and expanding access of those with disabilities to mainstream schools from pre-primary through tertiary education" (UNESCO, 2020a, p. 38).

The work undertaken in regard to inclusive education in Indonesia, and especially Yogyakarta Province, seeks to uphold the right of every child to a quality inclusive education. Like many countries, it also addresses Indonesia's obligation in ratifying the CRPD (United Nations, 2006). The work being undertaken around inclusive education is keenly watched by persons with disabilities, advocacy groups and all persons whose world is directly impacted by persons with disabilities. In observing developments and the promises of inclusive education, one can find outstanding examples of quality, contextually relevant inclusive education. There are, however, numerous examples of broken promises that come from the "mixaphobic" interpretations of quality inclusive education (Slee et al., 2019, p. 4). These examples are not unique to the Indonesian context, and parallel examples can be found across different borders.

Enacting inclusive education

As in many countries, the implementation of inclusive education varies widely in the Indonesian context. The concept of inclusive education is often perceived as students attending a regular school but being placed in special classes. The Ministry of Education has enacted a gradual process of building inclusive education (Kemdikbud, 2013). This was typified by the appointment of SPIEs and recently, all schools having to comply with Legislation 2020 to enrol and accept children with disabilities. The experiences of different actors within education have been varied. This section presents the voices of students, parents and teachers on their experiences of the development of inclusive education, prior to Legislation 2020.

Student's voice

Interrogating and analysing the nature of inclusive education within so-called inclusive schools through the student voice is critical. This form of inquiry is necessary to establish students' feelings of belonging and acceptance to better understand inclusion, its characteristics and existing deficits. It is essential to uphold the principles of inclusion (Carrington, Allen, & Osmolowski, 2007; Messiou, 2008; Nilholm & Alm, 2010).

From case studies of 'inclusive schools' in the Yogyakarta context, common messages voiced by students include the importance of play, hopes to move to the next grade, need for friendship, protection from bullying and isolation, and rejection of labelling practices. A key message from the students' voice was the use of the label 'inclusion' to identify and address students with disabilities (i.e., 'inclusion child'). This had an impact on the image and identity of students with disabilities who were seen as having a lower status by other members of the school community, and on their experiences of marginalisation both at the academic level and social level (Andriana & Evans, 2017, 2020).

At the social level, students with disabilities wished for a school that promoted social skills that allowed them to initiate or engage in interaction and play with all students. They also wanted to be accepted and to be part of a community that allowed them to make wider friendships from diverse backgrounds. Students with disabilities felt they had much to offer their peers without disabilities and school staff about acceptance and friendships. Friendship, from their point of view, should be inclusive of all members of the schooling community (Little et al., 2020).

Meanwhile, a study involving the voices of 100 children with disabilities in Indonesia, on accessibility in primary school, identified a typical problem relating to the limited number and range of resources. Access to learning, especially physical access and access to learning media, encounters the reality that it is complex and costly. The complexity refers to the diverse and specificity of needs among students with physical, sensory and/or intellectual disabilities (Sukadari et al., 2020). Reviewing those voices from children, it can be seen they are signalling the need for universal design both in the physical environment and the learning environment (i.e., curriculum design, learning related activities).

Teacher's voice

Through ongoing fieldwork by the researchers, it was found that many teachers held the belief that children with disabilities were being educated in an 'inclusive school' (i.e., not in a regular school). This way of thinking was evident, for example, by grouping students in the classroom based on their disability diagnosis, a practice frequently recommended by the medical profession. Teachers often referred students with disabilities to receive their lessons as part of the 'inclusion room', or allocated a special needs teacher to a student with disabilities individually, often at a cost to the family (Andriana, 2018). In some instances, schools required a parent of the student with disabilities to sit with their child in the classroom and support them.

In other examples teachers voiced that rather than 'forcing' classroom teachers to teach students with disabilities, it is better that special education teachers who have a special education needs background teach the students in mainstream classrooms (Poernomo, 2016). These practices created divisions between 'inclusion' children and 'regular' children, 'regular' education teachers and 'inclusion' teachers, and in some instances, between parents of students with disabilities and those without. This resulted in academic and social exclusion at the classroom and community level rather than inclusion.

At the very foundation, teachers need support, space and facilitation to discuss and reflect on what inclusive education really means for them in their context. Evidence from different projects in Indonesia (e.g., Andriana, 2018; Evans, Andriana, Setiani, & Kumara, 2018) indicates that many teachers view upholding the principles of inclusive education as a "one size fits all" formulaic undertaking (United Nations, 2016, p. 10). Professional learning opportunities that critically examine the diversity of contexts, students' strengths, supports available and teachers' professional knowledge, and how this impacts teacher practice for all learners, are key to promoting inclusive education across the multitude of contexts within the Indonesian archipelago.

Teachers need support, especially in the area of developing a flexible classroom curriculum that includes learning goals, method, assessments and materials (Andriana, 2018; Poernomo, 2016). Teachers need to have high expectations of all learners when designing classroom curriculum, where disability diagnosis does not impute expectations, or the level or type of accommodations to assist participation.

A quality, inclusive class curriculum needs to include flexible learning activities and assessments so that students with a diversity of learning needs and backgrounds are catered for, allowing them to proceed with peers to the next year level or secondary school (Andriana & Evans, 2020).

There is a need for schools, teachers and their communities to trial and reflect on practices that are inclusive for students in their local school. Developing these underpinning beliefs, schools and teachers can then move towards realising the principles of inclusion within their educational practices and policies. This contextually sensitive approach was provided to teachers in the original site for inclusive education: Gunungkidul, Yogyakarta Province. When supported with training on the principles of Universal Design for Learning (UDL), teachers in Gunungkidul developed learning environments inclusive of all students by enhancing the nature of their classroom planning, learning activities and assessments. The teachers provided a range of learning options that maximised students' interests and needs, and the resources of the community. The most significant change was the shift from reliance on the textbook as the sole method of representation in lessons to provide knowledge, to utilising alternative representations such as the use of everyday materials and engaging students in more interactive learning. The choices of ways given to students to demonstrate their learning were closely aligned with their use of a range of environmental resources to represent skills and knowledge (Evans et al., 2018). This use of environmentally relevant resources provided a range of options to teachers and students and prevented them from positing that the need for more resources was the only option in order for quality inclusive education practices to be implemented.

Parent's voice

Inclusive education has given broader options for parents of children with disabilities to send their children to be educated with their non-disabled peers. Many parents with children with disabilities in Indonesia experience stigma when they enrol their children in special schools. This psychological effect is greater in families who have high social and economic status (Primadata, Soemanto, & Haryono, 2015).

Families have the option to enrol their child with disabilities in a special school so they can access an education. The availability of special schools is limited compared to regular schools and often they are not geographically accessible. Most provinces in Indonesia have one special school in a municipality. In Yogyakarta Province, the ratio of special school to regular school at primary school level is 1:26; whereas the ratio at junior high school level is 1:8; and 1:7 at secondary high school level (BAPPEDA, 2020). Parents often have to travel significant distances so their child with disabilities can attend a special school. With special school hours being relatively shorter than regular schools, many parents stay at the school waiting for their children. For many parents, this situation has an impact on their economic life; as a result, many choose not to send their child to school or may stop taking their child to school. This lack of options and opportunity, along with difficulties in transporting their child to school, is a significant contribution to the low gross enrolment rate of students with disabilities in Indonesia. Therefore, the implementation of inclusive education was intended to reduce negative stigma, increase participation of children with disabilities in schools, and boost the opportunity for parents to contribute to the social and economic prosperity of their communities.

The promises of inclusive education for parents, however, has taken some down a road that can be challenging. For example, parents have raised their concerns regarding the limitations or quotas set by schools on the number of students with disabilities they will enrol. This practice has allowed some schools to give fewer opportunities to children with more severe disabilities to be accepted in their local or chosen school. In contrast, it also has allowed some schools to stop the flow of students with disabilities from schools that have refused enrolment to students with disabilities. This flow of students to schools previously designated as 'inclusion schools' has led to more than 50% of enrolled students being identified with disabilities (Andriana, 2018). The actions of schools and their teachers to enrol and teach students with mild disabilities in preference to students with more complex needs is supported from findings across several international contexts (Greece – Pappas, Papoutsi, & Drigas, 2018; Finland – Saloviita, 2015). Tejaningrum (2017) reported that parents of children with complex needs were required to go to several schools before they received an offer of enrolment. In other cases, students were required to enrol in special schools, or possibly be excluded altogether from schooling.

Parents of children with disabilities are generally positive about inclusive education. In a study with three primary inclusion schools in Yogyakarta, parents with children with disabilities reported that inclusive education provided greater interaction opportunities for their children (Andriana, 2018). This finding is supported by Tejaningrum (2017). Parents acknowledged that their children became more socially involved and gained greater motivation for learning. One mother described her optimism for inclusive education as it had changed her son's uncontrollable behaviour for the better. Further, Amka (2019) reported that almost 80% of parents of children with disabilities had positive beliefs and attitudes towards inclusive education.

A number of parents of students without disabilities were not supportive of their children being educated alongside peers with disabilities. The common reason for parents of children without disabilities rejecting inclusive education was their fear that the presence of children with disabilities will have negative impacts on the academic learning experiences of their children (Waki, 2017). However, most parents of children without disabilities do not mind their children having social interactions with children with disabilities (Amka, 2019).

Parents of students with disabilities voiced their concerns regarding the attitude of teachers and school members, particularly in enabling learning opportunities that were accessible to all students (e.g., joining the National Exam, school excursions, or access to computers). Parents believed there were low expectations of students with disabilities in the schools of their children. Further, parents also had concerns over the availability of learning support; for instance, parents could not afford to provide their own special education teacher for their children to enrol in regular schools that did not provide special education teachers. This issue is rooted in the understanding of inclusive education by schools, teachers and executive teams. Schools translate inclusive education as simply attaching special education teachers to students with disabilities in regular classrooms (Andriana, 2018). The systematic reforming of school ethos and goals for all students is often not undertaken, leaving parents with children with disabilities in regular schools on the outer with the same challenges of special education in a different guise (i.e., inclusive education).

Implication for the future of inclusive education in Indonesia

Inclusive education in Indonesia is being pursued earnestly and with vigour. This can be found within local communities that are being driven by strong community groups seeking greater access and participation at different levels of society. There have been a number of large-scale projects funded by international agencies (e.g., Australian Department of Foreign Affairs and Trade) that have supported the energy with which communities have taken up the principles of inclusive education. The path taken across a relatively short period of time has generated stories familiar from other countries (e.g., teacher attitudes, limited resources, system barriers), while other stories of positive outcomes can be found (e.g., the community of Gunungkidul). All efforts are to be congratulated, while learning from these stories is key to the future of inclusive education. Understanding some of the barriers and facilitators in the development of genuinely inclusive schools is important.

Conceptualisation of inclusive education

The key issue found in the Yogyakarta context is that inclusive education is characterised by the division between 'special' and 'regular', or 'inclusion' and 'regular'. This can be illustrated by the attachment of the label of 'inclusion' to children with disabilities ('inclusion' child), the special education teachers who support their learning (i.e., 'inclusion' teachers), designated rooms for students with disabilities who are pulled out from regular classes (i.e., 'inclusion' room), and schools charged with enrolling students with disabilities (i.e., 'inclusion' schools). This understanding of inclusive education serves to maintain the disparity between children of different backgrounds, skills and knowledge. It upholds traditional practices of the past where students were diagnosed with a disability, labelled, and then excuses made as to why they could not participate on the same basis as their non-disabled peers. These processes were often undertaken outside the context of the schooling environment, without consideration of the skills and knowledge of educators, community and students.

The current conceptualisation of inclusive education in the Indonesian context sustains the separation between special education and regular education; that students with disabilities are 'special' education's responsibility and students without disabilities are 'regular' education's responsibility. It seems that the community needs to reflect critically and consider that achieving inclusive education is not achieved by merely installing special education within regular education. Furthermore, in order to move inclusive education forward, perspectives need to be reconstructed with regard to exclusion (e.g., how current 'inclusive' practices are excluding students), a new conception of inclusion created, language rectified, and education policy and practice reforms pursued at all levels of education (Slee, 2011).

The division between 'special' and 'regular' or 'inclusion' and 'regular' has also led to curriculum, pedagogy, assessment and processes of exclusion in the name of inclusion. Students who do meet common standards are tested, diagnosed and transferred or 'marched' to 'inclusion' classes or schools; little reflection is given to the educational environment and how it disables students. Teachers and educators need to shift their understanding regarding individual differences and focus on learning as a shared activity (Florian, 2015). This can be done, sometimes without the need for an injection of substantial resources, as shown by the teachers in Gunungkidul where student differences are celebrated, shared and opportunities for learning designed for all learners, with all learners.

Strong policy

One of the facilitators for inclusive education in the Yogyakarta context is its strong policy commitment. Yogyakarta province aims to achieve its vision of all schools being transformed to schools that offer quality inclusive learning environments for all students by 2025. Several provincial regulations support inclusive education including child protection (*Peraturan Daerah DIY* No 4, 2013) and inclusive education resource support (*Peraturan Gubernur* No 21, 2013). Yogyakarta also has an Inclusive Education Action Plan (2015) that aims to guide the provision of non-discriminatory services through the identification of opportunities and challenges in accessing education for students with disabilities and strategies to develop the capacity for implementing inclusive education in Yogyakarta (Villeneuve et al., 2016).

In line with this, the education department of Yogyakarta City formed a Disability Service Unit that promotes and supports 'inclusion schools'. The supports include psychological assessments to diagnose disabilities and case conferences for special needs teachers to discuss cases of children with disabilities. The Disability Services Unit also offers a scheme to help parents of children with disabilities secure enrolment in regular schools. While this is judged to be a forward movement, it is a confused notion of inclusion. As discussed previously, the policy and the practice of the unit needs to revisit the conceptualisation of inclusive education. It would appear from the very beginning that being a separate unit from other parts of the education bureaucracy maintains the idea of exclusion. Undertaking case conferences with special needs teachers, for example, excludes other educators and maintains a separate educational track for students with disabilities. One way to promote principles and values of inclusion and build school capacity in inclusive practices is by inserting a Disability Service Unit within all levels of the education department. Supporting schools to build capacity to be inclusive of all learners in all domains of education would advance the re-conceptualisation of inclusion.

Community support

Within the unique context of Yogyakarta, there are examples of communities working together to support the development of inclusive education environments. Evans et al. (2018) provide an example of teachers from one Yogyakarta suburban school who had developed a proficiency in the use of the universal design for learning framework as part of their plan to become inclusive. Through working with teachers from rural Gunungkidul, a very different education context to their own, they co-designed learning experiences that applied the UDL framework, enhanced teacher capacity to be inclusive, and enriched the learning of all students. While supportive of teachers in Gunungkidul, the need to articulate their conceptualisation of inclusion provided the opportunity for teachers to reflect on their current practices, attitudes and beliefs.

These contextually relevant examples can be found throughout Indonesia where local communities have voiced and declared their desire to make education accessible for all (e.g., Kalimantan, Sulawesi). In another example, students with learning disabilities and without disabilities explored social inclusion and belonging within their community during service-learning projects that connected with their school curriculum using Photovoice. The project culminated with a public photo exhibition and presentations by the students. From the students' lens, students felt that friendship, respect, collaboration and the promotion of traditional culture made them feel included and part of their school and their community (Bonati & Andriana, 2021).

Community practice involving inclusive education implemented through *Kelompok Kerja Guru* (KKG/Teacher Working Group) and *Musyawarah Guru Mata Pelajaran* (MGMP/Subject Teachers Discussion Forum) are also evident in Yogyakarta. KKG and MGMP are non-structural teacher organisations in a school district. KKG consists of primary school teachers whereas members of MGMP are junior high school, secondary school and vocational teachers from several schools within a district. KKG and MGMP are strategic opportunities for teacher professional development as they enable teachers to learn collaboratively with colleagues. Teachers' collegiate learning facilitates their success in teaching. A study conducted by INOVASI (2019) found evidence of increased teachers' pedagogical abilities, attitudes and ways of thinking which in turn encouraged change in practice and better teaching through KKG in teaching literacy in two remote areas. Furthermore, KKG and MGMP enable teachers to arrange their professional development driven by their own needs. This practice motivates teachers as they can learn from each other about what works and does not work in their classrooms. This will enable teachers to learn from data to drive change at the pedagogical and cultural level (Mandinach, 2012).

Community commitment to inclusive education within schools is a positive start. Noted in a field visit to Sulawesi as part of the Australian Government Australia Award Fellowship, one province proudly and loudly celebrated their commitment to inclusive education. Public officials presented their vision to the community, the community was provided the chance to question these ideas, and students with a range of backgrounds presented their achievements. Yet this was the first day, and when a member of the audience articulated that making a verbal commitment to inclusion was different from being inclusive in every facet and feature of the school and community, a sense of reality set in. Changing attitudes and misconceptions and overturning traditional systems takes time, requires strong leadership, and needs to take students and community on the journey.

Vision for the way forward

The development of inclusive education in Indonesia has followed similar pathways as other countries. They have taken leads from other countries (e.g., United States, Netherlands, Japan, Australia) who have experienced their own trials and celebrations. Many of the key issues to achieving the full intent of inclusive education – "a process ... to provide all students ... with an equitable and participatory learning experience and environment that best corresponds to their requirements and preferences" – are similar, yet contextually different (United Nations, 2016, para. 11). The process requires the full support of all members of the community, from politicians through children and adolescents. Yet actions need to be louder than words – they need to be implicit and without the 'but' that often accompanies actions. Enrolment of students with disabilities in the local school is not inclusive unless it is accompanied by access to, and participation in, the same flexible curriculum as all other students. This enrolment will be inclusive when all students have the chance to celebrate their learning through flexible and dynamic assessment practices; when students can participate and progress with their peers without the need to jump the same standards fence.

Actions need to be for everyone, and by everyone. The ongoing devolution of educating students with disabilities to a special educator, shadow teacher, teaching assistant or parent is counter to the principles of inclusive education; it must be everyone's responsibility. Within the Indonesian context this devolution mirrors that in many countries (e.g., United States, Australia, China), yet with such a young movement towards inclusive education there exists a great opportunity for differing contexts to show their intentions to be inclusive of all students to the fullest extent.

Indonesia contributes to The Global Education 2030 Agenda, especially to SDG Goal 4, which aims to "ensure inclusive and equitable quality education and promote lifelong learning opportunities for all" (United Nations, 2021). An urgent call for action is that curricula should be flexible and dynamic, and employ interactive, learner-centred pedagogy alongside specially designed accommodations as required (UNESCO, 2020c). The teachers of Gunungkidul provide evidence of this positive movement, one that celebrates the local schooling and community context, demonstrates the power of collaboration and sharing, and ensures students with and without disabilities are not the collateral damage of the misappropriation of the principles of inclusion.

References

Amka. (2019). Sikap orangtua terhadap pendidikan inklusif. *Madrosatuna. Journal of Islamic Elementary School 3*(1). 15–26. https://doi.org/10.21070/madrosatuna.v3i1.2068.

Andriana, E. (2018). *Engaging with student voice through arts-informed methods: Exploring inclusion in three schools providing inclusive education in Yogyakarta, Indonesia.* [Doctoral Thesis, University of Sydney]. Sydney repository.

Andriana, E., & Evans, D. (2017). "Why I am chosen as inclusion child?": Listening to student voice on school experiences of inclusion in Indonesia. In V. Plows & B. Whitburn (Eds.), *Inclusive education: Making sense of everyday practice* (pp. 175–194). Rotterdam: Sense Publishers.

Andriana, E., & Evans, D. (2020). Listening to the voices of students on inclusive education: Responses from principals and teachers in Indonesia. *International Journal of Educational Research, 103*, 101644. https://doi.org/10.1016/j.ijer.2020.101644.

BAPPEDA (2020). *e-data.* Retrieved from http://bappeda.jogjaprov.go.id/dataku/data_dasar/index.

Bonati, M., & Andriana, E. (2021). Amplifying children's voices within photovoice: Emerging inclusive education practices in Indonesia. *British Journal of Learning Disabilities.* 00, 1–15. https://doi.org/10.1111/bld.12405

de Bruin, K. (2019) The impact of inclusive education reforms on students with disability: An international comparison, *International Journal of Inclusive Education, 23*(7–8), 811–826. https://doi.org/10.1080/13603116.2019.1623327.

Carrington, S., Allen, K., & Osmolowski, D. (2007). Visual narrative: A technique to enhance secondary students' contribution to the development of inclusive, socially just school environments – lessons from a box of crayons. *Journal of Research in Special Educational Needs, 7*(1), 8–15. https://doi.org/10.1111/j.1471-3802.2007.00076.x.

Directorate General of Primary and Secondary Education. (2003). Circular letter No 380/C.C6/MN/2003. *Inclusive school pioneering in municipality.* Author.

Evans, D., Andriana, E., Setiani, P., & Kumara, A. (2018). Universal design for learning to support learning in Gunung Kidul. In M. Best, T. Corcoran, & R. Slee. (Eds.), *Who's In? Who's Out? What to do about inclusive education* (pp. 71–87). Leiden: Brill-Sense Publisher. https://doi-org.ezproxy.library.sydney.edu.au/10.1163/9789004391000_010

Florian, L. (2015). Conceptualising inclusive pedagogy: The inclusive pedagogical approach in action. In J. Deppeler, T. Loreman, R. Smth, & L. Florian. (Eds.), *Inclusive pedagogy across the curriculum* (pp. 11–24). Emerald Group. https://doi.org/10.1108/S1479-363620150000007001

Gao, F., & Postiglione, G. A. (2015). Ethnicity and educational achievement, In J.D. Wright (Ed) *International encyclopedia of the social & behavioral sciences* (Second Edition) (pp. 130–135). Elsevier.

Gokdere, M. (2012). A comparative study of the attitude, concern, and interaction levels of elementary school teachers and teacher candidates towards inclusive education. *Educational Sciences: Theory and Practice, 12*(4), 2800–2806.

Government Regulation *(Peraturan Pemerintah).* (No. 13, 2020). *Reasonable accommodations for students with disability.*

Governor Regulation *(Peraturan Gubernur).* (No. 21, 2013). Implementation of inclusive education.

INOVASI. (2019). *KKG sebagai wadah pengembangan keprofesian berkelanjutan.* Retrieved from https://www.inovasi.or.id/wp-content/uploads/2019/10/Policy-Brief-8-KKG-1111.pdf.

Jayani, D. H. (2019, August 29). *Pada 2018, Hanya 5,48% Penyandang Disabilitas yang Masih Sekolah.* Databoks. https://databoks.katadata.co.id/datapublish/2019/08/29/pada-2018-hanya-548-penyandang-disabilitas-yang-masih-sekolah.

Kemdikbud. (2013). *Pedoman Penyelenggaraan Program Dikjas Adaptif Bagi PDBK Di Sekolah Inklusif.* Jakarta: Direktorat Pembinaan PKLK Dikdas Kemdikbud.

Little, C., de Leeuw, R. R., Andriana, E., Evans, D., & Zanuttini, J. Z. (2020). Social inclusion through the eyes of the student: Voices of students with disabilities on friendship and acceptance. *International Journal of Disability, Development and Education.* https://doi.org/10.1080/1034912X.2020.1837352

Mandinach, E. B. (2012). A perfect time for data use: Using data-driven decision making to inform practice. *Educational Psychologist, 47*(2), 71–85. https://doi.org/10.1080/00461520.2012.667064

Maulida, R., Atika, I. N., & Kawai, N. (2020). The pre-service teachers' attitudes towards inclusive education: An empirical study in Yogyakarta City, Indonesia. *Discourse and Communication for Sustainable Education, 11*(1), 65–73. https://doi.org/10.2478/dcse-2020-0007

Maulipaksi, D. (2017, February). *Sekolah Inklusi dan Pembangunan SLB Dukung Pendidikan Inklusi.* Kementerian Pendidikan dan Kebudayaan. https://www.kemdikbud.go.id/main/blog/2017/02/sekolah-inklusi-dan-pembangunan-slb-dukung-pendidikan-inklusi

Mayor Regulation (Peraturan Walikota Jogja). (No. 47, 2008). *Implementation of inclusive education.*

Messiou, K. (2008). Understanding children's constructions of meanings about other children: Implications for inclusive education. *Journal of Research in Special Educational Needs, 8*(1), 27–36. https://doi.org/10.1111/j.1471-3802.2008.00099.x

Ministry of National Education. (No 70, 2009). *Inclusive education for children with special needs and children with talent and giftedness.* Author.

Nasichin. (2001, October). *Kebijakan direktorat pendidikan luar biasa* A paper delivered in seminar of Special Education Department, Makassar, Indonesia.

Nilholm, C., & Alm, B. (2010). An inclusive classroom? A case study of inclusiveness, teacher strategies, and children's experiences. *European Journal of Special Needs Education, 25*(3), 239–252. https://doi.org/10.1080/08856257.2010.492933

Novembli, M. S., & Azizah, N. (2020). Bagaimana self-efficacy calon guru siswa dengan disabilitas di sekolah inklusi?: Studi di berbagai Perguruan Tinggi. *Persona: Jurnal Psikologi Indonesia, 9*(1), 51–66. https://doi.org/10.30996/persona.v9i1.2804

Pappas, M., Papoutsi, C., & Drigas, A. (2018). Policies, practices, and attitudes towards inclusive education: The case of Greece. *Social Sciences, 7*(6), 90. https://doi.org/10.3390/socsci7060090

Peraturan Daerah DIY. (No. 4, 2013). *Promotion, protection and fulfilment of the rights of persons with disabilities.*

Peraturan Menteri Pendidikan Nasional. (No. 70, 2009). *Inclusive education.*

Poernomo, B. (2016). The implementation of inclusive education in Indonesia: Current problems and challenges. *American International Journal of Social Science, 5*(3), 144–150.

Prasetiyo, W. H., Ishak, N. A., Basit, A., Dewantara, J. A., Hidayat, O. T., Casmana, A. R., & Muhibbin, A. (2020). Caring for the environment in an inclusive school: The Adiwiyata Green School program in Indonesia. *Issues in Educational Research, 30*(3), 1040–1057. http://www.iier.org.au/iier30/prasetiyo.pdf

Primadata, A. P., Soemanto, R. R., Haryono, B. (2015). Tindakan orang tua dalam menyekolahkan anak berkebuuhan khusus pada layanan pendidikan inklusif di sekolah dasar negeri 1 Tanjung, Kecamanatan Purwekerto Selatan, Kota Purwokerto. *Jurnal Analisa Sosiologi, 4*(1), 1–16.

Purbani, W. (2013). Equity in the classroom: The system and improvement of inclusive schools in Yogyakarta, Indonesia (a case study). *US-China Education Review, 3*(7), 507–518.

Rudiyati, S. (2011, May). *Potret sekolah inklusif di Indonesia.* A paper presented in AKESWARI seminar, Yogyakarta, Indonesia.

Runswick-Cole, K. & Goodley, D. (2015). Disability, austerity and cruel optimism in big society: Resistance and "The Disability Commons". *Canadian Journal of Disability Studies*, 4(2), 162–186.

Saloviita, T. (2015). Measuring pre-service teachers' attitudes towards inclusive education: Psychometric properties of the TAIS scale. *Teaching and Teacher Education*, 52, 66–72. https://doi.org/10.1016/j.tate.2015.09003

Savolainen, H., Engelbrecht, P., Nel, M., & Malinen, O. (2011). Understanding teachers' attitudes and self-efficacy in inclusive education: Implications for pre-service and in-service teacher education. *European Journal of Special Needs Education*, 27(1), 51–68. https://doi.org/10.1080/08856257.2011.613603

Sharma, U., Ee, J., & Desai, I. (2003). A comparison of Australian and Singaporean pre-service teachers' attitudes and concerns about inclusive education. *Teaching and Learning*, 24(2), 207–217.

Sheehy, K., & Budiyanto (2015) The pedagogic beliefs of Indonesian teachers in inclusive schools. *International Journal of Disability, Development and Education* 62(5): 469–485. https://doi.org/10.1080/1034912X.2015.1061109

Singh, R., & Mukherjee, P. (2018). Whatever she may study, she can't escape from washing dishes: Gender inequity in secondary education – evidence from a longitudinal study in India, *Compare: A Journal of Comparative and International Education*, 48(2), 262–280. https://doi.org/10.1080/03057925.2017.1306434

Slee, R. (2011). *The irregular school: Exclusion, schooling and inclusive education*. New York: Routledge.

Slee, R., Corcoran, T., & Best, M. (2019). Disability studies in education: Building platforms to reclaim disability and recognised disablement. *Journal of Disability Studies in Education*, 1, 1–11. https://doi.org/10.1163/25888803-00101002

Spandagou, I., Evans, D., & Little, C. (2008, November). *Primary education pre-service teachers' attitudes on inclusion and perceptions on preparedness to respond to classroom diversity*. Paper presented at the Australia Association for Research in Education National Conference, Brisbane.

Sukadari, J.M., Sentono, T., Huda, M., & Maseleno, A. (2020). Inequalities in access of learning in primary school: Voices from children with special needs. *International Journal of Psychosocial Rehabilitation*, 24(1), 356–366. https://doi.org/10.37200/IJPR/V24I1/PR200138

Sullivan, A. & Artiles, A. (2011). Theorizing racial inequity in special education: Applying structural inequity theory to disproportionality. *Urban Education*, 46(6), 1526–1552. https://doi.org/10.1177/0042085911416014

Tejaningrum, D (2017). Perspektif orang tua terhadap implementasi pendidikan inklusif di taman kanak-kanak. *Jurnal Konseling Pendidikan*, 1(1), 73–89.

United Nations. (2006). *Convention on the rights of persons with disabilities*. https://www.un.org/development/desa/disabilities/convention-on-the-rights-of-persons-with-disabilities.html

United Nations. (2016). *Convention on the rights of persons with disabilities: General comment No. 4*. https://www.refworld.org/docid/57c977e34.html

United Nations Educational, Scientific and Cultural Organization (UNESCO). (1994). *Salamanca statement and framework for action on special needs education*. Retrieved from http://www.unesco.org/education/pdf/SALAMA_E.PDF

United Nations Educational, Scientific and Cultural Organization (UNESCO). (2017). *A guide for ensuring inclusion and equity in education*.

United Nations Educational, Scientific and Cultural Organization (UNESCO). (2018). *Global education meeting: Brussels declaration*. Retrieved from https://unesdoc.unesco.org/ark:/48223/pf0000366394?posInSet=1&queryId=f00bbeb5-caf0-495d-9782-e4caad1e9e0f

United Nations Educational, Scientific and Cultural Organization (UNESCO). (2020a). *Global education monitoring report 2020: Inclusion and education - All means all.* https://en.unesco.org/gem-report/report/2020/inclusion

United Nations Educational, Scientific and Cultural Organization (UNESCO). (2020b). *Education for sustainable development: A road map.* https://www.gcedclearinghouse.org/sites/default/files/resources/200782eng.pdf

United Nations Educational, Scientific and Cultural Organization (UNESCO). (2020c). *Towards inclusion in education: Status, trends and challenges: The UNESCO Salamanca statement 25 years on.* https://reliefweb.int/sites/reliefweb.int/files/resources/374246eng.pdf

United Nations. (2021). *Sustainability development goals: Goal 4.* Retrieved from https://sdgs.un.org/goals/goal4

Villeneuve, M., Evans, D., Sadirin, S., Andriana, E., Bonati, M., Little, C., & Millington, M. (2016). *Collaborative action across health and education sectors for inclusion of children with disabilities in education: Establishing a policy vision and research agenda in Yogyakarta, Indonesia.* Sydney, Australia: Centre for Disability Research and Policy, University of Sydney. https://apo.org.au/sites/default/files/resource-files/2016-03/apo-nid64406_0.pdf

Waki, A. (2017). Persepsi orangtua terhadap pendidikan inklusif sekolah dasar di kecamatan Gunung Putri Kabupaten Bogor provinsi Jawa Barat. *Jurnal Basicedu 1*(1). 78–83.

Widagdo, C. (2016). Creatissng A fairer Indonesia for people with disabilities. *Global Policy Watch.* Retrieved from: https://globalpublicpolicywatch.org/2016/12/02/creating-a-fairer-indonesia-for-people-with-disabilities/

6

IS INCLUSIVE EDUCATION ENOUGH FOR AUSTRALIAN ABORIGINAL STUDENTS?

Making the case for belonging education to disrupt the normalised agenda of assimilation

Sheelagh Daniels-Mayes, Gary Fry, and Karen Sinclair

Introduction

For thousands of generations, Australian Aboriginal peoples have had their own sophisticated systems of educating their children. This process began as soon as the child moved in the mother's womb, as soon as it was known that there was a new responsibility (Price, 2012). Each day the child was observed to see what their contribution to the world would be. In the words of Eileen Lester (1975 cited in Price, 2012, p. 186):

> This one is a hunter, quick of eye; this one a leader, reflective and perceptive; this one is a scholar, quick of brain; this one a doctor, quick in learning about herbs; this one a linguist, quick to hear the speech; this one an astrologer, eager to understand the stars.

Education in Aboriginal society therefore was, and is, centred on the collective rather than the individual, connected to land with children learning alongside adults. Each person, no matter their 'difference' was constructed as being able to contribute to the community according to their identified ability. Tellingly, extensive research suggests that there exists no word in any Australian Aboriginal communities' language equivalent to the English words 'disability' or 'impairment' (Hollinsworth, 2013).

With the onset of colonisation in the late 18th century, much of this sophisticated system of strengths-based education was forced to adapt or perish. Eurocentric worldviews, constructed as being superior, were forced upon Aboriginal peoples, determined to replace long-established ways of knowing, being and doing (henceforth Aboriginal knowledges). Battiste (2002, p. 5) argues:

> Eurocentric thinkers dismissed Indigenous knowledge in the same way they dismissed any socio-political cultural life they did not understand: they found it to be unsystematic and incapable of meeting the productivity needs of the modern world.

Possession of Australia was accomplished through the fictional doctrine of terra nullius, Latin for 'land belonging to no one' (Reynolds, 1987). Colonisation dismissed and devalued Aboriginal society that had for thousands of generations been based on a holistic system that emphasised belonging, spirituality and relatedness (Martin, 2005). However, terra nullius not only facilitated the invasion of Australia, it established how relationships between Aboriginal and non-Aboriginal peoples within Australia were to operate (Mathews, 2012).

These relationships are most evident in our educational system where for more than two centuries Aboriginal education has been deleteriously shaped by discourses of deficit, exclusion and disadvantage (Foley, 2013; Price, 2012). From the very beginning of colonisation, Aboriginal children were constructed as being "uneducable" (Price, 2012, p. 32) or "unteachable" (de Plevitz, 2006, p. 48). Alternatively, colonisers deemed that Aboriginal children were only capable of learning menial tasks to become domestic servants, labourers and to tend livestock for the newcomers (Price, 2012). Undoubtedly, Aboriginal education policy and practice were grounded in discourses of racialised inferiority serving to justify the provision of second-class, often segregated education, well into the 20th century (Beresford, 2003; Foley, 2013).

In the 1930s, the policy of assimilation or 'absorption' emerged in response to the growing numbers of mixed-descent Aboriginal people and settler society's fears of racial miscegenation and degeneration (Foley, 2013). This policy strategised the biological and cultural absorption of Aboriginal peoples into 'white' Australia. Subsequently, tens of thousands of mixed-descent children were forcibly removed from their families and communities, a practice that persisted until the 1970s, in the belief that such children should not be exposed to the cultural influences of their Aboriginal parents (Beresford, 2003). Disparities of poor education outcomes between Aboriginal and non-Aboriginal learners in present-day Australia is borne out of this legacy of cultural genocide.

For generations, "the education system … through its curriculum and teaching strategies has attempted to 'de-Aboriginalise' Aboriginal people" (Heitmeyer, 1998, p. 198). Disturbingly, rates of segregation and exclusion – through both the provision of education in 'alternative' settings and disciplinary action – are on the increase. In New South Wales, for example, exclusionary discipline is used against Aboriginal students at alarming rates; in 2018, Aboriginal and Torres Strait Islander students made up around 24% of all short suspensions (lasting up to four days) and 29% of long suspensions (lasting up to twenty days) (NSW Department of

Education, 2018). Though education is commonly cited as a key factor in overcoming socioeconomic disadvantage, few benefits are evident for Australian Aboriginal students, their families or communities.

While our research projects differ in focus and methodology, as Aboriginal teacher educators, we share a distrust and scepticism of 'inclusive education', which has dominated Australian policy and practice in recent decades. In Australia, as with many other countries, inclusive education was initially adopted for the provision of schooling to students with a disability (Forlin & Bamford, 2005). Though it is now generally accepted that the meaning behind the term has expanded to focus on the provision of high-quality education to all students (Berlach & Chambers, 2011) it is still informed by a discourse of 'white privilege'. In other words, inclusive education was not about the inclusion of Aboriginal students or their cultural knowledges and practices, languages and identity, largely excluded since the onset of colonisation. Quite simply, inclusive education fails to recognise the role that encounters with racism continue to play in dispossessing Aboriginal children of their sense of belonging within education and wider society. Moreover, as will be shown, the terms 'inclusion' and 'belonging' are distinct and cannot be used interchangeably (Berryman & Eley, 2019).

In this chapter, we draw on our respective research projects beginning with making a case for belonging education. We then individually share stories from our research that briefly demonstrate the 'why' and 'how' of belonging education in the early years, through culturally responsive schooling, and in Northern Territory remote education. We will finish by bringing together our research and literature to provide our understanding of belonging education. But first, in accordance with Aboriginal protocols (Martin, 2005), we must first introduce ourselves and our research.

The research projects

This chapter draws on research from three Australian Aboriginal scholars, Kamilaroi Woman Sheelagh, Dagoman Man Gary, and Ngarrindjeri Woman Karen. We are teacher educators with lifetime histories of exclusion, inclusion and belonging. Each investigation complied with the Guidelines for Ethical Research in Indigenous Studies (AIATSIS, 2012) and secured human research ethics approval; Sheelagh and Karen's from University of South Australia, and Gary's from The University of Sydney. Additionally, each investigation secured ethics approval from the relevant education department.

Sheelagh's research sought to reveal and develop a counterstory of Aboriginal education success, shared by six community-nominated teachers at two sites in metropolitan Adelaide, South Australia. She utilised three theoretical frameworks: critical ethnography (Thomas, 1993), cultural responsiveness and Critical Race Theory. The principles of Indigenous storying methods known as yarning (Bessarab & Ng'andu, 2010) and Storywork (Archibald, 2008) provided methods for doing research 'proper ways' (borrowed from Aunty Nangala, personal communication,

23 June, 2013), meaning the research privileged the knowledges and practices of Aboriginal peoples. Sheelagh's research developed a framework referred to as Culturally Responsive Pedagogies of Success that centred Caring-Demander pedagogy for achieving academic success without sacrificing a student's Aboriginality.

Gary's research used Critical Race Theory, Aboriginalising its tenets to respond to the unique narrative of Northern Territory (NT) Aboriginal education. Drawing on research with remote North Australia Aboriginal principals, Aboriginal communities and educators, Gary investigated the intersecting roles of colonial history, 'race' and wealth inequality in the construction and deployment of Northern Territory remote Aboriginal education inequality. His investigation privileged the voices and stories of Northern Territory (NT) remote Aboriginal families, strengthened through his lived Aboriginal experience of 25 years employment as a teacher and senior education administrator in NT urban and remote communities. Gary's research advocated for a policy framework toward advancing NT remote Aboriginal education, factoring an Aboriginal political economy and community cultural capital (Yosso, 2005), wrapped around Indigeneity as a defining existential foundation.

Karen's mixed-method research utilised Foucauldian concepts of normalisation and governmentality (Foucault, 1980), Critical Race Theory and Indigenous Standpoint Theory to 'trouble' educators' perspectives on cultural competence. She sought to disrupt understandings of normalised concepts and to be receptive to other narratives of cultural competence. Her findings contributed to the development of a framework of positioning self in relationship to ways of knowing, being and doing cultural competence (Sinclair, 2017). Karen's framework assists educators to deconstruct understandings relating to authoritative constructions of cultural competence; develop cultural understanding through critical self-reflection; and engage with provocations presented in the framework.

Making the case for belonging education

While there is no single definition under which inclusive education is enacted, it is generally accepted that inclusive education is a discourse grounded in social justice (Dixon & Verenikina, 2007). Inclusive education aims to cease the practice of excluding students who do not fit within social constructions of normalcy and ability (Waitoller & Artiles, 2013). Furthermore, inclusive education is promoted as having the potential to break cycles of disadvantage (Snow & Powell, 2012), as well as to increase people's skills, leading to increased innovation and productivity and subsequently to long-term economic viability (Hoff & Pandey, 2004; OECD, 2017). In an inclusive education environment, teachers are encouraged and challenged to use a variety of pedagogies to cater for different learning needs, thereby having benefits for all students and not just for students of difference.

Yet the move to make the Australian education system more inclusive has had little success for Aboriginal students. There is, for example, an over-representation of Aboriginal students in segregated special education settings, and in-school suspension and expulsion rates. The reasons for this are complex, but the statistics cannot be ignored. As Sweller, Graham and Van Bergen (2012, p. 121) state:

> It cannot be claimed that increases in Indigenous enrolments in special education settings are due only to increases in the Indigenous population: If this were the case, the enrolments of Indigenous students should increase at similar rates for both mainstream and special settings.

Clearly, there is a 'significant gap' between envisioned inclusive education and the reality of what is happening in schools (Graham & Spandagou, 2011). If the current policies, strategies and pedagogies were working, the expectation would be that students, regardless of culture, background or ability, would be participating and succeeding at the same or similar rates as their non-Aboriginal counterparts. But this is not the case.

A sense of belonging has been shown to be an important schooling outcome in its own right, and for some students, is indicative of educational success and long-term health and well-being (OECD, 2004). Additionally, research reveals that feelings of being accepted by others at their school builds and sustains students' sense of belonging, stimulates motivation to learn and significantly reduces student attrition (St-Amand & Smith, 2017; Willms, 2003). PISA reports between 2003 and 2015 are therefore troubling as they reveal a 24% decrease in Aboriginal students reporting that they feel like they belong at school, a 17% decrease in their reports that they make friends easily at school, a 10% decrease in their reports that other students seem to like them, and a 14% decrease on items indicating that they felt like an outsider at school (ACER, 2018). Put simply, we do not believe that inclusive education is enough to overcome the pernicious legacy of exclusion, deficit and disadvantage embedded in the Australian education system. When Aboriginal students do not experience their own culture in their education, then education functions to assimilate by de-Aboriginalising them.

To successfully teach all students, not just those who most closely reflect the dominant culture, "[i]t is important for teachers to realise that they are inherently and consistently engaged in cultural production and reproduction" (Brayboy & Castagno, 2009, p. 37). Transforming educators' taken-for-granted understandings of the world requires critically questioning their beliefs, assumptions and prejudices to understand the cultural ways of others (Mitchell, 2015). Courageous conversations about the ongoing impact of racism would enable educators to purposefully interrogate their deficit constructions of Aboriginal students and their communities (Daniels-Mayes, 2020), thereby acquiring a new desire of knowing and understanding their students, and the cultures and communities to which they belong (Hale, Snow-Gerono & Morales, 2008).

Sands (2019) succinctly states: 'inclusion is a choice (you decide whether to include someone or not), but belonging is a feeling that can be enforced by a culture that you can purposefully create'. Watson (2005) takes the concept of belonging further, arguing that belonging is the way in which people feel accepted, respected, included and supported by a community in which they are involved. Furthermore, the need to belong has been identified as a fundamental human motivation, taking priority in human need over self-esteem and self-actualisation (Baumeister & Leary, 1995). For Aboriginal students who have been excluded and othered for generations, a sense of belonging at school and within the broader education system arguably becomes an even more significant issue. We now turn to our research and expand upon our understandings of belonging education.

Stories of belonging education

Across each of our investigations, the words 'belong' and 'belonging' are dominant. In the following three sections, we each demonstrate a need for belonging education and provide examples of how it can, and is, being enacted by educators despite many barriers.

Karen: Cultural competency in early years education

Cultural competence is a multifaceted 'slippery' social construct that is steeped in worldviews, values and assumptions. It is fraught with competing and opposing theories, representations and scholarship that undoubtedly influence curriculum approaches and pedagogies (Sinclair, 2017). Educators need to know the conventions of various discourses in order to challenge taken-for-granted assumptions in Aboriginal education, history, policy and curriculum that too often seeks to de-Aboriginalise learners. Here I focus on early years educators' views on diversity, inclusion and belonging, concluding by arguing that it is through a relational, dialogical process that "we develop an awareness and sense of self, of belonging and for coming to know our responsibilities and ways to relate to self and others" (Martin, 2003, p. 206).

Australia's first national approach to learning for young children, the *Belonging, Being and Becoming: The Early Years Learning Framework for Australia (EYLF)* (DEEWR, 2009), was developed to contribute to the Council of Australia Governments (COAG) aim to "improve outcomes for all children but specifically Indigenous children" (COAG, 2009, p. 13). Notably, *the framework* advocates strongly that a sense of belonging in early learning is critical to young children's well-being and is an essential aspect of quality care and education (DEEWR, 2009, 2010). Early childhood education prides itself on inclusivity. It performs 'nicely' at respecting diversity and making all children, no matter their background, feel that they belong. Problematically, the discourse within the EYLF (DEEWR, 2010) is dominated by non-Aboriginal voices and therefore is produced in a curriculum framework and pedagogy that privileges 'white interests' (Vass, 2012, p. 89). As stated by Said (1993, p. 100) "all cultures tend to make representations of foreign cultures the better to master or control them". As previously discussed, 'control' was achieved through constructing Aboriginal people as inferior and deficient from the earliest days of colonisation. Over the centuries, Aboriginal peoples have continuously fought to have their knowledges and pedagogies included in curriculum. Speaking of the importance of embedding culture in early childhood programs to ensure Aboriginal children form positive cultural identities, Bamblett and Lewis (2006) argue:

> The best protection we can offer any child is to give them a sense of belonging. Culture can provide that sense of belonging and through that belonging, resilience. That way we can begin the long process of creating a positive future for our children.
>
> (p. 66)

Similarly, the *National Aboriginal and Torres Strait Islander Education Plan 2010–2014* states:

> Participation in culturally inclusive, high quality early childhood education programs and care can assist Aboriginal and Torres Strait Islander children get the best start in life.
>
> (MCEECDYA, 2010, p. 9)

However, "cultural notions of belonging and unity among many social collectives are not only matters of discourse, but are also grounded in materialities, practices and 'real' space whose importance cannot simply be overlooked" (Fahlander, 2007, p. 26). Lieblein et al. (2018) contend that place belongingness in the symbolic sense refers to individuals feeling 'at home', comfortable, secure and emotionally attached to a place, a culture or a group (p. 2). Therefore, to feel a sense of belonging, children should be able to express their identity knowing that it will be acknowledged and respected.

All participating educators understood the importance of the educators' role to "recognise and promote culture in developing children's sense of being, becoming and belonging" (Sinclair, 2017, p. 84), illustrated in the following two comments:

> Educators having more understanding about cultural competence will benefit the service and the connections between cultures and each child having a sense of belonging.
>
> (Sinclair, 2017, p. 121)

And:

> Children's culture needs to be acknowledged and included as part of the whole child development.
>
> (Sinclair, 2017, p. 120)

Acknowledging the whole child means acknowledging the role culture, family, community and early childhood service play in children's development. Both Bronfenbrenner (1986) and Birch and Ladd (1997) uphold that educator–child and educator–family relationships are a priority in early childhood as this clearly informs children and families' sense of being and belonging within early childhood settings. The EYLF identifies secure, respectful and reciprocal relationships with children as one significant principle that underpins educators' practice (DEEWR, 2010). June, an Aboriginal Early Childhood educator, believes that collaborative work is imperative, stating:

> It is important that educators empower themselves to look for different ways of belonging, being and becoming in engaging with local Aboriginal children and their families.
>
> (Sinclair, 2017, p. 185)

Non-Aboriginal early childhood educator Ruth shares her view on the importance of developing an understanding of Australia's history:

> I think working in this community has increased my sense of accountability and responsibility for a shared history of Australia which includes our First Nations people and having a shared history, so you know belonging is central to being.
>
> (Sinclair, 2017, p. 152)

My research confirms that it is only through a relational, dialogical process with children and families that a sense of belonging can be established for children, families and communities.

Sheelagh: Belonging through culturally responsive schooling

> Our families are proud people, and our children grow up knowing that 'Black is beautiful' and learning to be 'Black and proud'. The home, the nurturing place of learning, teaches us a lot about ourselves, but unfortunately does not always prepare our children for the roller-coaster ride ahead of them.
>
> (Walker, 1993, p. 5)

According to my investigation, this 'roller-coaster ride' frequently begins on entering the mainstream educational system where Aboriginal students are quickly introduced to another set of values and beliefs, another set of experiences, language, and processes that differ markedly from their own (Gollan & Malin 2012). Likewise, Rahman (2013) argues that the learning 'rules' or 'hidden curriculum' evident in Australian schools are based on the values, practices and worldviews of the dominant culture, to which Aboriginal students are expected to assimilate. But as Brayboy (2014, p. 1) states, "the research is quite clear: there is no evidence that the assimilative model improves academic success". Culturally Responsive Schooling opposes long-standing agendas of assimilating Aboriginal students into the dominant culture by being student-centred, educating to and through a student's personal and cultural strengths, their cultural frames of reference, their intellectual capabilities, and their prior accomplishments (Gay, 2010; Ladson-Billings, 1994). As such, culturally responsive schools enable students to succeed academically, but not at the expense of their Aboriginality (Daniels-Mayes, 2016).

Gray and Beresford (2008, p. 208) state: "The impact on education from the historical legacy of Australia's racist past is impossible to overestimate, it is clear these effects are still being felt today". Within the institution of education Aboriginal students' Aboriginality and sense of belonging are often denigrated, ignored or simply rejected as having no value for academic success (Daniels-Mayes, 2016). Research participants intentionally seek to understand how to create schools of belonging for Aboriginal students, who may at varying times feel alienated or disengaged for various reasons. For example, at one school site there existed the Nunga Room: the office space of the Aboriginal Education Team (AET), a tutoring room, a meeting room and a gathering space. The room is divided into two halves with the AET working in a U-shape on one side and a group-work table and storage space existing in the other half. The walls are covered in Aboriginal art, often painted by students themselves; there are boxes of t-shirts from numerous Aboriginal-focused events; and, oftentimes, there are boxes of food ready for gathering or camping or a day's activity. Aboriginal students use this space for support, for studying or just to 'hang out'. It is into this space that I was welcomed upon arriving at this school, being invited to use the space as my base for the research.

During my many months spent in the Nunga Room I kept what Hayes, Johnston and King (2009) refer to as a 'Day Diary'. My purpose was to recount events in the Nunga Room as they occurred to provide a snapshot of the ebb and flow of this culturally safe space. What emerged was an understanding of the diversity, unpredictability and complexity of the Nunga Room in what it provides on a daily basis to support Aboriginal students as they gain their education. In one morning's entry, I noted the following: a student grappling with their Aboriginal identity ("Am I Nunga? Who's your mob?"); food is distributed to several students; another student is struggling with his desire to stay at school without his mates; and the planning of an event that will celebrate Aboriginal youth during Youth Week in 2015 (Field Notes: 5 November, 2014).

This randomly selected Day Diary entry is typical of the kind of happenings that take place within the Nunga Room. I witnessed art projects developing, sporting events being sorted, and discussions of racism and Aboriginal cultural identity taking place. Furthermore, with a high percentage of the senior students living independently, the Aboriginal Education Workers are often to be found sorting out the payment of bills, buying eyeglasses, negotiating with Centrelink on behalf of students, making medical appointments for students and providing breakfast and/or lunch as needed. Additionally, I have witnessed and participated in conversations with family and community members who either drop in spontaneously to discuss their children or who are regular collaborators on a diversity of matters.

The Nunga Room is a place of belonging located within the school that serves to ameliorate the ongoing impact of dispossessing colonisation discussed previously.

The Nunga Room's overall purpose is to increase the likelihood of Aboriginal students' academic success. However, staff do not relentlessly focus on academic excellence, but instead they are intentionally and purposefully creating a place of belonging (Berryman & Eley, 2019) where relationships are built, Aboriginal student/parent/community voices are privileged, and cultural safety and identity are centred. The question remains, however, of what will it take for whole schools to be a 'Nunga Room' rather than such a valuable space being only a segregated part of a school.

Gary: Belonging in northern territory remote aboriginal schools

> That Department [DoE]; you know, the people and the workers, whoever gets employed and, if we are going to make up a true collaboration and true partnership, let go! Let the community run it and they can feel, like we made a mistake, probably do this other way. And they know, eventually they will make any changes, but will be effective. I use my [Dreaming] logo. Slowly but surely you walk, but they look where they're walking (Aboriginal principal).
>
> (Fry, 2020, p. 224)

My research told the complex story of education policy failures aimed at Northern Territory remote Aboriginal children and their families. This necessarily long set of interconnecting stories revealed what transpires when Aboriginal voices are not included in educational policy (Gillan, Mellor & Krakouer, 2017). This failure is to be seen in, for example, the over-representation of Aboriginal youth in the NT juvenile justice system where in 2018 they made up 100% of the incarcerated population (NITV, 2018). My research goals were encapsulated in the National Aboriginal and Torres Strait Islander Education Policy (NATSIEP) (Australian Government, 1989). A key statement made by Indigenous Task Force members at the time argued, "A new approach to Aboriginal education can only succeed if the Aboriginal community is fully involved in determining the policies and programs that are intended to provide appropriate education for their community" (Gillan et al., 2017, p. 18).

But, as revealed in my research, 30 years later this has failed to happen. Instead, beyond the NT and Australian governments' moralising and good intentions, a destructive and costly trajectory of assimilation prevails, grounded in the dualistic entanglements of neoliberalism and neocolonialism that seek to ultimately de-Aboriginalise Australia's first peoples (Fry, 2020). This situation provoked my investigation into education policy responses to remote schooling in the Northern Territory and how student identity and belonging are central to redressing education policy dysfunction (Fry, 2020). My research emphasised the need for education policies that respond to NT remote Aboriginal peoples, including Aboriginal cultural inclusion, a more accessible form of remote education service provision, and pathways to employment and development on Country (Fry, 2020). Specifically, I wanted to know what policy approaches aimed at NT remote Aboriginal communities would enable students and their families to engage meaningfully and purposefully with a western education system. Here, I share one counterstory from my research that illustrates that when we listen to and privilege the voices of Aboriginal families in the education of their children, then remote NT Aboriginal communities become sites of community cultural capital (Yosso, 2005).

Most Aboriginal families located in NT remote Aboriginal communities continue to practice language, live by the key institution of Aboriginal customary law and resist a colonising and irrelevant education offering (Fry, 2020). But this abundance of community, cultural and social wealth/capital is persistently untapped by education policy designers (Fry, 2020). Employing a CRT lens, Yosso (2005) argued that marginalised communities are far from being empty vessels in need of filling with western culture, and instead advocates for nurturing cultural wealth through at least six forms of social and cultural capital. Applying Yosso's framework of community cultural capital enables us to re-imagine NT remote Aboriginal communities (Fry, 2020), and the following example illustrates this translation to community development.

In 2015 the NT remote Aboriginal community of Gunbalanya, East Arnhem Land, became the first, and so far, only, NT remote Independent Public School (IPS) (Gillan et al., 2017). This extraordinary achievement came about after decades of fighting for self control over their education services, as one research participant stated: 'We had to wrestle back control of education' (Department of Education) employee). Having increased autonomy concerning most aspects of schooling services, Gunbalanya's education performance has been outstanding, as highlighted in the recent Australian Education Review (Gillan et al., 2017):

> Since 2013 Gunbalanya School, situated in East Arnhem Land, has consistently outperformed all other remote schools across the Northern Territory in student achievement. The average student attendance rate in 2016 was 53 per cent with 8 per cent of students attending 90 per cent or more of the time. What sets Gunbalanya apart from most other very remote schools is its ability to consistently have a core of students graduate Year 12. Over the past 4 years, 27 students have graduated with this qualification and moved onto employment or tertiary education.
>
> (p. 69)

My research consistently found that if education is about preparing NT remote Aboriginal children to thrive within and contribute to a western world, then their identity needs to be strengthened and not de-Aboriginalised. My research found that this needs to be embedded within an education architecture that aligns with NT Aboriginal peoples' political economy and community development capacities (Brayboy & Castagno, 2009; Lowell & Devlin, 2010). That is, in a world of social complexity children, families and their communities develop a sense of belonging that reinforces social and emotional well-being for all, established through an education experience that gives purpose and existential foundations to community development.

Discussion and further pathways

In this chapter we have drawn from available literature our respective research investigations and our own lived experiences as Aboriginal teacher educators, to make the following cases:

- Embedded into the normalised narratives of Australia's educational system is a persistent racism borne out of two centuries of dispossessing colonisation that perniciously seeks to de-Aboriginalise and assimilate Aboriginal students;
- If all students are to reach their full potential and be able to contribute to society, then education needs to intentionally create places of belonging from early years to high school, and within policy domains, no matter the geography of the student;
- We need to recognise that inclusive education, underpinned by 'white privilege' is not enough to transform education so that it is of benefit to all students and not just those who are affiliated with the dominant culture;
- Belonging education requires the purposeful creation of a learning environment where children feel connected, accepted and respected by the schooling community that stretches to their families and communities whose voices are privileged.

In drawing our respective work together, what we have sought to briefly show is that there are significant differences between inclusion and belonging and these produce very different outcomes for Australian Aboriginal students in education. Quite simply, inclusive education is about making a choice to accommodate difference through reasonable adjustments but inclusive education continues to draw on the dominant 'white' cultural embedded narrative of how this is to be achieved and therefore has little value to Aboriginal children. Inclusive education is not about including Aboriginal student cultural knowledges and practices, languages and identity. That is, inclusion has functioned as a 'moralised form of ethics' that has become a defensible weapon to philosophic challenges. We argue that inclusion is an illusion because it situates external to the existential connectedness that children need in order to see the functionality and purpose of school – and importantly, to enjoy and be rewarded for the experience through their identity as the standpoint for engaging an external other.

Belonging education requires educators to centre students' Aboriginal knowledges in their learning; to see Aboriginality as an asset for learning and not a problem to be fixed; it is the identification and rejection of racialised deficit discourses of Aboriginality; and it is the creation and maintenance of culturally safe schools that promote belonging for Aboriginal students, their families and communities. Belonging education is relational, a dialogical process of coming to know, of refusing to tolerate failure; belonging education enables Aboriginal children and young people to succeed academically, but not at the expense of their Aboriginality; and Aboriginal children, like all children, are constructed as having the ability to contribute to a good society; belonging education is strengths-based (Daniels-Mayes, 2016; Fry, 2020; Sinclair, 2017).

In this chapter we have argued that inclusion in education is simply not enough for Aboriginal education success. It is projected as a moralising concept that hides the ongoing purpose of education to de-Aboriginalise and assimilate Aboriginal students into the Eurocentric education system. In contemporary times education needs to reflect a design that is responsive to the social complexity within school organisational spaces (Fry, 2020) and this means privileging Aboriginal knowledge and voices demonstrated in our three shared investigations. Our focus has been on the significance of a sense of belonging at school for Aboriginal students but we recognise too that a sense of belonging at school is critical for all students if they are to succeed. Our individual research projects did not set out to investigate the concept of 'belonging' per se. However, it is a theme that dominated our research findings. We recognise that further research is needed that explicitly focuses on the concept of belonging within all levels of education and the wider policy contexts within which they are embedded. There is still much unknown about how a sense of belonging can be purposefully created and sustained within education.

References

Archibald, J. A. (2008). *Indigenous storywork: Educating the heart, mind, body, and spirit*. Vancouver: UBC Press.

Australian Council for Educational Research. (2018). *PISA Australia in Focus Number 1: A Sense of Belonging at School*. Australian Council for Educational Research Ltd, Camberwell, Victoria.

Australian Government. (1989). *National Aboriginal and Torres Strait Islander education policy 1989* (pp. 1–19). Department of Education Employment and Training, Canberra, Australia.

Australian Institute for Aboriginal and Torres Strait Islander Studies (AIATSIS). (2012). *Guidelines for ethical research in Australian indigenous studies*. Canberra, Australia. https://aiatsis.gov.au/sites/default/files/docs/research-and-guides/ethics/gerais.pdf

Bamblett, M., & Lewis, P. (2006). A Vision for Koorie children and families: Embedding rights, embedding culture. *Just Policy: A Journal of Australian Social Policy, 41*, 42–46. https://doi.org/10.1017/cha.2014.28

Battiste, M. (2002). *Indigenous knowledge and pedagogy in First Nation's education: A literature review with recommendations*. National Working Group on Education and the Minister of Indian Affairs, Indian and Northern Affairs Canada (INAC). https://www.afn.ca/uploads/files/education/24._2002_oct_marie_battiste_indigenousknowledgeandpedagogy_lit_review_for_min_working_group.pdf

Baumeister, R., & Leary, M. (1995). The need to belong: Desire for interpersonal attachment as a fundamental human motivation. *Psychological Bulletin, 117*(3), 497–529.

Beresford, Q. (2003). The context of Aboriginal education. In Q. Beresford, & G. Partington. (Eds.), *Reform and resistance in Aboriginal education* (pp. 10–40). Perth: University of Western Australia Press.

Berlach, R., & Chambers, D. (2011). Interpreting inclusivity: An endeavour of great proportions. *International Journal of Inclusive Education, 15*(5), 529–539. https://doi.org/10.1080/13603110903159300

Berryman, M., & Eley, E. (2019). Student belonging: Critical relationships and responsibilities. *International Journal of Inclusive Education, 23*(9), 985–1001. https://doi.org/10.1080/13603116.2019.1602365

Bessarab, D., & Ng'andu, B. (2010). Yarning about yarning as a legitimate method in Indigenous research. *International Journal of Critical Indigenous Studies, 3*(1), 37–50. https://doi.org/10.5204/ijcis.v3i1.57

Birch, S. H., & Ladd, G. W. (1997). The teacher-child relationship and children's early school adjustment. *Journal of School Psychology, 35*(1), 61–79.

Brayboy, B. M. J. (2014). Culture, place, and power: Engaging the histories and possibilities of American Indian education. *History of Education Quarterly, 54*(3), 395–402. https://doi.org/10.1111/hoeq.12075

Brayboy, B. M. J., & Castagno, A. E. (2009). Self-determination through self-education: Culturally responsive schooling for Indigenous students in the USA. *Teaching Education, 20*(1), 31–53. https://doi.org/10.1080/10476210802681709

Bronfenbrenner, U. (1986). Ecology of the family as a context for human development: Research perspectives. *Developmental Psychology, 22*(6), 723–742. https://doi.org/10.1037/0012-1649.22.6.723

Council of Australian Governments (COAG). (2009). *Investing in the early years—national early childhood development strategy: An initiative of the Council of Australian Governments.* Canberra, Australia. http://www.startingblocks.gov.au/media/1104/national_ecd_strategy.pdf

Daniels-Mayes, S. (2016). *Culturally responsive pedagogies of success: Improving educational outcomes for Australian Aboriginal students.* Unpublished Doctoral dissertation. University of South Australia.

Daniels-Mayes, S. (2020). A courageous conversation with racism: Revealing the racialised Master Storys of Aboriginal deficit, disadvantage and failure for pre-service teachers. *The Australian Education Researcher, 47*, pp. 537–554. https://doi.org/10.1007/s13384-019-00360-0

Department of Education, Employment and Workplace Relations. (2009). *Belonging, being and becoming: The early years learning framework for Australia.* Canberra, Australia. http://www.deewr.gov.au/Earlychildhood/Policy_Agenda/Quality/Documents/Final%20EYLF%20Framework%20Report%20-%20WEB.pdf

Department of Education, Employment and Workplace Relations. (2010). *Educators belonging, being and becoming: Educators' guide to the early years learning framework.* Canberra, Australia. http://files.acecqa.gov.au/files/National-Quality-Framework-Resources-Kit/educators_guide_to_the_early_years_learning_framework_for_australia.pdf

Dixon, R. M., & Verenikina, I. (2007). Towards inclusive schools: An examination of sociocultural theory and inclusive practices and policy in New South Wales DET schools. Paper presented at the 2007 Learning and Socio-Cultural Theory: Exploring Modern Vygotskian Perspectives International Workshop. Wollongong, Australia.

Fahlander, F. (2007). Third space encounters: Hybridity, mimicry and interstitial practice. In P. Cornell, & F. Fahlander (Eds.), *Encounters / materialities / confrontations: Archaeologies of social space and interaction* (pp. 15–41). Newcastle upon Tyne: Cambridge Scholars Press.

Foley, D. (2013). Indigenous Australia and the education system. In N. Bagnall, C. Campbell, R. Connell, D. Foley, D. Hayes, H. Proctor, A. Sriprakash, M. Vickers, & A. Welch (Eds.), *Education, Change and Society* (3rd ed.) (pp. 131–157). South Melbourne, Victoria: Oxford University Press.

Forlin, C., & Bamford, G. (2005). Sustaining an inclusive approach to schooling in a middle school location. *Australasian Journal of Special Education, 29*(2), 172–181. https://doi.org/10.1080/1030011050290208

Foucault, M. (1980). *Power/Knowledge: Selected Interviews and Other Writings 1972-1977.* New York: Pantheon Books.

Fry, G. (2020). Indigeneity as a foundation for patterned Northern Territory remote Aboriginal student achievement within a stratified western education system (Unpublished doctoral dissertation). Sydney: University of Sydney.

Gay, G. (2010). *Culturally responsive teaching: Theory, research, and practice* (2nd ed.). New York, USA: Teachers College Press.

Gillan, K., Mellor, S., & Krakouer, J. (2017). *The case for urgency: Advocating for indigenous voice in education*. Victoria: ACER Press, Australian Council for Educational Research.

Gollan, S., & Malin, M. (2012). Teachers and families working together to build stronger futures for our children in school. In Q. Beresford, G. Partington, & G. Gower. (Eds.), *Reform and resistance in aboriginal education* (pp. 149–174). Crawley, Western Australia: UWA Publishing.

Graham, G., & Spandagou, I. (2011). From vision to reality: Views of primary school principals on inclusive education in New South Wales, Australia. *Disability and Society, 26*(2), 223–237. https://doi.org/10.1080/09687599.2011.544062

Gray, J., & Beresford, Q. (2008). A 'formidable challenge': Australia's quest for equity in Indigenous education. *Australian Journal of Education, 52*(2), 197–223.

Hale, A., Snow-Gerono, J. & Morales, F. (2008). Transformative education for culturally diverse learners through narrative and ethnography. *Teaching and Teacher Education*, 24, 1413–1425. https://doi.org/10.1016/j.tate.2007.11.013

Hayes, D., Johnston, K., & King, A. (2009). Creating enabling classroom practices in high poverty contexts: The disruptive possibilities of looking in classrooms. *Pedagogy, Culture and Society, 17*(3), 251–264.

Heitmeyer, D. (1998). The issue is not black and white: Aboriginality and education. In J. Allen (Ed.), *Sociology of education: Possibilities and practice* (pp. 195–214). Australia/New Zealand: Social Science Press.

Hoff, K., & Pandey, P. (2004). *Belief systems and durable inequalities: An experimental investigation of Indian Caste* (World Bank Policy Research Working Paper No. 3351).

Hollinsworth, D. (2013). Decolonizing indigenous disability in Australia. *Disability & Society*, 28(5), 601–615. https://doi.org/10.1080/09687599.2012.717879

Ladson-Billings, G. (1994). *The dreamkeepers: Successful teachers of African American children.* San Francisco: Jossey-Bass.

Lester, K. E. (1975). *Education by Aborigines for Aborigines.* Publisher unknown.

Lieblein, V. S. D., Warne, M., Huot, S., Laliberte Rudman, D., & Raanaas, R. K. (2018). A photovoice study of school belongingness among high school students in Norway. *International journal of circumpolar health*, 77(1), p. 1421369. https://doi.org/10.1080/22423982.2017.1421369

Lowell, A., & Devlin, B. (2010). Miscommunication between Aboriginal students and their non-Aboriginal teachers in a bilingual school. *Language, Culture & Curriculum*, 11(3), 367–389. https://doi.org/10.1080/07908319808666563

Martin, K. (2003). Ways of knowing, being and doing: A theoretical framework and methods for Indigenous and Indigenist research. *Journal of Australian Studies*, 27(76), 203–214. https://doi.org/10.1080/14443050309387838

Martin, K. (2005). Childhood, lifehood and relatedness: Aboriginal ways of being, knowing and doing. In J. Phillips, & J. Lambert. (Eds.), *Education and diversity in Australia.* New South Wales: Pearson Education Australia.

Mathews, C. (2012). Maths is storytelling: Maths is beautiful. In K. Price. (Ed.) *Aboriginal and Torres Strait Islander Education: An introduction for the teaching profession* (pp. 108–134). Port Melbourne: Cambridge University Press.

Ministerial Council for Education, Early Childhood Development and Youth Affairs (MCEECDYA)., Education Services Australia. (2010). *Aboriginal and Torres Strait Islander Education Action Plan 2010–2014.* http://scseec.edu.au/site/DefaultSite/filesystem/documents/ATSI%20documents/ATSIEAP_web_version_final.pdf

Mitchell, L. (2015). Intentionally creating a cultural identity and culturally responsive teaching practice workshop. *The International Journal of Diversity in Education*, 15(4) 1–7. https://doi.org/10.18848/2327-0020/CGP/v15i04/40132

NITV. (2018). 100% of children detailed in NT are Aboriginal. *National Indigenous Television Network*. https://www.sbs.com.au/nitv/nitv-news/article/2018/06/26/australia-aboriginal-detention-northern-territory

NSW Department of Education. (2018). *Suspensions and Expulsions 2018*. Retrieved October, 10, 2020, from https://data.cese.nsw.gov.au/data/dataset/c0a90a6f-2509-45c5-ba77-cf5b00350043/resource/5dccdd60-9c6b-4e80-a4c8-d1d485c1f736/download/2018-suspensions-and-expulsions_aa.pdf.

Organisation for Economic Co-operation and Development (OECD). (2004). *Learning for tomorrow's world – Final results from PISA 2003*. Paris, France.

Organisation for Economic Co-operation and Development (OECD). (2017). *PISA 2015 results (Volume III): Students' well-being*. Paris, France. https://doi.org/10.1787/9789264273856

de Plevitz, L. (2006). Special schooling for Indigenous students: A new form of racial discrimination? *Australian Journal of Indigenous Education*, *35*, 44–54. https://doi.org/10.1017/S1326011100004154

Price, K. (2012). A brief history of Aboriginal and Torres Strait Islander education in Australia. In K. Price. (Ed.), *Aboriginal and Torres Strait Islander education: An introduction for the teaching profession* (pp. 1–20). Cambridge University Press.

Rahman, K. (2013). Belonging and learning to belong in school: The implications of the hidden curriculum for Indigenous students. *Discourse: Studies in the Cultural Politics of Education*, 34(5), 660–672. https://doi.org/10.1080/01596306.2013.728362

Reynolds, H. (1987). *Frontier. Aborigines, settlers and land*. Abingdon, England: Allen & Unwin.

Said, E. (1993) *Culture and imperialism*. New York: Chatto & Windus.

Sands, A. (2019). *Diversity and inclusion aren't what matter: Belonging is what counts*. https://medium.com/@AnitaSands/diversity-and-inclusion-arent-what-matter-belonging-is-what-counts-4a75bf6565b5

Sinclair, K. (2017). *Educators' understandings and perspectives of Aboriginal and Torres Strait Islander cultural competence: A mixed methods study*. (Unpublished doctoral thesis). University of South Australia.

Snow, P. & Powell, M. (2012). Youth (in)justice: Oral language competence in early life and risk for engagement in antisocial behaviour in adolescence. *Trends and Issues in Crime and Criminal Justice*, *435*, 1–6.

St-Amand, J., & Smith, J. (2017). Sense of belonging at school: Defining attributes, determinants, and sustaining strategies. *IAFOR Journal of Education*, 5(2), 105–119. https://doi.org/10.22492/ije.5.2.05

Sweller, N., Graham, L., & Van Bergen, P. (2012). The minority report: Disproportionate representation in Australia's largest education system. *Exceptional Children*, 79(1), 107–125. Web. https://doi.org/10.1177/001440291207900106

Thomas, J. (1993). *Doing critical ethnography*. Newbury Park: Sage Publications.

Vass, G. (2012). So, what is wrong with Indigenous education? Perspective, position and power beyond a deficit discourse. *The Australian Journal of Indigenous Education*, 41(2), 85–96. https://doi.org/10.1017/jie.2012.25

Waitoller, F., & Artiles, A. J. (2013). A decade of professional development research for inclusive education: A literature review and notes for a sociocultural research program. *Review of Educational Research*, 83(3), 319–356. https://doi.org/10.3102/0034654313483905

Walker, Y. (1993). Aboriginal family issues. *Family Matters*, *35*, 51–53.

Watson, C. (2005). Classrooms as learning communities: A review of research. *London Review of Education* 3(1), 47–64.

Willms, J.D., Organisation for Economic Co-operation and Development (OECD). (2003). *Student engagement at school: A sense of belonging and participation. Results from PISA 2000*. Paris. https://www.oecd.org/education/school/programmeforinternationalstudentassessmentpisa/33689437.pdf

Yosso, T. J. (2005). Whose culture has capital? A critical race theory discussion of community wealth. *Race Ethnicity and Education*, 8(1), 69–91. https://doi.org/10.1080/1361332052000341006

PART II
Pragmatic innovation

7
VISIBLY REWARDING LEARNERS FOR ACADEMIC ACHIEVEMENT

The guise of excellence

Shakira Akabor

Introduction and background

Learners at school are rewarded for academic achievement visibly, tangibly and publicly. Elaborate ceremonious functions are usually held in the school hall and parents are invited to share the momentous occasion in recognition of their children's achievements. Photographs of learners with their rewards are displayed on the schools' website and social media pages (Akabor, 2020). This is not an uncommon scenario at many urban schools in South Africa. If the intentions behind reward programmes are for the recognition of the child's hard work and scholastic achievements, one might be inclined to believe there is no harm in this practice. At first blush, it appears a benign and beneficial practice that has existed for decades and is considered a normative part of schooling. But upon closer inspection, there lurks many issues that are worrisome, and some that might threaten the implementation of inclusive education. This chapter reports on insights from my doctoral study that interrogated the practice of rewarding learners at two urban high schools, where reward systems were found to be inherently problematic. I argue that reducing the mechanisms supporting academic competitiveness can encourage collaboration and cooperation, thereby creating environments that facilitate inclusive communities at schools.

Schools tend to reward in ways that are both traditional and unique. Some rewards can be seen visibly upon the learners' school uniform. These might be a differentiated tie or blazer in a colour distinguished from the rest of the learners (Akabor, 2020). Other common forms are tiny badges or pins worn on the lapel bearing words such as "Mathematics", "English" or "House Captain". These serve as a daily reminder of a learners' achievement, lasting well beyond the ceremony in which they were presented. Yet other forms of rewards are certificates or trophies presented to the learner in recognition of excellence in academic achievement.

DOI: 10.4324/9781003091950-9

In some schools, learners' names are engraved onto the school's honour board (Watkins, McInerney, Akande & Lee, 2003), with a listing of the learner's name and year in which the learner was recognised and the reason for the recognition. For instance, schools may reward one girl and one boy with a Dux Scholar award for the highest-ranking academic achiever in their respective genders. Rewards can be expected, or they can be awarded unexpectedly, at the discretion of the school (Jalava, Joensen & Pellas, 2014). Understanding reward and its relationship to inclusive education is made easier by knowing the context of inclusive education in South Africa. In this chapter, I will begin by providing a brief overview of the development and state of inclusive education in South Africa. A discussion of visible rewards and related concepts such as academic talent and merit follows. Then, a brief outline of my doctoral study and the discussion of a few findings are presented. Finally, I conclude with suggestions for change so that our schools' reward systems can become more inclusive.

Inclusive education in South Africa

The move towards inclusion in South African schools is a fairly recent development when compared to international trends. Although the foundation for inclusive education in South Africa had been laid in the Constitution (1996), initially in Section 29 (1), where it is stated that "everyone has the right to basic education", inclusive education as a policy in South Africa was introduced by the publication of *Education White Paper 6 (WP6): Special Needs Education: Building an Inclusive Education and Training System* (DoE, 2001). WP6 advocates a broad definition of inclusion, where the focus is not limited to learners with disabilities but includes all learners. According to WP6, inclusive education acknowledges the diversity of learners and their ability to learn. In order to meet the needs of all learners, WP6 outlines a plan that includes "enabling education structures, systems and learning methodologies" (DoE, 2001, p. 6) so that all learners can optimally benefit from the education system. Although WP6 was welcomed in South Africa as its policy is in line with international concern for and a move towards inclusive education, it became clear that WP6 needed further clarification and expansion for inclusive education to be applied practically in South African schools. Subsequently, policy documents offering practical support of WP6 followed. Schools now have a detailed system for the screening, identification, assessment and support of learners who might be experiencing barriers to learning, including physical disabilities, mental disabilities, mild to moderate learning disabilities, second-language acquisition, HIV-related impairments, and issues arising from poverty and/or malnutrition.

The provision of education in South African schools was unequal, fragmented and classified according to racial lines pre-1994, leaving the current post-apartheid government with an inheritance of multilayered inequalities (Sayed & Soudien, 2004; Walton, Nel, Hugo, & Muller, 2009). These inequalities of the past are inextricably linked to the diverse needs of learners today. In its broadest sense, inclusive education incorporates the South African goal of extending quality education to the whole population. Apartheid ensured the legally sanctioned racial oppression, disenfranchisement, and segregation of brown people, and matric results still reflect – rather than disrupt – racial and class divides (Spaull, 2015).

The available literature on the implementation of inclusive education in South African schools is not altogether positive. A variety of challenges including funding constraints, lack of clarity in policy, poor teacher attitudes towards inclusion, inadequate teacher training and inadequate support have been explored (Wildeman & Nomdo, 2007; Meier & Hartell, 2009; Walton, 2011; Donohue & Bornman; 2014; Majoko & Phasha, 2018). Walton (2011) states that apart from inclusive teaching strategies that are sorely needed, questions should be raised regarding the structures, practices and beliefs that continue to perpetuate exclusion in South African schools. Teachers themselves should be willing to challenge outdated beliefs and practices that act as barriers to inclusive education (Donohue & Bornman, 2014). It is clear that practices and processes at schools need rethinking towards inclusivity to ensure that inequalities are not perpetuated.

Promoting social cohesion, accepting diversity and accommodating all cultures was the priority of former white schools post-apartheid, but attempts at implementing inclusion had not been successful (Meier & Hartell; 2009). Earlier research shows that desegregation at two South African high schools resulted in a case of assimilating black learners into the school and its culture, with the result that the status quo is integrally maintained (Van Heerden; 1998). The implication is that new learners to the school come from educationally and culturally inferior backgrounds, resulting in lowering high standards in these former white schools when changing the curriculum to meet the newcomers' needs (Meier & Hartell; 2009). The problem is that no long-term attempts are made by schools to address deep-seated issues of racism and inequity (Carrim, 2009).

Recent research indicates a more targeted approach towards promoting inclusion (Majoko & Phasha, 2018; Engelbrecht et al., 2016; Walton, 2014; Walton, 2015). A number of implementation issues are identified in Majoko and Phasha's (2018) recent research report, including gaps in policy, a disjuncture between policy and practice, issues concerning the classroom environment, and the training of teachers. Additionally, physical access to school does not equate to equal access to learning opportunities, and there is still a risk of exclusion within an inclusionary framework (Majoko & Phasha, 2018). This is because all learners do not have equal access to the curriculum. The issue of epistemological access is further highlighted in Volmink's (2018) description of inclusive education as an interconnectedness between learners, educators and communities of learning – such that it provides a constructive environment that positively affects the self-worth, self-belief and achievement of all learners.

The Department of Education (2009) states that one of the major impediments to the realisation of inclusive education is that schooling remains fundamentally unchanged. In the same vein, Walton (2013) notes that the systemic school legacies and the current policies and practices that give rise to, and sustain, marginalisation and exclusion in schools needs interrogation. Walton (2013) indicates that a greater focus should be given to what exactly learners could be included into, highlighting the need for research in the social and peer group environment within South African schools. With this in mind, I believe that questioning the practice of visibly rewarding learners would make a significant difference to the implementation of inclusive education. As a cultural school practice that remains unchanged, visible rewards have the potential to entrench patterns of privilege and must be used cautiously and with cognizance of recognising excellence in all learners.

Visible rewards motivate learners?

Rewarding learners visibly and publicly motivates children to achieve is a concept widely believed by many teachers (Akabor, 2019). However, not all learners believe in the motivational power of rewards, and most parents disagree that visible rewards motivated their children to achieve. The literature indicates that rewards have negative effects on intrinsic motivation of learners (Deci, Koestner & Ryan, 1999; Levitt, List, Neckermann & Sadoff, 2012; Jalava, Joensen & Pellas, 2014). Given that rewards are visible, tangible and extrinsic this is not surprising. As Kohn (1994, p. 257) states, "what matters is not how motivated someone is, but how someone is motivated". Kohn's statement emphasises the importance of fostering meaningful participation via intrinsic motivation as opposed to the common but disturbing trend of "teaching to the test" (Jalava, Joensen & Pellas, 2014), which results in high achievement on paper but minimal mastery learning. All learners should be given opportunities to work on their strengths and develop their abilities through full participation and active engagement (Florian, Black-Hawkins & Rouse, 2017) rather than focusing on working towards outstanding achievements that rank them higher than their peers.

Since a handful of learners are rewarded, the value of the reward is heightened. As a result, there is an incentive to achieve not just As, but the highest mark in a single category. Learners compete with each other and outdo their peers in order to qualify for a reward. Thus the emphasis of learning is less about engagement with knowledge or a deep mastery of the subject, as mastery is not rewarded. Rather, assessment outcomes translate into a measuring tool for a small number of predetermined rewards. An intensely competitive environment pressures learners to achieve, and whilst some learners (likely award winners) find this motivating, most do not. Students should know where their strengths are and what they need to work on, not how they fit into our magical grading system (Courus, 2010).

Evidence suggests that not only learners benefit from the visible rewards system. Schools benefit in many ways from the achievements of their learners, among which is the school's reputation of providing excellence in academic achievement. As such, award-winning learners contribute to, and are beneficiaries of, the pride that schools hold when they are highly ranked for the number of As they produce at matric level (Akabor, 2019). "Matric" is a South African term that is abbreviated from word "matriculation" and refers to the grade 12 exit examinations, the results of which determine the learners' post-school options such as university entrance. Once matric results are released in January, newspapers and other online media provide evidence of the prestige associated with producing excellent matric results (Sobuwa, 2020, January 7). Schools and districts themselves are rewarded by the Minister of Basic Education for achieving excellent matric results. The public recognition of schools in the media thus incentivises schools and districts to produce better results. Consequently, schools end up privileging those learners who will elevate their status with respect to academic reputation and not much concern is given to those learners needing help to get up and climb higher academically. It is simpler, effortless and more beneficial for schools to make "celebrities" of their intelligent learners than to spend hours of extra classes on children who require support (Brantlinger, 2004) and are unlikely to garner schools those honours. In this way, the implementation of inclusive education can be threatened by a rewards/awards culture. Given that not all South African learners are motivated to achieve at school (Geduld, 2017) and a significant number of learners drop out of school before matriculating (Spaull, 2015), we should be questioning what motivates learners to achieve and how this can be encouraged for all learners. Official reasons for visibly rewarding learners appearing on school policy documents is the recognition of learners' hard work and academic talent (Akabor, 2020).

Academic talent

In South Africa, academic talent has been used politically to entrench discriminatory beliefs. Earlier research indicates that using IQ testing in definitions of academic talent within the socio-political interests of certain individuals in South Africa could promote notions of superiority of certain racial and ethnic groups, namely that white learners are stronger than black learners academically (Appel, 1998). Later research notes that the local literature has also evolved in accordance with international trends (Richards, 2015). The literature of the 1980s that focused on the giftedness construct mirrored the ideological traces of apartheid. Issues such as socioeconomic background, access to resources and quality of schooling received were largely ignored during the apartheid years, and the notion of scientific racism was widely accepted (McKenzie, 2020). Today however, a gradual shift towards more inclusionary definitions of academic talent and giftedness embrace areas such as creativity, leadership ability and personality attributes. Academic talent in the South African context has thus been identified by Richards (2015) as having an environmental basis, a multidimensional construct and contextual variability. Multidimensional perspectives on academic talent tend to be more culturally sensitive and encourage a broader view of intelligence. It can be argued that conceptions of giftedness include creativity, domain-specific abilities such as mathematical or verbal reasoning ability, and non-cognitive characteristics such as motivation (Olszewski-Kubilius, Subotnik & Worrell, 2015).

Whilst school prizes, rewards and awards are usually in place to create positive sentiments around the recognition of giftedness, a label itself which has been known to create animosity among peers (Phillips & Lindsay, 2006), schools are effectively catering for the well-being of what Gagné (2004) describes as the top 10% of age peers. The question of fairness in visibly rewarding such a small number of learners is immediately noticeable. Based on an inclusive approach in the classroom, the idea of recognising and celebrating the achievements of only 10% of learners should raise red flags as being deeply flawed and inequitable. Subsequently, 90% of age peers are left out of the recognition process, which brings us to question the notion of merit itself.

Who is deserving of merit?

In a society dominated by social class–related privilege, together with norms and values that legitimise and maintain the status quo, as stated earlier, the playing fields are not level for all learners in South Africa. Questioning the practice of visible rewards leads us to question a system of rewards based on merit that might be used to determine candidates for post-school scholarships, university entrance and job opportunities. These will no doubt contribute to forging the life paths of learners beyond their schooling careers. Meritocracy seemingly provides the 'infrastructure' that allows those who have the abilities to move up to higher positions since rewards are allocated according to their academic achievement and not on factors such as race, gender and social class (Young, 2001). In other words, the rationale in a meritocratic society is that anyone can work his/her way out of a low social class situation if they are able and motivated enough (Mijs, 2016). As stated by Brown and Tannock (2009), those defined as the 'best' are disproportionately rewarded, devaluing everything other than 'top' performance. This has inevitably impacted on education policy and practice, and demands a rethinking of education theory, goals and principles, particularly issues of equality, opportunity, inclusion and fairness (Brown & Tannock, 2009).

Meritocracy tends to be the status quo in many of the wealthier schools, both in the state and independent sector. In terms of functional state schools, South African schools are faced with a tug-of-war situation – on the one hand there are educational policies promoting inclusion, equality and learner collaboration that must be implemented. On the other hand, the functional schooling system that does exist is competitive, run like a business and is focused on outperforming other schools in terms of academic results (Akabor, 2020). Competitiveness with regards to academic results is seen as necessary by both independent and state schools in order to attract a specific type of learner (more importantly, the parent) from a middle-class background as future cohorts of the school (Fataar, 2009).

Based on the tensions between inclusive education and neoliberal schooling and the complex situation that South African schools find themselves in, the practice of rewarding learners appears to perpetuate inequalities and further entrench outdated ideas of merit being available to a select few. Some schools believe the fewer the better. As one teacher in my study stated,

> We're only rewarding 20 out of 300 in assembly ... in a way it is good, because there's only 20. They ARE the elite.

Our schooling system is underpinned by values that are in harmony with the aims and ideals of inclusive education, therefore it is therefore inconsistent to have hierarchical reward structures and a culture of competitiveness within schools that promote elitism. By providing symbolic representations of a sought-after school culture, these schools not only contribute to the entrenchment of value and commodification in the school, but also perpetuate what Gulson and Fataar (2011) argue as 'historically white schools' being privileged.

In a report on the condition of Gauteng's inclusive education implementation over the last two decades, Walton (2014) recommends that in order to improve their support of learning, schools should ensure that competitiveness does not result in the exclusion and marginalisation of learners who experience barriers to learning. Walton (2014) refers specifically to the level of competitiveness prevalent amongst high schools, such that learners who might affect the averages of the school are excluded from exams in an attempt to maximise the school's matric pass rate and maintain their lofty rankings. Given that a significant number of South African schools have a strong culture of awards and rewards, it is not uncommon for schools to exclude and deny learners the option of writing their matriculation examinations under the school's name, for fear of failure that would translate into schools losing their reputation for a '100% matric pass rate'. However, schools can oppose this meritocratic system by beginning to question the traditional school practice of rewards that do not contribute to quality education for all learners enrolled at the school. The awards/rewards culture promoted by many South African schools is a part of schooling that is not regulated by departmental policy from the Department of Basic Education, but rather remains the domain of internal school policy and differs per individual school. Thus schools can find ways in which they can interrogate and rework their own policies to become more inclusive.

The study

In this mixed methods study, I sought to interrogate the practice of visible rewards and to understand the perspective of learners, parents, teachers and school management on the rewards system from an inclusive education stance. Here, I report on the focus group interview data of the learners. I found that the *Index for Inclusion* (Booth & Ainscow, 2011) proved to be a useful tool to explicate issues of diversity, school culture, policy and transformation. I have used the *Index* as part of my theoretical framework, together with Johnson and Johnson's (1989, 2009) social interdependence theory.

The study was conducted at two public high schools in Gauteng, which I had called School A and School B to ensure anonymity. Both schools are established, well-resourced and spacious public schools amid beautifully tended gardens, manicured lawns and brown-brick buildings. The two schools are often represented in the media as being among the 'top public schools' in Gauteng, which is the smallest yet wealthiest province in South Africa. Student diversity with respect to gender, race and social

TABLE 7.1 Number of participants per phase in each school

	School A	School B
Phase 1: Quantitative		
Total enrollment 2018	1473 learners	1325 learners
Grade 11 Learners 2018	245 learners	228 learners
Grade 11 Learners	51 learner questionnaires received	53 learner questionnaires received
Parents	6 questionnaires received	11 questionnaires received
Phase 2: Qualitative		
Grade 11 Learners	8 learners in focus group 1 4 learners in focus group 2	6 learners in focus group 1 5 learners in focus group 2
Teachers	7 × grade 11 class teachers in the following subjects: Mathematics, English, Afrikaans, Life Sciences, Technology, Life Orientation, Maths Literacy	6 × grade 11 class teachers covering the teaching of the following subjects: Mathematics, English, Study Skills, Life Sciences, Business Studies, Technology
School Management	1 principal	1 principal
School Management	1 deputy principal	1 deputy principal
School Management	2 HOD's	1 HOD
Total number of participants: 141	68 participants	73 participants

class, as well as a wide range of learners from different socio-economic backgrounds were present in each school, despite being located within upmarket leafy suburbs.

This study comprised of two phases. In the first phase of the study, I used quantitative methods to gather data in order to determine the learners' and parents' values, beliefs and attitudes towards rewards, participation and achievement. In the second phase of the study, I used qualitative methods to gather data from the learners in focus groups, the teachers and the school management. At the end of the learner questionnaire, I had invited participants to participate in a focus group interview, which is data I am reporting on here (Table 7.1).

To better understand the inclusion and participation of all learners, I sought a mix of grade 11 award winners and non-award winners who were willing to share their opinions about the visible rewards system at school.

Results

Overall, visible rewards were found to be an outward manifestation of a competitive school culture that is concerned with valuing and privileging learners deemed to have merit, and therefore deserving of preferential treatment. Using richly descriptive multiple perspectives, this study found that visible rewards as a school-wide practice is inconsistent with the aims and ideals of inclusive education in a number of ways. A few insights will be discussed here.

A desire for recognition

Learners expressed a deep-rooted need for being recognised and valued, yet often were left feeling as though they were obscure as a result of not being visibly rewarded. A significant number of learners felt that they were not recognised for their efforts, talents and achievements via their school's reward systems. Due to their own understanding of what merit is, and of the value inherent in the rewards system, learners desperately sought recognition for their achievements. One girl, who was an award winner in the past but had narrowly missed the criteria to be included amongst the Top 20 learners twice in the last two years, was unequivocal that she deserved to be recognised for her efforts. She said:

> "But I just want to say, like ok, I've achieved. Can someone also just recognise that I have achieved?"

Learners expressed their discontentment with the narrow criteria for awards, and knew they had no influence or input into the rewards processes and procedures. These are solely determined by the respective committees at each school. Most learners felt their creative talents were ignored as it did not fall into the school's conceptualization of what was worthy of being rewarded. Another learner who had never won awards before felt that she had worked extremely hard in the past year to improve her marks from a C aggregate to a B aggregate. However, her achievements were not recognised by the school. She said:

> "No one is recognised for the small achievements in their lives. Children who are smart are shown to be better than everyone else and the learners who try and work hard to achieve their best are shunned".

Her testimony indicates her experience of exclusion from the programme designed to recognise achievement. Herein lies the dilemma that schools face: the system claims to reward achievement but cannot reward all learners that achieve without learners experiencing exclusion. The practice of rewarding learners can be considered an example of institutional discrimination (Booth & Ainscow, 2011).

Awards are subjective

From the learners' experience, rewards could not be transferred from school to school, therefore limiting their participation in the long-term rewards programmes available at their respective schools. Thus what might be considered as excellent in one school might fall short of being award-worthy at another. Presently, rewards are the domain of internal school policy, and each school has different qualifying criteria for awards. One learner had moved schools in grade 9 and had hopes of wearing a different coloured blazer in his matric (grade 12) year. In order to qualify for this, he must have produced an 80% average in all his subjects from grade 8 to 11. To his dismay, he found that his achievements from his previous school did not count. He had this to say:

> At my previous school, I was the top student and won awards all the time. Since I came here I only won two awards, but I was told that my As from my previous school are not recognised that I cannot work towards a white blazer.

Another girl felt extremely disappointed that she was never rewarded visibly despite having achieved the same aggregate as the boy who always won, which made her question the fairness of the system:

> I have a seventy-five and he also has a seventy-five, and he is going up, it's like what am I not doing? And then I recall: okay in grade ten you were there, in grade nine you were there, in grade eight you were there, is your name now engraved into the system or are you actually really working?

These learners' testimonies indicate that rewards are subjective. Thus the term excellence is not consistent and clear in every school and is at the discretion of school management. As such, a few people are responsible for deciding whose work is valuable and worthy of merit. Braunsteiner and Mariano-Lapidus (2014) suggest that the contribution of diverse stakeholders in the development of a school's culture and environment must grow. As such, the subjectivity of awards can be reduced.

Competitive learning environments

Although learners believed in the motivational power of visible rewards, the findings indicated that learners viewed their peers as rivals and had few opportunities to collaborate with each other with respect to learning within the classroom because some learners believed they were superior to others.

> And people that get the awards are very arrogant. They think they are better than everyone else. It's also because the teachers treat them differently.

The competitive school culture created discomfort in some learners' minds. They felt it was unethical and boastful to show off achievements to others who may not come from similar backgrounds as themselves. One learner insightfully articulated:

> Showing off your prize pupils in front of other pupils who do not achieve to that level is incredibly disheartening to the people who work really, really hard but just cannot reach that because of other factors, maybe they just aren't as motivated, or they don't have the opportunities to do so ….

Her reference to opportunities alluded to the awareness amongst learners of the link between socio-economic status and resources required to achieve and to be rewarded. Learners believed that their inability to win awards had implications on their sense of belonging within peer groups and resulted in a despondency towards school. One girl said the following:

> We are teenagers; I don't know if it's jealousy or hatred which I feel doesn't allow you to focus on your studies because you're just like I'm not gonna bother to study because I know the same people are constantly getting awards so why must I try.

This quote indicated that awards can actually demotivate some learners from achieving as they found the same learners won awards every year. Repetitiveness in award winners further indicates that excellence in academic achievement is limited to a select few learners.

Exclusionary beliefs and attitudes

It was apparent that teachers did not have high expectations of all learners. The language used by teachers indicated learners were of fixed abilities, situated on a bell-curve regarding their talents and their achievements. This indicated the exclusionary beliefs and attitudes of teachers (Booth & Ainscow, 2011) were endorsed in the visible rewards system. As a result, learners experienced a hierarchical structure within the school wherein learners were stratified according to their achievements and treated differently as a result. One learner said the following:

> If you always go up on stage, now you're automatically higher on the hierarchy. The teachers see you differently and it's very clear, it's very visible, the treatment between us and the teachers is very different, as soon as you are the one who is called up a lot on stage, we normally see, from principal to teacher to other learners themselves … you kinda get that, a little bit more respect type of thing.

The findings indicated that learners who won visible rewards were granted more opportunities than those who did not. The visible and tangible evidence of being an award winner was immediately recognisable to prospective university scouts, for instance. One learner described the visible nature of awards thus:

> Award-winners' uniforms are a different colour blazer or scrolls or badges and that presents them to outsiders as a person who can do these things; for a prospective university applicant that's very good because someone from a university sees you and they can scout you; the same for jobs and that kind of thing. It's brilliant for award-winners, they get all these opportunities in the world but for those who don't, they kinda left behind by quite a bit.

The identification of learners in this manner can be potentially harmful (Florian, Black-Hawkins & Rouse, 2017). Not all learners who have performed well or achieved good results will make it to the Top 20, nor will they be the most outstanding learner. Their own achievements, no matter how good or hard-won, fall short of recognition. This has the potential to hamper their meaningful participation as well as their attempts at accessing future opportunities. In claiming excellence, schools are instead unknowingly endorsing and legitimising inequities, thereby embodying exclusionary practices.

Discussion

Using social interdependence theory (Johnson & Johnson, 2002), the learner's testimonies in the preceding four points indicate that schools' reward policies lean towards the negative interdependence model. The negative interdependence model exists when there is a negative correlation among individuals' goal achievements. Individuals perceive that they can obtain their goals if and only if the other individuals with whom they are competitively linked fail to obtain their goals (Johnson & Johnson, 2002). Negative interdependence results in oppositional interaction, wherein individuals discourage and obstruct each other's efforts to complete tasks in order to reach their goals. On the other hand, inclusivity correlates to the positive interdependence model (Johnson & Johnson, 2002), associated with elements such as the success of one is dependent on the success of all, the inherent value of collaboration and cooperation for learners to increase their participation within the classroom, the absence of hierarchies that segregate learners according to abilities, or assumptions of their abilities and the welcoming attitude of the school in valuing a range of achievements. These inclusive elements can easily be facilitated by changing the competitive culture currently found at schools and by defining collaboration, cooperation, sense of belonging and egalitarianism as desired values and behaviours. As argued by Braunsteiner and Mariano-Lapidus (2014), "a truly inclusive education relies on a cultural shift that … views success through a lens not constructed of standardized test scores". Allowing some children to experience recognition of their achievements within the confines of the school's definition of success whilst the majority are left unrecognized is not excellence. Rather, it is a competitive culture that creates feelings of mistrust and division amongst learners (Johnson & Johnson, 2002).

Excellence in education should be available to all learners, and schools that deny some learners recognition of their hard work in favour of what they deem to be more prestigious achievements is not fair or equitable to all learners. As a result, excellence in academics is subjective (Jalava, Joensen & Pellas, 2014) and tends to exclude those who fall short of the narrow criteria. Hard work is not necessarily rewarded, as learners were bitterly disappointed to discover. Creativity is not rewarded, despite its relevance to the technologically advanced age we find ourselves in and to contemporary understandings of talent (Richards, 2015). These issues indicate that rewards are perhaps not the marker of excellence we imagine them to be, that excellence can exist outside the rewarded few, and that there are inherent harms in this practice with respect to inclusive education. Learners who actively work towards rewards yet fall short of being awarded are bitterly disappointed, eroding their intrinsic motivation, which is necessary for meaningful participation. Rewards that are given unexpectedly to learners have no effect on their intrinsic motivation, whilst expected rewards could cause intrinsic motivation to decrease, especially when learners did not receive the expected reward (Deci, Koestner & Ryan, 1999; Levitt et al., 2012; Jalava, Joensen & Pellas, 2014).

Where to from here?

A variety of possibilities exist for schools to rethink and reframe their rewards systems to enable schooling environments that are inclusive. To promote a collaborative, or cooperative situation, an award would only be given if in a particular class every learner has achieved a minimum requirement, for example 70% in a particular subject, therefore the class as a whole gets rewarded with an award for every learner. This reward scheme takes on the tournament or team reward structure outlined by Bigoni, Fort, Nardotto and Reggiani (2015), such that the success of all is considered valuable and worthy of recognition, rather than the success of a few individuals. Thus the efforts towards higher achievement of the class would change from concerns about individual learners' success towards the success of the whole group before any awards can be given out.

Another possibility is to use a model that rewards the bettering of one's own previous personal best, with no comparison to other learners and their achievements. This model may work to reduce the effects of a competitive environment but is a radical change from the formative way in which we assess learners at schools. Called ipsative assessment (Hughes, 2011; Hughes, 2014), it requires a change in the entire assessment process, not just the rewards process. Ipsative assessment has been known to increase motivation in learners (Hughes, 2011), which addresses previous concerns about the reduction of motivation to learn in rewards-based programmes (Deci, Koestner & Ryan, 1999; Deci, Koestner & Ryan, 2001).

Questioning the rewards systems at schools can be a creative process that schools must engage in with all stakeholders, including the learners themselves. As noted by Engelbrecht, Oswald and Forlin (2006) during their use of the *Index for Inclusion* in Western Cape schools, the honest reflection on school cultures, policies and practices can be a painful process at times. Revisiting and rethinking the awards programme is a process that is necessary for schools. The removal of the current system of visible rewards might sound drastic, but it has the potential to make schools seriously interrogate competitive practices that they might consider benign and beneficial to a few towards a school culture that is collaborative, cooperative and is genuinely concerned with raising achievement for all. Whilst there is little evidence in the literature of South African schools that follow this system of no rewards, alternative pedagogies such as Montessori, Waldorf and Reggio Emilia are known to be non-competitive environments that promote the learning of each individual learner without drawing attention to the achievement of others (Edwards, 2002).

Conclusion

Whilst rewarding learners is couched within the notion of recognising excellence, in reality the resultant competitiveness is problematic and exclusionary for many learners. Lomofsky and Lazarus (2010) argue that we need to recognise our interdependence on one another and, collaboratively, provide a quality education for all our learners. Excellence is a relative term, defined by those who are decision-makers, namely school management. In recognising the achievements of some and not others, we are sending out silent messages to children not only about their abilities, but about their future prospects post-school. Using overt messages and slogans that the school values and prides itself, it sets the tone for the dominant culture of the school (McMaster, 2015). In addition, rewards shift the focus to the achievement of some learners and away from the achievement of all learners. The use of the word "all" learners is not limited to learners qualifying for a specific educational service, nor is it reduced to groups of learners who have been identified with medical diagnoses. "All" as used in the South African context could be any learner that might face exclusion: the learner who is on the outside looking in, the learner who feels as though they do not belong, the learner who is limited in terms of their full and meaningful participation in the daily life of the classroom and within the school (Akabor, 2020). The ways in which we currently reward learners for academic achievement forms part of a larger school culture that leans towards academic competitiveness, leaving little room for cooperation and collaboration in the academic sphere. In doing so, we are raising children to believe that their success or failure in school equates to their success or failure at life itself.

References

Akabor, S. (2019). Are visible rewards congruent with inclusive education? *Inclusion in Education: Perspectives on Inclusive Education in South Africa*, 2 (1), 22–29. Accessed from http://www.included.org.za/wp-content/uploads/2019/07/Inclusion-in-Education-Vol-2.pdf

Akabor, S. (2020). *The intention and impact of visibly rewarding learners in two Gauteng high schools*. (Unpublished doctoral thesis). University of the Witwatersrand, Johannesburg.

Appel, S. (1998). Mining South Africa's 'children of gold' the rhetoric and discourse of educating the 'gifted'. *Critical Arts*, 5(1), 96–107.

Bigoni, M., Fort, M., Nardotto, M., & Reggiani, T. G. (2015). Cooperation or competition? A field experiment on non-monetary learning incentives. *The BE Journal of Economic Analysis & Policy*, 15(4), 1753–1792.

Booth, T., & Ainscow, M. (2011). *Index for inclusion: developing learning and participation in schools*. Bristol: Centre for Studies on Inclusive Education (CSIE).

Brantlinger, E. (2004). Chapter 1: Ideologies discerned, values determined: Getting past the hierarchies of Special Education. *Counterpoints*, 270, 11–31.

Braunsteiner, M. L., & Mariano-Lapidus, S. (2014). A perspective of inclusion: Challenges for the future. *Global Education Review*, 1(1).

Brown, P., & Tannock, S. (2009). Education, meritocracy and the global war for talent. *Journal of Education Policy*, 24(4), 377–392.

Carrim, N. (2009). Human rights and the limitations of releasing subaltern voices in a post-apartheid South Africa. In *International handbook of comparative education* (pp. 765–779). Springer, Dordrecht.

Courus, G. (2010). *The Impact of Awards*. Retrieved from http://georgecourus.ca/blog/archives/1079

Deci, E. L., Koestner, R., & Ryan, R. M. (1999). A meta-analytic review of experiments examining the effects of extrinsic rewards on intrinsic motivation. *Psychological Bulletin, 125*(6), 627.

Deci, E. L., Koestner, R., & Ryan, R. M. (2001). Extrinsic rewards and intrinsic motivation in education: Reconsidered once again. *Review of educational research, 71*(1), 1–27

Department of Education. (2001). *Education white paper 6: Special needs education: Building an inclusive education and training system*. Pretoria: Department of Education.

Donohue, D., & Bornman, J. (2014). The challenges of realizing inclusive education in South Africa. *South African Journal of Education, 34*(2), 1–14.

Edwards, C. P. (2002). Three approaches from Europe: Waldorf, Montessori, and Reggio Emilia. *Early Childhood Research & Practice, 4*(1), n1

Engelbrecht, P., Nel, M., Smit, S., & Van Deventer, M. (2016). The idealism of education policies and the realities in schools: The implementation of inclusive education in South Africa. *International Journal of Inclusive Education, 20*(5), 520–535.

Engelbrecht, P., Oswald, M. & Forlin, C. (2006). Promoting the implementation of inclusive education in primary schools in South Africa. *British Journal of Special Education*. 33(3). 121–129.

Fataar, A. (2009). Schooling subjectivities across the post-apartheid city. *Africa Education Review, 6*(1), 1–18.

Florian, L., Black-Hawkins, K., & Rouse, M. (2017). *Achievement and inclusion in schools*. Second edition. New York, NY: Routledge.

Gagné, F. (2004). Transforming gifts into talents: the DMGT as a developmental theory. *High Ability Studies, 15*(2), 119–147.

Geduld, B. (2017). Personal and contextual influences on township school learners' motivation and self-regulated learning. *Africa Education Review, 14*(2), 122–139.

Gulson, K. N., & Fataar, A. (2011). Neoliberal governmentality, schooling and the city: Conceptual and empirical notes on and from the Global South. *Discourse: Studies in the Cultural Politics of Education, 32*(2), 269–283.

Hughes, G. (2011). Towards a personal best: A case for introducing ipsative assessment in higher education. *Studies in Higher Education, 36*(3), 353–367.

Hughes, G. (2014). *Ipsative Assessment: Motivation through marking progress*. Chicago: Springer.

Jalava, N., Joensen, J. S., & Pellas, E. (2014). Grades and rank: Impacts of non-financial incentives on test performance. *Journal of Economic Behavior & Organization, 115*, 161–196.

Johnson, D. W., & Johnson, R. T. (1989). *Cooperation and competition: Theory and research*. Edina: Interaction Book Company.

Johnson, D. W., & Johnson, R. T. (2002). Learning together and alone: Overview and meta-analysis, *Asia Pacific Journal of Education, 22*(1), 95–105. DOI: 10.1080/0218879020220110.

Johnson, D. W., & Johnson, R. T. (2009). An educational psychology success story: Social interdependence theory and cooperative learning. *Educational researcher, 38*(5), 365–379.

Kohn, A. (1994). *The Risk of Rewards*. Retrieved from ERIC Digest (ED376990).

Levitt, S., List, J., Neckermann, S., & Sadoff, S. (2012). The Behavioralist Goes to School. *NBER Working Paper, 18165*. Accessed from: https://www.nber.org/papers/w18165.pdf

Lomofsky, L., & Lazarus, S. (2010). South Africa: First steps in the development of an inclusive education system. *Cambridge Journal of education, 31*(3), 303–317.

Majoko, T., & Phasha, N. (2018). *The state of inclusive education in South Africa and the implications for teacher training programmes*: Research Report December 2018. British Council South Africa.

McKenzie, J. (2020). Intellectual Disability in inclusive education in South Africa: Curriculum challenges. *Journal of Policy and Practice in Intellectual Disabilities, 18*(1), 53–57.

McMaster, C. (2015). "Where is _____?": Culture and the process of change in the development of inclusive schools. *International Journal of Whole Schooling, 11*(1), 17–34.

Meier, C., & Hartell, C. (2009). Handling cultural diversity in education in South Africa. *SA-eDUC Journal, 6*(2), 180–192.

Mijs, J. J. (2016). The unfulfillable promise of meritocracy: Three lessons and their implications for justice in education. *Social Justice Research, 29*(1), 14–34.

Olszewski-Kubilius, P., Subotnik, R. F., & Worrell, F. C. (2015). Conceptualizations of giftedness and the development of talent: Implications for counsellors. *Journal of Counseling & Development, 93*(2), 143–152.

Phillips, N., & Lindsay, G. (2006). Motivation in gifted students. *High Ability Studies, 17*(1), 57–73.

Richards, Z. (2015). Conceptions of academic talent: implications for talent identification and development. *South African Journal of Higher Education, 29*(1), 270–293.

RSA (Republic of South Africa). (1996). Constitution of the Republic of South Africa (Act 108 of 1996). *Government Gazette No. 25799.*

Sayed, Y., & Soudien, C. (2004). Decentralisation and the construction of inclusion education policy in South Africa. *Compare: A Journal of Comparative and International Education, 35*(2), 115–125.

Sobuwa, Y. (2020, January 7). Angie Motshekga congratulates "best of the best" from Class of 2019. *The Sowetan.* Retrieved from https://www.sowetanlive.co.za/news/2020-01-07-angie-motshekga-congratulates-best-of-the-best-from-class-of-2019/

Spaull, N. (2015). Schooling in South Africa: How low-quality education becomes a poverty trap. *South African Child Gauge, 12,* 34–41.

Van Heerden, M. E. (1998). *What's Happening in Practice? A Comparative Study of Teaching and Learning in Two Desegregated South African Public High Schools.* Department of Anthropology and Archaeology, UNISA.

Volmink, J. (2018). Foreword. T. Majoko & N. Phasha. *The state of inclusive education in South Africa and the implications for teacher training programmes: Research Report December 2018.* (pp. 9–10). British Council South Africa.

Walton, E. (2011). Getting inclusion right in South Africa. *Intervention in School and Clinic. 46*(4), 240–245.

Walton, E. (2013). Inclusion in a South African high school? Reporting and reflecting on what learners say. *International Journal of Inclusive Education, 17*(11), 1171–1185.

Walton, E. (2014). Working towards Education for All in Gauteng. In F. Maringe & M. Prew (Eds). *Twenty Years of Education Transformation in Gauteng 1994 to 2014.* (pp. 210–227). Johannesburg: African Minds.

Walton, E. (2015). *The language of inclusive education: Exploring speaking, listening, reading and writing.* London: Routledge.

Walton, E., Nel, N., Hugo, A., & Muller, H. (2009). The extent and practice of inclusion in independent schools in South Africa. *South African Journal of Education, 29*(1), 105–126.

Watkins, D., McInerney, D., Akande, A., & Lee, C. (2003). An investigation of ethnic differences in the motivation and strategies for learning of students in desegregated South African schools. *Journal of Cross-Cultural Psychology, 34*(2), 189–194.

Wildeman, R. A., & Nomdo, C. (2007). *Implementation of inclusive education: How far are we?.* IDASA-Budget Information Service.

Young, M. (2001). Down with meritocracy. *The Guardian, 29*(6), 01.

8
DIAGNOSIS, INTEGRATION, AND INCLUSION

The experiences of schools and families in Cambodian policy and practice

Anne E. Crylen

Introduction

Since 2008, the Royal Government of Cambodia's Ministry of Education, Youth and Sport (MoEYS) has supported inclusion of students with disabilities. However, the focus was on accessibility to education, limited to physical disabilities, and lacked support for students with cognitive impairments including Down syndrome and autism spectrum disorder (ASD).

In 2017, the MoEYS established the National Institute for Special Education with a focus on teacher training in teaching students with disabilities, building capacity on disability education, developing programs to support curriculum standards, and priming the job market for the needs of people with disabilities. The need of special education continues to rise as the Cambodian Socio-economic Survey (2017) reports 4.6 percent of children ages 6–17 years do not attend school due to a disability or due to a long-term (over 3 months) illness.

This chapter illuminates the challenges parents face while navigating the dynamics of parental, medical, and academic systems of support for school-aged children with ASD in Cambodia. Their journey is captured through narratives describing a special school in Phnom Penh highlighting mental health, intellectual disability, the rise of a "new" diagnosis of ASD in Cambodia, and the shifting placement of disability within the government structure. The narratives from parents of children with ASD articulated parallels made to the "experience of acquired disability" as explored in the researcher's previous work on return-to-learn following traumatic brain injury (2019). Both groups of parents were on a search for answers to explain why their children were behaving differently, later explained with a diagnosis of a disability not generally recognized in their community or supported through educational accommodations.

As a focus two main questions will be addressed. First, what are the experiences of Cambodian parents/families of children with ASD in the medical and rehabilitative community and educational and social contexts? Next, what resources and strategies do schools use to meet the educational needs of children with ASD? Using this premise, we address some barriers to accessible services for individuals with ASD and other "invisible disabilities" by considering stigma within the Cambodian culture and provide future recommendations.

Disability in Cambodia

Historically in Cambodia, physical disabilities are generally more recognized than cognitive and developmental disabilities, due in part to the Cambodian genocide carried out by the Khmer Rouge regime under the leadership of Pol Pot. In addition to landmine accidents, physical disabilities are often caused at birth and by traffic accidents. Traditional belief in karma blames a wrong in one's past life as the reason they are disabled (Edmonds, 2005). This belief of karmic curse is slowly changing with the younger generation twice removed from the war, who recognize that the loss of sight, hearing, and mobility may be due to other causes. However, intellectual and developmental disabilities that are not clearly evident or explained by complications at birth or from disease are not readily culturally accepted.

Structural supports for disability

Since the restoration of the monarchy in 1993, the Kingdom of Cambodia has struggled to establish a strong infrastructure and provide universal health care and education. In 2012, Cambodia signed and ratified the United Nations Convention on the Rights of Persons with Disabilities (CRPD). Likewise, the United Nations Convention on the Rights of the Child (CRC), the Sustainable Development Goals, and the strategic goals of Education for All were all implemented to address disparities in the health and education system for individuals with disabilities. At the signing/ratification of the various conventions and instruments, the Royal Government of Cambodia spent 1.9 percent of the GDP on education (UNESCO Institute for Statistics, 2021), and there is a continued need to address quality support, staffing, and resourcing for which the government relies on support from non-governmental organizations and support through international aid organizations.

Resources and services are provided to children with disability through multiple agencies like MoEYS, the Ministry of Health (MoH), and the Ministry of Social Affairs, Veterans and Youth Rehabilitation (MoSAVYR). These different ministries are tasked by the general assembly with specialized projects to promote the success of a national policy supporting children with disability (Table 8.1).

There is little collaboration among the siloed branches of the government, causing a disconnect of services and positioning the child with disability in the middle of the three ministries, leaving families on their own to navigate between the different

TABLE 8.1 Disability agencies in Cambodia

Sector	Government Agency	Non-Government Agency	International Agencies
Education	Ministry of Education Youth and Sport (MoEYS)	Rumdul School	Aide-et-Action International UNICEF
Health	Ministry of Health (MoH)	Clinic for Youth Mental Health (CYMH)	World Health Organization (WHO)
Disability	Ministry of Social Affairs, Veterans and Youth Rehabilitation (MoSAVYR)	Disabled Peoples Organization (DPO)	United Nations Committee on the Rights of the Persons with Disabilities (UNCRPD)

agencies. Policy defines the services to be provided by each ministry, yet alignment and synergy of those services is absent in the current structure.

When MoEYS first developed the Policy on Education for Children with Disabilities in 2008 it did not specify the types of disabilities included (Kingdom of Cambodia, 2018). The MoEYS accommodates students with physical disabilities by providing access to buildings with ramps but does not provide formal special education instruction for any students with cognitive or developmental disabilities. Families living in Phenom Pehn may find special schools in the capitol, however those in the farther provinces rely on the community-run afterschool programs supported by the local chapter of the Disabled People's Organization under MoSAVYR. The gap in special education services, resources, and education support are ongoing challenges in Cambodia's 2,873 rural schools with 3,018 teachers across 24 provinces (Kingdom of Cambodia, 2019a, b). As the National Institute for Special Education has begun to train teachers on supporting students with hearing and visual disabilities (Thmey, 2020), the challenge of teaching students with ASD rests upon special schools.

Autism spectrum disorder in Cambodia

The Center for Disease Control defines ASD as a "developmental disability that can cause significant social, community and behavioral challenges" (CDC, 2019). In April 2021, the World Health Organization stated, "It is estimated that worldwide, about one in 270 people has ASD" (WHO, 2021). ASD can encompass a wide range and spectrum of symptoms ranging in severity. The "range of conditions are characterized by some degree of impaired social behavior, communication and language, and a narrow range of interests and activities that are both unique to the individual and carried out repetitively" (WHO, 2013).

ASD is not diagnosed at birth. As in many countries, characteristics of ASD go unnoticed or are explained away in the child's first years by an unknown developmental delay. ASD is a new phenomenon in Cambodia, and most participants reported being assured by others that the child is just "late to talk" (Arun Chann, personal communication, 2014). However, the elders of their community often use the Khmer word, ឆ្កួត (*chhkuot*), translated as "go mad" or "crazy", and reinforce the traditional belief in karmic curse. Therefore, it is concerning when the child shows non-communicative symptoms. It is common for the parent to hide their child in the house with fear of stigmatization from the community. Seeking out a medical diagnosis for ASD proves difficult culturally as well as logistically.

In Cambodia, ASD is commonly understood as a mental health disability as it does not have physical characteristics such as Down syndrome or cerebral palsy. As, the national health system does not conduct assessment of "mental health" it does not recognize the diagnosis of ASD. The Royal Government of Cambodia has charged the MoH to only provide medical procedures and rehabilitation therapies to Cambodians with physical disabilities at no charge. Therefore, parents searching for an expert to explain how their child is different from their peers is a lengthy and costly process. Likewise, many parents have sought answers by crossing the border into Vietnam; public hospitals in Phnom Penh are beginning to refer all cases of intellectual disability to the Clinic for Youth Mental Health (CYMH) located just outside the capital.

The clinic, funded by an international non-governmental organization, falls under the MoH and employs one international doctor and two Khmer doctors. The clinic provides assessment, diagnosis, and initial therapies and then refers the family to Rumdul School for additional "education." Instead of "autism," clinical therapists use the Khmer word for "triangle" to describe the "cardinal attributes" of ASD: abnormal play, loss of language skills, and lack of social communication. While at CYMH, families are divided into two main groups, those with ASD and those with Down syndrome, although they take classes together to learn how to care for and teach their children about basic needs. Upon request, parents are referred to a special school if so desired. This research followed several families of children diagnosed at CYMH with ASD who enrolled at Rumdul School for further education.

Multi-case study

This qualitative multi-case study was conducted at the only special school for children with disabilities in Phnom Penh, the capital of Cambodia. Rumdul School was identified as the unit of study at the recommendation of several key informants in the field of mental health and pediatric disability. Rumdul School services children with intellectual disabilities, ASD, Down syndrome and cerebral palsy. CYMH refers patients to Rumdul School at parents' request. No official reports or records of a child's health or diagnosis follow them throughout the referral process. Children entering the school are assessed by the educator team and placed in one of four tiers of classes according to their strengths and needs. At the time of this study, Rumdul School was introducing a special classroom on a public-school campus to promote social inclusion.

Over the course of six months, the researcher followed the journey of families and their children with ASD through the process of identification, diagnosis, medical treatment, and education, delving deeper into the inquiry of the presence and knowledge of the medical and educational services provided to children with ASD.

Families with ASD

The families attending Rumdul School represent communities from Cambodia's 24 provinces and 76% of its rural population on the lower end of the median annual income of $1,500 (World Bank, 2020). Five families at Rumdul School were identified among students enrolled across the three tiers of programming at the school, aligned with national standards in preschool, kindergarten, and lower elementary grades. All families were referred to the school after diagnosis at CYMH and their home communities outside of the capitol province which required temporary living arrangements. Two teachers, also parents of children with ASD, and the school's leadership team, which included the school founder/director and the business manager, were also interviewed to gather cultural, political, and economic context of education for children with ASD (Table 8.2).

Employing qualitative survey methodology, all interviews were guided by a semi-structured protocol that served as an agenda of the study questions. The interview protocol was used both as "an instrument of inquiry – asking questions for specific information ... as well as an instrument for conversation about a particular topic" (Castillo-Montoya, 2016). Parents were asked to *think aloud* their responses to scaffold questions about disability, the process of seeking a diagnosis of ASD, and the current state of education for students with ASD. This methodology provided opportunities for participants to elaborate their thoughts, "revealing reasons for the responses" (Desimone and Le Floch, 2004) and giving a running commentary of their thought process as they answer an illicit question "what is a clear and accurate reflection of their experience, what is ambiguous or awkward, and what is absent" (Desimone and Le Floch, 2004). From this given response, the researcher used a protocol of questions to further assess how well the respondent understood the question/issue.

All families wanted to share their stories and engaged in one-hour–long discussions at the school. To ensure communication, cultural nuances and expectations were clearly conveyed and understood and all participants spoke in Khmer, the national language, and were interpreted into English by a certified translator.

Grounded theory was used throughout the data analysis, which included thematic coding. Given that ASD presented as a "new" diagnosis in Cambodia's medical, educational, and cultural contexts, the researcher used the Three Spheres of Support Model for School Re-entry after TBI (Crylen, 2015) to find the medical and educational spheres were joined in the hierarchy of government services. Organizing the three agencies of support highlighted the clear division of responsibilities and services for the child with ASD between the MoH, MoEYS, and MoSAVYR. For the purposes of this research, the family of the child with ASD is at the core of the model, yet caught in the crease between the MoH and MoEYS and their delivery of services as illustrated in Figure 8.1.

TABLE 8.2 Study participants overview

Name	Gender	CYMH Medical Diagnosis	Rumdul Education Program
Dara	Female	Medium Autism – infant-like behavior, rarely speaks, slow to process	Readiness Class – matches objects with numbers, lower threshold of frustration and increased happiness
Pich	Female	Medium Autism – isolated in own world, no speech, selective hearing, did not follow directions	Readiness Class – relates to others including family members, plays with blocks, can dress herself
Sokun	Male	Low Autism – No eye contact, plays alone, late to speak	Integrated Room – recognizes colors, reads and writes his name, loves song and dance
Thom	Male	Low Autism – no eye contact, no speech, no social interest	Integrated Room – plays with classmates, recognizes colors and letters, follows directions
Visoth	Male	Low Autism – no speech, no social interest	Special Class – high intellectual capacity with strong conceptual mathematical knowledge, literate in English and Khmer, emotionally immature

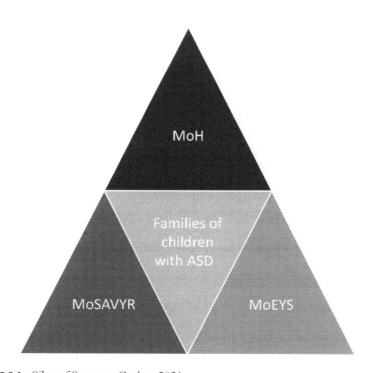

FIGURE 8.1 Silos of Support. Crylen, 2021.

Findings

This study explored the dynamics of parental, medical, and academic systems of support for school-aged children with ASD in Cambodia guided by two main questions: 1) What are the experiences of Cambodian parents/families of children with ASD in the medical and rehabilitative community and educational and social contexts? 2) What resources and strategies do schools use to meet the educational needs of children with ASD? Four themes emerged from the data related to identification, diagnosis, treatment, and a national response for change.

Identification in reconciling difference

The Cambodian health system does not provide standard pediatric check-ups after postnatal care; therefore, parents rely on social observations to ensure their children are healthy. One mother stated, "I noticed that she was not as bright as the other children in the community" (Maly's parent, personal communication, 2015). As much of Cambodia is rural, many parents work in agriculture and are away from home during the day. This further challenges parents to see their child in social settings and leans on their own relationship with their children. "I noticed that he was afraid to look at me and the relationship between me and him seemed to be not close. He didn't care about my return from work or anywhere when I come home" (Sokun's parent, personal communication, 2015). While the parent reconciles that their child is different, they must embark on a complicated search for answers. The runaround between clinics leads to an undefined diagnosis and a deflated family.

As a cultural norm in Cambodia, many parents of children with ASD relied on the advice of their village elders before seeking medical advice. Conventional wisdom relayed to concerned parents alluded to physical growth. "When I ask others about ASD, they just said my son has big tongue. They understand that my son is stuttering and say when he grows up he can speak. They have *Sokum* [hope]" (Thom's parent, personal interview). Adhering to this advice, several parents tried to send their children to public school. In most cases, the classroom experience included bullying from other students and discrimination by teachers (Sokun's parent, personal communication, 2015).

Seeking clear and consistent information about ASD from official sources proved difficult. The lack of equity of access to health care in Cambodia contributed to parents waiting to find answers. As the only advocates for their children with difference, parents' worries intensified throughout the identification process.

Once parents made their way to medical clinics, guilt and grief were exacerbated as parents received reassurance by government doctors that was later shattered at the international non-governmental clinic for mental health. As one parent shared, "I discuss [his difference] with doctors at pediatric hospital [who] said no problems happen to him. But when I took to the [CYMH] clinic, the doctor said he has ASD (Visoth's parent, personal communication, 2015). Additionally, parents were unsatisfied with lack of a defined medical cause of ASD and thus no known cure for the condition. "The doctor said ASD is inborn disease and right now we don't have research to know how it is caused" (Dara's parent, personal communication, 2015). As parents met other parents with children of ASD, they began to come up with their own answers

Diagnosis as confused definition

Compounded with the guilt and grief of parents reconciling difference in their child, confusion overwhelmed many families once they entered the medical system. For some, the public health system did not provide a diagnosis but rather a category of mental illness. As one parent shared, "Doctors (at the public hospital) said they did not look after on such an illness for a child. [Then] The doctor (at the clinic) told me that my son has mental weakness" (Sokun's parent, personal communication, 2015).

For those parents that did receive a diagnosis, the explanation remained in the broader use of intellectual disability, an abstract concept for many parents. "They [doctors] just tell me that my granddaughter has ASD. No they didn't give anything [information]. They [doctors] said it was a brain disability" (Pich's parent, personal communication, 2015). Other parents were confused by the vocabulary because the term ASD didn't exist in the Khmer language. "At the public infant hospital (doctors) told me my daughter is suffering from ASD, but they didn't say anything in Khmer. They said in Khmer it is a kind of mental disability or intellectual disability (Maly's parent, personal communication, 2015). Once the diagnosis of ASD was given, the parents continued to seek for the meaning of this foreign word and concept in Cambodia.

At CYMH, doctors used the symptoms of ASD as the definition of the condition. Using visual metaphors to explain how the symptoms contribute to the diagnosis, the international doctors use the concrete images of a wobbly three-legged stool. Each stool leg represents one major symptom of ASD: impaired social behavior, communication and language, and a narrow range of interest and activities.

After rendering a diagnosis of ASD at CYMH, several parents continued to make public school work for their child. These parents tried to intervene and talk with the teachers and found themselves with a burden of educating teachers. As one parent stated:

> When I went to Public School, I talk about ASD. But teachers there don't know what ASD is. I tried to explain them, but they don't understand. I think that in public school that patience and love is only for children without ASD.
>
> (Sokun's parent, personal communication, 2015)

With the lack of a formal definition of ASD recognized by the MoH, the international clinic's explanation of ASD became an official explanation of the condition. The clinic's working definition aligned with the deficit-oriented medical model of disability, grounded in dependency rather than independence, and supported children remaining at home rather than going to school.

Dilemma of medical treatment or social education

Recognizing parents wanted a treatment for ASD, CYMH offered 6-week long classes for caregivers. These one-hour classes were offered once a month focusing on how to parents could teach basic life skills to their diagnosed children including dressing themselves, brushing their teeth, and feeding themselves (Thom's parent, personal interview). For many of the parents, these classes became the substitution of public schooling for their children.

> At the hospital, the doctor asks all the parents to get together. They teach me to draw, they show the pictures and I draw the picture like I teach my daughter. The doctor means that this is what I should teach my daughter. He means is that it is very different to teach the children with ASD like this
> (Dara's parent, personal communication, 2015).

For some parents, the classes offered at CYMH were not enough and asked for more education. Upon request, the international clinic offered parents a referral to the only special school in Phnom Penh.

For those referred to Rumdul School, the school administrators saw a pattern and concluded the international clinic had identified children as severe on the ASD Spectrum Disorder, using a 1-3 scale as Mild-Moderate-Severe/Profound. One being Mild ASD which is high-functioning ASD requiring low levels of support, two being Moderate ASD requiring supports, three being Severe/Profound ASD requiring substantial supports with severe deficits in all three symptomatic areas (Framingham, 2020). However, that was rarely disclosed to parents.

> The doctor told [parents] to bring all their sons to the special school. Those that are high [ASD] they come to the special school and those that are low [ASD] go to the integrated public school. That means the degree of ASD
> (Dara's parent, personal communication, 2015).

While at CMYH, parents understood that some students with ASD could be integrated back into Public School right away, but that other students with more challenge were referred to Rumdul School. The school administration later clarified that students that were referred to return to public school eventually found their way to Rumdul School after failed attempts at integration.

During enrollment, Rumdul School starts from scratch as parents rarely bring an official medical report with the diagnosis of ASD. The director uses an assessment tool of his own design to determine where the child is on the spectrum before determining placement in a class. The director talked with parents to re-define their educational goals for their children with ASD.

We have different goals for each child. We have individual education plan. Our goal we want the children to be more independent (living). We don't expect them to read or write or become a doctor, a teacher or booker. This is more independent (academic). We only focus on the present.

(Arun Chann, personal communication, 2014)

Moving beyond self-care and hygiene, students were in classrooms according to their ability levels with differentiated curriculum that included literacy and numeracy, communication and socialization, and vocational training as illustrated in Figure 8.2.

While parents have tempered their education goals for their children with ASD, they expressed the universal desire for their children to grow up independently and be accepted. As one parent expressed, "From her [life] experience she needs warmth. I notice that she wants the parents and guardians to love her. Also, when she comes to school, she wants teachers to love her" (Maly's parent, personal communication, 2015). As Rumdul School has grown, the administrator has trained interested parents to become instructors in the absence of government certified special education teachers.

Parents at Rumdul School have seen their children grow more independent as they learn to navigate their world through language, socialization, and basic skills. "He understands a lot now. He knows about love. He likes to be hugged and he needs his mother to comfort him. And I hope he has a bright future, and he can help himself in the society" (Sokun's parent, personal communication, 2015). With reconciliation of their child's difference, many parents express hope for their children's future.

Instructional Tiers	Parent Participants		Skill Focus
Readiness Class: 4-12 years old *Preschool*	New to school >1 year	Second year	Language: eye contact Literacy: matching items Hygiene: toileting, self-care Social: build attention
Special Class: 4-12 years old *Kindergarten, 1st grade*	Progressed from readiness class	Same level +2 years	Language: speech Literacy: writing, tracking, drawing Hygiene: basic living (dressing) Social: social
Integrated Class: 12-14 years old *2nd, 3rd grades*	Progressed from special class	Same level +2 years	Improved skills Vocational Training

FIGURE 8.2 Rumdul School Matrix of Instruction. Rumdul School, 2015.

What I want is she can help herself. I don't hope she can learn as good as the other kids or have a better job. I don't think so. But what I want is she can help herself live in society. That is enough.

(Maly's parent, personal communication, 2015)

For students who matriculated through all the leveled classrooms, Rumdul School has begun to partner with the MoEYS to start integrated classes at public schools. "At the [integrated public school] they have two parts. There is the public school and then two rooms for the integrated. They want the kids to know and see if the other kids will play around" (Dara's parent, personal interview). At the time of the study, the public school housed Rumdul School in the middle of the campus both for physical accessibility to the rooms as well as building awareness and integration with general education students.

The special school welcomed students from CYMH and adopted the practice of teaching both parents and the children about ASD through a social model of building independence. For some parents, the welcome was a wave of relief in the reconciliation process. "In the special school they understand ASD. They know the methods to teach them, they love the children and have patience with the children" (Sokun's parent, personal communication, 2015). Word of mouth about Rumdul School spread within the newly formed community of families with ASD, leaving some parents to go around the CYMH referral system. "At first the teacher said the school was full, so I begged the teachers to let my son study in the special school here because he's afraid of the Public School" (Sokun's parent, personal communication, 2015). At the time of this study, Rumdul school had started a social media presence on Facebook and a new website.

A national call for inclusion

The common thread for parents interviewed was a misconstruction of ASD as mental illness rather than a disability. They spoke to a universal desire for their children to grow up independently and be accepted socially. Many parents expressed after having gone through the experience of identification, reconciliation of difference, diagnosis of ASD from an international clinic and receiving educational programming at Rumdul School, that a lack of information leads to misunderstandings in the community that could be remedied by the Royal Government of Cambodia. "The MoH should formally declare about ASD because if the ministry does the community will learn about ASD better," (Maly's parent, personal communication, 2015). Additionally, parents have hopes that the Royal Government of Cambodia will recognize ASD as it does other invisible disabilities. "I think the royal government [will] also focuses on ASD. A few days ago, I saw (Prime Minister) Hun Sen and his wife give gifts to the deaf and mute children" (Sokun's parent, personal communication, 2015).

With support from the MoSAVYR, the first of the ministries to recognize Down syndrome and ASD, a collective of parents of children with ASD have formed an advocacy group. "We (parents) just talk about what we worry and the symptoms of the ASD, but we don't know how to find the solutions" (Pich's parent, personal communication, 2015). Together the parents organized a national ASD Day modeled after the US based Autism Speaks organization. At the time of this research, it was attended by representatives of the MoEYS as well as the MoSAVYR with sponsorship from various international aid organizations.

Discussion

These narratives bring forward the voice of families of children with ASD who have not always been heard and understood within their home communities or considered part of inclusive education practice in Cambodia. For many, they are isolated from their villages and find themselves running between the MoH, MoEYS, and MoSAVYR as they seek answers about their child's difference, see Figure 8.1. For those parents fortunate to find CMYH, they receive a medical identification of ASD and are then referred to Rumdul School with hopes that their goals of social independence for their child are further actualized. However, this is achieved outside of the national health care and education systems and available to few families in Cambodia.

Families exhausted from running between these silos of support, have called for a national movement of inclusion from the MoH, MoEYS, and MoSAVYR to recognize and meet the needs of their children with ASD. Moving from silos to a trifecta of support surrounding each individual child with disability regardless of type, would create sustainable synergy to identification, diagnosis, treatment, and education, see Figure 8.3. This integrated Trifecta of Support of the three agencies would require systemic change. Using a common language of diagnosis, referral documentation and accountability of support for disability would propel social inclusion of children with ASD in their community and schools.

Additionally, the Trifecta of Support would open multiple entry points for families on the search for answers. Should a family go to their local health clinic, they

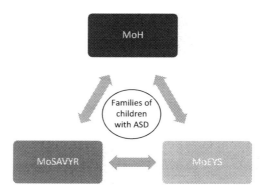

FIGURE 8.3 Trifecta of Support. Crylen 2021.

would be referred through the existing tiered national health system to seek medical diagnosis at a regional hospital with documentation to take to their local school. Conversely, if the family was concerned with their child's performance in class, the school could make the referral to the regional hospital for diagnosis and consult with the local DPO chapter to help make transportation arrangements to the larger city. This Trifecta of Support extends the outreach of the agencies at the same time identifying and welcoming families across the rural provinces into organized groups of advocacy for inclusion much like the Special Olympics of Cambodia has created.

This integrated model of support echoes the collaborative spirit of the international non-governmental organizations Cambodia has partnered with over the last 40 years in the areas of health, nutrition, poverty, and disability. With full support from Royal Government of Cambodia, it will strengthen its sustainability in meeting the needs of the whole child. Much like the experiences of families of children with TBI from which this model is based, the families of children with ASD will find this wrap around support offering both the opportunity for medical diagnosis with clarity and a prognosis for quality of life complete of educational, medical, and social services.

Collective diagnosis

The lack of a word for ASD in Khmer continues to keep the diagnosis at arm's length from the Cambodian collective socially. Much like physical disability was socially embraced by Cambodians with an understanding of its cause by injury following the war or accident and eventually folded into national healthcare, non-physical disabilities including deafness and blindness are gaining the attention of the Prime Minister as deaf-blind schools are being transferred into the National Institute for Special Education. Once recognized in the official language of Cambodia and with formal identification by the Royal Government and its agencies including MoH, MoEYS, and MoSAVYR, ASD will gain awareness and acceptance on local and national levels, following its global partners.

As Cambodia is a fully engaged member party of the United Nations and a member state of the World Health Organization, it is recommended that the MoH and MoEYS work with the WHO Cambodia Representative Office to review the Sixty-seventh World Health Assembly adopted resolution, "Comprehensive and coordinated efforts for the management of autism spectrum disorders" (WHO, 2016). Developing a common classification system for ASD, used in the medical and educational fields will alleviate the stress and confusion parents faced in the experienced shared in this study. Additionally, a collective language among the governmental agencies will provide for more accurate statistical tracking of children with disabilities.

In the United States, socio-cultural norms position the medical sphere with more authority than the educational sphere, as instituted through the federal legislation, Individuals with Disabilities Education Act of 1990. The medical diagnosis of disability drives the necessity for special education evaluation, planning, and implementing an Individualized Education Plan or 504 plan to access a Free

Accessible Public Education (Individuals with Disabilities Education Act, 1990). In the research with families of children with TBI, after being given the medical director's letter of recommended accommodations, families looked to the school to take the lead as they navigate the Return-to-Learn process. Cambodian families of children with ASD followed the same informal process with CMYH and Rumdul School providing a model to scale in the public sector for referrals of ASD once a common definition and diagnosis is recognized in Khmer.

Prognosis of inclusive education

The findings show, a diagnosis of ASD is only half of the answer parents seek on their quest to understand their child's difference. A common thread woven in each narrative was the desire for an independent life for their child achieved through education. This prognosis of reassurance of a good quality of life is a universal desire of every parent. In this study, it is a prominent need given the current stigma and lack of resources for children with "invisible" disabilities including ASD.

Cambodia places education as a high priority for the nation as evidenced in the implementation of Education For All and its response to SDG 4 (Kingdom of Cambodia, 2019a, b). Leveraging Cambodia's strong alliance with UNICEF already established, it is recommended MoEYS use Rumdul School as a springboard to design and implement inclusive education for all students including those with physical, intellectual, and cognitive challenges.

Rumdul School has developed a grass roots approach to special education with a foundation in the social model of disability. The director of Rumdul School based its programming on the American model of special education and understanding of ASD as a spectrum disorder. Learning along the way, the director and staff gather tools and strategies from dated textbooks and US publications available online. The director is regarded as the expert in non-physical disability education and is regularly called on by the various disability councils to lead national awareness campaigns. In recent years, the director has hosted MoEYS officials at Rumdul School for workshops on intellectual, cognitive, and developmental disabilities and lead teacher training for the development of a national special education plan.

Moving forward, MoEYS will need to commit financial and human capital resources to take Rumdul School to scale. Although dedicated to the school, many of the teachers are not formally trained in education and do not hold teaching licensure through the MoEYS. While this has not been a formal challenge to the school, it does raise a concern as more students advance into the integrated tier of classes and the school expands into inclusion settings on the public-school campuses. The National Institute for Special Education would serve as a strong center for parent educators in addition to its pre-teaching certification program.

Furthermore, the MoH and MoEYS will need to formalize a true partnership of CMYH and Rumdul School with two-directional communication and collaboration. As of now, CMYH issues a diagnosis to the parents, but does not send any documentation to Rumdul School. It is essential to collaboration that medical documentation be shared with Rumdul School with detailed diagnosis of deficits and strengths to support the education evaluation process. In turn, Rumdul School should collaborate with CMYH on clinic classes and a transition process for parents referred to the school. The development of wrap-around services for children with ASD will further support the national call for inclusion.

As the findings show, understanding the cultural context of the rise of ASD in Cambodia is critical to the development of education policy inclusive of non-physical disabilities. There is a significant need for more schools specializing in non-physical disabilities including ASD and trained special education teachers across the public school system. To do so, the Royal Government of Cambodia needs to align the definition and diagnosis of ASD across the MoEYS, the MoH, and the MoSAVYR. A shift of dependance on foreign aid to a collaboration with non-governmental organizations will ensure sustainability of the development and implementation of an education policy and practice inclusive of all students.

Conclusion

For more than 40 years, disability in Cambodia has been visually recognized as physical impairments due to the atrocities of war, which have been culturally absorbed in the nations' rebuilding and the healing process of the Khmer Rouge trials. The reliance on international non-governmental organizations to field the need of prostheses, wheelchairs, and rehabilitation services while providing medical diagnosis of a disease or treatment for an injury associated with an accident that resulted in disability was normalized. As the generations of the genocide pass, Cambodia is seeing a new emergence of invisible disability including cognitive, intellectual, and developmental delays. A concerted effort on equal access and participation in society emphasized in the CRPD and CRC now shifts to equitable inclusion in society through the SDGs particularly in education. Within half a century, Cambodia has seen its nation fall, pick itself up from the rubble, rebuild, and respond to new change. As the findings of this study show, the invisible disability of ASD brings a different set of needs for identification, diagnosis, treatment, and inclusion. It will provide families with a diagnosis and a prognosis that will shape their child's quality of life. Utilizing a new integrated trifecta of support model for the three agencies of health, education, and disability rehabilitation in Cambodia will promote common language, and strengthen channels of communication and equitable education services, promoting social inclusion for those with invisible disabilities.

References

Centers for Disease Control (CDC). (2019). Autism Spectrum Disorder (ASD) Fact Sheet. Retrieved from https://www.cdc.gov/ncbddd/autism/facts.html

Crylen, A. E. (2015). Socio-emotional support needs for re-entry to school after traumatic brain injury. In *Including learners with low-incidence disabilities (International Perspectives on Inclusive Education, Vol. 5)*. Bingley: Emerald Group Publishing Limited, pp. 159–179. https://doi.org/10.1108/S1479-363620140000005009

Desimone, L. M. and Le Floch, K. C. (2004). Are we asking the right questions? Using cognitive interviews to improve surveys in education research. *Education Evaluation Policy Analysis*, 26(1), 1–22.

Edmonds, L. J. 2005. *Disabled people and development.* Asian Development Bank, 2–5. http://hdl.handle.net/11540/5360

Framingham, J. (2020). Autism. Psych Central. Retrieved on August 1, 2020, from https://psychcentral.com/autism/

Individuals with Disabilities Education Act, 20 U.S.C. § 1400 (2004).

Kingdom of Cambodia. (2018). Policy on Inclusive Education. Phnom Penh, Cambodia: Ministry of Education, Youth and Sport. Retrieved from https://static1.squarespace.com/static/5940eb9a414fb5787b3436ac/t/5e3b131449b9d50287aa5b8f/1580929822677/Inclusive+Education+Policy_EN_2018.pdf

Kingdom of Cambodia. (2019a). Cambodia's Voluntary National Review 2019 on the Implementation of the 2030 Agenda for Sustainable Development. Retrieved from https://sustainabledevelopment.un.org/content/documents/23603Cambodia_VNR_PublishingHLPu.pdf

Kingdom of Cambodia. (2019b). The Education Statistics and Indicators 2018-2019 Book. Retrieved from http://www.moeys.gov.kh/index.php/en/emis/3071.html

Thmey, K. (2020). *Teachers training.* Krousar Thmey. Retrieved from: http://www.krousar-thmey.org/en/education-for-deaf-or-blind/teachers-training/

UNESCO Institute for Statistics (UIS), http://uis.unesco.org/en/country/kh#slideoutmenu, April 25, 2021.

Willis, G. B. (2005). *Cognitive interviewing: A tool for improving questionnaire design.* Thousand Oaks, CA: Sage.

World Bank. (2020). Cambodia GDP. Retrieved from https://www.macrotrends.net/countries/KHM/cambodia/gdp-gross-domestic-product

World Health Organization (WHO). (2013). Meeting report: autism spectrum disorders and other developmental disorders: from raising awareness to building capacity: World Health Organization, Geneva, Switzerland 16–18 September 2013.

World Health Organization (WHO). (2016). World Health Assembly resolution on "Comprehensive and Coordinated Efforts for the Management of Autism Spectrum Disorders" Agenda item 13.4, WHA 67.8 2016.

World Health Organization (WHO). (2021). *Autism spectrum disorders.* World Health Organization. Retrieved from: https://www.who.int/news-room/fact-sheets/detail/autism-spectrum-disorders

9
TALKING ABOUT SELF

Exploring the potential of teacher's talk in professional learning communities for inclusive pedagogy

Wacango Kimani

Introduction

Teacher education is the well-worn response to research that reveals the challenges of implementing inclusive education. While the need for increased skills and knowledge – particularly in special education – have been a recurring recommendation (Materechera, 2020), Woodcock and Hardy (2017a) demonstrate that such knowledge alone did not engender inclusive teaching that considered all learners in a classroom. This chapter takes a new direction, arguing that simply acquiring knowledge and skills for inclusive teaching misses the need for shifts in teacher identity and agency.

The shaping of professional identity and agency is necessary when teachers are required to take up a new practice (Eteläpelto, Vähäsantanen, Hökkä & Paloniemi, 2014). Inclusive education, a relatively new concept and practice in South Africa, was not part of initial teacher education for many in-service teachers (Walton & Moonsamy, 2015). Therefore, many teachers do not perceive themselves as educators capable of implementing inclusion (Walton et al., 2014). Research on professional learning for inclusive education has considered teacher perceptions, attitudes, and experiences about implementing inclusive education (Walton et al., 2014). However, Swart & Oswald (2008) found that teachers' identity and agency can be impacted by professional learning for inclusive education when teachers learn collaboratively. Studies elsewhere suggest that understanding teacher agency and identity is important to practicing inclusive pedagogy (Lyons, Thompson & Timmons, 2016).

Additionally, the focus of professional learning needs to shift: from understanding barriers that some learners face, to pedagogical solutions that consider the learning of all children in classrooms with diverse educational profiles. Florian and Spratt's (2013) inclusive pedagogy provides a framework for inclusive teaching that

DOI: 10.4324/9781003091950-11

is achievable by all qualified teachers. Rather than imposing knowledge from the experts, a focus on teacher professional identity and agency begins with teachers – where they are at, what they know and what they do. This approach is more likely to encourage teachers' buy-in. Prevalent notions of inclusion that focus solely on learners with barriers who can only be taught by teachers with 'special education' knowledge do not engender buy-in. Buy-in may be facilitated when teachers engage knowledge that gives them perceptions of themselves as capable of teaching inclusive classrooms with their current qualifications. Teacher professional identity and agency are self-vision oriented and empowering because teachers see themselves first; they see their successes and their ability to teach diverse learner populations.

Drawing on Wenger's (1998) theory of learning as social practice and Sfard and Prussak's (2005) "narrative as identity", this chapter argues that teacher talk within Professional Learning Communities (PLCs) reflects teachers' re-negotiation of their professional identity and agency, necessary markers for learning inclusive practices in complex contexts. An analysis of teacher talk in relation to Florian and Spratt's (2013) inclusive pedagogical approach in action (IPAA) framework offers avenues to understand how learning could happen, be curtailed or be promoted in PLCs. The form, content and change in teacher talk in PLCs indicates the extent to which teachers may be learning inclusive pedagogy.

Teacher education for inclusion

Professional learning for inclusion is linked to the definition of inclusive education that the professional learning programme adopts. When inclusion is defined as including learners with disabilities to access regular education, then the professional learning will focus on identifying ability differences and the specific ways to teach learners with different disabilities. The models for professional learning based on special education needs reinforce deficit perceptions of learners (Woodcock & Hardy, 2017a). Professional learning programmes that focus on instructional practices, such as universal design for learning and differentiation, are intended to move beyond identifying the barriers that learners face and have been perceived by teachers to be disconnected from their school practices (Deppeler, 2010). Since skills development has not sufficiently prepared teachers for diversity (Waitoller & Kozleski, 2010), then professional learning for inclusion must be "reframed from something that is *done to teachers* to something that *teachers continue to do together*" (Deppeler, 2010 p. 182). When collaboration is espoused both as a principle of inclusion and as a skill and strategy for implementing inclusive education, professional learning would broadly interpret inclusion within a school-wide approach that also considers marginalisation and exclusion of any learner inside and outside the classroom.

PLCs have been recommended as a viable professional learning model for inclusion (DBE, 2009; Walton et al., 2014). PLCs, as communities of practice, focus on teacher identity as the vehicle for learning in and through action and activity (Waitoller & Kozleski, 2010). Teacher identity is continuously renegotiated through participation in the PLCs. Teachers reconstruct their identity by how they interpret their role in school, what they see as the purpose of education, and how they fit within this purpose (Waitoller & Kozleski, 2010). This constant renegotiating of their identity builds their professional growth. Engagement in PLCs mediates between teachers' current realities and an imagined better future. Identity work is important since teachers learn in the present by drawing from the past, imagining the future, and creating new tools for future situations (Sfard and Prusak, 2005). Becoming an inclusive teacher is an identity-formation process where teachers and their surrounding context write another page of the teachers' biography (Waitoller & Kozleski, 2010). Since learning is becoming a different person and thus renegotiating identity (Wenger, 1998), professional learning programmes need to provide experiences that support the development of inclusive teacher identities.

Conceptual framework

Meaningful teacher learning is "a slow and uncertain process" (Borko, 2004, p. 6) involving change. Collaborative professional learning provides an environment for individual change as well as social change, where communities create professional knowledge through interaction in ways that challenge previous assumptions and create new meanings (Timperley, 2011). Professional learning communities (PLCs) foster collaborative learning, which has been shown to influence teacher professional identity and agency and improve the quality of education (Chauraya, 2016). The PLC, theorised here as 'learning as social practice', acknowledges that teachers can take ownership of their learning, and that community can provide a conducive professional learning environment to impact teacher change and shift teacher identity (Chauraya, 2016).

Using Wenger's (1998) "learning as social practice" for the theoretical framework counters the general assumption that learning "has a beginning and an end; that it is best separated from the rest of our activities; and that it is the result of teaching" (Wenger, 1998, p. 3). Wenger (1998) challenges the separation of learning from other social activities, contending that learning happens everywhere and is a social process of participation. Learning is the "process of becoming a member of a sustained community of practice" (Lave, 1991, p.65); of people who are engaged in a domain – a passion that defines the identity of the community (Wenger, 2010).

Wenger's (1998) theory emphasises participation as key to learning, and not just mental representation as previously described in cognitive theories of learning. Participation is not the outcome or the process of learning; by definition, learning *is* participation. Traditionally, researchers studied learning as if it were a "process contained in the mind of the learners" and ignored the "lived-in world" (Lave, 2009,

p. 202). Because learning is not a product, it happens in unmarked, unintended ways and happens everywhere (Lave, 2009). Analysis of learning is thus analysis of peoples' involvement in social activities, where the engagement constitutes learning: "participation is learning ... a process of changing understanding in practice, that is, as learning" (Lave, 2009, p. 201). One individual's participation in a social setting enables other members to learn, not only from what that individual does, but also through what all members "do" together. The community learns from individuals participating in community.

Inclusive pedagogy – the subject of discussion for teachers participating in the PLCs – is defined by the acceptance of differences between learners as an ordinary aspect of human development (Florian & Spratt, 2013). Inclusive pedagogy begins with decisions about what is being taught and by whom, and with teachers who are responsive to diverse student and learning needs. When inclusion is broadly conceptualised, teachers can identify the way they teach, and their teacher's craft (Black-Hawkins & Florian, 2012), as being inclusive. The inclusive pedagogical approach in action (IPAA) (Florian & Spratt, 2013) articulates inclusive pedagogy as social justice, arguing that teachers are capable of implementing inclusive education using their knowledge and professional craft. The IPAA defines inclusive pedagogy based on how a teaching strategy is used rather than the choice of strategy. It emphasises teachers' active role in producing knowledge from and for their teaching practice, hence shaping their professional identity and agency as inclusive educators. The IPAA framework is undergirded by three key principles: difference as an essential aspect of human development; teachers' belief in their capability to teach all children; and development of the profession through collaboration among teachers and other professionals. Florian and Spratt (2013) note that this approach fosters collaboration among mainstream teachers and specialists to support all learners, not just those identified as needing additional support.

To understand teachers' identity as a trajectory of learning, the analysis considered Wenger's (1998) three modes of belonging – engagement, imagination and alignment – as the "process of identity formation and learning" (Wenger, 1998, p. 173). Through engagement, imagination and alignment, people create a picture of themselves as participants in a community of practice. Engagement relates to practice and an individual's direct experience and competence or incompetence in the practice. Imagination entails a teacher's construction of the world that helps her/him understand how s/he belongs or does not belong. Engagement and imagination also entail an alignment with the context, including following the norms of the community. The school context can enable and constrain teachers' engagement in a PLC (Walton et al., 2019). Juxtaposing Wenger's (1998) Modes of belonging with the IPAA–enabled analysis of teacher professional identity.

Table 9.1 is a grid categorising the aspects of identity. Each element of Wenger's Modes of belonging is matched to the principles of the IPAA. Data that reflected each IPAA principle was matched to the corresponding element of Wenger's Modes.

Talking about self   **155**

TABLE 9.1 The IPAA with Wenger's Modes of belonging

IPAA Principles	Identity: Modes of belonging		
	Engagement: *active involvement in mutual processes of negotiating meaning*	**Imagination**: *entail teacher's construction of the world that helps her/him understand how s/he belongs or does not belong.*	**Alignment**: *with common goals and with the context*
1. Learner profile			"Our School"
2. Teachers' capability		They're specially trained	
3. Working together	Small groups are good		

Source: Florian & Spratt (2013); Wenger (1998)

Li & Ruppar's (2020) consolidated framework for teacher agency for inclusive education was used to analyse teacher professional agency. Li and Ruppar (2020) define teacher agency for inclusive education as:

> a temporal, individual, and collective engagement (Priestley et al., 2016) in active decision making on curriculum, assessment, and every-day inclusive education practice, mediated by given educational contexts, to negotiate the benefit of inclusive education and to work against practices that perpetuate norms of ability and differences.
>
> (Li and Ruppar, 2020, p. 11)

Li and Ruppar's (2020) framework for teacher agency draws on nine international empirical studies about teacher agency for inclusive education and Pantić and Florian's (2015) aspects of teacher agency. Combining the IPAA Framework with teacher agency for inclusion is shown in Table 9.2.

IPAA Principle One – Learner Profile – corresponded with inclusive professional philosophy. Principle Two – Teachers' Capability – aligned with inclusive teacher identity and professional competence. Principle Three – Working Together – aligned with Reflexivity. Even though the analysis followed the matchings assigned in Table 9.2, these divisions are not fixed and the constructs are not mutually exclusive. This was especially so with the aspect of autonomy and professional competence that were evident as Teachers' Capability and Working Together.

The context: "City Primary School"

The three-year study informing this chapter was conducted in a full-service/inclusive school, given the pseudonym "City Primary School" in Johannesburg, South Africa, where teachers had ordinary/mainstream diplomas and degrees in education. In partnership with a local university, PLCs were established and all teachers participated. The university team, which also comprised researchers, created discussion guidelines based on the IPAA as shown in Table 9.3.

TABLE 9.2 The IPAA and aspects of teacher agency for inclusive pedagogical practice

IPAA Principles	Aspects of teacher agency	Description
Learner Profile	Inclusive professional philosophy	Attitudes and perceptions toward teaching, learning, and ability
Teachers' Capability	Inclusive teacher identity	Professional roles, moral roles, and motivation
	Professional competence	Knowledge and practice of inclusive pedagogy
Teachers' Capability	Autonomy	Individual and collective efficacy, decision making, and collaboration with other actors
Working Together	Reflexivity	Reflection, monitoring, and regulation of one's own actions and social contexts

Source: Adapted from Florian and Spratt (2013); Li and Ruppar (2020); Pantić and Florian (2015)

PLC Sessions and Topics

The university team prepared each discussion topic based on the teachers' expressed needs and met with facilitators a few days before each PLC session to acquaint them with the topic for discussion. The facilitators received two handouts. One was a guide for facilitators on how to conduct the PLC session and keep the discussions focused. The second was the teachers' handout on the topic for discussion, which was often a worksheet with questions and spaces for teachers to record their understanding.

PLC sessions were scheduled at the beginning of the school year. At each session the university team was available for clarification where necessary. The discussions were audio recorded with the teachers' permission. Teachers sat in mixed-grade groups with a colleague as facilitator. Three PLC sessions were held in Year 1; four in Year 2 and four in Year 3 (Table 9.3). At the outset, teachers expressed concerns that learners did not listen to them during teaching. Therefore, the first project year was dedicated to topics related to listening and understanding: what enabled and constrained learners' hearing; the different components for effective listening; and building vocabulary from comprehension. The research team would have preferred to have more sessions but this was impossible, given teachers' commitments to other school activities. Each PLC session began with a review of the previous session and teachers sharing their experiences of incorporating what they had learned into the classroom. Teachers were encouraged to express their feelings, the successes and challenges of teaching learners with diverse needs.

Method

The PLC discussions were audio recorded and transcribed. Each recording was about 45 minutes long. While audio recording captured all the discussions, it may also have inhibited teachers from talking for fear of exposure (Cohen, Manion &

TABLE 9.3 List of PLC sessions

Year	Month	PLC Session	Topic
1	February	1	Effective Listening
	June	2	Whole Body Listening
	August	3	Building Vocabulary for Comprehension
2	February	4	Inclusive Teaching and Learning
	May	5	Cooperative Learning 1
	July	6	Cooperative Learning 2 ★Think-Pair-Share
	August	7	Cooperative Learning 3 ★Write-Think-Pair-Share ★Pair-Coaching
3	February	8	Sentence Starters
	May	9	Meaningful Engagement
	August	10	Bell-Curve Thinking & Inclusive Pedagogy 1
	September	11	Bell-Curve Thinking & Inclusive Pedagogy 2

Morrison, 2018). Teachers gave consent to the recording and expressed their preference for group discussions rather than lectures in a workshop setting. This preference could have minimised possible trepidation about participating in the PLC discussions.

Once the data was collected, an in-depth data analysis was conducted that involved coding and identifying themes and patterns (Cohen, Manion & Morrison, 2018) that would answer the research question:

> What does teacher talk, that takes place in PLCs that focus on inclusive pedagogy, reveal about teacher professional identity and agency?

The conceptual framework provided the lens to ascertain where teachers' discussion of inclusive pedagogy indicated incidences of teacher professional identity and agency. The analysis began with reading the PLC transcripts, followed by a second reading in conjunction with listening to the audio recordings to identify any significant nuances in meaning.

A limitation of the study was the inability to identify the different speakers in the PLCs. Therefore, the extracts presented here delineate the different speakers with 'T' (for teacher) and a numeral to denote the number of teachers speaking in that extract.

Findings

The PLCs provided an environment where teachers could share experiences, challenge perceptions, and indicate their engagement with inclusive practices. The opportunity to discuss their practice via their stories enabled teachers to deliberately engage their identities through enacting inclusive pedagogy. They grappled with what it means to be an inclusive teacher in the South African context.

Teacher Professional Identity: I am not an inclusive educator

Though teachers do not self-identify as inclusive teachers, they display characteristics of inclusive teachers. Teacher talk shows their identity as concerned with all learners, caring teachers and as life-long learners (Pantić & Florian, 2015). These roles reflect the Principles of the IPAA.

IPAA Principle 1: Concern for all learners

Teachers see their role as extending beyond teaching to concern for the learners' well-being beyond the school. They discuss learners' home circumstances, sharing information about how this impacts the learners' behaviour and achievements. They consider how to engage with guardians and parents. In Session 8 teachers were presented with sentence starters and were required to define a full-service school with inclusive teachers.

T1 *Our school is different from other kinds of schools… .*
T2 *so we can write about their disability … mentioning barriers…those other ones, that we know they're struggling. When we do lesson planning, we have to lower the grade; the standard of their learning so as to suit all of those learners. Right?*

T1 states a common understanding about where they belong. "Our school" aligns to a goal of their school and their role as teachers. Perceptions about "disability" and "barriers" lead teachers to conceive that when dealing with such learners, they will plan their lesson with lower standards than the curriculum requires. The teachers align themselves with their school and they show concern for their learners by imagining what will suit the learners who experience barriers to learning. However, this engagement and apparent misunderstanding about differentiation suggests that teachers may need deeper knowledge to enable them perceive themselves as inclusive teachers.

IPAA principle 2: Teachers' capability and self-perception

When teachers create and share images of the world, they make connections across time and space by extrapolating beyond their own experience. Imagination transcends the teachers' current realities and is rooted in sharing experiences and interactions. Imagination offers another way for the individual and the community to construct reality and an identity. However, imagination also invokes the possibility of "losing touch with a sense of efficacy by which our experience of the world can be interpreted as competence" (Wenger, 1998, p. 175).

Even when teachers described their ability to teach learners with diverse abilities, they chose to not acknowledge themselves as inclusive educators. Their perspective on inclusive education is primarily regarding barriers to learning.

T3 *An inclusive teacher is different from the teachers because*
T4 *they're specially trained*
   [Teachers murmur in agreement]
T4 *they're specially trained for inclusive education.*
T3 *Which makes it easier for them to also identify these learners.*

The teachers do not self-identify as inclusive teachers even though they teach learners with disabilities. Their notion of an inclusive teacher is one who "easily" identifies learners with barriers, underlining an obvious disconnect between themselves and who they believe is an inclusive teacher – one that is specially trained. This disconnect between their current practice with learners, their type of school and their belief in their ability to teach is emphasised when they request the university team to give them tips on how to teach. One teacher requests a member of the university team to instruct them on how to teach:

T3 *You know, I've become a bit worried. Are you also going to help us with some of the ways that we can use to help these learners in the class, because most of the time it's like us, us, us talking and you are not giving us any development [chuckles] or something.*

Teachers have differing perceptions of themselves as teachers based on their beliefs about what it means to be teachers (Vähäsantanen, 2015; Lasky, 2005). Some teachers focussed on educating students or teaching their subject, while others were more oriented towards their own skill deficiencies, and yet others were keen on collaboration through shared experiences and mutual learning. Teachers do understand that their role in school is reflected in their talk about themselves.

IPAA principle 3: Teachers as life-long learners

Engagement in Wenger's (1998) modes of identity relates to practice and an individual's direct experience and competence or incompetence in the practice. Teachers negotiate meaning through shared histories of learning and active involvement with practice and community relationships. Engagement considers current realities as a vital start to achieving purposeful ends. It enables teachers to jointly establish and define the meaning of their activities. With engagement, teachers create a shared reality within which they can act and construct their identities.

When the project began, teachers discussed the meaning of each word of the PLC. They identified that working in small groups – that is, the PLC groups – was better than workshops because the groups made learning personal. The teachers noted that workshops did not encourage participation.

T1 *In a big group I can relax and not participate*
T2 *Small groups are good because you feel encouraged. Even though you're sitting with challenges you get ideas from others.*

The anonymity in workshops means teachers do not need to work. However, this relaxation is not a good thing because teachers do want support for the challenges they experience. Sharing in a small group provides helpful ideas, where teachers learn from others who willingly share knowledge and experience.

Teacher professional agency: It works for me

Teacher agency is a present-time decision-making process, built on past experiences. It considers how an act would impact the future. As an initiative taken in the present and in a social setting, agency invites accountability from members. A common expression in the PLC sessions was "It worked for me", which captures teachers' professional agency for inclusion. The statement encapsulated their purposiveness, especially in their response to problematic situations (Biesta & Tedder, 2007).

IPAA principle 1: Teaching all learners

Teachers create and show meaning through decision making; teacher talk reflects options being weighed and choices being considered. Choices may be determined between personal and group agreement and disagreement. Pantić and Florian (2015) found that when teachers are committed to social justice, they go the extra mile to accommodate all learners; they develop competencies in inclusive pedagogical approaches, including working under unfavourable conditions; and they make a difference.

When a teacher experiences difficulties in teaching some learners and requests assistance, this implies that she/he can teach all learners but needs help to learn how to do so.

T1 *What works for me to support those learners I really want to support, I have to do group work.*

Teachers' agency reflects their self-perception as pedagogical experts who have the capability to intentionally and responsibly manage new learning situations (Toom, Pyhältö & Rust, 2015). Even if the situation primarily affords that teacher control of learners, the teacher's decision is focused on helping learners meaningfully engage with their learning.

Teacher agency in inclusive settings is a negotiated practice between assessment requirements and teachers' concerns about learners (Li & Ruppar, 2020). Teachers concerned about annual assessments may view differentiation as "downgrading" the standards for those learners who experience barriers to learning. Teachers are keen to keep "standards" but are also concerned about their schools' assessment. Accommodating learners' individual needs while maintaining overall assessment frameworks can be difficult.

Teacher professional agency influences learner achievement. Teachers spoke confidently about their ability to help learners succeed. When they imagined their learners' success, teacher talk revealed their control over decision making. Teachers make meaningful decisions by considering a learner's abilities vis-à-vis classroom management. By challenging bell-curve thinking, teachers were encouraged to find innovative ways of teaching.

IPAA principle 2: Teaching with confidence

The ease with which teachers felt they could apply a teaching practice is significant. Through sharing what works, teachers indicated how they adapt time-management strategies and content-delivery methods. Teachers express confidence when relating what works in their classrooms. Even when seeking assistance regarding strategies that could work for them, they believe in their capacity to implement these strategies, which worked for other colleagues. During critiques or professional disagreements regarding a shared practice, teachers' confidence about their strategy's success demonstrates belief in their ability to teach all learners. Successful strategies benefit both teachers and learners. When learners are working well, teachers feel fulfilled regarding the efficacy of their teaching.

T3: *I become very happy when I see them in action doing whatever that I instructed them to do. So to me it works because I can see they are all taking their pencils, they are all getting down to write, they all raise up their hands, 'Ma'am I'm done. Ma'am, I'm done.' So for me it works.*

Taking initiative is determined by asking questions to identify problems and opportunities that enable teachers to learn new skills. Preceding action, teachers consider whether actions align with their personal beliefs, values and goals, and whether fellow teachers encourage the initiative. Taking initiative to create meaningful classroom experiences is considered in light of the current circumstances, including any difficulties a teacher could be facing.

In a session on cooperative learning held in year two, teachers discuss how to use a strategy after they have watched a video.

T1 *Now if the school doesn't have worksheets for each and every child we can still improvise and put one worksheet there ...*
T3 *We need to improvise, come up with new stuff, at the same time use our own hands and everything, our creativity. That's very good Ma'am. Learner respect each every member's contribution to the group...*
T4 *Ja, I wish we had time for that. You know sometimes, because there's so much to do, this co-operative learning's sometimes going to be difficult... .*
T5 *It's not easy to do it because you want attention, you want this, this must happen, so when have co-operative it's not, it's not easy like you want...it's not that easy as in the books.*
T2 *Ja, it's not easy but I think it goes back to, don't you think Ma'am it goes back to a subject that you are teacher? For instance Life Skills*

T1 *Ja, that's true. It may depend on the subject.*
T3 *and the topic, themes and also the number of the class also contributes, because maybe with a small group in class you can achieve this, you see.*

Teachers are keen to try out the strategy and realise they need to be creative about how to enact the practice. However, they also must contend with practical difficulties that arise: class size, time to complete a topic, material resources.

Teachers talk about enacting inclusive pedagogy was linked to particular topics of the PLC, the form of engagement, and other teachers' reported successes. When teachers were provided with specific practices, e.g. whole body listening and think-pair-share, in subsequent sessions they reported how they had enacted the practice. Some PLC sessions had deep discussions and divergent views, with teachers indicating their considerations afterward. The intense discussions in Session Ten about bell-curve thinking were recalled in Session 11 with further intensity. Bell-curve challenged existing narratives about learning, and teachers were driven to reflect on how they spoke about themselves and what they do. Teachers' professional identities are sometimes challenged when they are expected to venture into new ways of teaching. Teachers' responses to such challenges can indicate whether they have shifted their professional identity and agency.

Constraints to enacting inclusion were both personal and structural. A "fixed mind-set" about learners and bell-curve thinking were personal beliefs that inhibited inclusive pedagogical practice. The quick-paced curriculum and assessment requirements also constrained inclusive practice.

IPAA principle 3: Accountability in learning together

Asking accountability questions enabled teachers to gauge the group's commitment to a shared goal and to seek approval for the intended action. Accountability questions also indicate a teacher's shift from being a victim of circumstances, to not blaming others, including learners, for action and inaction. Accountability also indicates teachers' belief in their capacity to try new ways of teaching

In discussing learners' different abilities, teachers critique the ways the learners are only considered from an academic achievement standpoint:

T1 ... *if we are doing that we are, we are killing their confidence*
T2 *Yes, yes. Sometimes a learner is good in sports*
T1 *So it is important to give them time*
T3 *A chance*

In this excerpt the teachers challenge a teacher's impatience with a learner who is only considered as being good at sports. They urge different ways to help the learner. The teacher is held accountable for his/her perspective of the learner and encouraged to be patient. This is an inclusivity perspective, with the teachers offering suggestions to consider the abilities of all learners rather than sidelining one learner who apparently finds it difficult to keep up with the others.

Teachers note that bell-curve thinking also keeps learners in interventions that may be problematic:

T5 *I've got a learner there who, who always for intervention by the psychologist. She's not good in writing, not good in reading, but when I'm doing the other activities .... She's good ...*
T1 *these are the, the problematic results of bell curve thinking. We make judgment about what some learner can and cannot do.*
Some teachers: *Ja*
T2 *We, we limit learning*
T7 *Like now that one, maybe we are, we are limiting her learning by saying she can't.*
T5 *what I'm trying to say is that you can't judge that person ... .*
There's no person that you can judge him or her as bad ...
T4 *An no, no child is born blank.*

These teachers' critique of psychological interventions may be an example of miscommunication with other professionals about what the child needs. However, their concerns indicate they are interested in pedagogical responses to children who may not be achieving at the same level as other learners.

Speaking about what is successful in the classroom affirms teacher self-perception. When ideas from PLC meetings appear to be relatively easy to practice and incorporate into the classroom, teachers are more likely to take initiative and discuss how they would use the "tip". Teachers share what they believe they can do. Teacher professional agency for inclusion is conditional, but can be positively exercised within professional learning environments where teachers have autonomy to deliberate what enables or constrains their agency towards a particular action.

Discussion: Productive dissonance

Professional learning that does not give teachers opportunities to "story" their own learning may merely encourage the outward rhetoric of a proposed pedagogy (Graven, 2012). Sfard and Prusak's (2005) *Identity as Narrative* provides a further lens to explain teachers' identity through the stories they tell about themselves regarding inclusive pedagogy. These stories are reifying, significant and endorsable (Sfard & Prussak, 2005). They reify their identity by saying that they are teaching all learners. They make their stories significant by defining the features of their practices and defending the practices with, "It worked for me". The endorsement of the identity is the agreement by members of the community with the storyteller's account.

The teachers' stories identify them as being inclusive educators because their stories also show their practice has pertinent features of inclusivity. Learning could be about bridging the gap between saying one is not an inclusive teacher – the current identity – to saying, I am an inclusive teacher – the designated identity. While holding these seemingly disconnected stories, the teachers still meaningfully engaged in the PLCs. Because the teachers say they are not inclusive teachers they are willing to learn. Even though the teachers judged themselves as not-inclusive teachers, they talk about achieving success with practicing inclusive strategies. This is productive dissonance.

Productive dissonances have been recorded of teachers in inclusive schools (Naraian and Schlessinger, 2018; Florian & Spratt, 2013). Teachers may experience dissonance in their identity between their perception of what it means to be inclusive after teacher education and what is actually required of them in practice at school. Some teachers may negotiate with their school what practice they choose to enact as being inclusive, rather than what the school defines as inclusive (Florian & Spratt, 2013). For other teachers the dissonance is in "agentive maneuverings" (Naraian & Schlessinger, 2018), where teachers make choices by mediating their practical-evaluative dimension of agency – the present – with the professional roles expected of them at school. The exercise of agency was determined by context and teachers chose different enactments based on context rather than only on their identity as inclusive teachers (Naraian and Schlessinger, 2018). The dissonance between identity and agency talk generate "productive dissonances" that could transform professional learning for inclusive pedagogy. If dissonances are allowed to co-exist without being resolved to only one way of practice, teachers could develop creative practices applicable to their peculiar classroom situations.

Teachers' conceptualisation of inclusion limits their practice. It is problematic to consider inclusion as only about identifying barriers to learning. Additionally, when teachers view their role towards learners who experience barriers to learning as "charity", they are unlikely to see themselves as inclusive educators. The medical and charity perspectives on inclusive education, rooted in teachers' beliefs and assumptions, have been a longstanding concern and need to be addressed in professional learning (Symeonidou & Phtiaka, 2009).

The productive dissonance finding further dents the binary perspective about inclusion (Woodcock & Hardy, 2017b). Teachers are not either inclusive or not inclusive. Teachers at "City Primary School" are "trapped between two conflicting identities" (Graven, 2012, p. 18). They are in a full-service school and therefore are expected to be inclusive teachers but do not consider themselves inclusive teachers because they are "not trained". This gap needs to be reconceptualised because:

> [a] perceived persistent gap between actual and designated identities … is likely to generate a sense of unhappiness.… As implied by the common wisdom that "success begets success and failure begets failure" stories of victories and losses have a particular tendency toward self-perpetuation.
> (Sfard & Prussak, 2005, p18)

The seeming contradiction identified in this study provides an insight on how to develop professional teacher education for inclusion. I propose a re-authoring of teacher professional identity and agency for inclusion. Agreeing with Graven (2012), I suggest that teacher educators need to narrate teachers' current identities as experienced teachers, who have some inclusive practices. This acknowledges the value of teachers' present practices, knowledge and experience. Both teachers and teacher educators agree that increased knowledge and skills are necessary to meet ever-changing classroom dynamics. Therefore, the teachers' designated identities would be as lifelong learners who are willing to learn and self-identify as inclusive educators.

Pedagogy and identifying barriers are seemingly contradictory enactments of inclusion. Due to a dearth of detailed special education lessons in their initial teacher education and in professional learning, teachers do not self-identify as inclusive educators. However, the discussions of inclusive pedagogy in the PLCs indicate that they still exercised pedagogical agency and found ways to teach all learners in their classrooms. As considerate teachers with the desire to teach all their learners, the teachers resolved a purposiveness about their professional identity.

Teachers need to be involved in developing professional learning programmes. The frequently cited complaint about teacher learning programmes offered at the end of the school day needs to be taken seriously. PLCs need to be embedded in the school practice and therefore the school needs to reorganise the school day to allow teachers to meet regularly for their own learning. Seeing teachers as learners and producers of knowledge and not mere receivers of knowledge would change notions that teachers need more "training". This requires acknowledging that teachers have knowledge, skills and experience and are best placed to give meaningful feedback on curriculum and teaching practices, including in the context of professional learning (Graven, 2012). Wenger's (1998) conceptualisation of identity as becoming paints teachers as objects in the identity construction – what is being done to them. Combining Wenger's (1998) concepts of imagination, alignment and engagement, with Sfard and Prussak's (2005) narrative as identity, teachers are the subject of their identity construction – it is what *they* are doing and saying. Teachers construct their identity by authoring their imagination, their alignment and their engagement. In becoming (Wenger, 1998), teachers author their "designated identities" (Sfard & Prussak, 2005). When learning programmes value teachers' experiences, there could be a more realistic construction of practice. This could generate teachers' buy-in, since expectations of teachers would be based on cooperation. Additionally, if teachers are aware of their current and designated identities, their involvement could foster greater buy-in and creative solutions. Grounding programmes on teachers' existing knowledge and experience can be a fruitful base for further learning (Graven, 2012).

Conclusion

Teacher talk in PLCs revealed that even though teachers enacted inclusive pedagogy, they did not self-identify as inclusive educators. They were confident with sharing the classroom practices they had successfully used to teach learners with diverse abilities but did not consider themselves inclusive educators, since the latter have had special education training to "manage learners with special needs" (PLC 8). Because they had not had "special education training", they did not acknowledge themselves as inclusive educators. This productive dissonance is meaningful for professional learning.

Teacher educators need to appreciate the biographical histories and traditions that teachers bring into a professional learning programme and help them become conscious of values and beliefs that inform their teaching. Teachers would record their everyday experiences in the classroom and share interpretations of their practice in PLCs as a conscious identity renegotiation. A conscious reshaping of teachers' normative assumptions about learners and learning through such "identity projects" would help teachers view the "reciprocal dance in which they influence and are influenced" by their classroom enactments (Waitoller & Kozleski, 2010).

The findings of this study also contribute a conceptual understanding of the interplay between teachers' professional identity and the sociocultural contexts of PLCs and how teacher talk mediates teacher learning for inclusive education. The teachers in this study made choices aligned with their working conditions and constraints, for systemic and personal reasons. This study addresses the "well-worn complaint" about "untrained", "insufficiently trained" and "more training required" conclusions reached by studies on inclusive education with questions. If teachers *are* inclusive in their practice but do not perceive themselves as inclusive educators, what kind of professional learning do they require? Even where teachers have had special education training they still appear to grapple with inclusion (Naraian & Schlessinger, 2018; Woodcock & Hardy, 2017a).

Teacher identity and agency require integrated approaches of both sociocultural and critical perspectives which acknowledge teachers' inherent empowerment and so provide a discursive environment. Such approaches could also disentangle the bifurcation of inclusion and special education from a social justice standpoint. The "productive dissonances" arising from the gap between identity talk and agency talk could transform professional learning for inclusive pedagogy, with teachers developing creative practices suitable for their unique situations. If the tension is considered productive, it invites wide-ranging possibilities. The desire for, and expectation of, certainty when challenges arise can be misleading. The resolution may lie outside the current construction of learning.

Professional learning that values teachers' voice and experience encourages connections between teachers. Teacher-driven PLCs recognise teachers' professionalism and value their insights, providing a platform for teachers to express and develop the capacity to act purposefully and constructively for their own learning and for their learners.

Implementing inclusive education is an onerous and sometimes vague undertaking. Inclusive classrooms can sometimes appear to be "*a mess*" (Teacher, PLC #5). The term inclusive education denotes many things; it is large and wide. Therefore, collaboration and community cannot be overemphasised (Walton et al., 2019). When inclusion is presented as an approach, such as the IPAA, teachers may not perceive inclusion as an impossible ask or an individual teacher's burden, but a practice in collaboration with colleagues.

References

Biesta, G., & Tedder, M. (2007). Agency and learning in the lifecourse: Towards an ecological perspective. *Studies in the Education of Adults, 39*(2), 132–149. https://doi.org/10.1080/02660830.2007.11661545

Black-Hawkins, K., & Florian, L. (2012). Classroom teachers' craft knowledge of their inclusive practice. *Teachers and Teaching, 18*(5), 567–584.

Borko, H. (2004). Professional development and teacher learning: Mapping the terrain. *Educational Researcher, 33*(8), 3–15.

Chauraya, M. (2016). The importance of identity in a teacher professional learning community. *Professional learning communities in South African schools and teacher education programmes*, 196–213.

Cohen, L., Manion, L., & Morrison, K. (2018). *Research methods in education* (8th ed.). Oxon: Routledge.

DBE. (2009). *Guidelines for full-service/inclusive schools*. Pretoria: Department of Basic Education.

Deppeler, J. (2010) Professional learning as collaborative inquiry: Working together for impact. In C. Forlin, (Ed), *Teacher education for inclusion. Changing paradigms and innovative approaches* (pp. 180–188). Abingdon, UK: Routledge.

Eteläpelto, A., Vähäsantanen, K., Hökkä, P., & Paloniemi, S. (2014). Identity and agency in professional learning. In *International handbook of research in professional and practice-based learning* pp. 645–672. The Netherlands: Springer.

Florian, L., & Spratt, J. (2013). Enacting inclusion: a framework for interrogating inclusive practice. *European Journal of Special Needs Education*, 28:2, 119–135. https://doi.org/10.1080/08856257.2013.778111

Graven, M. (2012). Changing the story: Teacher education through re-authoring their narratives. In C. Day (ed.), *The routledge international handbook of teacher and school development* (pp. 127–138). Abingdon, UK: Routledge.

Lasky, S. (2005). A sociocultural approach to understanding teacher identity, agency and professional vulnerability in a context of secondary school reform. *Teaching and Teacher Education, 21*(8), 899–916.

Lave, J. (1991). Situating learning in communities of practice. In L. B. Resnick, J. M. Levine, & S. D. Teasley (Eds.), *Perspectives in socially shared cognition* (pp. 63–82). Washington, DC: American Psychological Association.

Lave, J. (2009). The practice of learning. In K. Illeris (Ed.), *Contemporary theories of learning: learning theorists… in their own words*. (pp. 200–208). New York: Routledge.

Li, L., & Ruppar, A. (2020). Conceptualizing Teacher Agency for Inclusive Education: A Systematic and International Review. *Teacher Education and Special Education: The Journal of the Teacher Education Division of the Council for Exceptional Children*. https://doi.org/10.1177/0888406420926976

Lyons, W. E., Thompson, S. A., & Timmons, V. (2016). 'We are inclusive. We are a team. Let's just do it': commitment, collective efficacy, and agency in four inclusive schools. *International Journal of Inclusive Education, 20*(8), 889–907.

Materechera, E. K. (2020). Inclusive education: why it poses a dilemma to some teachers. *International Journal of Inclusive Education, 24*(7), 771–786.

Naraian, S., & Schlessinger, S. (2018). Becoming an inclusive educator: Agentive maneuverings in collaboratively taught classrooms. *Teaching and Teacher Education, 71*, 179–189. https://doi.org/10.1016/j.tate.2017.12.012

Pantić, N., & Florian, L. (2015). Developing teachers as agents of inclusion and social Justice. *Education Inquiry, 6*(3), 27311. https://doi.org/10.3402/edui.v6.27311

Priestley, M., Biesta, G., & Robinson, S. (2016). *Teacher agency: An ecological approach.* London: Bloomsbury Academic.

Sfard, A., & Prusak, A. (2005). Telling identities: In search of an analytic tool for investigating learning as a culturally shaped activity. *Educational Researcher, 34*(4), 14–22. https://doi.org/10.3102/0013189X034004014

Swart, E., & Oswald, M. (2008). How teachers navigate their learning in developing inclusive learning communities. *Education as change, 12*(2), 91–108.

Symeonidou, S., & Phtiaka, H. (2009). Using teachers' prior knowledge, attitudes and beliefs to develop in-service teacher education courses for inclusion. *Teaching and Teacher Education, 25*(4), 543–550.

Timperley, H. S. (2011). *Realizing the power of professional learning.* UK: McGraw-Hill Education.

Toom, A., Pyhältö, K., & Rust, F. O. C. (2015). Teachers' professional agency in contradictory times. *Teachers and Teaching, 21*(6), 615–623.

Vähäsantanen, K. (2015). Professional agency in the stream of change: Understanding educational change and teachers' professional identities. *Teaching and Teacher Education, 47*, 1–12.

Waitoller, F. & Kozleski, E. (2010). Inclusive professional learning schools. In C. Forlin (Ed) *Teacher education for inclusion: changing paradigms and innovative approaches* (pp. 65–73). Abingdon, UK: Routledge.

Walton, E., Carrington, S., Saggers, B., Edwards, C., & Kimani, W. (2019). What matters in learning communities for inclusive education: a cross-case analysis. *Professional development in education, 2019*, 1–15.

Walton, E. & Moonsamy, S. (Eds.) (2015). *Making education inclusive.* Newcastle upon Tyne: Cambridge Scholars.

Walton, E., Nel, N. M., Muller, H., & Lebeloane, O. (2014). 'You can train us until we are blue in our faces, we are still going to struggle': Teacher professional learning in a full-service school. *Education as Change, 18*(2), 319–333.

Wenger, E. (1998). *Communities of practice: learning, meaning, and identity.* Cambridge, UK: Cambridge University Press.

Wenger, E. (2010). Communities of practice and social learning systems: the career of a concept. In C. Blackmore (Ed.), *Social learning systems and communities of practice* (pp. 179–198). London, UK: Springer.

Woodcock, S., & Hardy, I. (2017a). Probing and problematizing teacher professional development for inclusion. *International Journal of Educational Research, 83*, 43–54.

Woodcock, S. & Hardy, I. (2017b). Beyond the binary: rethinking teachers' understandings of and engagement with inclusion. *International Journal of Inclusive Education, 21*(6), 667–686. https://doi.org/10.1080/13603116.2016.1251501

10
LOCALIZING A UNIVERSAL CLAIM

Applying universal design strategies to support inclusion in Armenia

Armenuhi Avagyan, Christopher Johnstone, Ofelia Asatryan, Lilia Khachatryan, and Aleksandr Shagafyan

Introduction

Architect Ron Mace first coined the term "Universal Design" to describe a philosophy and approach to structural design that was intended to promote accessibility for all humans. Mace's perspectives came from his own experience as a wheelchair user, but his focus was explicitly *not* on persons with disabilities alone. Rather, Mace posited that "Universal design is the design of products and environments to be usable by all people, to the greatest extent possible, without the need for adaptation or specialized design" (Center for Universal Design, 2008). Connell et al. (1997) further operationalized Universal Design by providing a series of principles to which architects could adhere in order to promote accessibility in the built environment and avoid costly retrofitting at later stages. Connell et al.'s principles included: 1) Equitable Use; 2) Flexibility in Use; 3) Simple and Intuitive Use; 4) Perceptible Information; 5) Tolerance for Error; 6) Low Physical Effort; and 7) Size and Space for Approach and Use.

The Universal Design Principles proposed by Center for Universal Design (1997) provided practical and philosophical guidance to architects seeking to promote accessibility but did not have the rigidity of specific codes such as those outlined in disability accessibility laws in the United States. While Mace and others agreed that such laws were imperative to set minimum standards for disability accessibility, the Universal Design Principles were published in an effort to provide a general framework for design that allowed for flexibility based on the local context, artistic vision, and functional needs of the specific environment.

The core philosophies found in the Universal Design Principles inspired researchers in other fields to examine how accessibility could be promoted through processes of forethought, design thinking, concern for all end users, and consideration for human differences. In the 1990s, scholars in the field of education began

DOI: 10.4324/9781003091950-12

to examine how Universal Design could be used in the field of education. In its early days, educationists used the terms Universal Design for Instruction (UDI) (Orkwis & McLane, 1998; Scott, McGuire, & Shaw, 2003). Later, the term Universal Design for Learning (UDL) (Rose & Meyer, 2002) came to describe the process of enhancing accessibility for all learners in inclusive classrooms and based on the assumption that learning occurs as a result of interactions between all members of classroom communities and its resources. In time, UDL became the terminology most commonly used by scholars and practitioners because of its holistic focus on the teaching and learning process.

Similar to the Center for Universal Design's Principles of Universal Design, the Center for Applied Special Technologies (CAST) originally provided three simple guidelines for UDL: 1) Multiple means of engagement; 2) Multiple means of representation; and 3) Facilitating multiple means of action and expression (CAST, 2018a). In time, a series of nine "Checkpoints" developed as indicators of the original three guidelines to support teacher thinking and classroom-based activity (CAST, 2018b). Version 2 of CAST's guidelines foregrounded education that was engaging and active, rather than simply relying on an original conception of student "response" in classrooms that was an original consideration of UDL (Rose & Meyer, 2002). CAST's updated guidelines include student goals, which aim for students to be 1) purposeful and motivated in learning (through engagement), 2) resourceful and knowledgeable (through representation), and 3) strategic and goal directed (through action and expression) (CAST, 2018a).

UDL provided a framework for new research and was frequently employed as a strategy enhancing the engagement and learning of students with disabilities (King-Sears, 2009; Pisha & Coyne, 2001; Hitchcock & Stahl, 2003). Throughout the early 2000s and 2010s, UDL began to be seen as means for supporting flexibility in lesson planning (Spooner, Baker, Harris, Ahlgrim-Delzell, & Browder, 2007) in order to enhance accessibility for all learners, including those with disabilities. CAST's guidelines, similar to the Center for Universal Design's principles, encouraged localization of implementation and the discretion of the designer (in this case, teachers) to create classroom environments that were accessible in nature.

The UDL 'revolution' inspired educators to think about lesson plans as a design project and as a mechanism for enhancing accessibility for diverse learners. Strong case evidence exists related to student engagement through UDL (Dalton & Proctor, 2007; Rose, Hasselbring, Stahl, & Zabala, 2005; Dolan, Hall, Banerjee, Chun, & Strangman, 2005), but scaled-up experimental designs are difficult given the flexibility of UDL. By its very nature, UDL is designed to be localized to the classroom level and responsive to the particular learning needs of the children in a given classroom.

This chapter aims to further consider localization of UDL, expand case knowledge of UDL pedagogies and investigate the 'universality' of universal design. In the following sections we present a contextualized case example of how commitments to accessibility and inclusion often align with principles of UDL but can be applied in diverse ways. Following, we present the case of Ofelia, a teacher in Yerevan, and describe how she creates an accessible environment for students. Her activities align well with UDL principles, but reflect the cultural ways of knowing, resource opportunities and constraints, and national curriculum of her Armenian classroom. We therefore argue that UDL need not be a replication of CAST's original vision but can provide a set of core inclusionary commitments that can be interpreted and implemented to fit specific settings.

Review of global literature: UDL

There are seemingly endless options for UDL in global education environments. However, the vast majority of UDL studies have shared two commonalities. First, most studies have taken place in the United States, which has a unique context of policy, teacher autonomy, and the availability of particular resources. Related to this, nearly all of the studies cited in the preceding sections employed some form of digital technology to support classroom learning. Recently, however, UDL has become a topic of interest in relation to global education, with potential localized applications for different contexts around the world (Hayes, Turnbull, & Moran, 2018; Johnstone, 2014). Hayes et al.'s (2018) and Johnstone, Avagyan, & Marutyan (2019) contributions provide an overview of UDL concepts and applications in classrooms with diverse levels of access to digital technology, but only cite a few case examples. The following section provides readers with an overview of other studies of UDL in a variety of national contexts.

We share these global examples not to imply that the word "universal" in UDL should be read as uniformity of implementation across settings or even classrooms. Such a purpose would be impossible and contrary to the spirit of UDL guidelines. Rather, the purpose of this chapter is to report on how UDL can be implemented in a setting outside of its origin. In this study, we use classroom case evidence from Armenia to add new context to existing knowledge on UDL. Our purpose is not to prove whether or not UDL is effective by any normative categories, but rather to provide comparative insights into how UDL can be implemented in a completely different context than how it was originally conceived.

As stated previously, there is scant but emerging evidence from outside of the United States related to Universal Design for Learning. Recent research points to both the importance of flexibility of the guidelines as well as opportunities for teachers to be empowered to make changes in their own classrooms. In Canada, for example, "the UDL framework allowed [teachers] to address various students' needs, provide options, and plan on overcoming barriers in instruction and assessment through intentional planning" (Lowrey, Hollingshead, Howery, and Bishop, 2017, p. 230). Further, Dalton, McKenzie, and Kahonde (2012) introduced a group of teachers and therapists to the main concepts of UDL in a workshop in the Republic of South Africa. An evaluation of the workshop found that teachers felt that UDL's guidelines aligned well with South Africa's national policy on inclusive education and the opportunities and constraints presented in South Africa's classrooms, but the evaluation did not follow up on its implementation in classrooms.

Alternatively, Mavrou and Symeonidou (2014) conducted a qualitative analysis of the New National Curriculum (NNC) in Greek-Cypriot schools in Cyprus. The authors concluded that the NNC states a commitment to inclusive education, but that the goals of the curriculum were inflexible and did not allow for variation or differentiation based on students' diverse needs. Using UDL as an evaluative and analytic framework, Mavrou and Symeonidou concluded that the curriculum does not allow for multiple means of representation, action, expression, or engagement, and therefore may not be as inclusive as purported. In their conclusions, Mavrou and Symeonidou proposed that UDL might be used as a framework to enhance the inclusiveness of the NNC and act as a starting point to empower teachers to develop more inclusive classrooms.

The potential global nature of UDL has also been documented in postsecondary settings in Australia and Belgium. Hitch, Macfarlane, and Nihil (2015), for example, found that 32% of Australian higher education institutions claimed to be implementing UDL in their instructional practice. A closer look at practice, however, revealed that professional development workshops mainly focused on learning accommodations for specific groups of students. Individualized accommodations are part of a broader rights-based framework of inclusive education, but the ultimate goal of a UDL–informed framework is accessible practices for all students (Schwanke, Smith, & Edyburn, 2001). Hitch et al. critiqued the purported inclusiveness of higher education practice in Australia, noting that such inclusiveness was only focused on accommodating "other" students who are not deemed as part of the norm in Australia (i.e., Aboriginal, international, or having a disability), avoiding approaches to change higher education systems for greater accessibility. Hitch et al. proposed a UDL framework that allowed instructors to define and incorporate accessibility into an overall framework of effective teaching and learning for all students.

Finally, Griful-Freixenet, Struyven, Verstichele, and Andries (2017) interviewed Flemish university students with disabilities in order to understand the students' perspectives on best teaching practices for postsecondary education. The authors found that student perspectives often aligned with UDL guidelines, but specific teaching ideas often contradicted one another. Specifically, strategies that benefit one student might create a barrier for another. In such circumstances, Griful-Freixenet et al. suggest that UDL is a helpful framework for facilitating accessibility, but that instructors must be vigilant in asking students questions about ways to continually enhance accessibility in the classroom. Unlike Universal Design in the built environment, lessons and their requisite activities change daily, meaning that how UDL is implemented may have differential impacts on students. Griful-Freixenet's contribution to the UDL literature is the addition of student questioning for design purposes. Such questions align with universal design concepts of "end user" feedback (Johnstone, Altman, & Moore, 2011) and may further support the contextualization of UDL across educational and national boundaries (see also Johnstone, Avagyan, & Marutyan, 2019).

Methods

The methodology for this paper was adapted from two distinct qualitative methods – qualitative single case studies (Creswell, 2012) and Most Significant Change evaluation techniques (Davies & Dart, 2005). These methods informed the practical data collection for a larger non-governmental organization project focused on enhancing inclusive education in Armenia. The single case study of a classroom in Yerevan was the main source of data for this paper. Over several months, two of the authors of this paper participated – as researcher and teacher – in a series of observations and interviews related to classroom accessibility. These interviews led to a series of small monographs which highlighted the most significant change (Davies & Dart, 2005) experienced in the classroom, according to the teacher. These monographs were then reviewed a second time by all authors to identify relevant themes that might inform the way that UDL is understood in global contexts.

Policy context

Inclusive education is, by definition, aimed at improving educational opportunities and outcomes for all children. Within the context of Armenia, however, children with disabilities have faced historic exclusions through either segregated schooling (a Soviet-era practice for children with moderate to significant disabilities in urban areas) or exclusion from school (rural children with disabilities have remained at home due to lack of infrastructure and exclusionary policies in schools). Since the 1990s, however, Armenia has adopted several important policies, both international and national, that contributed to the expansion of inclusive education policies and practices in the country. Armenia ratified the UN Convention on the Rights of the Child (CRC) in 1992, the Inclusive Education Concept Paper was adopted in 2005, and the UN Convention on the Rights of Persons with Disabilities (CRPD) was ratified in 2010 (Tichás, Abery, Johnstone, Poghosyan, & Hunt, 2018). Finally, Article 55 of Armenia's 2015 Education Law stated that

> Learners aged 6,5 years and older, having been admitted to the first year at schools of general education from 2001 to 2005 inclusive, as well as in 2006, shall continue their education under educational programmes approved for the eleven-year secondary school of general education".
>
> (Republic of Armenia, 2015)

The new law paved the way for teacher development and classroom-based activities focused on inclusion and accessibility for all students. One such classroom is the subject of this study. Details of the study are provided in the following paragraphs.

Key informant

As noted, this study examines the activities of one teacher – Ofelia – who is a history teacher based in a Yerevan public secondary school. Although Ofelia's classrooms had always had learners with diverse learning needs and preferences, Ofelia's teaching shifted in 2016 when she was introduced to accessibility guidelines similar to those in the UDL guidelines. Her new strategies were put to the test when Ofelia's class included a child with a significant hearing impairment. The combination of reflection on accessibility and enhanced understanding of student diversity led Ofelia to make changes to her lessons, which will be reported in the findings section.

Procedures

The study draws upon the collection of lessons through a series of observations and self-reflection over the course of one academic year in a Yerevan-based secondary school where Ofelia Asatryan teaches. The data were collected as part of a larger initiative from the project 'Strategies for Inclusion – Making history and citizenship education more inclusive and accessible' led by European Association of History Educators (EUROCLIO) in partnership with Armenian Center for Democratic Education (Armenian-CIVITAS) and aimed at supporting the implementation of inclusive education strategies in schools. Original data were collected in a collaborative process with Avagyan, and Asatryan taking notes on specific strategies that were attempted in her classroom, the rationale behind the strategy, and observed impacts.

Analysis

A secondary analysis was then conducted on the written reflections and highlights that emerged from the project. The secondary qualitative analysis was conducted by an international team of researchers who deductively read and coded the products generated from the project described above in search of specific themes related to UDL and its applications in Armenia. The analysis used an adapted Most Significant Change (Davies & Dart, 2005) framework by re-examining stories selected at the local level. In Davies' and Dart's evaluative framework, organizational representatives evaluate locally generated stories for significance to the organization. In this adapted method, the local and international authorship team of researchers examined themes for significance related to how UDL is enacted globally and locally.

Findings

In the following paragraphs, we present four pedagogical strategies employed by Ofelia, followed by a short discussion on each strategy that relates strategies back to CAST's guidelines on UDL. The following paragraphs present a synopsis of field notes taken by Avagyan, discussed with Asatryan.

The Kingdom of Van

When Ofelia teaches about the 6th-century Van kingdom, she makes two PowerPoint slide decks in advance. These decks contain pictures of historical events, important people, symbols of the era, and representations of historical concepts. Each picture has a description that describes the picture and the historical concept it represents. For each slide, Ofelia follows each slide that has a picture and description with a second slide that has the same picture as the previous slide, but no description. When Ofelia shows the second slide, she asks students to select one of three cards that potentially describe the event, person, or symbol. Only one of the three cards holds an accurate description of the picture. Students place their selected answer card on the blackboard. Ofelia quickly assesses student answers. She makes a mental note about which students understand and do not understand the concept, then removes incorrect notes from the board. If a particular student answers incorrectly, she asks students for an "alternative answer" but never says that an answer is "wrong." Although Ofelia may technically tell students they are wrong if they select the wrong card, she is careful to tell students to select a new answer. In this case, mastery may take two or three tries, but can always be reached (Avagyan, 2017a).

In her "slides" lesson Ofelia presents her material in different ways (with and without text); uses a creative way of supporting students to respond (through selecting cards with correct answers and assessing student choices); and keeps students engaged in class through the scaffolding of description of events (first with, then without text), through kinesthetic movement to the board, and through emotionally supportive responses such as searching for "alternative answers" rather than telling student they are ever "wrong." In sum, Ofelia engages her students. The visual and kinesthetic classroom activities are supportive to all children but were reported to be particularly supportive of a child with a significant hearing impairment in Ofelia's classroom.[1] In this lesson, UDL appears to be at work in a way that is unique to the resource and pedagogic context of Armenia.

The color of victory

In order to facilitate comprehension of reading passages, Ofelia created a set of activities that utilized colored pencils to help students make connections between historical concepts. During this activity, Ofelia asks her students to read their textbooks in small groups. As students read, they underline important passages using colors that correspond with particular emotions that students feel when they read about a historical event. Ofelia introduces these emotions using gestures (e.g., pride, sadness, etc.). Each emotion has a corresponding color.

For example, when describing victory, Ofelia pointed to the color red, which was associated with happiness and positive emotion. If defeat was in the paragraph, the student used a dark grey pencil that symbolized tragedy as an important event and sadness as an emotion. When the book described peace, the student pointed to a blue pencil, which symbolizes peace as a historical event, and spiritual harmony as an emotion. For homework, Ofelia assigns students to read the topic at home and to highlight each paragraph with a pencil having the relevant emotional color that students choose, thus showing what historical event it is about, and what emotion is connected to it. This gives Ofelia an opportunity to figure out how the students comprehend and engages their emotional intelligence in order to process historical events. She can check for understanding just by scanning the student's book in the classroom.

As the class worked through the book and pencil activity, Ofelia discovered that not all students had the same emotional reactions to events and responded differently to historical events. For example, one student suggested that red is "the color of blood" and not associated with either victory or happiness. In time, Ofelia allowed students to use colors that they selected, provided they gave a rationale for why color was selected and what a particular color represents (Avagyan, 2017b).

Ofelia presented information in this lesson through a typical textbook but allowed for student response through underlining text in color. This particular response limited writing requirements, was highly visual in nature, and allowed for students who used speech and sign language to communicate equally through symbolic color responses to the text. If there was a child who experienced visual difficulties or colorblindness, Ofelia may have adjusted activities accordingly.

Ofelia facilitated student engagement by allowing students to respond to historical events emotionally. At first, Ofelia standardized how students used colors to express emotions, but later allowed students to deviate from original instructions as long as they could justify a response. UDL examples from high-income countries often involve the use of digital technologies to enhance accessibility. In this case, Ofelia provided a flexible means of student communication and a high engagement activity through the use of colored pencils. In this case, UDL guidelines provided an overall framework for the lesson, but culturally specific activities such as understanding students' emotional reactions to history demonstrated that the specific pedagogies used may vary greatly across contexts. Ofelia's example provides evidence that customization of UDL guidelines can occur within particular national, cultural, or resource contexts. Ofelia found the use of colors helps students organize their work and tells students that their color coding is a process of "arranging the paragraphs in the appropriate shelves" (Avagyan, 2017b, p. 2).

Not your mother's quiz

Ofelia uses quizzes as a way of engaging students and checking for understanding. Typically, quizzes are understood as individualized assessments in which students answer questions and submit papers to the teacher. Recent innovations in educational technologies have allowed for students to take assessments with audio components (i.e., students can listen to test questions being read by an automated screen reader) (Johnstone, Higgins, & Fedorchak, 2019). No such technologies, however, are available in Ofelia's class. Rather, Ofelia creates quizzes with an audio representation that she reads herself. The result is an audio administration that allows students to both read the words of the quiz on paper and hear them read by Ofelia. Further, Ofelia attempts to enhance engagement (UDL Guideline 3) in her class by allowing students to answer in a participatory manner. When Ofelia reads a quiz question, students respond by holding up one of four cards that say A, B, C, or D and correspond to answer choices (for further discussion on the research behind response cards, see Cavanaugh, Heward, & Donelson, 1996). After students respond, Ofelia scans the room for correct and incorrect answers. If she notices students answering incorrectly, she will provide information on the test item to the entire class, and never identify which students answered correctly or incorrectly. Such a response style is an alternative representation style that allows for kinesthetic activity and further allows for students with different communication needs to participate in class activities equally.

Ofelia uses these "quizzes" as an informal assessment. She keeps mental notes and quietly jots down the names of students who consistently answer quiz questions incorrectly. She later meets with these students and provides supplemental tutoring as needed. Although Ofelia notes that she would prefer a tablet or other digital technology for this activity, her focus on accessibility aligns well with general UDL guidelines and provides case evidence that such guidelines can be implemented in ways that are appropriate to school context (Avagyan, 2017c).

Multi-sensory groups

Group work is a relatively standard approach to enhancing student engagement in classrooms worldwide. Often students attempt to solve a problem or discuss an issue and report back to the whole class on their results. In order to ensure that all students could participate and benefit from discussions, Ofelia added an additional component to her group work. Johnson and Johnson (1999) suggest assigning roles to students in cooperative groups like facilitator, timekeeper, etc. Based on the demographics of her classroom, Ofelia decided that an additional necessary role would be a "drawer." The drawer (or illustrator) added to group activities by creating visual representations of the assignment at hand. The role served two purposes. It first provided one student, who was a gifted artist but had communication challenges with her classmates, with an opportunity to use her strengths in class (Avagyan, 2017d). The illustrator role also allowed students in other groups to have an additional means of representation or material and response to group discussions. In this case, Ofelia added the simple additional element of drawing to group projects in order to facilitate additional means of representation, response, and engagement.

Discussion

In many ways, Ofelia's approach to UDL exemplifies how concepts created in one context, like UDL, can be useful in other contexts only if they are adapted in ways that are meaningful to the end user. As noted, UDL principles emerged in the United States with a high reliance on digital technologies to help reduce participation and achievement barriers. Ofelia demonstrated that the most important elements in UDL for low-technology applications are a commitment to accessibility and lesson design that follows. In each lesson reviewed here, Ofelia carefully designed lesson plans with curricular prototypes for representation, response, and engagement. She used her own informal action research data collection to understand how students were responding to lessons and for providing further support to those who were not.

For this reason, more research is needed in comparative studies of inclusive education on how UDL is adapted and transformed. UDL has become shorthand for classroom accessibility and now terms such as "universal usability" are being used to keep the focus of accessibility on students themselves (Edyburn, 2021). As greater numbers of global organizations begin to advocate for UDL usage as a focal area (Hayes et al., 2018), further investigation is needed on how UDL is useful for teachers in inclusive classrooms, in specific contexts. Nearly two decades ago Phillips and Ochs (2003) predicted that once policy interactions occurred across national lines, a predictable pattern of decision making, implementation, and internalization would occur in countries that are "attracted" to approaches from other nations. We hope to point out through this data that UDL should not create a standardized set of rules that should dictate how teachers engage with students, but rather create a set of core ideals about accessibility and inclusion that can be enacted in agentic and localized ways by teachers (Ball, 2008).

Armenia has a relatively new policy on inclusive education and teachers are just beginning to find ways to promote accessibility in the classroom. The circumstances for Armenia are similar to several countries in Central and Eastern Europe. Inclusive education is being implemented through policy change and the day-to-day work of teachers. One strategy being used by teachers is to embrace UDL guidelines in lesson planning. The adaptability of UDL has made it attractive to teachers like Ofelia, but there is little research on its effectiveness.

In this chapter, we argue that it is nearly impossible to evaluate the effectiveness of UDL guidelines because they are not linked to a specific set of pedagogies. There is no feasible way to examine UDL on a large scale because the guidelines themselves are reliant on the day-to-day decision making of teachers and their understanding of the accessibility needs in their classrooms. This is not to say that teachers cannot use evidence-based practices as part of the UDL planning process. Such usage would likely enhance the pedagogical power of UDL's implementation (Hayes et al., 2018). However, how teachers interpret and utilize UDL is highly contextualized in terms of national education environment, cultural understandings of what "learning" means, and resource considerations. Because of this, one way to better understand UDL is through localized case studies.

In this study, Ofelia provided an important finding related to the global transferability of UDL. A common thread throughout all of the examples shared in this chapter was that Ofelia purposefully planned activities that provided equal access to her students. Ofelia's class was heterogeneous in terms of the way that they could receive and respond to curricular information. Rather than create lesson plans aimed at presumed homogeneous children and reliance on specialist support for those who did not fit normative expectations, Ofelia found a way (through creative visualization, alternative means of artistic and kinesthetic response, and engaging students' emotional response to content) to create a classroom where every child had an opportunity to participate and succeed.

In this case, UDL is not a replication of a pedagogical approach that could be tested for fidelity to its original conceptualization. Rather, UDL was merely a framework for helping Ofelia to organize and design her lessons for accessibility that made sense for her students, within her context, and in relation to her own philosophies about teaching. As comparative education scholars begin to examine how UDL will be applied in global settings, Ofelia's examples provide important guideposts.

To this end, there are important considerations we feel we must mention in relation to global education organizations. Ofelia's example shows us that there may be inherent danger in low-level "training" for teachers to do UDL. An excellent example of this from a different setting is Song's (2015) findings about teachers in Cambodia who were trained in child-friendly schools but ended up implementing in superficial ways because they never fully reflected on underlying purposes of child-friendly pedagogies. One-off or shallow training may actually undercut core principles of design that appeared to be the most important elements that guided Ofelia's teaching. Specifically, UDL appeared to work in Ofelia's classroom because she knew the curriculum, she knew the children well, and she knew what resources she could and could not employ. This example of UDL in Armenia demonstrates that teachers can be exposed to UDL guidelines, but from there need to be the key architects who design lessons. The reason for this is that no other individual will fully understand the strengths, complexity, or overall ecosystemic conditions of a classroom than the teacher. Such a conclusion places great responsibility on teachers but acknowledges that inclusive education is a systemic initiative (not an individualized initiative for children with special education needs). National policies, resource considerations, and classroom dynamics will impact the system of inclusion in individual classrooms. Providing teachers with general UDL guidelines and principles, then supporting the hyper-local design, innovation, prototyping, and revisions may support the development of inclusive classrooms that are culturally relevant to teachers and students and not simply an ill-fitting replication of a foreign educational concept.

Further work related to UDL and teacher autonomy, phronesis (Florian & Graham, 2014), enactment (Ball, 2008) and other teacher-focused theories may inform this work. Further, we recommend that further research on UDL be conducted either with single cases, such as Ofelia, to demonstrate how a single teacher makes sense and promotes accessibility in a way that is hyper-local (classroom level, within municipal and national systems). In this way, the universality of Universal Design for Learning could be viewed as a metaphorical constellation of stars who teach and promote accessibility in ways that make sense in localities rather than a set of standards to be replicated across settings.

Note

1 Readers should note that the child has residual hearing and speech, and does not use sign language to communicate.

References

Avagyan, A. (2017a). *The use of matching exercises to assess the internalization of notions.* The Hague: European Association of History Educators. Retrieved from: https://euroclio.eu/resource/the-use-of-matching-exercises/

Avagyan, A. (2017b). *"Match!": Making a connection between concepts and symbols in an entertaining manner.* The Hague: European Association of History Educators. Retrieved from: https://euroclio.eu/resource/match-making-connection/

Avagyan, A. (2017c). *Silent learning: The use of quizzes to motivate and assess participation in the classroom.* The Hague: European Association of History Educators. Retrieved from: https://euroclio.eu/resource/silent-learning-the-use-of-quizzes/

Avagyan, A. (2017d). *Silent learning: The use of small-group learning and sharing to ensure full participation in the classroom.* The Hague: European Association of History Educators. Retrieved from: https://euroclio.eu/resource/silent-learning-the-use-of-small-group-learning/

Ball, S.J. (2008). *The education debate.* London: Policy Press

Cavanaugh, R. A., Heward, W. L., & Donelson, F. (1996). Effects of response cards during lesson closure on the academic performance of secondary students in an earth science course. *Journal of Applied Behavior Analysis, 29*(3), 403–406.

Center for Applied Special Technology (CAST) (2018a). *Universal design for learning guidelines version 2.2 [graphic organizer].* Wakefield, MA: Author.

Center for Applied Special Technology (CAST) (2018b). *Universal design for learning guidelines version 2.* Wakefield, MA: Author. Retrieved from http://udlguidelines.cast.org

Center for Universal Design (2008). *About UD.* Wakefield, MA: Author. Retrieved from: https://projects.ncsu.edu/design/cud/about_ud/about_ud.htm

Connell, B.R.; Jones, M.; Mace, R.; Mueller, J.; Mullick, A.; Ostroff, E.; Sanford, J.; Steinfeld, E.; Story, M.; & Vanderheiden, G. (1997). *The principles of universal design.* Raleigh, NC: Center for Universal Design, North Carolina State University. Retrieved from: https://projects.ncsu.edu/design/cud/about_ud/udprinciplestext.htm

Creswell, J. (2012). *Qualitative inquiry and research design: Choosing among five approaches* (3rd ed.). Thousand Oaks, CA: Sage.

Dalton, E. M., McKenzie, J. A., & Kahonde, C. (2012). The implementation of inclusive education in South Africa: Reflections arising from a workshop for teachers and therapists to introduce Universal Design for Learning. *African Journal of Disability, 1*(1), 1–7.

Dalton, B., & Proctor, C. P. (2007). Reading as thinking: Integrating strategy instruction in a universally designed digital literacy environment. In D.S. McNamara (Ed.). *Reading comprehension strategies: Theories, interventions, and technologies,* 423–442. New York: Psychology Press.

Davies, R., & Dart, J. (2005). *The 'most significant change'(MSC) technique. A guide to its use.* London: CARE International.

Dolan, R., Hall, T. E., Banerjee, M., Chun, E., & Strangman, N. (2005). Applying principles of universal design to test delivery: The effect of computer-based read-aloud on test performance of high school students with learning disabilities. *The Journal of Technology, Learning and Assessment, 3*(7).

Edyburn, D. (2021). Ten years later: Would you recognize Universal Design for Learning if you saw it? *Intervention in School and Clinic, 56*(5), 308–309.

Florian, L., & Graham, A. (2014). Can an expanded interpretation of phronesis support teacher professional development for inclusion?. *Cambridge Journal of Education*, *44*(4), 465–478.

Griful-Freixenet, J., Struyven, K., Verstichele, M., & Andries, C. (2017). Higher education students with disabilities speaking out: Perceived barriers and opportunities of the Universal Design for Learning framework. *Disability & Society*, *32*(10), 1627–1649.

Hayes, A., Turnbull, A., and Moran, N. (2018). *Universal design for learning to help all children read*. (First Edition). Washington, D.C.: USAID. Retrieved from: https://www.edu-links.org/sites/default/files/media/file/Literacy%20for%20All%20toolkit_v4.1_0.pdf

Hitch, D., Macfarlane, S., & Nihill, C. (2015). Inclusive pedagogy in Australian universities: A review of current policies and professional development activities. *International journal of the first year in higher education*, *6*(1), 135–145.

Hitchcock, C., & Stahl, S. (2003). Assistive technology, Universal Design, Universal Design For Learning: Improved learning opportunities. *Journal of Special Education Technology*, *18*(4), 45–52.

Johnson, D. W., & Johnson, R. T. (1999). Making cooperative learning work. *Theory into Practice*, *38*(2), 67–73.

Johnstone, C.J. (2014). *Access to school and the learning environment II: Universal design for learning*. New York: UNICEF. Retrieved from: http://www.inclusiveeducation.org/sites/default/files/uploads/booklets/IE_Webinar_Booklet_11.pdf.

Johnstone, C.J., Altman, J.R. & Moore, M. (2011). Universal design and the use of cognitive labs. In M. Russell and M. Kavanaugh (Eds.). *Assessing students in the margins* (pp. 425–442). Charlotte, NC: Information Age Publishing.

Johnstone, C.J., Avagyan, A., & Marutyan, M. (2019). Universal design for learning. In Tichá, R., Abery, B., Johnstone, C., Poghosyan, A., & Hunt, P. (Eds.). *Inclusive education strategies: A textbook*. Minneapolis, MN, USA: University of Minnesota; Yerevan, Armenia: UNICEF Armenia & Armenian State Pedagogical University.

Johnstone, C., Higgins, J., & Fedorchak, G. (2019). Assessment in an era of accessibility: Evaluating rules for scripting audio representation of test items. *British Journal of Education Technology*, *50*(2), 806–818.

King-Sears, M. (2009). Universal Design for Learning: Technology and pedagogy. *Learning Disability Quarterly*, *32*(4), 199–201.

Lowrey, K.A., Hollingshead, A., Howery, K., & Bishop, J.B. (2017). More than one way: Stories of UDL and inclusive classrooms. *Research and Practice for Persons with Severe Disabilities*, *42*(4), 225–242

Mavrou, K. & Symeonidou, S. (2014). Employing the principles of universal design for learning to deconstruct the Greek-Cypriot new national curriculum. *International Journal of Inclusive Education*, *18*(9), 918–933.

Orkwis, R., & McLane, K. (1998). *A curriculum every student can use: Design principles for student access*. Washington, DC: ERIC/US Department of Education Office of Special Education Programs Topical Brief.

Phillips, D., & Ochs, K. (2003). Processes of policy borrowing in education: Some explanatory and analytical devices. *Comparative Education*, *39*(4), 451–461.

Pisha, B., & Coyne, P. (2001). Smart from the start: The promise of Universal Design for Learning. *Remedial and Special Education*, *22*(4), 197–203.

Republic of Armenia (2015). *Law of the republic of Armenia: Official translation*. Yerevan: Ministry of Justice of the Republic of Armenia. Retrieved from: http://www.anqa.am/en/about-us/legal-field/laws/law-of-the-republic-of-armenia-on-education/

Rose, D. H., Hasselbring, T. S., Stahl, S., & Zabala, J. (2005). Assistive technology and universal design for learning: Two sides of the same coin. In D. Edyburn, K. Higgins, & R. Boone (Eds.). *Handbook of special education technology research and practice*, pp. 507–518. Whitefish: Knowledge By Design Publishers.

Rose, D. H., & Meyer, A. (2002). *Teaching every student in the digital age: Universal Design for Learning*. Alexandria, VA: Association for Supervision and Curriculum Development.

Schwanke, T.D., Smith, R.O., & Edyburn, D.L. (2001). A3 model diagram developed accessibility and universal design instructional tool. *RESNA Annual Conference Proceedings, 21*. Washington, DC: RESNA Press.

Scott, S. S., McGuire, J. M., & Shaw, S. F. (2003). Universal Design for Instruction: A new paradigm for adult instruction in postsecondary education. *Remedial and Special Education, 24*(6), 369–379.

Song, S. (2015). Cambodian teachers' responses to child-centered instructional policies: A mismatch between beliefs and practices. *Teaching and Teacher Education, 50*, 36–45.

Spooner, F., Baker, J. N., Harris, A. A., Ahlgrim-Delzell, L., & Browder, D. M. (2007). Effects of training in universal design for learning on lesson plan development. *Remedial and Special education, 28*(2), 108–116.

Tichá, R., Abery, B., Johnstone, C., Poghosyan, A., & Hunt, P. (Eds.) (2018). *Inclusive education strategies: A textbook*. Minneapolis, MN, USA: University of Minnesota; Yerevan, Armenia: UNICEF Armenia & Armenian State Pedagogical University.

United Nations (n.d.). *Fact sheet: Inclusive education in Armenia*. Yerevan: UNICEF Armenia. Retrieved from: https://www.un.am/up/library/Inclusive%20Education_eng.pdf.

11
CRITICAL REFLEXIVITY AS A PEDAGOGY FOR INCLUSIVITY IN TEACHER EDUCATION

Levan Lim and Thana Thaver

Introduction

The significance of reflexivity is undeniable in our diverse world. Our 21st-century world order of global interconnections and ceaseless change have accelerated the interface, intermixing and intermingling of people from diverse nations and cultures to the point that the cultural identities of societies, communities and individuals across the globe are incessantly subjected to the process of change and transformation, thereby rendering them dynamic, fluid and negotiable. This universal characteristic and condition of our global context has vastly reinforced the notion that the world we live in and its gamut of identities and differences, which are in themselves changing and re-emerging in new forms, mixtures and hybrids, are not to be taken as a given or for granted but are being constantly constructed and reconstructed. It is no wonder that when it comes to understanding how people consider themselves in relation to their social contexts to make sense and respond to rapid change and diversity, reflexive deliberations that allow the filtering of personal subjectivities that can influence and shape human responses to others is an imperative in our current global context (Archer, 2010, 2012).

This reflexive imperative has become a normative requirement in phenomenological approaches to doing qualitative and ethnographic research across many fields in the social sciences and education (e.g., Dean, 2017; Lazard & McAvoy, 2020; May & Perry, 2011) where the ethics of not practicing reflexivity can raise questions about the integrity and credibility of the research process and subsequent findings. With regards to the professional practice and development of personnel in fields or disciplines apart from anthropology and its closely related field of sociology, the concept of reflexivity has been adopted and emphasized to different extents in fields across the social sciences, education and management at the tertiary higher education level and in their respective professional industry-based practices.

DOI: 10.4324/9781003091950-13

Fields of study that have incorporated the concept of reflexivity or critical reflexivity (to emphasize its critical dimension though all reflexivity involves a level of criticality; hence these two terms are used interchangeably in this chapter) demonstrate evidence of the adoption of this concept within their disciplinary content and discourse to enhance personnel professionalism through the questioning of their own epistemic knowledge base and assumptions underpinning normative practices. These fields include social work (e.g., D'Cruz, Gillingham & Melendez, 2007; Houston, 2015; Watts, 2019), occupational therapy (e.g., Kinsella & Whiteford, 2009; Phelan, 2011), medicine and health professions (e.g., Ingrassia, 2011; Ng, Wright & Kuper, 2019; Setchell & Dalziel, 2019) and management education (e.g., Barge, 2007; Cunliffe, 2002, 2004, 2009; Hibbert & Cunliffe, 2015; Maclean, Harvey & Chia, 2012).

While there is an emerging body of literature within teacher education on the role of reflexivity in shaping the epistemology of teacher development and practice (e.g., Brownlee, Ferguson & Ryan, 2017; Cole & Knowles, 2000; Feucht, Brownlee & Schraw, 2017; Hofer, 2017), critical reflexivity has yet to gain a foothold within teacher education concerning the preparation of teachers for inclusive education or inclusivity. A review of the literature in teacher education revealed only a few applications of critical reflexivity in fostering teachers to be more inclusive of diverse students (e.g., Bentley-Williams & Morgan, 2013; Bentley-Williams, Grima-Farrell, Long & Laws, 2016). These studies showed that by engaging pre-service teachers in reflexive learning to deepen their own understanding of themselves and others by considering the influence of biographical real-life experiences, questioning their own assumptions and actions, and having professional discourses about inclusive education while engaging in situated learning experiences, the pre-service teachers were able to develop themselves personally and professionally as inclusive practitioners.

The purpose of this chapter is to introduce relevant literature on (critical) reflexivity drawn from various fields of study to define and illuminate its meanings and functions, its elements and features, and its significance and relevance to the professional growth, development and practice of personnel involved in inclusive education. This chapter also describes how critical reflexivity and its various elements can be weaved as a pedagogical practice within teacher education for the professional development of teachers to become more inclusive practitioners.

Critical reflexivity

The concept of reflexivity in modern times has its foundations in the social psychology of George Herbert Mead, who studied the social processes for the formation of the human individual. In his writings, such as *Mind, Self, and Society*, which was published posthumously in 1934, he emphasized the social nature of the formation of the individual through regular interaction with others and declared that "the individual mind can exist only in relation to other minds with shared meanings" (Miller, 1982, p. 5). Mead recognized reflexivity – the turning back of the experience of the person upon oneself – as the essential condition, within the social process, for the formation of a person's mind and self (Mead, 1934; Salzman, 2002; Strauss, 1956) since "there is no knowledge of the world that is not a knowledge of our experience of it and in relationship to it" (Goulder, 1970, p. 28).

In the decades that followed, the concept of reflexivity has become more prominent, in varying degrees, across fields in the social sciences. In the field of anthropology in particular, encounters between persons from different cultures highlight the requisite role of reflexivity in cautioning the observer to be aware of interpretive bias, the bidirectionality of influence between the observer and the observed, and personal subjectivities in reading and responding to the external world. Anthropological encounters therefore rely on reflexivity to achieve a greater objectivity in understanding others through a higher subjectivity of how one forms knowledge about others. This accounts for why reflexive understanding and hermeneutic mediation of what is observed and how it is interpreted are vital in the field of anthropology (Nazaruk, 2011; Scholte, 1972, Salzman, 2002).

According to Scholte (1972), the emphasis on reflexivity in anthropology represents a paradigm shift from the objectivist, value-neutral scientific approach to an interpretive, hermeneutic approach that values the 'perspectivist' perceptions and subjective emic meanings held by those who are observed rather than a primary reliance on interpretations by the observer. In the encounter and interaction between individuals, reflexivity also plays a pivotal role in mediating the interactions between the subjectivities of individuals (i.e., human inter-subjectivity – a term coined by Fabian, 1971). In such interactions where individuals are reflexively turning back the experience with others upon self in order to gain an awareness of the influence of personal subjectivities on relating with the other, they are actually engaged in the process of (re)constituting new meanings and views of the other person.

The work of Donald Schön has contributed enormously to many fields, including teacher education, for professionals to become reflective practitioners (Schön, 1983). In fact, reflection is a cornerstone of teacher education where Schön's differentiation of reflection into reflection-on-action (a retrospective evaluation of past action), reflection-in-action (constructing an understanding of a situation while in it), and reflection-for-action (to inform on improvements in future actions) comprise fundamental standard practice for teachers to learn from processing experience and gain insights into one's practices for future improvements. Pedagogical strategies such as problem-based learning, action learning/research, the use of self-assessment questionnaires and case studies are common examples in teacher education where reflection is routinely used as a pedagogical process to enhance reflective practice in teachers.

Reflexivity, while involving aspects of reflection, goes beyond reflection to the critical dimension of interrogating one's situatedness within the sociocultural and historical conditions that have influenced the construction of knowledge, values, assumptions and perspectives. Reflexivity extends beyond reflection to invite the self to 'bend back' to recognize and see more clearly one's own position in the world so that one can understand the limitations of one's knowing and appreciate the social realities of others (Ng et al., 2019). The process of engaging in reflexivity involves 'an unsettling' of long-held assumptions, discourses and practices to describe and relate to reality (Pollner, 1991). As noted in the literature reviewed across various fields, the prefix 'critical' is added to emphasize the element of critically appraising and accounting for how the self has been influenced and shaped by prevailing and dominant cultural practices and their discourses to imbibe (most often, unintended) certain values, assumptions, beliefs and perspectives from the contexts that one is embedded or situated in. Critical reflexivity asks us to think critically about the world and its ways that we accept and take for granted, and furthermore to recognize and claim our complicity and responsibility in (re)shaping our individual and collective mindsets and responses to (re)create the social structures and realities that we are a part of.

Critical reflexivity therefore involves the act of interrogating one's situatedness in society, history and culture to arrive at a critical awareness of how we have constructed knowledge out of our everyday learning experiences and interactions (which are linguistically mediated through oral and written language) as well as a greater consciousness of our own human agency in rethinking, reimagining and reshaping our values, beliefs, identities, aspirations and perspectives (Cunliffe, 2004; Ferguson, 2003; Ng et al., 2019; Phelan, 2011). In practicing critical reflexivity, the self is the site of learning, relearning and unlearning to deconstruct influences on one's personal biographical history and knowledge constructed through interaction with others, and to reconstruct new meanings and possibilities for self and others in relation with self.

Critical reflexivity draws from social constructivist theories that emphasize a critical subjective situated approach to understanding the influence of social interactions, interpersonal relations, and communication on learning (Bentley-Williams et al., 2016; Wilder-Bassett, 2005) and highlights the operation of power relations within interactions and relationships (Badwell, 2016; D'Cruz et al., 2007; Ng et al., 2019; Phelan, 2011); for example, in the relations between professionals and their clients or teachers and their students. Critical reflexivity is hence not just another technique but a philosophically driven approach and practice that recognizes and questions the informal ways of making sense and tacit knowledge generation that are embedded and situated within the experience of everyday life through conversations, interactions and relationships with others, upon which we construct and narrate our own accounts of our perceptions, judgments, actions, identities and relationships with others (Cunliffe, 2002, 2004).

The relevance of critical reflexivity to inclusive education

Critical reflexivity is relevant to inclusive education as it turns one's reflexive gaze back to interrogating one's situatedness within the sociocultural and historical conditions that contribute to and influence contemporary and dominant discourses surrounding equity, social justice, inclusion, exclusion, and the differential treatment of certain members of society (e.g., persons with disabilities). As pointed out by

Slee (2011), to discuss inclusion is to first examine and understand the phenomenon of exclusion as more complex than addressing unequal access and outcomes for certain groups of students. The act of dismantling exclusion involves the understanding that we live, act, and interact within politically charged and historically contingent sociocultural contexts where the dynamic flow, contestations and negotiation of meanings about being in the center or at the margins affect how inclusion and exclusion are constructed around difference (Waitoller & Artiles, 2013). In order to understand and renegotiate the margins that exclude certain members within society, it is necessary to engage with the complexity of local contexts and their own unique sociocultural and historical influences and legacies (Lim, Thaver & Strogilis, 2019).

It is acknowledged that inclusive education is situated within larger societal contexts with their own unique sociocultural *habitus* and sociohistorical legacies, but researchers in inclusive education have not sufficiently considered the influence of these contextual complexities on how inclusive education is construed, interpreted and implemented (Kozleski, Artiles & Waitoller, 2011; Lim et al., 2019). In reviewing the professional development literature about supporting teachers for inclusive education, Waitoller and Artiles (2013) recommend teachers need to understand local contextual forms of exclusion that are situated within historically evolving activity systems (i.e., contexts) through the meaning-making process they and their local members have constructed about difference. This self-interrogative and introspective process of scrutiny and exploration of how one's personal and professional forms of knowledge and sense making are linked with prior subjective life experiences arising from interactions in situated learning contexts provides an account of how one's subjective life biography is influenced by discursively construed social norms and values.

Critical reflexivity and human agency

In our dynamic and rapidly changing global context foregrounded by uncertainty, complexity and a multiplicity of differences, relativism has de-centered traditional authorities and universal dogmas in defining and governing moral and ethical behavior to the onus of the individual. In such a social climate where reality is constantly being constituted and reconstituted through our individual and collective actions, what is highlighted is that we all have a potential agentive capability through reflexivity (Kögler, 2017) in changing the world for the better by living the axiom (attributed to Mahatma Gandhi) to 'be the change you want to see in the world'. Critical reflexivity therefore reinforces the idea that professionals in the social sciences are also moral practitioners (Cunliffe, 2004) who deal with a wide variety of situation-specific ethical issues in their practice, which require a constant reassessment of one's judgments and responses and whether they align with one's moral values and ethical position.

The potential moral agency within us that can be activated through critical reflexivity offers an opportunity to expand existing conceptual boundaries of inclusive education by exploring a new space to refresh and reconsider in educational thinking and practice within the field – i.e., the site of self – for developing personal and professional capabilities in assessing the conditions we find ourselves in and responding in morally desirable actions with others that correspond with one's ethical position. This new direction is an outgrowth of problematizing the currency of inclusive education as the application of universal rules by stakeholders to transform education systems to become inclusive through policies, guidelines and indexes, regardless of context-specific characteristics and variables (Lim et al., 2019).

Ethical and moral behaviors and positions regarding social justice, equity, inclusion, exclusion and differential treatment cannot merely result from the application of universal rules and guidelines subscribing to the translation of inclusive education across contexts. Rather, ethical goals and decisions are made in response to our self-reflexive interrogations to question our own stances or positions on issues that are situation-specific and which can be influenced by socially mediated values, beliefs, assumptions and perspectives. Critical reflexivity is of particular relevance in helping professionals to consciously clarify and shape their own ethical decisions and responses in a relativistic social world, and therefore can be leveraged upon newer disciplines and fields of study, such as inclusive education, for enhancing professional development and practice.

Reflexivity and the dialogical self

According to Archer (2007), reflexivity enables individuals to filter their own personal subjectivities that can influence and shape their responses and actions with others. This personal capability for reflexivity occurs through internal conversations within the dialogical self – a concept of the self as possessing a dynamic multiplicity of *I*-positions within an individual that can move from one position to another with changes in situation and time. The *I* can also move and shift among different and opposing positions and has the imaginative capacity to endow different positions with voices to enable dialogical relations between the positions. Hence, the *I* in one position can agree, disagree, oppose, understand the *I* in another position. The dialogical self is 'social' in that other persons can occupy positions in a multi-voiced self (Hermans, 2001, 2003). As described by Bakthin (1981), the dialogical self is polyphonic in that it speaks with a polyphony of many voices in co-existence.

This concept of the dialogical self is useful for framing reflexive deliberations as a dialogical multi-voiced process within the individual's internal conversations which is also susceptible to the influence of other people's voices. The dialogical self, with its imaginative capacity to bestow each *I*-position with a voice, is able then – through the sheer power of the imagination – to construe and more deeply understand the position of others through imaginatively occupying their position and also imagining the others occupying one's position. Learning about and responding to others through the reflexive dialogical process draws upon the power of the imagination to (re)construct new perspectives of how others and self may think and feel in relation to a particular situation.

Appadurai (1990) claimed that the world we live in ushers in a new role for the imagination in social life as "the imagination is now central to all forms of agency, is itself a social fact, and is the key component of the new global order" (p. 5). The role and value of the imagination, as harnessed in reflexive dialogical practice to re(constitute) the social world we live in, is therefore particularly relevant to enhancing the agentive capabilities of professionals across fields in the social sciences and education, including inclusive education (e.g., to deepen one's understanding of 'the other' in relation to self). Besides the role of the imagination in the reflexive process, the literature in reflexivity more recently has been emphasizing the role of emotions in our perceptions and responses (e.g., Burkitt, 2012; Holmes, 2010) and that emotions are central to reflexive processes.

The arising of feelings, no matter how negative or how vulnerable one can feel as a result, are a natural emergence of practicing self-reflexivity and are to be acknowledged as multiple voices of the *I*-positions of the dialogical self which can change due to interactions with other *I*-positions. Feelings or emotions can color and inform reflexivity as well as motivate or de-motivate human agency in (re) constructing new ways to respond to and relate with others and the social world. The combination of feelings with imagination within reflexive dialogical practice holds much potential in creating new embodied insights and perspectives in learning about and responding to oneself, others and the social world.

Weaving critical reflexivity into teacher education

Teacher education programs are crucial in developing epistemologies of inclusivity on the part of teachers in responding to differences in students and educational inequity. The use of critical reflexivity within teacher education carries the potential of encouraging deeper consciousness within teachers to question normative assumptions, challenge conventional thinking, realize the susceptibility of social structures and reality to transformation, and one's responsiveness to enact change. This section of the chapter describes how we, as teacher educators at the National Institute of Education in Singapore, weaved in elements of critical reflexivity into coursework to introduce pre-service and in-service teachers to working with students with disabilities.

Establishing a rationale for an exploratory 'space' for self

We first established a rationale and justification for adopting critical reflexivity as a pedagogy for inclusivity by recognizing the limitations of solely focusing on providing information on strategies on how to work with and include students with disabilities. This 'technicist' approach to equipping teachers with the knowledge and skills to work with students with disabilities has been demonstrated to be of limited impact in developing more favorable attitudes towards students with disabilities and their inclusion (e.g., Forlin & Chambers, 2011; Tait & Purdie, 2000). In addition to learning the knowledge and skills to be inclusive practitioners, we wanted our teachers to develop more inclusive values by first making visible and conscious their own values, beliefs and attitudes towards persons with disabilities.

We were therefore explicit in informing our students that we were offering them an exploratory 'space' to critically examine how they have been socialized throughout their lives in Singapore to perceive and relate to disability. The rationale used to explain to our teachers for the affordance of this exploratory space was that without the deliberate attempt to deconstruct their own baggage of values, beliefs and assumptions about disability and how these came about, it would be difficult to reconstruct new positions and ways of thinking about disability as well as generate new ideas, meanings and possibilities for the lives of persons with disabilities in Singapore. In other words, we clearly positioned the self as the site for educational learning and change in that the teachers were guided into a personal encounter with their own attitudes towards disability.

To facilitate the creation of a safe space for teachers to explore and interrogate their own experiences and attitudes towards disability, we conveyed that their learning journey in encountering themselves regarding their own values, beliefs, assumptions and perspectives concerning disability might be challenging, uncomfortable and evoke cognitive and emotional dissonance that can be unsettling, but that such feelings and thoughts are a natural and legitimate part of their learning trajectory. Understanding ahead that their learning trajectories would bring them to a place where learning can be confronting, uncomfortable, challenging and even confusing assisted the teachers' acceptance of their learning encounters with their own attitudes towards disability (which surfaced when teachers became aware of their reflexive subjective responses during class activities/discussions and the viewing of videos portraying the lives of persons with disabilities, which they noted in their reflection journals and shared in their individual assignments).

We asked the teachers to acknowledge and not judge and repudiate their own subjective thoughts and feelings (especially their negative ones) about disability, which they could keep to themselves and note in their journals. By doing so, we emphasized that they were holding space for and being inclusive of their own subjective thoughts and feelings including moments when they were struck by insights and spontaneous personal reactions, all of which offer important learning opportunities to be reflexive of self and self in relation with others. The act of acknowledging their own subjective thoughts and feelings was made possible through our explicit instruction for them to note and write in their journals their thoughts and feelings on what they were experiencing during class lectures, discussions, activities, and video presentations.

The subjective and situated biographical life-history

Critical reflexivity recognizes the role of contextual influences, the situatedness of learning in everyday life about social realities, and the subjective meanings and interpretations one forms in association with social realities. Any critique through reflexive inquiry is therefore situated in self, practices and context rather than abstract concepts and ideologies (Chia, 1996). Hence, the subjective thoughts and feelings related to teachers' experiences with disability accrued from their everyday lives of schooling, working and living in Singapore comprise legitimate funds of tacit knowledge that have influenced their values, beliefs, assumptions and attitudes about persons with disabilities. We mentioned to our teachers that they have somehow already been 'introduced' to disability through the crucible of their own informal learning histories, and therefore they needed to re-understand these funds of prior learning about disability.

To facilitate the reflexive engagement of individual teachers with their own relational experiences and sense making of disability as situated in their biographical life histories, we posed to our teachers questions which they reflected upon and shared with their peers, such as: (i) What images and thoughts come to your mind in association with the word 'disability'? (ii) Have daily or regular experiences afforded you the opportunity to meet and interact with persons with disabilities? (iii) Do you personally know anyone with a disability? (iv) If you do, how did you come to know this person? (v) If not, how did you learn about what you presently know about disability? What sources of information and learning have influenced your beliefs, images and ideas about people with disabilities? (vi) Where there have been moments of contact and/or interactions with persons with disabilities, what meanings did you construct in your mind about these individuals? and (vii) How do you think the public and media have portrayed persons with disabilities? How has that influenced your perceptions of people with disabilities?

How teachers responded to these questions (in their journals and dialogues in class) reflected their own personal life experiences with persons with disabilities (or lack of), and their espoused values, beliefs and meanings related to the experience of disability. We stated that it is entirely possible for a person who has never had the direct experience of interacting with any person with a disability to adopt certain ideas about people with disabilities based on 'second-hand' information gained through others and/or public/media images. Many teachers, having grown up in a dual system of education where students with and without disabilities were generally seen as belonging to separate systems of education – i.e., the mainstream and special education systems (Lim & Nam, 2000; Lim & Quah, 2004; Lim & Thaver, 2018) – recognized that without opportunities for regular direct interactions with peers with disabilities throughout their school years and working lives, they were influenced by dominant discourses that perpetuate negative beliefs and attitudes within society about disability.

For example, when teachers were asked to say what immediately came to mind (i.e., reflex responses) when the word 'disability' was mentioned and flashed on PowerPoint, many negative words and associations were shared even though many teachers admitted they had little or no direct personal experiences and relationships with persons with disabilities. The teachers were then requested to locate the sources of their negative images associated with disability as situated within their life experiences in Singapore society. Many of these negative images can be traced to informal discourse about disability within family and home settings, superstitions, cultural perceptions and beliefs, media images, charity television shows to raise funds for disability organizations, the absence of positive representations of persons with disabilities in the public sphere, and the pervasive lack of interactions and relationships between Singaporeans with and without disabilities in society.

Through an individual assignment which asked teachers to narrate their own biographical experiences with persons with disabilities (or the lack of) and how they have come to understand their own attitudes towards persons with disabilities and the sources of influence on how they have been 'introduced' to disability, the teachers were provided the platform to consciously interrogate their own sense making of disability as situated in their subjective biographical life experiences. This assignment assisted the teachers to explore and 'restory' in hindsight their personal biographies of how they saw disability through gaining a critical awareness and understanding of how society has constructed its position towards disability (e.g., institutional arrangements, dominant beliefs and assumptions) and how the self has participated through its own alignment with society's position.

Through this exploration and narration of their biographical histories, the teachers gained insight into how their subjective personal histories contributed to their own positions, comprising of their own values, beliefs and assumptions, towards disability. The teachers thus also learned about positionality (which is a significant feature of critical reflexivity) in terms of where they situated themselves in connection with persons with disabilities, which they learned through course lectures to recognize as 'the other' – someone whom they do not know, understand and experience, who poses questions that challenge and even contradict their way of knowing, assumptions and worldviews. More importantly, the teachers learned that by questioning and becoming conscious of their own assumptions and attitudes about disability, they realized that their own positions are not fixed or static but can be altered and changed in accordance with what they can imagine of themselves that resonates with new aspirations to become more inclusive of persons with disabilities.

Awareness and human agency

Interrogating the biographical formation of their own attitudes and sources of influence also facilitated teachers, as evident in class discussions, to become more aware of the social and institutional structures and conditions (as evident in the recollections of their schooling and educational experiences) that have contributed to their own attitudes. More importantly, they became aware of their own tacit complicity as members of society in taking for granted and assuming the normalcy of social and institutional structures and conditions that can contribute to exclusionary practices for students with disabilities (e.g., the dual system of education, the intense pressure to succeed academically in mainstream schools, high stakes examinations, and a strong emphasis on meritocracy in Singapore society).

Critical reflexivity is of particular relevance to arousing an awareness of self and a greater consciousness of one's implicit and complicit role and responsibility in social realities. We explained to teachers the example that an entire system (economic, cultural, political and education) can beckon and instill in teachers to think about children with disabilities as belonging to the special education system where special education schools are considered the best placement for their learning needs. That is, behind the personal and private thoughts, opinions, feelings, decisions and actions of ordinary citizens concerning persons with disabilities stands an entire system that manifests, expresses and maintains society's position towards them. These interconnections between the self and the social world were presented in a lecture in which we show the interrelatedness between the social and individual human actions, public knowledge (i.e., second-hand imbibed knowledge), personal practical knowledge (knowledge from lived experiences) and worldviews (Lim, Thaver & Slee, 2008).

This awareness can be unsettling (and it was the case for some teachers who expressed this during class discussions) because it clarifies that we all in society are, to a certain degree, complicit in participating in the social construction of disability in society. However, we highlighted that awareness can also be liberating in that one becomes aware of one's human agency that somehow, one can play a part, no matter how minor or small, indirectly or directly, to influence and affect the experience of disability in Singapore. To ignite the impetus for our teachers to consider their own human agency for change after gaining greater self-awareness, we included within their individual assignment a section on how they would pivot what they have learned in the course about inclusion into their future as educators. To guide the teachers in thinking about and imagining their aspirations as inclusive practitioners, we posed questions for them to reflect upon, such as (i) How would you like to grow, develop and evolve as an educator in the future? (ii) What would be your new emphases in your thinking and practice as an educator? and (iii) How would you like to (re)position and evolve yourself in your vision/mission/meanings of being an educator? The teachers were also given the opportunities to share their future aspirational thoughts and plans with their peers in a group sharing session towards the end of the course.

Another example of a class activity that was designed to provoke teachers to reconsider their positioning and agency on the part of our teachers in how they situated their connections with persons with disabilities was conducted with teachers to arrive at an understanding of the shared humanity between people with and without disabilities. In this activity, we asked our teachers to individually and collectively envision what a desirable quality of life for persons with disabilities would comprise of. After this exercise whereupon they would realize that a desirable quality of life for people with disabilities would be the same or similar with people without disabilities (e.g., inclusion in society, close relationships with family and friends, good health, a sense of belonging, etc.), the teachers were then asked to consider whether the status quo of society's position and attitudes towards persons with disabilities was aligned with supporting them to achieve a desirable quality of life (to which they would consistently respond with a negative reply) and to think about the barriers to an inclusive society for persons with disabilities.

The reconstruction of new meanings, positions and possibilities

A key tenet of critical reflexivity is that our knowledge is constructed and reconstructed through situated learning experiences and interactions with others and in the process taking note of the subjective thoughts and feelings that arise during learning activities. The deconstruction of contextual influences on one's biographical life history in relation to disability set the stage for us to then present new conceptions of disability and inclusion to our teachers upon which they could reconstruct new ideas, meanings and perspectives about disability and inclusion. We informed our teachers that they needed to interact with what they were learning by reflecting upon and writing in their journals their subjective thoughts and feelings in response to their learning (e.g., to lectures, course readings, questions, discussion, class activities and videos). Our teachers were also provided the opportunity to share and dialogue with their peers and lecturers their responses to what they were learning.

Once again, their personal subjective responses provided the funds of tacit knowledge upon which they were guided through class discussions to reconstruct new meanings, positions, and possibilities to consider in thinking about disability and inclusion. To facilitate teachers' reconstruction of new meanings and positions of themselves of educators for inclusion, we showed videos of positive local and international stories of the lives of persons with disabilities engaged in productive and fulfilling lives that were made possible through the support of educators and professionals as well as videos that highlighted how negative social attitudes can have deleterious impact upon the lives of persons with disabilities. Where possible at certain times, we also invited persons with disabilities to share their life stories and perspectives with our teachers followed by interactive conversations.

In addition to the first section of their individual assignment on their (past) biographical histories on how our teachers were socialized to think about and relate to disability in the Singapore context, and the third section which contained their (future) aspirational thoughts and plans to become inclusive educators, the middle or second section of their individual assignment asked for teachers to write about the (present) impact and influence of what they were currently learning during the course. To guide them in their reflections, we asked questions such as: (i) How have these learning experiences influenced your awareness, knowledge, understanding, insight, vision, meaning and purpose of your work as educators? and (ii) Which specific learning experiences were significant or meaningful to you? How were they significant and/or meaningful? (can be positive or negative or both); and (iii) How have these learning experiences influenced or impacted you? To work on this section on the impact of the course on them, the teachers drew themes from their journal reflections on how they responded in terms of their subjective thoughts and feelings to what they meaningfully experienced in their learning within situation-specific learning activities during the course (e.g., a particular class activity or watching a certain video).

The teachers' narrations of their learning journeys about disability and inclusion in the three parts of their individual assignment, comprising of the past, present and future, illustrated the process of reflexivity as occurring through internal conversations within the dialogical self where a dynamic multiplicity of interactive and fluid *I*-positions allows the negotiation *for* change to occur over time and space. As these *I*-positions within an individual are susceptible to the influence of other people's voices in the past (within their situated biographical experiences) and present (e.g., of lecturers and peers within dialogue class sessions and that of persons with disabilities as shown in videos or in person), we could see a shift in the dominant positions voiced by teachers towards disability and inclusion in their reflections across these three parts of their individual assignment.

Just like characters in a story, the voices of the *I*-positions across the three parts of the teachers' individual assignment are all parts of a complex narratively structured self and all have a story to tell of their own experience (Hermans, 2003), and therefore need to be acknowledged in the form of the subjective thoughts and feelings expressed by the teachers. The interactions with other voices of *I*-positions as influenced by conversations and learning activities with others (such as lecturers and course mates) encouraged and led teachers to new perspectives and possibilities in reconstructing alternative thoughts, feelings, responses and actions towards oneself and others (e.g., parents of students with disabilities whom they have interacted with before and held certain views about).

In taking note of the roles of the imagination and emotions in reflexive deliberations and motivating moral and ethical agency in teachers towards becoming more inclusive and empathetic practitioners, we were intentional in creating a safe space within our course for teachers to self-innovate through acknowledging the presence of the dialogical multi-voiced self within themselves. To facilitate the creation of a safe space within the course for teachers to engage with their dialogical self in arousing their consciousness of feelings, thoughts, judgments and responses to their relational experience of disability, as narrated and witnessed in their internal conversations and journal writing, we prepared teachers on the nature of such an inward learning journey. The affordance and permission of a safe space that is inviting and conducive to being vulnerable and open to self-innovation is notably an important condition for teachers to optimally engage in this dialogical process of critical reflexivity.

Conclusion

This chapter describes and discusses how we at the National Institute of Education (Singapore's sole teacher accreditation body) facilitated the use of critical reflexivity on the part of our teachers to gain greater awareness and criticality of their own assumptions and positions towards persons with disabilities, and how they have been shaped by their sociocultural and sociohistorical influences within Singaporean society to possibly reproducing exclusionary attitudes and practices. The perspective of the individual self as historically and culturally contextualized provides the aperture for the self to be critically reflexive of one's socially constituted position and responses to persons with disabilities and invites the individual to be awakened by the imagination to new and refreshed perspectives and possibilities in reconstituting meanings and actions in relating with and advocating for the inclusion of persons with disabilities. As such, critical reflexivity is itself a "pedagogy of hope" (Freire, 1992; hooks, 2003) as well as a "pedagogy of possibility" (Simon, 1992, p. 4).

The value of critical reflexivity in invigorating the processes for learning, relearning and unlearning in a dynamically changing world has been recognized in several fields and disciplines, most notably in social work, the health professions and management education. These fields have thus employed the use of critical reflexivity to enhance the personal and professional development and practice of personnel. The uptake of using critical reflexivity as a pedagogical practice within teacher education for fostering inclusivity has, in contrast, not received a similar level of interest and practice-based applications in the field of inclusive education. We hope that this proposed direction in opening up a new space for considering critical reflexivity as a pedagogy within the current discourse and practice of preparing teachers to be inclusive and for inclusion will elicit interest and motivation from within the field of inclusive education itself to be reflexive of its own identity and conceptual boundaries.

References

Appadurai, A. (1990). Disjuncture and difference in the global cultural economy. *Public Culture, 2*(2), 1–24.

Archer, M. S. (2007). *Structure, agency and the internal conversation.* Cambridge: Cambridge University Press.

Archer, M. S. (2010). Introduction: The reflexive re-turn. In M. Archer (Ed.), *Conversations about reflexivity* (pp. 1–14). London, UK: Routledge.

Archer, M. S. (2012). *The reflexive imperative in late modernity.* New York: Cambridge University Press.

Badwell, H. (2016). Critical reflexivity and moral regulation. *Journal of Progressive Human Services, 27*(1), 1–20.

Bakthin, M. (1981). *The dialogic imagination.* M. Holquist (Ed), C. Emerson & M. Holquist (Trans.). Austin: University of Texas Press.

Barge, J. K. (2007). Reflexivity and managerial practice. *Communication Monographs, 71*(1), 70–96.

Bentley-Williams, R., Grima-Farrell, C., Long, J., & Laws, C. (2016). Collaborative partnerships: Developing pre-service teachers as inclusive practitioners to support students with disabilities. *International Journal of Disability, Development and Education, 64*(3), 270–282.

Bentley-Williams, R., & Morgan, J. (2013). Inclusive education: Pre-service teachers' reflexive learning on diversity and their challenging role. *Asia-Pacific Journal of Teacher Education, 41*(2), 173–185.

Brownlee, J. L., Ferguson, L. E., & Ryan, M. (2017). Changing teachers' epistemic cognition: A new conceptual framework for epistemic reflexivity. *Educational Psychologist, 52*(4), 242–252.

Burkitt, I. (2012). Emotional reflexivity: Feeling, emotion and imagination in reflexive dialogues. *Sociology, 46*(3), 458–472.
Chia, R. (1996). The problem of reflexivity in organizational research: Towards a postmodern science of organization. *Organization, 3*(1), 31–59.
Cole, A. L., & Knowles, G. (2000). *Researching teaching: Exploring teacher development through reflexive inquiry*. Needham Heights: Allyn & Bacon.
Cunliffe, A. L. (2002). Reflexive dialogical practice in management learning. *Management Learning, 33*(1), 193–213.
Cunliffe, A. L. (2004). On becoming a critically reflexive practitioner. *Journal of Management Education, 28*(4), 407–426.
Cunliffe, A. L. (2009). Reflexivity, learning and reflexive practice. In S. J. Armstrong & C. C. Fukami (eds.), *The SAGE handbook of management learning, education and development* (pp. 405–418). London: SAGE Publications Ltd.
D'Cruz, H., Gillingham, P., & Melendez, S. (2007). Reflexivity, its meanings and relevance for social work: A critical review of the literature. *British Journal of Social Work, 37*(1), 73–90.
Dean, J. (2017). *Doing reflexivity: An introduction*. Bristol, UK: Policy Press.
Fabian, J. (1971). Language, history and anthropology. *Philosophy of the Social Sciences 1*(1), 19–47.
Ferguson, H. (2003). Welfare, social exclusion and reflexivity: The case of child and woman protection. *Child and Family Social Work, 2*(4), 221–234.
Feucht, F. C., Brownlee, J. L., & Schraw, G. (2017). Moving beyond reflection: Reflexivity and epistemic cognition in teaching and teacher education. *Educational Psychologist, 52*(4), 234–241.
Forlin, C., & Chambers, D. (2011). Teacher preparation for inclusive education: Increasing knowledge but raising concerns. *Asia-Pacific Journal of Teacher Education, 39*(1), 17–32.
Freire, P. (1992). *Pedagogy of hope: Reliving pedagogy of the oppressed (translated by Robert Barr, 1992 original version)*. New York: Bloomsbury Publishing.
Goulder, A. W. (1970). *The coming crisis in Western sociology*. New York: Basic Books.
Hermans, H. J. M. (2001). The dialogical self: Toward a theory of personal and cultural positioning. *Culture & Psychology, 7*(3), 243–281.
Hermans, H. J. M. (2003). The construction and reconstruction of a dialogical self. *Journal of Constructivist Psychology, 16*(2), 89–130.
Hibbert, P., & Cunliffe, A. (2015). Responsible management: Engaging moral reflexive practice through threshold concepts. *Journal of Business Ethics, 127*(1), 177–188.
Hofer, B. K. (2017). Shaping the epistemology of teacher practice through reflection and reflexivity. *Educational Psychologist, 52*(40), 299–306.
Holmes, M. (2010). The emotionalization of reflexivity. *Sociology, 44*(1), 139–154.
hooks, B. (2003). *Teaching community: A pedagogy of hope*. New York: Routledge.
Houston, S. (2015). Enabling others in social work: Reflexivity and the theory of social domains. *Critical and Radical Social Work, 3*(2), 245–260.
Ingrassia, A. (2011). Reflexivity in the medical encounter: Contributions from post-modern systemic practice. *Journal of Family Therapy, 35*(2), 139–158.
Kinsella, E. A., & Whiteford, G. E. (2009). Knowledge generation and utilization in occupational therapy: Towards epistemic reflexivity. *Australian Occupational Therapy Journal, 56*, 249–259.
Kögler, H-H. (2017). Reflexivity and globalization: Conditions and capabilities for a dialogical cosmopolitan. *Human Affairs, 27*(4), 374–388.

Kozleski, E. B., Artiles, A. J., & Waitoller, F. R. (2011). Introduction: Equity in inclusive education: Historical trajectories and theoretical commitments. In A. J. Alfredo, E. B. Kozleski & F. R. Waitoller (Eds.), *Inclusive education: Examining equity on five continents* (pp. 1–14). Cambridge, MA: Harvard Educational Press.

Lazard, L. & McAvoy, J. (2020). Doing reflexivity in psychological research – What's the point? What's the practice?. *Qualitative Research in Psychology, 17*(2), 159–177.

Lim, L., & Nam, S. (2000). Special education in Singapore. *Journal of Special Education, 34*(2), 104–109.

Lim, L., & Quah, M. M. (2004). Foresight via hindsight: prospects and lessons for inclusion in Singapore. *Asia-Pacific Journal of Education, 24*(2), 193–204

Lim, L., & Thaver, T. (2018). Inclusion of persons with disabilities in Singapore: An evolutionary perspective. In S. Hsu (Ed.), *Routledge handbook of sustainable development* (pp. 373–393). United Kingdom: Routledge.

Lim, L., Thaver, T., & Slee, R. (2008). *Exploring disability in Singapore: A personal learning journey.* Singapore: McGraw-Hill.

Lim, L., Thaver, T., & Strogilis, V. (2019). Contextual influences on inclusivity: The Singapore experience. In M. J. Schuelka, C. J. Johnstone, G. Thomas & A. J. Artiles. *The SAGE handbook of inclusion and diversity in education* (pp. 496–508). London, UK: Sage Publications.

Maclean, M., Harvey, C., & Chia, R. (2012). Reflexive practice and the making of elite business careers. *Management Learning, 43*(4), 386–404.

May, T., & Perry, B. (2011). *Social research and reflexivity: Content, consequence and context.* London: Sage Publications Inc.

Mead, G. H. (1934). *Mind, self and society* (edited by C. W. Morris), Chicago: University of Chicago Press.

Miller, D. L. (Ed.). (1982). *The individual and the social self: Unpublished essays by G. H. Mead.* Chicago: University of Chicago Press.

Nazaruk, M. (2011). Reflexivity in anthropological discourse analysis. *Anthropological Notebooks, 17*(1), 73–83.

Ng, S.L., Wright, S. R., & Kuper, A. (2019). The divergence and convergence of critical reflection and critical reflexivity: Implications for health professions education. *Academic Medicine, 94*(8), 1122–1128.

Phelan, S. K. (2011). Constructions of disability: A call for critical reflexivity in occupational therapy. *Canadian Journal of Occupational Therapy, 78*(3), 164–172.

Pollner, M. (1991). Left of ethnomethodology: The rise and decline of radical reflexivity. *American Sociological Review, 56*(3), 370–380.

Salzman, P. C. (2002). On reflexivity. *American Anthropologist, 104*(3), 805–813.

Scholte, B. (1972). Toward a reflexive and critical anthropology. In D. Hymes (Ed.), *Reinventing anthropology* (pp. 430–455). New York: Pantheon Books.

Schön. D. (1983). *The reflective practitioner: How professionals think in action.* New York: Basic Books.

Setchell, J., & Dalziel, B. (2019). Using critical reflexivity to enhance clinical care: A clinician perspective. *Journal of Humanities in Rehabilitation,* May, 1–20. Retrieved from: https://www.jhrehab.org/wp-content/uploads/2019/05/Setchell_Spring19_CriticalReflexivity.pdf

Simon, R. I. (1992). *Teaching against the grain: Texts for a pedagogy of possibility.* New York: Bergen & Garvey.

Slee, R. (2011). *The irregular school: Exclusion, schooling and inclusive education.* Oxon, UK: Routledge.

Strauss, A. (1956). *The social psychology of George Herbert Mead.* Chicago: University Chicago Press.

Tait, K., & Purdie, N. (2000). Attitudes towards disability: Teacher education for inclusive environments in an Australian university. *International Journal of Disability, Development and Education*, *47*(1), 25–38.

Waitoller, F. R., & Artiles, A. J. (2013). A decade of professional development research for inclusive education: A critical review and notes for a research program. *Review of Educational Research*, *83*(3), 319–356.

Watts, L. (2019). Reflective practice, reflexivity, and critical reflection in social work education in Australia. *Australian Social Work*, *72*(1), 8–20.

Wilder-Bassett, M. E. (2005). CMC as written communication: A critical social-constructivist view of multiple identities and cultural positioning in the L2/C2 classroom. *The Computer Assisted Language Instruction Consortium*, *22*(3), 635–656.

12
RE-TURNING INSIGHTS ON BELONGING

An international collaboration between Flanders and New Zealand

Hanne Vandenbussche, Elisabeth De Schauwer, Evelyn Christina, Missy Morton, and Geert Van Hove

Introduction

The analysis and discussion in this chapter is an outgrowth of earlier – initially separate – projects in Flanders and New Zealand that are grounded within a Disability Studies in Education (DSE) framework. In-depth conversations and exchanges about our separate projects led to the desire to engage together on the shared project described in this chapter. We begin with a brief overview of what we each brought initially to the engagement.

In New Zealand, an early example of drawing on DSE is the series of developing the approach of narrative assessment (for more detail see, for example, Morton et al., 2012). Our research and experience had shown that traditional special education and psychological approaches to assessment were marked by a grammar of testing, diagnosis, prescription (teaching) and focus on the decontextualised individual (problem) student. This grammar of schooling was, and often still is, a barrier to inclusion and to learning. Such traditional approaches positioned special education students firmly outside the curricula and formative assessment approaches available to most students. Our work on narrative assessment started from the premise that changing understandings and approaches to assessment for disabled students was an important entrée to changing understandings and approaches to curriculum and pedagogy; to helping teachers understand the importance and value of making the New Zealand curriculum accessible to all learners. As researchers and teacher educators on the project we found ourselves looking outside traditional special education to understand what we were able to see, to notice, recognise differently and to share with others. Māori principles and values also supported us to recognise classrooms with what we came to characterise as cultures of belonging (Macfarlane et al., 2012). Rather than looking at belonging as an individual trait, or belonging as something to be bestowed by others, we thought of cultures of belonging as

DOI: 10.4324/9781003091950-14

assemblages of time, space, beings. While there are a number of Māori values that intersect to support cultures of belonging, two in particular are drawn on in the rest of this chapter: Ako describes the idea of teacher and student learning from and with each other. Manakitanga describes the idea of recognising, valuing and upholding the mana, the integrity, of every person. We underpin our work in initial teacher education and professional learning, working with new and experienced teachers to recognise, build and maintain cultures of belonging in their classrooms and schools (Morton et al., 2021).

In Flanders, we plugged the conceptual tools of posthuman and new materialist frameworks in our working with DSE. We tried to map our making sense of belonging through different research projects (Vandenbussche & De Schauwer, 2018; Vandenbussche, De Schauwer, & Van Hove, 2019). We immersed ourselves into belonging and approached it from the inside. It was very difficult to define the meaning and importance of belonging; it could not be fixed, it had a lot of different meanings. Belonging became understood as a relational process, where it is necessary to be attentive to the complexity of connections between children and places, children and matter, children and other people. Belonging was very much related to and interwoven in the local context. We saw the importance of intensive moments where there were opportunities to affect and to be affected, not only for students, but also for teachers, support workers, parents. Belonging was unspeakable and could not be determined in an 'objective way' – tangible. The desire for belonging was large, a desire for connections and interactions was woven into complex assemblages in which the place, people and its history were all part of its potential for belonging. In connectedness, multiple lines of belonging were released, new constellations of intensities could grow, new imaginaries emerged, new ways of moving forward could be devised. Belonging had transformative power to create more inclusive school environments.

In our collaborative paper we argue that taking up the conceptual tools of 'ritual', 'waiting' and 'almost-nothing' provide us with means to avoid the trap of searching for reasons to explain (away) the failures of students, the failures of inclusion, the failures of belonging. Rather, we notice movements toward what is yet to come, what is not there yet and how we can actively support children, young people, teachers, movements so that they may flourish. We argue for affirmation of the work that is already being done, of the strengths of teachers and learners and of the little movements and variations in the participation and learning processes of every child, which requires a close attention to each child's story. We rethink belonging not as a procedural given but as a powerful becoming-process in schools that entails radical relationality.

Inclusief [Inclusive]: a Flemish documentary[1]

In 2018, Ellen Vermeulen made a documentary about the practices of inclusion in the regular classrooms of four children and their families in Flanders, Belgium. The Flemish authors were intensely involved in the making process of this documentary.

The documentary maker and the authors cooperated closely, giving input to which children could be contacted, the storylines presented and the choice of images in the montage process. We exchanged ideas through email and phone and met on a regular basis to discuss the participation of the disabled students and the shifting positions of others involved. The documentary maker wanted to move her viewers beyond judgement about the place where these children should belong. Instead, spectators become part of the stories and the negotiations in the classroom and at home as they followed the children's desire for recognition and belonging. Consequently, the documentary ultimately posed the question of 'is this inclusion?' and created space to think about what matters for the children and their parents. Ellen Vermeulen wanted to tell another narrative than the often-dominant focus on the resistance against inclusion in regular education and the lack of means and sufficient support.

Methodology – Our way of working

Our starting point for this chapter was our common interest in belonging, from which we worked back and forth between researchers in Flanders and New Zealand. We wanted to step into our earlier work and continue the (re)configuring of belonging in inclusive classrooms. This was not a straightforward and fully traceable process; rather, it occurred in the exchanges between the five authors of this paper as we wrote and plodded along.

We draw on the work of Karen Barad (2014), a new-materialist scholar who approaches the concept of *re-turning* from an ethico-onto-epistemological account. This refers to the complex entanglements of ontology (discussing questions about 'what is there – being'), epistemology ('what we can know – knowledge') and ethics. These domains cannot be separated, they are interwoven and change each other. Re-turning is about an entangled process taking the past and the future into account. Concepts can also be re-turned, which means we approach them from different, but connected, angles over and over again. This requires an attentiveness to how the concept moves and changes in surprising and unexpected ways, always rooted into phenomena built from relationality between people, places, things, ideas, concepts, and so on.

The shared materials and analysis included the contents of the documentary Inclusief, as well guided discussions and reactions to the documentary by teachers and public audiences in Flemings that were recorded and transcribed. The documentary was used as part of a research project (www.potentialtoteach.be) where seven teacher teams were guided in their reflections on the documentary. These discussions were recorded and transcribed. The documentary was also shown in cinemas across Flanders and discussions afterwards were guided by the documentary maker and the Flemish authors. We reflected on the reactions from the teachers and the spectators who watched the documentary in the cinema or at school through guided discussions.

All five of us watched *Inclusief* several times, and we each selected a number of fragments from this documentary that were greatly inspired from our own contexts

Re-turning insights on belonging 203

and experiences in connection with belonging. We read and discussed the reactions from Flemish teachers and audiences. We exchanged our own reactions and beginning analyses through shared writing in an online document and through our weekly conversations on Zoom. In the discussion we brought in links with other classroom events from different research projects in New Zealand and Flanders. During these conversations, it became increasingly clear that we experienced the use of time as a very important and recurring phenomenon. We focused on this perspective and elaborated on three concepts: 'refrain', 'waiting' and 'almost-nothing' or the importance of small changes. We worked from several scenes in the film that are discussed in this article to re-turn belonging "to not merely change what it will have done after the fact but to change who/what it will have been, that is, its very ontology" (Barad, 2014, p. 180; see also Davies, 2018).

Moment 1 – Rosie and rituals[2]

'Can you do it, Camille?' The teacher helps a little girl to put a plate on the wall. 'You can wake up Ruudje.' The teacher helps another child. 'And you can sit over there, there is some

PICTURE 1–6 Rosie during the morning ritual in preschool.

room left with Robin.' Rosie sits in a small circle with the other children. The teacher whispers, 'All hands behind your back'. Rosie points her finger at the other children and repeats, 'Hands behind your back!'

'Hands behind your back, very good Rosie', the teacher says. The teacher starts to sing, 'Ruudje Rube, Ruudje Rube, where are you?' The children sing along. Rosie is looking around, fascinated and interested. She observes the other children and the teacher very closely. She sings some words with them and laughs at the end where the teacher says, 'Hello little friends, good morning everybody!' Rosie repeats some words.[3]

At the start of going to school, Rosie was hiding in a playhouse and would not come out. Recognising her fears and anxiety about what was new at school, she started at her own tempo and participated in ways that were possible for her. In this scene, Rosie is taking part in the circle. She observes the other children and she speaks, repeating the words she already knows and can utter. The teacher is respecting Rosie's pace unconditionally and encourages her, even if it feels disruptive at times. The connection with the morning ritual and Rosie's small steps in participating slowly moves their relationship into one of temporary resonance. The morning ritual established in a class situation enables participation: it provides a grip and offers a key to belonging. We argue the power of the ritual can be important in inclusion processes to attend to the way rituals are helpful for some children to find a recognisable place in the classroom, to understand better what is expected from them as a learner and to have returning opportunities to show what they are able to do.

A multi-rhythmic analysis from Davies (2021) is helpful in unravelling the many workings of rituals. Davies draws on the work of Deleuze and Guattari who invented the *ritornello* [ritual] as a philosophical concept in a search for consistency. Rhythm and milieu are basic in the *ritornello*, just as the way territories work and are inhabited. The rhythm and milieu of Rosie's class using the song, the structured organisation, the way the teacher introduces the doll, the returning behaviour codes of 'hands on the back' and how the teacher responds to the children in her classroom are all part of this welcoming ritual to start a new day. This ritual becomes familiar for Rosie; she can rely on what will happen and what she is expected to do. It takes time – more time than most of her peers need – but the images and the description (see pictures 1–6) show that there is a lot more to take into account than just Rosie's verbal response; her smile, her contribution, and her enthusiasm offer new possibilities to look at belonging and open up the often narrow understandings of what can be meaningful goals for children with special educational needs. The *ritornello* opens up the space for Rosie to become Rosie who is eager to learn and to be part of whatever is going on in the classroom. At the same time, it holds challenges for her to take steps in several learning processes. This ritual works in many directions. Repeatedly it can be witnessed in how Rosie is watching her peers and through imitation learns to master the morning ritual. Her peers inspire her and make sure that she can fall back in when she loses track. The teacher finds new entrances to get to know Rosie, to see her in this becoming-process. All these elements influence each other and matter when we want to say something about Rosie's belonging, with this teacher, in this group, in this preschool and at this time of the day.

In what follows, we look deeper into the movements of the refrain and what it can mean for Rosie in this class context. Davies explores three interdependent components of refrain: holding the world safe, establishing a safe plot of land, and throwing the world back into chaos (Davies, 2021, p. 81).

In the first movement, repetition is essentially imaginary; that is, it is imagination bringing together what is in existence to be seen as repetition. In repetition, the ultimate element is difference standing out from the 'identical' form of representations (Deleuze, 2011/1968, p. 98). Repetitions – habituated thoughts and practices – can hold the world safe. The first movement of the *ritornello* starts with Rosie hiding in a playhouse. For a long time, Rosie needed distance and her own safe space in order to gain confidence to take bigger 'risks' in becoming part of the group. The safety of having an idea about what is coming offers contours to experiment with her participation in what is going on and expected in the classroom. This requires not only a lot of patience and persistent invitations from the teacher, but also an unconditional belief in Rosie's potential. The teacher did not consider difference as problematic; she was not forcing Rosie to come out of the playhouse but gave Rosie time to find her way into the group and kept insisting on making connection with Rosie.

A second way the ritual can work is by establishing a safe plot of land. This is about creating control, a marked terrain, a home (Deleuze and Guattari, 1987). In a classroom, rituals enable students to experience clarity, stability, and tranquillity. The repetition is supportive, providing some hooks to hold on to in an environment like the classroom or playground that can be chaotic and unpredictable. The morning ritual is a moment where Rosie really feels as a part of the class: the circle with the little bench seats, the pictures on the wall, the puppet Ruudje, the teacher, the children, the songs and the habits have become familiar – a safe haven has been created. This does not mean it stays safe all the time; when new activities are offered, when some patterns are disturbed, Rosie seeks another spot in the classroom where she feels at ease. Teachers can judge children who differ from the normative standards as disturbing and insufficient, and thus ignoring or minimising the smaller steps in a learning process, like that of Rosie's.

This brings in a third component of refrain through which the new emerges (Davies, 2021, p. 84). This third movement ensures that the created safe spot does not become a jail, and that borders can be overstepped. The safe spot offers Rosie a liminal space for 'becoming Rosie', in a complex entangled way (Land, Meyer & Baillie, 2010). Rosie creates her own territory for change and discovery, starting from the playhouse where she can hide, and then growing to take part in the circle moment shared with the class group. She experiments with the *ritornello*, searching for how to keep the chaos at bay and marking reference points (the song and the singing, the doll, the teacher, hands on your back, etc.), so that she finds her place. She knows that it is necessary to put her hands on her back, she reminds her peers, she watches who is taking action, she sings the last words of the sentences and her expression is showing interest to start the day. The teacher is encouraging her in the steps she takes and gives her opportunities to take into account her strengths and difficulties and let her grow in this stimulating, regular class context.

The refrain of the ritual is transformative (Davies, 2021). The ritual unravels difference and repetition as entwined dynamics in a search for balance, not giving up on all markers and collapsing into pure chaos but also preventing stagnation into fixed identities and frames of reference in our daily classroom actions.

Moment 2 – Irakli and waiting time[4]

Teacher: '*I will repeat the words*: eigenaardig [extraordinary], porselein [porcelain], spookrijder [ghostrider]) *and* vijand [enemy].'

Irakli is still typing, going from one letter to the other slowly but focusing on the letters and on his movement. His support worker is repeating the words quietly while Irakli is progressing. The class writes and afterwards waits patiently.

It is very quiet in the room.

The teacher goes further, while he watches the class. 'And now the sentences: De operatie is geslaagd [The operation has succeeded].'

Class: 'De operatie is geslaagd.'

Again, the class is writing it down. Irakli is typing, very slowly; we see he is still writing the first dictated word of the sentence. He moves his body to move his finger in the correct direction on his keyboard. He stretches his finger and moves across the adapted board. Each time the support worker helps put the cursor on the right spot and to leave space between the different words.

The teacher pauses. He holds and waits for Irakli. The other children are ready and wait silently.

Irakli is working as fast as he can on his one-finger typing of every letter of every word, the doubt: geslaagt *or* geslaagd. *His support worker whispers:* 'Think hard.' *He chooses the wrong one.*[5]

Irakli's presence disrupts a lot of prejudices. He speaks Dutch, French, English, and Georgian and shows strong ability and interest in languages. Teachers get confused by his story. Irakli appears to be intelligent, but upon confrontation with his fragile and unruly body, the teachers decide that he does not belong in a regular school. For many teachers, Irakli is not recognisable as one of their students. There is a confrontation with another pace, where efficiency and speed dominate when thinking about 'good learning'. Ableist time governs, which means that Irakli has to be creative in finding his own ways to participate, by using reasonable accommodations and extra support (e.g., his computer, his support worker, not having to write everything down, downsizing the amount of exercises, etc.). The teacher and the class need to provide adjustments, producing tension with what is familiar in a sixth grade.

In this scene, the teacher is mindful of Irakli: he waits. The class is used to it; they know Irakli, and they also wait and show patience. Although Irakli is more than slow – several rhythms are at play – his slowness here is an invitation to think about inclusion and belonging. The question of whether Irakli really belongs is often raised by teachers. His vulnerable body challenges our normal standards of what a 'good

Re-turning insights on belonging **207**

PICTURE 7–11 Irakli is doing his dictation in class.

student' is, and how he/she should look like. It is difficult for the teachers and the spectators of the documentary to express the feelings and organize the thoughts that these images had awakened. It is undoubtedly clear that Irakli is only able to participate when ways of teaching and learning are thoroughly differentiated. However, this is not only seen as an invitation to change our habitual educational practices but also, more often than not, it makes teachers wonder about the authenticity of Irakli's participation and belonging. It brings belonging down to an individual characteristic, instead of envisaging it as a collective responsibility that occurs in deeply relational work between Irakli and his context.

Teachers question the possibility of waiting for a student like Irakli. They experience discomfort over the time Irakli needs. In the following, the focus will lie on this complexity of time in the processes of inclusion and belonging. The waiting time in this fragment will be rethought and its potential in relation to belonging will be explored. Farman (2018) considers how, during waiting, time flows through us and changes us. He argues that waiting is noticed and lived, and often makes people feel uncomfortable, uncertain and anxious. In many environments waiting times are seen as hurdles between us and our plans, as burdens and obstacles; the larger structural reasons for why this is experienced are rarely noticed (Farman, 2018, p. 186). This was also happening when teachers watched this fragment of Irakli. People get out of balance when other rhythms come across, and in this case, the teacher spectators in the audience experience 'empty time' when Irakli's teacher waits. Discomfort over the time Irakli needs awakens the reflexivity of the teacher spectators, who state that it is not possible for *their* class to wait so long. They claim that it is not good for the other children and that Irakli needs to understand that he does not belong there.

Foucault describes the value of an *ethic of discomfort*. Referring to Merleau-Ponty's teaching, Foucault explains both the essential philosophical task and an ethic of discomfort require us to

> never to consent to being completely comfortable with one's own presuppositions … remembering that in order to give them the necessary mobility one must have a distant view, but also look at what is nearby and all around oneself.
>
> (Foucault, 1994, p. 448)

Here, the discomfort arises from disruption to the habitual way of teaching, where teachers do not always demonstrate the openness and flexibility required in inclusive education. In their discussion of this part of documentary, the spectator teachers begin to question their own presuppositions about time and the 'best' uses of time.

The disturbance in the dictation caused by Irakli's slowness makes teachers very aware of the high tempo in educational practices. Speed has redefined space and time and has overtaken our body movement (Vannini, 2002). While the teachers reflected and discussed the documentary, it becomes clear that teachers also express the need to have more time. Teachers need time – non-linear time – to help them notice belonging and what helps to achieve it. In the feelings of discomfort, they start to think about time differently, about time as a multitude. Linear time will always be present and is also necessary, but despite the comfort this offers, there remains a lot of not knowing and unexplored terrains. The conception of flowing time is helpful to consider what happens and moves in a class setting; here, Irakli helps us to comprehend this more clearly because of his different needs. The waiting time in particular is interesting because it illustrates how discomfort can have many layers, and it can challenge teachers and others to consider other possibilities for becoming and learning—Irakli's, his peers', the teachers' and the viewers'.

Waiting time forces people to think about time, about slowing down, and about children's belonging. According to Farman (2018), waiting is not an in-between time but rather a silent force shaping our social interactions; waiting can be fruitful and we risk losing the ways in which waiting shapes vital elements like social intimacy, the production of knowledge and creative practices (p. 18). The waiting time during the dictation gives students extra time to repeat, write and reread. It gives time for Irakli to follow in typing all the words on his computer and mobilizing enough physical effort. He receives support from his personal assistant who whispers the word again, when he is behind. The negotiation on how to use time in different ways during the dictation is the result of experimentation and asks for collaboration between all parties involved. Waiting opens up new lines of flight to wonder about possibilities, the new and the unexplored for everyone and everything involved. Irakli, his teacher, his support worker and his peers experienced what it can do and silently agreed to go along with it. This does not mean that waiting is a technique to use in each classroom during dictation.

Time becomes an investment in the social fabric that connects persons, places and matter. The awareness of time can also be collective rather than individual (Farman, 2018). The time that Irakli needs is an investment of the teacher and the students in a collective event. It is not always, and in each situation possible or necessary. Waiting can be essential for certain modes of learning, for creativity and connecting, and for encouraging social change, not only for Irakli, but for everyone involved in the classroom, 'as we realize that not everyone is afforded the same agency for how time is used' (Farman, 2018, p. 193). Irakli—unintentionally—is offering other ways of dealing with time, creating opportunities to challenge static ways of teaching, learning and approaching children. This implies that the relationship between Irakli and his teacher can be conceived of as interdependent, where they both transform and produce resistance to how teaching should be done, taking into account Irakli's desires, as well as those of the teacher and the other students.

Small changes: The need of an attentive gaze to notice *presque-rien* [an 'almost-nothing']

From the moments of Rosie and Irakli, we learn that it is important to look at the very small changes to 'notice' and to 'respond to' how a child belongs in an inclusive learning environment (Morton et al., 2012). We think the importance of listening attentively in order to notice what a child desires and needs is an inherent capability present in every person. Teachers who dare to take the time to divert from the often restrictive pathways that push them to teach according to strict curricula, and teachers who take the time to listen with all of their senses and experiment from that point with other options of taking part in their classes, are opening new opportunities for a lot of students. That is why we want to draw attention to the significance of small movements in a continuous experimentation with learning and teaching.

In the refrain of the morning ritual and in the story of waiting very small changes occur: Rosie looking at what the others do, Rosie imitating the others, repeating some of the words, asking others to participate; Irakli's teacher holding, repeating the same words or sentences a little more, the class waiting, repeating, rereading, Irakli putting in focus and effort to type each word letter by letter, etc. It is a challenge to grasp what these little differences are and what they mean for inclusive education. Jankélévitch, a French philosopher, tried to understand the little differences that happen in life and are very small but also very meaningful. He describes these small shifts as *presque-rien* [an 'almost-nothing'] and *je-ne-sais-quoi* [an 'I-don't-know-what']; this *presque-rien* is the infinitesimal which form the basis of the charm; why we feel excited or enchanted by what is happening (Jankélévitch, 1980). It prompts us to approach certain events not only with our minds. The *je-ne-sais-quoi* and *presque-rien* are connected in a sustainable way and refer to the perplexity and unrest people experience when unable to define or express something in words. This is also how belonging is noticed with Rosie and Irakli.

Belonging happens in intense moments (repeatedly) in a constant duration of time; as such, it is always changing and keeps slipping through our hands when we try to take possession of its meaning. We cannot represent or hold belonging. We tried to show small movements in belonging by not putting Rosie, Irakli or the concept of belonging in a certain category, where conditions for a possible experience are set as a general knowledge (Deleuze, 2011/1968). Often, these movements are not even recognised but are obstructed by an impatient way of looking at learning and progress of students in a classroom. Teachers experience doubt if they are just muddling around and are not seeing enough change at the rhythm that they are used to. Rosie's teacher is happy with every small achievement in Rosie's becoming-process in the classroom and is *not* focusing on what is not there yet or what Rosie is not able to do in comparison with peers. A similar process happens in the interaction between Irakli and his teacher. A resonant relationship arises, where Irakli can be challenged in his learning and at the same time gets the support he needs to be able to start learning and participating. Irakli is part of the class, in his own way, but in the middle of the group and without prejudice, presuming his competence. Irakli is seen as the avid student, longing to be there.

Rosie and Irakli ask to be recognised in all their differences and talents, and in all their desires to persist in trying to take part in the learning and belonging at school. In the morning ritual we see Rosie in a deeply relational way. Her peers sometimes change their interactions with her, inviting her to participate in their play, or leaving her at peace when she wants to play alone. Also, Irakli's peers take Irakli's need for more time as evident and not disturbing: the other rhythms offer opportunities for their own learning. Peers invite him to play along in the playground, with the wheelchair as a perfect holder for the rubber band when jumping. The teachers affirm Rosie and Irakli in their experimenting and insist on continuing to invite them to take part in the class activities in their own way. Recognition is intimately tied to difference, where difference is both a problem in its deviance from the norm, and simultaneously an affirmation of life (Davies et al., 2013). The questions shift. It is no longer important to determine what is exactly wrong with Rosie or Irakli and how to address this better in their learning. The focus moves towards what is yet to come, what is not there yet and how we can support. It is a recommencement time and again: a beginning that never ends to begin (Jankélévitch, 1966). Seeing Rosie and Irakli in this deeply relational way is important to notice how learning and belonging work and are emergent through the interplay with the material and non-material context that surrounds both of them.

In conclusion: Re-turning belonging

In the process of discussing the two stories from across the contexts of Flanders and New Zealand, we were re-turning our own understandings of belonging to comprehend the opportunities these open up for student and teacher learning. Re-turning belonging forces us to stand still and see and feel how belonging works for Rosie and Irakli. We connect with theoretical insights about little changes, time and rituals, and we connect with the perspectives of teachers, parents, support workers, and children. This does not require a lot of means. Diving into the small stories and re-turning them makes us response-able[6] as a student, teacher, spectator and researcher.

In what follows, we offer three propositions, which resonate with a sort of revolt against schools as bureaucratic places where control and efficiency are held up high. Schools are places to experience and facilitate belonging, connection, and desire.

We believe these propositions can be related to the 'grammar of schooling'; these are elements so deeply embedded in educational organisations that they seem natural and stay relatively unquestioned, for example, schooling as a mechanism for sorting students by perceived ability (Mehta & Datnow, 2020, p. 491). In recent years there have been a range of efforts moving us away from the century-old grammar of schooling. We suggest the grammar of schooling needs another turn, needs to move a little bit, where we hold close to the actions, didactics, interactions that work, but stretch them from the inside so it opens the space for children as Irakli and Rosie to find their way and belong. Rituals and working with 'time' are essential in this grammar, and are recognisable by teachers around the world. The re-turning practices we attempted here help us see that in this very grammar of schooling options for belonging for every child can be found. There is no need for a big turn or a struggle against what is known; we can start from what is already there and make little shifts or movements within, opening small changes with potentially big consequences.

The first proposition we come up with is about the importance of a child being noticed and recognised in order to be able to belong. This idea is concerned with the notions of noticing, recognising and responding that we have learned to use in the narrative assessments in New Zealand (Morton et al., 2012). This is connected to developing the necessary response-ability for teachers to make sure every learner in her/his class feels valued. It focuses on the many talents and powerful teaching skills available in every child and teacher; that is, noticing each student's potential to teach other students and the teacher.

This relates to a second proposition, which prompts teachers to break out of an ordered, structured way of working that relies only on themselves in feeling responsible for the learning processes in class. Teachers need to find a balance in dealing with the chaos, using reference points in a flexible way and experiencing learning as a *collective responsibility* of becoming for every person involved. It asks for teachers to see the many ways in which time works and to be daring to take the time that they need to let each child participate in learning. It is a revolt against (only) ableist time, against (only) timetables – a rebellion time. We argue for the importance of *time* in pedagogy to feel resonance with each student, to attune to the multiple/different paces, and to learn together with students and support workers in order to foster those multiple rhythms in a performative way. This opens up space for an ethical encounter. Teachers can gain the luxury of time by giving a lesser focus to progress or gain, which leads to a lot of not noticing, not attending and not responding.

The third proposition we offer is for teachers to stay with the discomfort that accompanies their practices, as in waiting. This feeling of discomfort does not have to be resolved, because it is challenging and teaches us something about ourselves and our school practices. We argue for taking some risks in dealing with discomfort; taking the job as a teacher seriously, aiming to get the most out of every child and focusing on learning *and* belonging. We do not plead for turning away from all that is done or that is known, but for re-turning over and over again: keep doing what is valuable and moving further to what is not there yet, to the new, as in the *ritornello*.

The focus on belonging – in all its complexity and multi-layeredness – helps us to re-think inclusion, not as a procedural given but as a powerful becoming-process in schools that entails deep relationality. Focusing on belonging puts teachers in the position of learners and experimenters, not knowing all of the answers but exploring materials and ideas together with the children present in the classroom, going for small adventures (Jankélévitch, 1966).

Notes

1 Trailer: https://vimeo.com/307219668l – The documentary was made as part of a research project, Potential (www.potentialtoteach.be).
2 Pictures 1–6 by Jonathan Wannyn.
3 To see this part of the documentary: https://www.youtube.com/watch?v=sQzDn9xKvmw&feature=youtu.be (min: 3:00–3:50).

4 Pictures 7–11 by Jonathan Wannyn.
5 To see this part of the documentary: https://www.youtube.com/watch?v=jmZkI3w3Lf E&feature=youtu.be (min. 3:55–6:00).
6 Response-ability is a concept used by Barad. Every one of us is able to respond to a situation, to take action in a situation, to respond to every child, including when this child has different needs. Barad states that 'responding—being responsible/response-able—to the thick tangles of spacetimematterings that are threaded through us, the places and times from which we came but never arrived and never leave, is perhaps what re-turning is about' (2014, p. 184). The concept of spacetimemattering refers to the complex entanglement of relations between spaces, time and matter, what new materialism is very much attended to.

References

Barad, K. (2014). Diffracting diffraction: Cutting together apart. *Parallax*, 20(3), 168–187. https://doi.org/10.1080/13534645.2014.927623

Davies, B. (2018). The persistent smile of the cheshire cat. Explorations in the agency of matter through art-making. *Qualitative Inquiry*, 26(7), 707–715. https://doi.org/10.1177/1077800418809742

Davies, B. (2021). *Entanglement in the world's becoming and the doing of new materialist inquiry*. London: Routledge.

Davies, B., De Schauwer, E., Claes, L., De Munck, K, Van De Putte, I., & Verstichele, M. (2013). Recognition and difference: A collective biography. *International Journal of Qualitative Studies in Education*, 26(6), 680–690. https://doi.org/10.1080/09518398.2013.788757

Deleuze, G. (2011). *Verschil en herhaling. [Difference and repetition]*. Amsterdam, the Netherlands: Boom. (Original work published 1968)

Deleuze, G., & Guattari, F. (1987). *A thousand plateaus: Capitalism and schizophrenia*. London, UK: Athlone Press.

Farman, J. (2018). *Delayed response, the art of waiting from the ancient to the instant world*. New Haven and London, UK: Yale University Press.

Foucault, M. (1994). For an ethic of discomfort. (R. Hurley and others, Trans.). In J. D. Faubion (Ed.), *Essential works of Foucault (1954–1984), volume 3: Power*, (pp. 443–448). London, UK: Penguin Books.

Jankélévitch, V. (1966). *De beleving van de tijd: avontuur, de verveling, de ernst. [The adventure, boredom and seriousness]*. Antwerp, Belgium: Het Spectrum.

Jankélévitch, V. (1980). *Le Je-ne-sais-quoi et le Presque-rien: 2. La méconnaissance. [The I-don't-know-what and the almost-nothing: 2. The ignorance]*. Paris, France: Editions du Seuil.

Land, R., Meyer, J. H. F., & Baillie, C. (2010). Editors' preface: Threshold concepts and transformational learning. In J. H. F. Meyer, R. Land & C. Baillie, (eds.) *Threshold concepts and transformational learning* (pp. ix–xlii). Rotterdam, The Netherlands: Sense Publishers.

MacFarlane, A. H., Macfarlane, S., Savage, C., & Glynn, T. (2012). Inclusive education and Māori communities in Aotearoa New Zealand. *Teaching in inclusive schoolcommunities*, 163–186.

Mehta, J. & Datnow, A. (2020). Changing the Grammar of Schooling: an appraisal and a research agenda. *American Journal of Education*, 126, 4, 491–498.

Morton, M., McIlroy, A. M., Macarthur, J., & Olsen, P. (2021). Disability studies in and for inclusive teacher education in Aotearoa New Zealand. *International Journal of Inclusive Education*, 1–16.

Morton, M., McMenamin, T., Moore, G, & Molloy S. (2012). Assessment that matters: The transformative potential of narrative assessment for students with special education needs. *Assessment Matters*, 4, 110–128.

Vandenbussche, H., & De Schauwer, E. (2018). The pursuit of belonging in inclusive education–insider perspectives on the meshwork of participation. *International Journal of Inclusive Education*, 22(9), 969–982. https://doi.org/10.1080/13603116.2017.1413686

Vandenbussche, H., De Schauwer, E., & Van Hove, G. (2019). Diffractive lenses catching stories: The meaning of belonging through the voice of adolescents. In I. Berson, M. Berson, & C. Gray (Eds.), *Participatory methodologies to elevate children's voice and agency* (pp. 275–294). Charlotte, NC: Information Age.

Vannini, P. (2002). Waiting dynamics: Bergson, Virilio, Deleuze, and the experience of Global Times. *Journal of Mundane Behavior*, 3(2), 193–208.

PART III

Methodological innovation

13
BEING SEEN AND HEARD

Using photovoice methodology in inclusive education research

Alisha M. B. Braun

FIGURE 13.1 Out of Bounds

"Out of Bounds" is the title of the photo in Figure 13.1, taken by a co-researcher with a mobility disability in a photovoice research project conducted in Ghana (Braun & Naami, 2021). The title aptly expresses the dejection felt by Evans (pseudonym) every time he wheeled by the campus library that is shown in the photograph. He wanted to study there but was unable to do so unless he sought assistance from friends to physically carry him up the staircase leading into the building entrance. There was no accessible entrance that would allow Evans to independently enter the library building.

Inclusive education activists and scholars do not want Evans or any other student to ever feel that spaces of learning are "out of bounds" for them. Likewise, no

DOI: 10.4324/9781003091950-16

student should feel that their participation in inclusive education research is "out of bounds." Honoring its inherent philosophy, inclusive education research should indeed be inclusive. It is uniquely positioned to enhance the visibility and amplify the voices of those who are marginalized by educational and social systems around the globe. Photovoice is presented in this chapter as an innovative methodology for inclusive education researchers to foster an inclusive research space for all.

The chapter begins by summarizing the historical origins and theoretical tenants of this participatory action methodology characterized by using a combination of photographs and narratives throughout the research process. Next, the central aims of photovoice are reviewed and a procedural overview is provided to familiarize readers with the practical side of this innovative approach to research. An argument is then presented for why photovoice is aptly suited for inclusive education research due to its accessibility, flexibility, and capacity for power redistribution. A research exemplar of an empirical study recently conducted by the author and colleagues in Ghana closes the chapter to provide an in-depth look at how photovoice can be used in inclusive education research for the experiences of marginalized students to be seen and their stories heard. Select photographs and corresponding narratives from the research project are shared to illustrate the collective power of the multi-faceted approach to provide a means for the global and local community to both see and hear the lived experiences of those who are often overlooked or silenced.

Historical origins and theoretical underpinnings of photovoice

Photovoice was borne in the early 1990s out of the seminal work by Wang and Burris (1994), who originally termed the research methodology *photo novella*. Their initial research study used photo novella to study women's health in rural China. As Wang et al. (1997, 1999) further developed this qualitative research methodology by strengthening its roots in feminist and empowering theories, the term photo novella was replaced with photovoice to give credence to the methodology's prioritization of participant voice. In photovoice, the prioritization of participant voice is achieved by equipping participants with cameras to express their perspectives both visually in the form of photographs as well narratively by sharing their stories through critical discussion and analysis of their captured images. This dual representation of voice as spoken and visual expression allows participants to be both seen and heard, which is a defining feature of this methodology. Accordingly, I chose to frame the Ghana research exemplar that closes this chapter in a way that delineates the seeing and hearing contributions of the methodology to highlight this duality.

The empowering and participatory tenants of photovoice epistemologically situate the methodology within the realm of participatory action research (PAR). Consistent with other PAR methodologies, photovoice assumes that participants are experts about the issues they are experiencing in their communities, so should be actively involved in the production of knowledge about those issues (Bisung Elliott, Abudho, Schuster-Wallace, & Karanha, 2015; Castleden, Garvin, & First Nation, 2008; Wang & Burris, 1997). Also consistent with a PAR approach, scholars recommend that photovoice participants serve as co-researchers to become equal partners at all stages throughout the research process (Castleden et al., 2008; Whyte, 1991). As I have argued elsewhere (Braun, 2020), the empowerment of researched populations as experts in a co-researcher capacity helps dismantle power inequalities and facilitates more inclusive research spaces for marginalized populations.

Finally, in reviewing the historical and theoretical underpinnings of photovoice, it is important to pay tribute to the centrality of marginalization to photovoice. Historically, the voices of people who are socially, culturally, economically, and politically marginalized have been highlighted using photovoice. For example, the rural Chinese women in Wang and Burris' (1994) original photovoice study were systematically marginalized by their community. The centrality of marginalization to photovoice has persisted over time and has expanded to encompass additional marginalized voices, such as youth deemed 'at-risk' (Baker, 2016), rural adolescent girls in India (Shah, 2015), students with fetal alcohol spectrum disorder (Brenna, Burles, Holtslander, & Bocking, 2017), and 'outsider' Quallunaat teachers in Inuit communities (Mueller, 2006). Given the ongoing pursuit of the inclusive education movement to enhance educational outcomes and global participation for marginalized student populations, the historical and enduring centrality of marginalization to photovoice cannot be underemphasized.

Aims and procedural overview of photovoice

The three central aims of photovoice are to: 1) record people's everyday realities, 2) promote critical dialogue and knowledge about community strengths and concerns, and 3) reach policymakers and community leaders (Wang, 2006). To meet the first aim, this participatory method positions participants (herein referred to as co-researchers to emphasize the participatory dimension of the method) as experts with cameras which they use to take photographs that are representative of their everyday lived experiences and perspectives. The second aim of photovoice is met during the next phase of the research process, whereby co-researchers meet to discuss their photographs. During these group discussions, co-researchers engage in storytelling to contextualize their images and collaboratively identify themes or issues that are represented by the photographs. Critical dialogue during in-depth group discussions is often facilitated by following the SHOWeD mnemonic line of questioning (Wang, 2006, p. 151):

- What do you *S*ee here?
- What's really *H*appening here?
- How does this relate to *O*ur lives?
- *W*hy does this situation, concern, or strength exist?
- What can we *D*o about it?

Finally, to bring about advocacy and community action, co-researchers plan a format to share their photographs and stories with policymakers and community leaders. This frequently takes the form of a community exhibition to showcase photographs, enhance public awareness of community strengths and concerns that are depicted in the images, and share recommendations to policymakers and community leaders.

If using photovoice, in addition to complying with institutional research ethics requirements (i.e., university institutional review boards), it is important to be aware of the photovoice ethics guidelines developed by Wang and Redwood-Jones (2001). There are unique ethical considerations to keep in mind when conducting photovoice research, such as the multifaceted process of acquiring informed consent. In addition to obtaining informed consent at the beginning of the research study prior to participation (as is common practice), consent should also be obtained by photographers before taking any photos of people throughout the duration of the project, as well as at the conclusion of the study for participants to grant permission for the publication of any of their work in community exhibitions or other forms of research dissemination (Wang & Redwood-Jones, 2001).

The utility of photovoice in inclusive education research

A relatively small but growing body of literature exists in inclusive education research that uses photovoice methodology (e.g., Baker, 2016; Brenna et al., 2017; Miles, 2011). Despite this, I argue that photovoice is an underutilized method that is especially well suited for inclusive education research due to its 1) accessibility, 2) flexibility, and 3) capacity for power redistribution. Each of these three reasons will be elaborated upon in the following sections.

Accessibility

One primary reason why photovoice is such a powerful research method for inclusive education researchers is its accessibility. The epistemological parameters of more traditional qualitative research methods often used in inclusive research, such as interviews and focus groups, can be exclusionary because they implicitly favor a particular level of cognitive ability (Klotz, 2014). A relatively high level of cognitive ability is required to be able to interpret and respond to interview questions, as well as discuss complex issues in focus groups. Unfortunately, many traditional research methods are discriminatory against people with learning disabilities, for instance due to their epistemological rules (Aldridge, 2007). In effect, inclusive education research that uses these methods contributes to the marginalization of people with learning disabilities that it is paradoxically aiming to circumvent. It is therefore essential for inclusive education researchers to be mindful of the research methods they are selecting and in doing so critically question whether they are accessible for people of varying cognitive abilities, processing capacities, verbal communication abilities, and social interaction abilities.

Photovoice can be effectively used with heterogeneous populations to ensure that all voices are represented, irrespective of cognitive ability and regardless of whether they are communicated in spoken or nonverbal forms. The joint use of photographs and narrative provides a multimodal opportunity for the sharing of perspectives and experiences, which is an asset when considering varying ability levels. The power of communicating through photographs can be especially beneficial in a study of the inclusion of students who are nonverbal, for example. Depending on the needs and abilities of co-researchers, accommodations and adjustments to the preceding photovoice procedure may be needed. Fortunately, the methodology provides space for adaptations to be made to suit the needs of those included in the photovoice research process due to its flexibility.

Flexibility

Closely related to the issue of accessibility, a benefit of photovoice is the flexibility of the method to be used with a variety of ability levels as opposed to other conventional research methods that may be exclusionary. For example, Cluley (2016) used photovoice to include people with profound and multiple learning disabilities in inclusive research. Photovoice was chosen for their study because it could be tailored to the abilities of people with profound and multiple learning disabilities, who are generally unable to express and cognitively process abstract questions or concepts without support. Accordingly, many people with learning disabilities require 'allies' to do research (Walmsley, 2001), so Cluley's study included care workers (i.e., carers) as co-researchers to serve as allies for the people with learning disabilities. All co-researchers, including the people with profound and multiple learning disabilities and their paid carers, were given cameras to take photographs. Deliberate steps were taken to give as much agency as possible to the people with disabilities while being realistic about their abilities, such having carers only take photographs when a participant showed signs it was okay to do so. During the second critical dialogue phase of photovoice research reviewed in the previous section, in Cluley's study carers facilitated the communication of the people with disabilities and also added additional details that the people with disabilities could not. In this way, the inclusion of the voices of carers in their own right added layers of meaning, while the photovoice method's emphasis on visual communication gave nonverbal co-researchers with profound and multiple learning disabilities a means to share their complex lives. Cluley's mediated approach to the inclusive research process would not have been possible without the epistemological flexibility of photovoice.

Power redistribution

Photovoice methodology provides an opportunity to redistribute power and reconceptualize the researcher-participant relationship by acknowledging participants' competency and agency (Sauer, 2013). Inclusive education research focuses on those who are excluded from educational systems and social structures at large. While inclusive education research is continuously broadening the populations under study, students with disabilities are a primary population under analysis within our field. Sauer (2013) calls for further action and research on the researcher-participant relationship for the disability population specifically because people with disabilities are often assumed unable to express their own opinions. Photovoice methodology has the power to challenge these sorts of deficit-based assumptions and instead empowers those with disabilities and other marginalized populations by affording them the opportunity to express their own opinions and experiences through the research process.

For example, as part of a collaborative action research study, photovoice enabled groups of Zambian students, with an average age of 12 years, across seven schools to express their own opinions about the inclusivity of their school environments (Lewis, 2004; Kaplan, Lewis & Mumba, 2007; Miles, 2011). A forum for action was created in this study through a poster exhibition at one of the schools where the study took place by having students present their reflections and images. The empowering nature of this methodology and redistribution of power is evident in how Lewis (2004) and Miles (2011) report that it was the first time that adults genuinely listened to the views of these young students. The photovoice research process employed in this study, culminating in the poster exhibition, gave students the forum to express their opinions to Zambian teachers and led to awareness raising.

Seeing and hearing: The collective power of photographs and narrative

To illustrate the power of photovoice methodology for inclusive education research, a combination of photographs and narratives are shared from data analyzed in a recent research study that I published in collaboration (Braun & Naami, 2021). Note that some chosen examples were previously published in the aforementioned article, while others are from the same data collection but are previously unpublished. Our research study features the voices of two students with mobility disabilities (pseudonyms: Felix and Evans) as they share barriers experienced when accessing their respective postsecondary campus environments in Ghana. In addition to documenting accessibility challenges that serve to impede their inclusion and full participation, the academic and emotional impact of their lived experiences was explored. To increase local and global community awareness to inform inclusive education policy and practice, we chose photovoice as our research methodology to share the lived experiences of postsecondary students with disabilities in Ghana firsthand and represent student voice in the academic and policy arena.

I purposefully selected the images and corresponding narratives that follow from our data collected in the aforementioned research study to feature the duality of the methodology that together brings about a collective impact on the audience that is greater than the sum of its parts. The duality of photovoice is aptly captured by Mueller (2006), who describes how the photographs in and of themselves are not necessarily revealing but the reflections that are initiated by the photographs are.

Mueller goes on to say that the camera provides a voice through which participants represent their challenges and "the photographs become metaphors to illustrate complex issues" (p. 437). The respective value that reflective narratives add to the photographs, and in turn that which the photographs add to the narratives, is explored in the subsequent two sections on hearing and seeing.

Hearing: The added value of narratives

On its own, Figure 13.2 appears to be a random university campus building with an uneven staircase leading to its entrance. Equipped with the background knowledge of the research study being on the topic of campus accessibility, one might infer that the jagged cement, stairs, and absence of a ramp renders the building inaccessible to a wheelchair user. This inference is not incorrect, but it is only part of the story. The full emotional depth of the lived experience being represented by the photograph is not unveiled until after reading the co-researcher's emotionally charged title "My Heart Jumps" together with Evan's corresponding narrative:

FIGURE 13.2 My Heart Jumps. *Note.* From "Access to Higher Education in Ghana: Examining Experiences through the Lens of Students with Mobility Disabilities," by A. M. B. Braun, and A. Naami, 2021, *International Journal of Disability, Development and Education, 68*(1), p. 104 (https://doi.org/10.1080/1034912X.2019.1651833). Copyright 2021 by Taylor & Francis www.tandfonline.com. Reprinted with permission.

> Anytime I see this building my heart jumps. This is supposed to be my primary department but because the building is not disability friendly, changes were made for me. The lecture halls have staircases which are not accessible for a wheelchair user. In view of the architectural design of the department, my courses were changed from economics, mathematics and statistics to sociology, social work and religion. Some of my classes of these new courses were

also held in inaccessible buildings. One of them, interestingly, was held in the Mathematics Department. I feel I have been denied the opportunity to read the course of my choice.

(Braun & Naami, 2021, p. 109)

Multiple emotions such as anxiety, anger, betrayal, resentment, and disappointment that are represented in the photograph for Evans are brought to the surface in his narrative. We learn that the depicted building represents a violation of his academic freedom. Due to the building's inaccessibility, the university forced Evans to switch his program of study, which ironically included coursework that took place in the very building that prompted the change.

Figure 13.3 displays another example of the added value of narrative. The photograph shows two able-bodied students walking through a turnstile entrance. Similar to the initial interpretation of Figure 13.2 postulated above, with the background knowledge of the study's topic on accessibility, one could reasonably infer that the co-researcher is unable to navigate that portion of the physical campus environment in the same way. This presupposition is confirmed by Felix's comment at the beginning of the photograph's narrative that he cannot use the depicted entrance to the university because it is difficult and risky. However, analogous with the value added by the emotionally charged narrative of Figure 13.2, here too the emotional consequences of the campus' physical inaccessibility do not become evident until fully reading the corresponding narration. Only then do we come to appreciate Felix's feelings of his personhood being invalidated caused by the inability to use the

FIGURE 13.3 I Am Not a Car. *Note*. From "Access to Higher Education in Ghana: Examining Experiences through the Lens of Students with Mobility Disabilities," by A. M. B. Braun, and A. Naami, 2021, *International Journal of Disability, Development and Education*, *68*(1), p. 105 (https://doi.org/10.1080/1034912X.2019.1651833). Copyright 2021 by Taylor & Francis www.tandfonline.com. Reprinted with permission.

pictured entrance, coupled with the fact that in lieu of using that entrance he is told by gatekeepers to use the car entrance instead. His chosen title "I Am Not a Car" powerfully captures the relationship of the image to his identity and personhood. The full narration follows:

> This is the main entrance to university. It is a turning start entrance which I cannot use due to my condition. It is difficult to push through and risky as well. The security men at the entrance sometimes ask me to use the entrance for cars, which is more accessible, but I do not feel good about it because I am a human being, and I should use the entrance for people and not the one for cars. I feel I am being treated unfairly by the university management by not providing an accessible entrance.
> (Braun & Naami, 2021, p. 105)

In addition, the portion of the narrative that calls out Felix's perceived injustice of being treated unfairly by university management is reminiscent of Evan's previously stated experience with university management taking away his right to choose his program of study. Both narratives highlight the power dynamics at play and give co-researchers an opportunity to reclaim some of the power that is lost by bringing these issues to light during the critical discussions of stage two and the community awareness raising of stage three of the photovoice research process.

The collective power of photographs and narrative is illustrated in these examples by showcasing the emotional depth and power dynamics that undoubtedly add layers of meaning to the images. Applying Mueller's (2006) assertion that photovoice allows photographs to serve as metaphors, Figure 13.2 serves as a metaphor for Evan's constrained academic freedom and Figure 13.3 as a metaphor for Felix's invalidated personhood. These powerful metaphors would not exist without the joint contributions of photographs and narratives to the photovoice process. The unique value that is added to the photographs by the reflective narratives allow historically marginalized voices to be heard more loudly and clearly compared to what can be communicated through photographs alone.

Seeing: The added value of photographs

Conversely, in photovoice methodology, photographs add value to narratives by providing the audience with imagery to illustrate what is being expressed in the narrative. For example, in the following narrative Evans walks the reader through the numerous steps that are required to enter a lecture theatre that is supposedly accessible to wheelchair users because it has a ramp:

> To get to the entrance of this lecture theater, you first have to cross an open gutter, then you can see the chippings which is also extremely difficult for wheelchair users. Then, when you get to the ramp, there is [a] huge step to get on the ramp which will also require assistance for a wheelchair user. You see,

there are several issues/barriers to enter one building: open gutter, stone chippings, and then a huge step before one can use the ramp provided for access to this lecture theater. It is sad. There is no way a person in a wheelchair can access this building on their own without help. No way!

(Braun & Naami, 2021, p. 102)

Figure 13.4 illustrates the first step of crossing the open gutter. Figure 13.5 illustrates the second step of crossing the stone chippings (i.e., loose gravel) as well as the third

FIGURE 13.4 Depend on People Always – Step 1, previously unpublished.

FIGURE 13.5 Depend on People Always – Steps 2 and 3. *Note.* From "Access to Higher Education in Ghana: Examining Experiences through the Lens of Students with Mobility Disabilities," by A. M. B. Braun, and A. Naami, 2021, *International Journal of Disability, Development and Education, 68*(1), p. 102 (https://doi.org/10.1080/1034 912X.2019.1651833). Copyright 2021 by Taylor & Francis www.tandfonline.com. Reprinted with permission.

Being seen and heard **227**

step of rising over the steep edge of the concrete ramp. The numbers 1, 2, and 3 have been added to the original images to show the three steps that Evans articulates in his narrative.

Evans titled the photographs "Depend on People Always," because, as he explains, "When I see these kinds of structures, I feel like society is telling me to continually depend on others because I have no place to live on my own" (previously unpublished). Evans is unable to complete these three steps independently without assistance from others. While his detailed explanation of the numerous steps required to enter the building helps readers imagine the various challenges along the way, having the accompanying photographs helps readers put themselves in Evans' shoes and navigate alongside him. The photographs provide a window into Evans' lived experience of trying to go to class by way of an inaccessible wheelchair ramp.

The final example, Figure 13.6 titled "House Arrest," corresponds to the following narration by Felix:

> This is a pathway where I live. It is difficult for me [to] walk on this muddy and rubbish filled path. When it rains, it becomes even more challenging and renders me immobile. I cannot go to school, church, or to work. I feel bad because I cannot use the path.
>
> (previously unpublished)

The path is described as muddy and rubbish filled and that is particularly challenging for Felix to traverse when it rains. It may be difficult for a reader to visualize what the path looks like based on the narrative description alone, but having the corresponding photograph helps the reader understand Felix's lived experience and

FIGURE 13.6 House Arrest, previously unpublished.

more accurately picture what it would be like to navigate the challenging terrain on a dry day. The photograph also provides a starting point for readers to envision the path during the rainy season and imagine how much more challenging it would be to traverse with pouring rain running down the slanted hillside, thick mud, and puddles amongst the rubbish. The presence of the cinderblock house structure in the frame is also effective in aiding the audience in imagining the helpless feeling of being under house arrest due to the immobility experienced on rainy days.

Conclusion

Photovoice methodology is an innovative research practice that inclusive education researchers can use to enhance inclusivity throughout the research process. Photovoice has the power to make a profound impact in society, in research, and on the co-researchers participating in the research process themselves. Each of these three areas of application will be discussed next, moving from micro to macro levels of impact and benefit.

Unlike conventional research methods that may perpetuate power inequalities between researchers and those who are being researched, the empowering and participatory characteristics of photovoice methodology have the potential to equalize power disparities and create inclusive research spaces for marginalized populations. Rooted in participatory action research, photovoice is a mutually beneficial methodology that promotes the active involvement of marginalized populations in all phases of the research process as equal partners serving as co-researchers. Repositioning people who have been excluded as experts by equipping them with cameras to showcase their lived experience and facilitating opportunities for critical dialogue and community advocacy is empowering and action focused. Not only are marginalized populations actively involved in the production of knowledge about the daily issues that they face, but this methodology inspires true change and community improvement. Photovoice methodology also affords epistemological flexibility, which increases the accessibility and inclusivity of the research process for people of varying abilities. This epistemological flexibility is advantageous to continue to enhance the diversity of populations whose perspectives and experiences are represented in inclusive education research.

The research exemplar featured in this chapter illustrates the collective power of photographs and narrative to make the experiences and perspectives of children and youth who are systematically excluded from education systems be both seen and heard. Photovoice allows researchers to employ participatory data collection methods and innovative analytical tools such as the SHOWeD technique (Wang, 2006) to collaboratively interpret photographs and narratives in ways that further enrich research. Compared to other conventional inclusive education research methodologies such as attitude surveys, photovoice research studies can make a greater impact by telling people's stories and by featuring visual images. These visual and narrative dimensions provide a uniquely multifaceted depth to the research process and to the findings, thereby enhancing the overall impact of the research. Not only do people who are participating in the research have the opportunity to explore and experience the research in a multisensory manner as they take and critically discuss photographs, but the methodology allows outsiders to bear witness to the co-researchers' lived experiences from their vantage point and through their words.

The combination of firsthand stories and photographs have the unique ability to draw an audience in and deepen their understanding, eliciting emotional and empathetic reactions that can inspire change. Photovoice allows for a stronger message to be communicated during research dissemination and for greater advocacy for inclusion in society. As one of photovoice's three central aims reviewed in this chapter, community advocacy is an inherent component of the methodology. This research aim aligns with the advocacy interests of many inclusive education policymakers, researchers, educators, and stakeholders. Photovoice is a powerful tool to bring about advocacy and community action by enhancing public awareness of the challenges faced by those who are excluded and by showcasing the benefits of inclusion in action.

References

Aldridge, J. (2007). Picture this: The use of participatory photographic research methods with people with learning disabilities. *Disability and Society*, 22(1), 1–17.

Baker, A. M. (2016). The process and product: Crafting community portraits with young people in flexible learning settings. *International Journal of Inclusive Education*, 20(3), 309–330. https://doi.org/10.1080/13603116.2015.1047656

Bisung, E., Elliott, S., Abudho, B., Schuster-Wallace, C., & Karanha, D. (2015). Dreaming of toilets: Using photovoice to explore knowledge, attitudes and practices around water-health linkages in rural Kenya. *Health and Place*, 31, 208–215. https://doi.org/10.1016/j.healthplace.2014.12.007

Braun, A. M. (2020). Amplifying the voices of people with disabilities in comparative and international education research with PhotoVoice methodology. In E. Anderson, S. Baily, Call-Cummings, M., R. Iyengar, C. Manion, P. Shah, & M. Witenstein (Eds.), *Interrogating and innovating comparative and international education: Decolonizing practices for inclusive, safe spaces* (pp. 166–184). Brill.

Braun, A. M. B., & Naami, A. (2021). Access to higher education in Ghana: Examining experiences through the lens of students with mobility disabilities. *International Journal of Disability, Development and Education*, 68(1), 95–115. https://doi.org/10.1080/1034912X.2019.1651833

Brenna, B., Burles, M., Holtslander, L., & Bocking, S. (2017). A school curriculum for fetal alcohol spectrum disorder: Advice from a young adult with FASD. *International Journal of Inclusive Education*, 21(2), 218–229. https://doi.org/10.1080/13603116.2016.1193565

Castleden, H., Garvin, T., & First Nation, H. (2008). Modifying photovoice for community-based participatory indigenous research. *Social Science and Medicine*, 66, 1399–1405. https://doi.org/10.1016/j.socscimed.2007.11.030

Cluley, V. (2016). Using photovoice to include people with profound and multiple learning disabilities in inclusive research. *British Journal of Learning Disabilities*, 45, 39–46. https://doi.org/10.1111/bld.12174

Kaplan, I., Lewis, I., & Mumba, P. (2007). Picturing global educational inclusion? Looking and thinking across students' photographs from the UK, Zambia and Indonesia. *Journal of Research in Special Educational Needs*, 7(1), 23–35.

Klotz, J. (2014). Sociocultural study of intellectual disability: Moving beyond labeling and social constructivist perspectives. *British Journal of Learning Disabilities, 32*(2), 93–104.

Lewis, I. (2004). *Using images to explore and promote inclusion: Experiences from Mpika schools.* Manchester: EENET. http://www.eenet.org.uk/resources/docs/report_zambia_yes.pdf

Miles, S. (2011). Exploring understandings of inclusion in schools in Zambia and Tanzania using reflective writing and photography. *International Journal of Inclusive Education, 15*(10), 1087–1102. https://doi.org/10.1080/13603116.2011.555072

Mueller, C. (2006). Creating a joint partnership: Including Qallunaat teacher voices within Nunavik education policy. *International Journal of Inclusive Education, 10*(4–5), 429–447.

Sauer, J. S. (2013). Research, relationships and making understanding: A look at Brantlinger's Darla and the value of case study research. *International Journal of Inclusive Education research, 17*(12), 1253–1264. https://doi.org/10.1080/13603116.2013.781237

Shah, P. (2015). Spaces to speak: Photovoice and the reimagination of girls' education in India. *Comparative Education Review, 59*(1), 50–70.

Walmsley, J. (2001). Normalisation, emancipatory research and inclusive research in learning disability. *Disability & Society, 16*(2), 187–205. https://doi.org/10.1080/09687590120035807

Wang, C. C. (1999). Photovoice: A participatory action research strategy applied to women's health. *Journal of Women's Health, 8*(2), 185–192.

Wang, C. C. (2006). Youth participation in photovoice as a strategy for community change. *Journal of Community Practice, 14*(1–2), 147–161.

Wang, C. C., & Burris, M. A. (1994). Empowerment through photo novella: Portraits of participation. *Health Education & Behavior, 21*(2), 171–186.

Wang, C. C., & Burris, M. A. (1997). Photovoice: Concept, methodology, and use for participatory needs assessment. *Health Education & Behavior: The Official Publication of the Society for Public Health Education, 24*(3), 369–387.

Wang, C. C., & Redwood-Jones, Y. A. (2001). Photovoice ethics: Perspectives from Flint photovoice. *Health Education & Behavior, 28*(5), 560–572.

Whyte, W. F. (1991). *Participatory action research.* Los Angeles: Sage.

14
COLLABORATIVE B-LEARNING AS A TOOL TO STUDYING AND PREPARING FOR INCLUSION IN A CULTURALLY DIVERSE ENVIRONMENT

Silvia Romero-Contreras, Ismael García-Cedillo, and Gabriela Silva-Maceda

Introduction[1]

Inclusive education emerged as a process that could reverse the effects of poor-quality education that is generally offered to students who belong to groups in vulnerable situations. So far, in most regions of the world, schools have not managed to reduce social inequalities (UNESCO, 2005). Therefore, a change toward an education accessible to all, that is not determined by the personal, social or family conditions of the student body is needed. Thus, this new educational model seeks to offer quality education to all students to enable successful educational paths.

Implementing inclusive education requires an educational policy oriented toward promoting, initiating, and maintaining efforts in favor of inclusion. The ideal scenario would be to have very flexible national curricula that allow teachers to make adjustments considering the context and the characteristics of the students; in other words, that schools and teachers had a certain degree of autonomy. Schools need resources to remove physical, administrative and methodological barriers that hinder student participation and learning. They also need collaborative mechanisms to define, along with the parents, their mission and the values to be promoted. Along with all these elements, the implementation of inclusive education requires school principals who are academic leaders, as well as committed and well-trained teachers.

Inclusive education requires teachers with a highly developed value system that genuinely allows them not only to tolerate or even respect but also to positively value diversity in their classrooms. These values should be reflected in their belief system about the nature of disability (Jordan, Schwartz & McGhie-Richmond, 2009) and in the development of favorable attitudes toward the inclusion of traditionally excluded students (Forlin, García-Cedillo, Romero-Contreras, Fletcher & Rodriguez-Hernández, 2010). Teachers should possess extensive knowledge of the curriculum and methodological strategies to make learning accessible to all their students. This accessibility implies having a high sense of self-efficacy to teach all students (Forlin et al. 2010) to implement inclusive practices in the classroom and effective teaching strategies that enable learning for all their students. Teachers must also have a genuine interest in each and every one of their students and high academic expectations for all of them.

In sum, building the professional, physical and administrative structures for inclusive education is a very long process. One necessary step is to offer professional development for pre-service and in-service teachers to sensitize them on the relevance of inclusive education and offer them didactic tools to teach all their students. This chapter describes the design and implementation of such professional development with a large number of teachers (and other professionals) from a South American country and reports on the impact of this strategy on the participants' attitudes, knowledge and self-perceptions of their practices.

The concept of inclusive education

Ainscow, Booth and Dyson (2006) are probably the most widely recognized promoters of inclusive education (IE). In 2006, they defined inclusive education as: "an approach to education embodying particular values ... concerned with all learners and with overcoming barriers to all forms of marginalisation, exclusion and underachievement" (p. 5). Such an approach, according to Ainscow et al., demands the transformation of the educational system in terms of culture, policies and practices, to reduce exclusion so that all students are able to attend and remain in school, as well as to participate and learn at the best of their capacities.

In order to fully implement inclusive education, educational systems should go beyond responding to the needs of some learners to bring them to the mainstream and assume a decisive and full responsibility of responding to the diversity of all learners (UNESCO, 2005). UNESCO points out that inclusive education implies changing teachers and learners' ideas about diversity to "see it as a challenge and enrichment of the learning environment, rather than a problem", while, at the same time, leaving "open the possibility of personal choice and options for special assistance and facilities for those who need it" (p. 15).

Inclusive education in Latin America: Where do we stand?

Latin America is the region of the world with the deepest structural inequalities and the most stratified societies (Blanco & Duk, 2011), in addition to presenting a culturally diverse population (Blanco, 2014). All these characteristics have played an important role in the unequal progress attained by the countries of the region in the implementation of inclusive education. Educational inequalities regarding access, permanence and completion, as well as quality are present at all educational levels; however these deepen at the higher educational levels (high school and college) (Blanco, 2014).

It is fair to say that practically all countries in the region have progressive laws and regulations; in addition, most have laws in favor of inclusive intercultural education (Tomé Fernández & Manzano García, 2016). Nevertheless, in many countries it is necessary to establish mechanisms to advance their compliance (Blanco & Duk, 2011; García, 2009; Samaniego de García, 2009). Among the mechanisms that can support the implementation of inclusive education are awareness raising and pre-service and in-service teacher training, as teachers are the central agents of change. According to Blanco and Duk (2019), under the current circumstances in Latin America, it is necessary to create "policies that articulate pre-service and in-service teacher professional development, job placement, professional career, the improvement of working conditions and a greater appreciation of the teaching profession" (p. 38). Through teacher training, it is possible to influence attitudes, beliefs, conceptions and competencies aimed at offering quality education to all students.

There are different models to attend to diversity, which are also reflected in several models for teacher training. Nash and Norwich (2010) classify teacher training models into three categories: a) One-way model, where all teachers are prepared to serve all students including those with specific educational needs; b) Two-track model, where special education teachers are trained separately from regular education teachers, and c) Multiple-track model, where all teachers share a common foundation and then specialize in a particular area. Many countries in the region have adopted the two-track model, e.g., Ecuador (Vélez-Calvo, Tárraga-Mínguez, Fernández-Andrés & Sanz-Cervera, 2016) and Mexico (Romero-Contreras, Garcia-Cedillo, Forlin & Lomelí-Hernández, 2013). This model, unfortunately, is insufficient to prepare teachers to face the challenge of implementing inclusive education, as the members of each track learn very little about the other and end up having to work in inclusive environments without such perspective, so they have difficulties collaborating and understanding the other's point of view.

In sum, given the current situation, the Latin American region has the challenge of continuing to work toward inclusion mainly through changes in policy and teacher preparation. Governments need to design policies that: a) at the school level, foster flexible curricula so that schools and teachers can have greater autonomy while receiving sufficient support, such as systematic initial and in-service training for inclusion; and b) at the family level, guarantee the right of parents to enroll their children in the nearest school and to have access to assistive technologies (Molina-García, Molina-García & Rodríguez-Abelarde, 2019). Pre-service and in-service programs need to focus on developing teachers' competencies in order to positively value diversity from a human rights perspective, be willing to work collaboratively, have the ability to flex and diversify the curriculum, and manage inclusive learning environments (Duk, Cisternas & Ramos, 2019).

Designing a blended learning program

In the 21st century, virtual learning in Latin America has been widely extended but it is still scarce compared to other regions of the world. Countries such as

Venezuela, Costa Rica, and Colombia had their first higher education virtual learning experiences in the 1970s, while others started in the 1980s and 1990s or even later (Verdún, 2016).

Virtual learning comprises many formats and options that make it difficult to characterize it as one type of learning, but as Verdún (2016: 77) states, it is exactly the "versatility of combining various means in one environment" that makes it unique. Asynchronous virtual learning is even more versatile to design, organize and manage for administrators, teachers and tutors and to follow for students (Verdún, 2016). Virtual learning belongs to the fourth generation of distance learning, which started a few years after the creation of the World Wide Web. Prior to this, other modalities of distance learning were based on regular mail, radio, telephone and TV networks, and some basic WWW–based resources (Verdún, 2016).

According to Verdún (2016) e-learning, m-learning and b-learning are among the most common virtual learning formats nowadays. Electronic or *e-learning* refers to online or total virtual learning, in the sense that it is delivered and received through technology. While at first it emphasized the delivery of information, this modality is now geared toward creating asynchronous interactive learning communities. Mobile or *m-learning* incorporates mobile devices to e-learning, which facilitates access even when people are in transit. This modality appears to be a common type of non-formal learning. Blended or *b-learning*, also known as *mixed-learning*, combines face-to-face learning with e-learning. This modality has the potential of merging the best attributes from the two worlds and offers flexibility in the design and delivery of information and knowledge construction (Verdún, 2016).

B-learning presents various advantages for adult learning, higher and in-service education and a wide variety of educational resources (González Guerrero, Padilla Beltrán & Rincón Caballero, 2011). In this modality, the cost is lower when compared to full face-to-face learning in terms of the use of facilities and transportation. Given that students can manage their study time more flexibly, it is more compatible with other activities, such as work or home chores. By combining multimedia and online resources with face-to-face interaction, students have more opportunities to achieve higher levels of understanding and to further develop their problem-solving abilities.

Effective planning and managing of a b-learning program requires a well-trained educational staff in order to conduct various activities, such as designing the educational plan and the instructional materials, facilitating learning and access to technology, managing resources and offering assistance and feedback (González Guerrero et al. 2011). Moreover, a conceptual model of learning and content structure must guide these activities (Alonso, López, Manrique & Viñes, 2005). Alonso et al. (2005) propose a b-learning instructional approach based on three psychopedagogical prescriptions or principles: structured content, effective cognitive processes and effective collaborative activities. These principles involve integrating the course contents into "coherent information structures that help build knowledge schemas in the learner's minds" (p. 220) to allow for effective cognitive processes to occur as the learner interacts with content as well as with others within a learning community. The model consists of seven phases: analysis, design, development, implementation, execution, evaluation and review.

The next sections describe the context and the stages of design followed through the b-learning course on inclusive education that was recently delivered to a large group of teachers and other educational professionals in a South American country.

Context

The course was designed under the request of offering a specialization course at the graduate level for in-service teachers and other professionals in a country, which had recently made legislative changes in favor of inclusive education. Three parties organized the course: the Ministry of Education, a private local university and the local office of an international organization. The latter was responsible for selecting and appointing the group of professionals who would be in charge of designing, implementing and evaluating the specialization (from now on "international or design team"[2]). The local office of the international organization (from now on "local team") was also responsible for administering the resources and supervising the development of the course. The course was designed following the principles and phases proposed by Alonso et al. (2005) for b-learning.

Psychopedagogical principles

Course structure

The course consisted of a 360-hour-course: 100 face-to-face hours, 200 online work hours and 60 on-site practicum hours, organized in five monthly modules with an introductory face-to-face one-week session and online independent work. All educational resources (videos, readings, presentations, questionnaires, assignments) were managed through an open-source course management system.

Effective cognitive processes

The course was designed to serve as a model to teach diverse populations, so activities were designed following universal design for learning (UDL, CAST, 2011), differentiated instruction (DI, Tomlinson, 2017), inclusive pedagogy (Florian, 2010; Spratt & Florian, 2013), collaborative work guidelines (Barkley, Cross & Howell, 2007) and a disciplinary research-based approach to teaching with specific reading, writing and math content (Romero-Contreras, 2014). It included guided and independent, collaborative and individual activities, which involved oral and written discussion and decision-making tasks, in order to offer participants several opportunities to advance their competencies in attitude, management, organization and critical thinking as they had been appointed by the government and were expected to go back to their school communities to initiate or continue the process of inclusion. Most activities demanded participants to reflect on their practice and conduct, short surveys, assessments or interventions at their workplace to advance their final project and practicum.

Effective learning communities

The course was delivered in two cohorts of 550 participants each, divided into learning communities of 50 to 70 students at various locations in the country. The international team trained a group of inclusive education specialists on the program, the materials and the dynamics, who then led the learning communities. Technology tutors provided assistance to access the materials and upload the assignments to the platform. During face-to-face sessions, members of the international team delivered videoconferences to all groups in the cohort to introduce or expand on the topics to be discussed, to offer general guidelines and to exchange opinions and concerns. Most face-to-face activities included small-group and whole-class discussions; online activities included participation in fora and teamwork products. Team members were regularly part of the same school community, workplace or school level, so they shared common knowledge and interests.

Course design, phases

Analysis

Before designing the course, the international team with the support of the two local partners conducted a thorough analysis of the country's characteristics such as its educational system, laws and regulations regarding general education, special education and inclusive education, teachers' characteristics, and teacher preparation programs. The local partners also kept the international team informed of all the decisions they made as to the number of students, the number and location of the groups, the profile of the students registered, and the resources available at each location for participants and facilitators.

Design

The total number of course-hours and the distribution between face-to-face and online hours were defined by the two local parties as part of the terms of reference. Based on this parameter and the course's general purpose – to offer a professional development course for in-service teachers, principals, supervisors and other educational authorities, to advance the implementation of inclusive education in the country, following the laws and regulations recently issued – the international team defined a five-module course structure. The main contents of the course are presented in Table 14.1.

Other bodies of content, basic knowledge and strategies for managing technology resources, academic language resources and disciplinary/subject area-based strategies for teaching were organized cross-sectionally (see Figure 14.1).

Development and implementation

Modules were organized into thematic units. The instructional model included: an introduction to the topic, further theoretical information or data, integration

TABLE 14.1 Description of core content in each module

Modules	Core content description
I **The evolution of inclusion and inclusive education.**	The main international agreements and conventions, as well as local laws and regulations on inclusion, were revised, discussed, analyzed and assessed in light of the real progress attained at participants' workplaces and communities.
II **Attitudes on inclusive education.**	The history and tensions of the right to education, special education and inclusive education were reviewed and analyzed considering the main concepts, typologies, milestones and dilemmas in the field. Particular attention was given to the concept of resilience through the analysis of real cases and prototypical examples.
III **Serving and teaching students from diverse populations and groups.**	A typology of target populations by disability (sensory, motor, intellectual, psychosocial), personal conditions (language, attention, behavior) and living conditions (poverty, migration, HIV, chronic disease, etc.) was introduced to organize some of the key content and historical periods. Real cases and prototypical examples of diverse students were presented and discussed considering socio-emotional, educational, family-oriented, and legal perspectives, as well as the principles of inclusive pedagogy, universal design for learning and differentiated instruction.
IV **Promoting inclusive education (Methodology I).**	The characteristics of the ideal classroom and socio-emotional skills, classroom climate and organization and resources of inclusive pedagogy and evaluation were revised and reflected on. Special attention was given to serving students in poverty, from diverse cultural backgrounds, chronic disease and without family ties (in foster homes or institutions).
V **Designing projects for inclusive education (Methodology II).**	The process of planning and implementing inclusive education was reviewed and mentored. Mentoring was conducted throughout the whole course; however, this module was mostly devoted to revising and adjusting participants' projects.

exercises and an online review activity or project. The introductory activity had the purpose of either activating previous knowledge or presenting a problematic situation for participants to analyze. The topic presented was followed by the relevant information to advance on the topic in the form of text, video-clip, infographics, slides presentation and conceptual map, among others. Participants were asked to further investigate the topic, discuss, and integrate the information on an individual or group product such as a summary, response to questions, survey, artwork

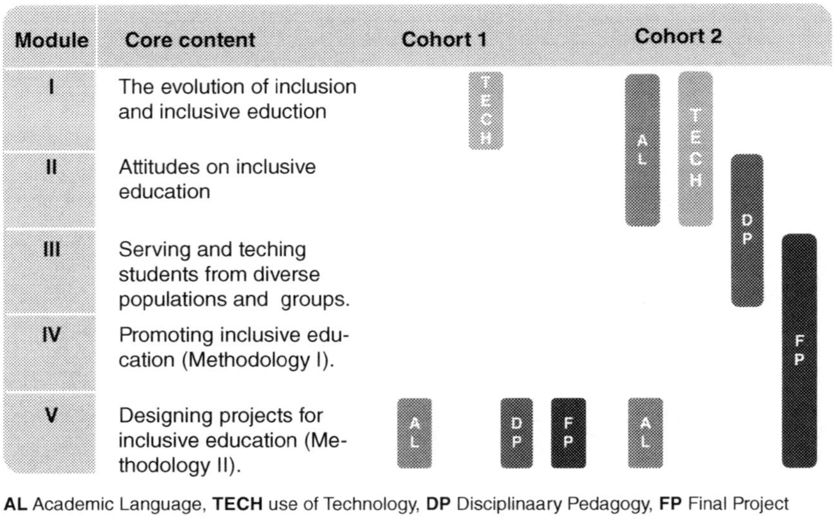

Module	Core content	Cohort 1	Cohort 2
I	The evolution of inclusion and inclusive eduction	TECH	AL / TECH
II	Attitudes on inclusive education		DP
III	Serving and teching students from diverse populations and groups.		
IV	Promoting inclusive education (Methodology I).		FP
V	Designing projects for inclusive education (Methodology II).	AL / DP / FP	AL

AL Academic Language, **TECH** use of Technology, **DP** Disciplinaary Pedagogy, **FP** Final Project

FIGURE 14.1 Distribution of cross-sectional content in Cohort 1 and Cohort 2.

(i.e. create a poem or a song). After the face-to-face meetings, participants had one online assignment per thematic unit, which commonly required connecting theory and practice within their work contexts.

Execution. The course was implemented sequentially for two cohorts of 550 participants each and distributed in ten sites in six regions across the country; inclusive education specialists and b-learning tutors delivered the course. Members of the international team provided intensive training and permanent support to the local specialists and also participated on-site during the face-to-face sessions as class facilitators and coordinators, answering questions or doubts about the materials to the inclusive education specialists and tutors (via instant messaging), and delivering a daily one-hour videoconference to keep all sites simultaneously informed so they could advance together.

Evaluation

During each module, participants, facilitators and tutors filled out different questionnaires on the relevance and quality of the activities; suggestions were also welcomed. These responses were useful to adjust upcoming activities and also, among other resources, to revise the design between the first and the second cohort. After each module, participants had a three-week period to revise selected activities conducted during the face-to-face sessions in order to round them up, improve them and submit them for assessment and grading. They also had to complete activities and/or advance on their final projects. In addition, at the end of each module, participants completed an online assessment with close and open-ended questions. At the beginning and at the end of the course, participants were administered several instruments on their demographics, attitudes, teaching practice and knowledge on inclusive education (see instruments, ahead).

Review

The course was revised prior to, during and after its execution. The Ministry of Education and the local team conducted extensive and systematic revisions to the course content before each execution offering suggestions that were timely attended. During the training sessions conducted prior to each face-to-face session, the local specialists revised the materials and identified dialectal differences and/or imprecisions regarding specific local laws, regulations or procedures involving general, special or inclusive education. At the end of the first cohort the course was revised based on a variety of resources obtained with the first cohort to improve its overall quality before its delivery to the second cohort.

The general strengths of the course, upon completion with the first cohort, were:

- Most participants had a positive opinion on the quality and the professionalism of the inclusive education specialists and other staff responsible for delivering the course.
- The themes, dynamics, materials, readings, videos and cases were highly valued.
- Most participants attended all sessions, did so on time and engaged enthusiastically in the activities.
- The local team and the Ministry of Education offered good and timely support to face and resolve the difficulties that arose.

The most important difficulties were related to the following aspects:

- Many participants had limited digital skills; the initial training offered was insufficient to overcome these difficulties, so they required very close support from course staff and classmates.
- Internet access was limited at some of the sites.
- The facilities, at some of the sites, were inappropriate for the number of participants.
- In general, participants needed support to comply with academic standards (quality of papers and plagiarism were especially sensitive issues), mainly those who had long completed their undergraduate studies.
- Some activities, particularly the final project, required very intense academic work; the time allocated to carrying them out was considered insufficient.
- Subject area activities (reading, writing and math) were valued but considered insufficient.

The main changes for the second cohort were:

1. A more comprehensive and relevant course was offered to support students with digital skills deficiencies, in addition to more consistent support.

2. The content and workload were reduced, so that participants could focus on the quality of their work.
3. Internet connectivity was improved at all sites.
4. Course requirements and grading criteria were more clearly specified from the beginning and throughout the course; all assignments and rubrics were systematically analyzed with the class to offer timely clarification.
5. Academic standards were made explicit; several resources were offered to help participants improve the quality of their work and avoid plagiarism.
6. Even though it was not always possible to change the location of overcrowded groups, a better distribution of participants was achieved, which somewhat alleviated the overcrowding issue.
7. More subject area teaching activities were included following the participants' suggestions.
8. Participants' final projects were initiated earlier to allow for more direct and close support during face-to-face meetings.

Impact of the program

In order to identify how the described 360-hour b-learning collaborative course impacted participant attitudes and beliefs toward inclusion, as well as their teaching practices and knowledge about strategies to promote learning in inclusive environments, we conducted pre- and posttest online assessments of both cohorts using various self-report instruments.

All participants were asked at the first and last face-to-face meetings to answer the online versions of the instruments and to give their consent for the anonymous use of their results. In both cohorts, the turnaround was very high for the pretest and rather low for the posttest, as participants still had a tight work agenda and several assignments to complete for the course. The results presented as follows include only those participants who answered both rounds of testing, pre and post.

Characteristics of the instruments

Instruments were administered online. Digital versions were copies of the paper versions in terms of the content with a few additional questions to secure consent and participants' identification to cross-reference pre- and posttest results. The format, on the other hand, had to be adapted according to the online resource. Similar to the paper copy, no time limit was set to answer each instrument, however the system was configured to accept only one full answer per participant and for a specific period of time, regularly one week.

Six instruments were administered. Two to assess attitudes, two for teaching practices, one for concept knowledge and one for digital abilities. Reliability data of previous studies with Spanish-speaking populations are reported whenever available. Two instruments did not have psychometric information (ESTRAT, IE-CON) and one reported a low Cronbach's alpha for one subscale (SACIE), so reliability measures were obtained with the present data (see Table 14.2).

TABLE 14.2 Summary of instrument characteristics

Instrument	Subscales (Crombach's alfa)	Validation studies
Attitudes		
SACIE	Total (.716)★ (.732)	Mexican preservice teachers
15 items	Sentiments (.609)★ (.643)	Romero-Contreras et al.
4-point Likert	Attitudes (.625)★ (.812)	2013★
scale – agreement	Concerns (.366)★ (.637)	This study
TEIP	Total (.941)	Mexican pre-service
18 items	Inclusive instruction (.865)	teachers
6-point Likert	Collaboration (.845)	Romero-Contreras et al.
scale – agreement	Managing disruptive behavior (.855)	2013
Teaching practices		
	Total (.847)★ (.963)	
	Classroom layout (.812)	
	Planning (.878)	
	Use of time (.737)	
GEPIA	Teaching methods (.912)	Mexican teachers
58 items	Assessment (.858)	García-Cedillo et al.
4-point Likert	Student-teacher relationship (.874)	2018★ (total only)
scale –frequency	Interaction with support personnel (.937)	This study (total and subscales)
	Inclusive education awareness (.708)	
	Professional development (.763)	
	Collaboration with special ed. (.906)	
	Collaboration with families (.788)	
ESTRAT		
34 items		
4-point Likert scale	Reduced version, 17 items (.898)	This study
– frequency		
Concept knowledge		
IE-CON		
10 multiple choice single items	Total (.534)	
3 cases with various binary decision-like questions (correct/incorrect) each.	Concepts (.408) Case analysis (.658)	This study
Digital abilities		
TPACK	TK Technological Knowledge (.906)	Spain and Latin-American
19 items	PK Pedagogical knowledge (.951)	pre-service teachers
5-point Likert scale	TPK Technological-pedagogical	Cabero Almenara et al.
– agreement	knowledge (.912)	2015

Instruments for the assessment of attitudes

SACIE – The Sentiments, Attitudes and Concerns about Inclusive Education Scale (Forlin, Earle, Loreman, & Sharma, 2011). On this scale, teachers report on three areas: their attitudes toward the positive potential of educating people with different disabilities in the regular classroom (i.e., attention deficit, language impairment, sensory impairment); their negative sentiments regarding their interaction with people with disability and the idea of having a disability; and the concerns they face when incorporating students with disabilities into their class. On this scale, it is expected that as awareness and knowledge about inclusive education increase, scores on attitudes increase and those on sentiments and concerns decrease.[3]

TEIP – Self-efficacy in Implementing Inclusive Practices Scale (Sharma, Loreman & Forlin, 2012). TEIP assesses the self-perception of teachers regarding their possibilities of implementing inclusive practices in their classrooms. Self-perception is related to their abilities to control the disruptive behaviors of some students, to respond appropriately to the most capable students, to promote collaborative work among their students, to evaluate them appropriately, to communicate activities clearly, to support families to help children and to become involved in school activities and in collaborative work with other professionals. (For SACIE and TEIP Spanish versions, see Forlin et al. 2010; Romero-Contreras, Garcia-Cedillo, Forlin & Lomelí-Hernández, 2013).

Instruments for the assessment of teaching practices

GEPIA (*Guía de la Evaluación de las Prácticas Inclusivas en el Aula-Auto-reporte/* Inclusive Teaching Practices Assessment Protocol-Self-report, García-Cedillo, Romero-Contreras, Escalante-Aguilar & Flores-Barrera, 2018). This instrument is based on the index of inclusion (Booth, & Ainscow, 2002). On this instrument, teachers report on their classroom practices to promote inclusive education regarding classroom management and organization, planning, use of time, teaching methods, assessment and student participation. They also report on their collaborative practices with parents and professionals within the school, as well as their attitudes toward diversity and the training they have received to promote inclusion.

ESTRAT Self-Rating Scale. Strategies for Learning: Teacher Questionnaire (Mitchell, 2015a, 2015b; Spanish version study: Ramos-Estrada, García-Cedillo, Sotelo-Castillo, López-Valenzuela, & Murillo-Parra, 2020). This instrument is based on the analysis of best practices for inclusion and consists of a list of such practices where teachers report how often they use each of them. For this research a short version of ESTRAT was used. It includes practices to promote students' collaborative work, social skills, self-esteem and cognitive processing (memory, problem solving, reading comprehension), as well as the use of strategies based on direct instruction, use of technology and assistive devices, differentiated instruction and assessment, universal design for learning (UDL) and positive school and classroom climate.

Instrument to assess inclusive education concepts

IE-CON. The Questionnaire on Inclusive Education was designed *ad hoc* to assess participants' conceptual knowledge on inclusive education. This instrument includes two sections. The first is a series of multiple-choice questions on basic facts and concepts on inclusion. The second part presents three cases for participants to make decisions based on their attitudes, knowledge and strategies to deal with students with disabilities and vulnerable conditions.

Instrument to assess digital abilities

TPACK. In this research, teachers were administered a reduced version of a tool for assessing participants' digital abilities based on the TPACK model (http://www.matt-koehler.com/tpack-101/; Schmidt, Baran, Thompson, Mishra, Koehler & Shin, 2009; Spanish version: Cabero Almenara, Marín Díaz & Castaño Garrido, 2015). Three out of five scales were administered: Technological knowledge, to assess participants' familiarity with the use of hardware and software; pedagogical knowledge, to assess teachers' general pedagogical practices and technological pedagogical knowledge to assess teachers' use of technology for teaching purposes.[4]

Characteristics of the participants

As mentioned before, not all participants responded to the pre- and posttest. For the first cohort, participation in the posttest was minimal, so only participants from the second cohort are included here. The impact analysis was conducted on a total of 517 participants: 70 male and 447 female, ages between 24 and 59 years from six geographical areas of the county (metropolitan area and five other regions) where the course was delivered. Table 14.3 presents the main characteristics of the participants.

Differences between pre- and posttest

Mean pre- and posttest results of each instrument were compared using the Student t test (see Table 14.4). The number of responses per test varied between 273 and 401 (see n value). Results showing a significant difference after the course are shown in Table 14.4. Total non-significant results were included when subscales were significant.

The main impacts of the course, based on the t-test results, appear to be contradictory, as a few unexpected decreases were found. However, these seem to reflect the complex cognitive process of relating theory to practice. On the one hand, the greatest impact was a significant increase in concept learning (IE-CON-Concepts), which indicates that participants improved their knowledge of and understanding on inclusive education. Similarly, they also showed moderate but significant post-course

TABLE 14.3 Characteristics of the participants

Category	Subcategories	Percentage
Current position	Classroom teacher	51.2
	Other: Coordinator, Vice-principal, Administrator (in school or at the Ministry of Education)	33.7
	School paraprofessional	7.37
	Principal, general school	3.78
	Special Ed. teacher in general school	2.59
	Supervisor	1.20
	Principal, special ed. school	0.20
Educational level served	Early education 0 to 3–4 years	1.99
	Preschool – 3–5 years	3.98
	Elementary – 6–12 years	22.71
	Secondary – 13–15 years	19.32
	High school – 16–18 years	19.72
	Other: All levels, college or nonspecified	32.27
School organization	Complete	75.30
	Multigrade	3.59
	Not working in school	8.17
	Other	12.92
Location – course site	Metropolitan area	56.67
	Non-metropolitan area	43.33

increases on their attitudes toward inclusive education (SACIE-Attitudes), their overall sense of self-efficacy to implement inclusive education in their own classroom (TEIP-Total) and their teaching strategies also improved modestly but significantly (ESTRAT). A modest yet significant increase was shown also for how participants perceived the specialization course could help them address their school's inclusive education needs (GEPIA-Professional Development).

On the other hand, participants also experienced an unexpected decrease in their perceptions regarding the adequacy of their teaching methods (GEPIA-Teaching methods), their decisions on how they would deal with hypothetical cases (IE-CON-Case Analysis) and evidenced higher awareness or concerns of having students with disabilities in their classroom (SACIE-Concerns).

Considering that the second cohort had received the redesigned course with digital skills as part of the course content, post-evaluations showed that participants also significantly advanced on their digital abilities (TPACK-Total).

In the following section, we further explore the impact of the program on the participants' knowledge and teaching practices through regression models.

Predicting change in knowledge and teaching practices

The ultimate goal of the program was for these teachers and administrators to improve their knowledge and teaching strategies in order to meet the needs of their

TABLE 14.4 Pre- and posttests results of attitudes, teaching practices, concept knowledge and digital abilities measures

Instrument	N	Mean pretest	Mean postest	p value	E.S. Cohen's d
Attitudes					
SACIE Total	304	22.89	22.41	.273	0.07
• Sentiments	304	3.57	3.14	.027	0.13
• Attitudes	304	11.51	12.98	<.001	0.36
• Concerns	304	6.29	7.82	<.001	0.48
TEIP Total	305	93.30	97.44	<.001	0.34
• Inclusive instruction	305	31.72	32.81	<.001	0.27
• Collaboration	305	31.64	32.97	<.001	0.34
• Managing disruptive behavior	305	29.94	31.65	<.001	0.38
Teaching practices					
GEPIA Total	350	150.62	148.29	.037	0.12
• Teaching methods	357	21.43	18.87	<.001	0.76
• Professional development	355	10.63	10.88	.009	0.15
ESTRAT	401	41.77	43.88	<.001	0.29
Concept knowledge					
IE-CON Total	273	21.20	21.09	.597	0.036
• Concepts	273	3.67	5.18	<.001	1.12
• Case analysis	282	17.52	15.9	<.001	0.59
Digital abilities					
TPACK Total	327	77.1	79.13	.003	0.21
• TK Technological Knowledge	327	26.76	27.64	.010	0.18
• PK Pedagogical knowledge	327	29.56	30.18	.010	0.18
• TPK Technological-pedagogical knowledge	327	20.84	21.31	.015	0.17

diverse students. For that purpose, the three variables that showed to be the most susceptible to change were selected: teaching practices as measured by the full scale ESTRAT, inclusive classroom practices related to the adequacy of teaching methods measured by GEPIA-Teaching methods, and knowledge of inclusive education concepts measured by IE-CON-Concepts (Table 14.5).

Predictor variables for each regression analysis were identified from bivariate correlations between each pretest and posttest variable with the outcome variable, to examine how they could contribute to participants' teaching practices and inclusive education knowledge. In cases when only the posttest variable was significantly correlated with the outcome variable, the pretest variable was still included in the analyses as a predictor to examine both the baseline of the variable and its growth after attending the program.

A first hierarchical regression analysis was aimed to predict the final teaching practices around inclusive education in the full scale ESTRAT. Results showed that

246 Silvia Romero-Contreras et al.

TABLE 14.5 Summary of hierarchical regression analyses for variables predicting final teaching practices (GEPIA-Teaching methods & ESTRAT), and final knowledge (IE-CON-Concepts)

	Final teaching practices				Final knowledge	
	ESTRAT		GEPIA – Teaching methods		IE-CON – Concepts	
Predictor variable	R^2	R^2 change	R^2	R^2 change	R^2	R^2 change
Initial self-efficacy[a]	0.083	0.083★★★	0.082	0.082★★★		
Final self-efficacy[a]	0.143	0.059★★★	0.218	0.136★★★		
Initial perceived usefulness of professional development[b]	0.177	0.034★★				
Final perceived usefulness of professional development[b]	0.223	0.046★★★				
Initial sentiments toward inclusive education[c]			0.219	0.001		
Final sentiments toward inclusive education[c]			0.219	0.000		
Initial attitudes toward inclusive education[d]					0.017	0.017★
Final attitudes toward inclusive education[d]					0.041	0.024★

NB: a = TEIP, b = GEPIA-Professional Development, c = SACIE-Sentiments, d = SACIE-Attitudes
★p<.05, ★★p<.01, ★★★p<.001

initial self-efficacy beliefs contributed a significant 8.3% of explained variance, but once controlling for the baseline self-efficacy, the final self-efficacy accounted for a smaller but significant 5.9% of unique variance in the final teaching practices. Then, controlling for both measures of self-efficacy, the participants' perceived usefulness of professional development at baseline in GEPIA-PD predicted an additional 3.4% of unique variance, while the change from baseline, that is the growth, predicted an additional 4.6% of unique variance. In total, the last model encompassing all four variables predicted 22.3% of the variance in final teaching practices in inclusive education.

A second hierarchical regression was performed to predict a significant decrease found in final self-reported teaching practices around inclusive education using

GEPIA-Teaching methods. This analysis showed that even when initial self-efficacy beliefs contributed a significant 8.2% of explained variance in the final self-report of teaching practices in GEPIA-Teaching methods, it was the change between the final self-efficacy and the baseline, which accounted for an additional 13.6% of unique variance in the final measures. Nonetheless, once accounting for self-efficacy beliefs at both points in time, the sentiments about inclusive education did not contribute additional explained variance to GEPIA-Teaching methods, suggesting self-efficacy alone could predict the change in teaching practices.

A final hierarchical regression was performed to predict final inclusive education knowledge using IE-CON-Concepts. This analysis showed that in this group of education professionals, their knowledge was slightly but significantly influenced by their initial attitudes about inclusive education as reported in SACIE-Attitudes. Then, controlling for these attitudes, their final attitudes' scores contributed an additional 2.4% of explained variance. In sum, these two variables explained a 4.1% of the participants' change in conceptual knowledge about inclusive education.

Discussion of results

The inferential tests comparing initial and final scores showed that teachers and administrators attending this large b-learning course were able to improve some of their teaching strategies, their self-efficacy beliefs, their knowledge of inclusion concepts, as well as their attitudes and concerns about inclusion. These findings fall in line with other teaching training programs and courses that have achieved increases in inclusive education knowledge (Forlin & Chambers, 2011), attitudes (Avramidis & Kalyva, 2007), self-efficacy beliefs (Miller, Wienke & Savage, 2000; Chao, Sze, Chow, Forlin & Ho, 2017) and teaching practices (Edwards, Carr, & Siegel, 2006).

Regarding technological skills learning, the tests showed that participants were able to successfully increase their digital abilities through the explicit teaching of digital strategies within a b-learning course aimed at facilitating the development of inclusion strategies. Baseline and final self-efficacy played an important and similar role in two outcome measures with different results: final perception of teaching methods, which decreased when compared to its baseline, and final perception of teaching strategies, which increased. We argue that while both scales measure what teachers do in the classroom, the first one, (ESTRAT) focuses on systematic and reflective methods to attain a particular outcome, while the second (GEPIA-Teaching methods) focuses on the presence and frequency of good, but isolated, practices.

For the first measure (ESTRAT), participants are asked to rate how often they perform a certain activity, such as: use of peer tutoring, offer students strategies to improve their memory, help students improve their reading comprehension. After taking the course, it seems plausible that participants were doing these activities much more often than before, as the relevance and procedures of many of these practices were discussed in the course. In this regard, self-efficacy translates into the possibility of recognizing and using good practices.

For the second measure (GEPIA-Teaching methods), participants are asked to reflect on the frequency with which they implement the principles of inclusive education in their classrooms. Most questions start with a fairly deterministic phrase (Do you make sure that …?). Therefore teachers need to rate, for example, how often they ensure that all students understand the concepts and tasks performed and take into account each student's style and pace of learning and prior knowledge. The fact that participants rate themselves significantly lower after taking the course than before could be the result of a more critical view of their own practice as they develop a deeper understanding of the complexities of teaching for diverse students, which is consistent with findings from Mexican teachers (Serrato Almendáez & García Cedillo, 2014). In this regard, self-efficacy translates into the possibility of being more critical of their own practice.

These two findings regarding an increase of teaching strategies accompanied by a more self-critical stance toward their teaching methods converge with previous results of an increase in knowledge coupled with an increase in concern after attending a training course in inclusive education (Forlin & Chambers, 2011).

The regression analyses offered evidence that participants' self-efficacy beliefs play a critical role, both at the baseline and its change, suggesting a role for developing courses that work on this level. Previous studies have documented strategy improvements for teaching in inclusive education environments (Edwards, Carr, & Siegel, 2006). However, the present study has identified that the initial and course-mediated change in self-efficacy beliefs are the ones that account for a significant proportion of teaching strategy increases.

In addition, regarding teaching practices, the perceived professional development course's usefulness at the end of the course, which could be interpreted as an evaluation of this course, was combined with self-efficacy beliefs to improve these self-reported teaching practices to facilitate inclusion of all students.

The finding for the ESTRAT model, that almost a fourth of the total explained variance was accounted by these self-efficacy ratings as well as professional development perceptions, highlights the importance of attending to teachers' thoughts and reflections about their practice and about their own perceived abilities. It also emphasizes the fact that having a positive attitude toward a specific professional development course could have a slight but significant additional effect on the teachers' inclusive practices, proposed in other studies (Di Gennaro, Pace, Zollo, & Aiello, 2014).

Regression analyses showed that participants' learning of inclusive education concepts is only slightly explained by baseline and final attitudes toward inclusive education. Thus, it could be that other factors not systematically measured here, such as study habits, compliance with activities, and participation, could have played a more important role on this outcome measure.

Taken together, these results highlight the critical role of self-efficacy for the improvement of teaching practices that benefit students in a large-scale course in a Latin American country. Similar findings have been reported with a reformed program emphasizing inclusive education topics in Mexico's pre-service teachers (Forlin et al. 2010).

Lessons learned

In this chapter we have presented the design process and the results of a large-scale b-learning teacher preparation course in a South American country to advance the implementation of inclusive education. After this experience, we identified several key elements that contributed to making this a successful experience that could be useful to inform inclusive education professional development programs.

The most important element for the success of this process was the collaborative spirit of all involved parties. Teams from different countries collaboratively planned, designed, executed and revised the program; teams from diverse regions of the target country worked collaboratively to reach members of the educational system within the country who, in turn, collaboratively supported the learning process of their peers. As staff members of different schools and different educational backgrounds (regular teachers, special education teachers, psychologists, rehabilitation specialists, administrators, etc.) engaged in the problem-solving and discussion activities specifically designed (Alonso et al. 2005) to promote collaboration as recommended by inclusive education specialists (i.e., Duk, Cisternas & Ramos, 2019), they strengthened their abilities within and across schools to continue reflecting and working together toward inclusion. We argue that the multidisciplinary nature of the groups was an asset that contributed to improving participants' understanding of the perspective and expectations of other professionals. This was particularly relevant for special and regular education teachers who, in the target country, are trained under the two-track model (Nash & Norwich, 2010).

Another critical element was conducting the course in the b-learning modality, which made it possible to offer various educational resources and facilitated the process for all involved in many ways (González Guerrero et al. 2011). On the one hand, the course management system guaranteed that all participants had access to the same materials, dynamics, content, and evaluation forms. It facilitated access to the course materials so that participants could review them at any time depending on what suited them best. It also allowed instructors to have all the materials organized and to keep track of participants' progress. The course management system became the unique form of communication. All course-related issues were dealt through it; participants and teaching staff did not have to check or use other resources (e-mail, instant messaging, etc.), which improved the communication flow. On the other hand, the face-to-face component allowed for more in-depth discussions and, through collaborative learning, facilitated the establishment and/or strengthening of support networks to continue, within the school communities, the work initiated in the classroom. The regional design of the face-to-face meetings, moreover, allowed participants to take the course simultaneously with peers from different regions of the country, sparing the cost and time of travel.

Another critical element was working with an inclusive approach to design and execute the program; given that the main topic and purpose was inclusive education, this choice was not only obvious but necessary. Participants learned through their own experience, and not only in theory, the principles and methods of inclusion

(UDL, DI, inclusive pedagogy, positive classroom environment, mindfulness, etc.), so that they would be more prepared to promote them and use them within their educational communities.

This experience showed that the implementation of b-learning teacher professional development programs in Latin American countries and others that have similar characteristics such as poor connectivity, limited technological resources and teachers with basic digital skills, can be a good alternative for innovative quality and massive teacher professional development. However, in our experience, several measures need to be taken prior and during the design and delivery of the courses to maximize their success. We would like to highlight some of the most relevant.

Improving connectivity and offering free or low-cost Internet access to teachers before conducting an e-learning or b-learning professional development program would be desirable. However, less-costly alternative measures can also be implemented, such as providing external memory devices (USB or hard drives) with the program and all materials to participants and granting them access to Internet-equipped computers (at public or private facilities) to upload their work. In our experience, Internet access was improved for the second cohort, and alternative measures were offered upon request during face-to-face meetings with the support of technology tutors.

Participants' diversity in terms of digital skills and attitudes might, as in our case, range from only handling mobile phone functions to a fairly good understanding of various devices, apps, software and learning platforms or course management systems. Learning about participants' digital abilities is crucial to plan and deliver specific and differentiated support. For those participants with basic or below basic skills it would be useful to have a preliminary or introductory course. If this were not possible, they should have a more personalized digital tutor and peer support throughout the course. In our experience, we found that peer support was an excellent way of reducing the fear or anxiety, also called technophobia (van Dijk, 2006), that is commonly associated with less-competent digital users.

Participants also tend to have different levels of academic skills: some might have graduate studies, while others might only have the required undergraduate degree for teaching. In this regard, having a very flexible design of the curriculum in such a way that materials, contents, dynamics and forms of evaluation can be modified or adapted, along with activities designed to improve participants' academic language and skills, can be key to addressing this challenge. In our experience, we made various adaptations to meet participants' academic needs in the first cohort and most substantial changes for the second cohort, as we had a clearer idea of the different profiles.

Finally, we would like to end this chapter pointing out the relevance of this work under the current context derived from the COVID-19 pandemic, which has certainly propelled the transformation of educational settings and processes.

Despite the efforts made, the digital divide is still very wide, so it is likely that children and youth in the region will be seriously affected in their learning as a result of the closing of schools. However, those with a disability will surely be the most affected, as they have been relegated from the measures adopted by governments to face this situation (Murillo & Duk, 2020). Currently, up to 97% of children in Latin America and the Caribbean have lost the opportunity to continue their education on a regular basis. An estimated 137 million children have ceased to have face-to-face education (UNICEF, 2020). SEND students have been particularly affected since the beginning of 2019 due to "the loss of social contact [and] the difficulty to development and implement curricular adaptations which has caused the blurring of inclusive education and hindered the application of universal design parameters of learning /instruction"(Moreno-Rodríguez, 2020, pp. 5–6).

In the current situation, those teachers who studied the specialization with the b-learning modality are hopefully more likely to face the challenges of the COVID pandemic, since they not only learned about inclusion and improved their digital skills but also lived the experience of a semi–face-to-face learning with an inclusive orientation. In this sense, the purposeful use of technology in service of education is a valuable way of preparing teachers for their regular practice, and also to better respond to critical situations such as the one we are now experiencing.

Notes

1. This chapter refers to work conducted in a Latin American country during a transition period. While all participants agreed to the use of the data with academic purposes, changes in the administration of the two local entities involved hindered the possibility of obtaining signed permission to explicitly name the country.
2. All authors of this chapter are part of the international team.
3. To avoid this apparent contradiction, in some research reports, the scores for sentiments and concerns are reversed; however, in this study scores were all treated equally.
4. Due to an administrative request, this instrument was administered anonymously, without information to cross-reference participants' pre and post scores.

References

Ainscow, M., Booth, T., & Dyson, A. (2006). *Improving schools, developing inclusion*. London: Routledge. https://doi.org/10.4324/9780203967157

Alonso, F., López, G., Manrique, D., & Viñes, J. M. (2005). An instructional model for web-based e-learning education with a blended learning process approach. *British Journal of Educational Technology*, *36*(2), 217–235. https://doi.org/10.1111/j.1467-8535.2005.00454.x

Avramidis, E., & Kalyva, E. (2007). The influence of teaching experience and professional development on Greek teachers' attitudes toward inclusion. *European Journal of Special Needs Education*, *22*(4), 367–389. https://doi.org/10.1080/08856250701649989

Barkley, E. F., Cross, P., & Major-Howell, C. (2007). *Técnicas de aprendizaje colaborativo. Manual para el profesorado universitario*. Ediciones Morata.

Blanco, R. (2014). Inclusión educativa en América Latina: caminos recorridos y por recorrer. In A. Marchesi, R. Blanco & E. Hernández. (Coords.), *Avances y desafíos de la educación inclusiva en iberoamérica* (pp. 11–63). Organización de Estados Iberoamericanos. https://panorama.oei.org.ar/_dev2/wp-content/uploads/2018/05/Metas_inclusiva.pdf

Blanco, R., & Duk, C. (2011). Educación inclusiva en América Latina y el Caribe. *Aula*, *17*, 37–55. https://doi.org/10.14201/8394

Blanco, R., & Duk, C. (2019). El legado de la Conferencia de Salamanca en el pensamiento, políticas y prácticas de la educación inclusiva. *Revista Latinoamericana de Educación Inclusiva*, *13*(2), 2–43. http://dx.doi.org/10.4067/S0718-73782019000200025

Booth, T., & Ainscow, M. (2002). *Index for inclusion. Developing learning and participation in schools*. Center for the Studies on Inclusive Education. https://www.eenet.org.uk/resources/docs/Index%20English.pdf

Cabero Almenara, J., Marín Díaz, V., & Castaño Garrido, C. (2015). Validación de la aplicación del modelo TPACK para la formación del profesorado en TIC. *@tic, Revista D'innovació Educativa*, *14*, 13–22. https://doi.org/10.7203/attic.14.4001

CAST. (2011). *Universal design for learning guidelines version 2.0*. Wakefield, MA: Author. https://udlguidelines.cast.org/binaries/content/assets/udlguidelines/udlg-v2-0/udlg_fulltext_v2-0.doc

Chao, C. N. G., Sze, W., Chow, E., Forlin, C., & Ho, F. C. (2017). Improving teachers' self-efficacy in applying teaching and learning strategies and classroom management to students with special education needs in Hong Kong. *Teaching and Teacher Education*, *66*, 360–369. https://doi.org/10.1016/j.tate.2017.05.004

Di Gennaro, D. C., Pace, E. M., Zollo, I., & Aiello, P. (2014). Teacher capacity building through critical reflective practice for the promotion of inclusive education. *Problems of Education in the 21st Century*, *60*, 54–65.

Duk, C., Cisternas, T., & Ramos, L. (2019). Formación docente desde un enfoque inclusivo. A 25 Años de la Declaración de Salamanca, Nuevos y Viejos Desafíos. *Revista Latinoamericana de Educación Inclusiva*, *13*(2), 91–109. http://dx.doi.org/10.4067/S0718-73782019000200091

Edwards, C. J., Carr, S., & Siegel, W. (2006). Influences of experiences and training on effective teaching practices to meet the needs of diverse learners in schools. *Education*, *126*(3), 580–592.

Florian, L. (2010). Special education in an era of inclusion: the end of special education or a new beginning? *The Psychology of Education Review*, *34*(2), 22–27.

Forlin, C., & Chambers, D. (2011). Teacher preparation for inclusive education: Increasing knowledge but raising concerns. *Asia-Pacific Journal of Teacher Education*, *39*(1), 17–32. https://doi.org/10.1080/1359866X.2010.540850

Forlin, C., García-Cedillo, I., Romero-Contreras, S., Fletcher, T., & Rodriguez-Hernández, H. J. (2010). Inclusion in Mexico: Ensuring supportive attitudes by newly graduated teachers. *International Journal of Inclusive Education*, *14*(7), 723–739. https://doi.org/10.1080/13603111003778569

Forlin, C., Earle, C., Loreman T., & Sharma, U. (2011). The Sentiments, Attitudes and Concerns about Inclusive Education (SACIE) scale for measuring pre-service teachers' perceptions about inclusion. *Exceptionality Education International*, *21*(3), 50–65. https://doi.org/10.5206/eei.v21i3.7682

García, I. (2009). *La educación inclusiva en Latinoamérica y el Caribe. El caso mexicano*. San Luis Potosí: Banco Mundial-UASLP.

García-Cedillo, I., Romero-Contreras, S., Escalante-Aguilar, L., & Flores-Barrera, V. J. (2018). Algunas propiedades psicométricas de las guías para evaluar prácticas inclusivas en el aula. *Revista Española de Orientación y Psicopedagogía*, *29*(2), 8–28. https://doi.org/10.5944/reop.vol.29.num.2.2018.23150

González Guerrero, K., Padilla Beltrán, J. E., & Rincón Caballero, D. A., (2011). Fundamentos conceptuales para la evaluación del docente en contextos *b-learning*. *Revista Virtual Universidad Católica del Norte*, No. 34, 220–243. https://revistavirtual.ucn.edu.co/index.php/RevistaUCN/article/view/336

Jordan, A., Schwartz, E., & McGhie-Richmond, D. (2009). Preparing teachers for inclusive classrooms. *Teaching and Teacher Education*, 25(4): 535–542. https://doi.org/10.1016/j.tate.2009.02.010

Miller, K. J., Wienke, W. D., & Savage, L. B. (2000). Elementary and middle/secondary educator's pre and post training perceptions of ability to instruct students with disabilities. *Rural Special Education Quarterly*, 19(3), 3–14. https://doi.org/10.1177/875687050001900 3-402

Mitchell, D. (2015a). *Strategies for enhancing learning: Teacher questionnaire. A self-rating scale.* Taylor and Francis Group. https://routledgetextbooks.com/textbooks/_author/mitchell-9780415623230/rating.php

Mitchell, D. (2015b). Inclusive education is a multi-faceted concept. *Center for Educational Policy Studies Journal*, 5(1), 9–30.

Molina-García, P. F., Molina-García, A. R., & Rodríguez-Abelarde, I. (2019). La educación inclusiva en Latinoamérica, el Caribe y el caso de Ecuador. *Revista Científica Dominio de las Ciencias*, 5(2), 673–690. https://dominiodelasciencias.com/ojs/index.php/es/article/view/1116/1701

Moreno-Rodríguez, R. (2020). Prólogo. In R. Moreno-Rodríguez, A. Tejada-Cruz, & M. Díaz-Vega (Coords.). *COVID-19. Educación inclusiva y personas con discapacidad: fortalezas y debilidades de la teleeducación* (pp. 5–6). Colección iAccessibility Vol. 23. La Ciudad Accesible. https://www.observatoriodelainfancia.es/ficherosoia/documentos/7181_d_COVI19-EducacionInclusiva.pdf

Murillo, F. J., & Duk, C. (2020). Editorial: El Covid-19 y las brechas educativas. *Revista Latinoamericana de Educación Inclusiva*, 14(1), 11–13. http://dx.doi.org/10.4067/S0718-73782020000100011

Nash, T., & Norwich, B. (2010). The initial training of teachers to teach children with special educational needs: A national survey of English post graduate certificate of education programmes. *Teaching and Teacher Education*, 26(7), 1471–1480. https://doi.org/10.1016/j.tate.2010.06.005

Ramos-Estrada, D. Y., García-Cedillo, I., Sotelo-Castillo, M. A., López-Valenzuela, M. L., & Murillo-Parra, L. D. (2020). Validación de un instrumento de estrategias para fortalecer el aprendizaje. *Revista Electrónica Educare*, 24(1), 1–15. http://doi.org/10.15359/ree.24-1.6

Romero-Contreras, S. (2014). Aportes de la psicopedagogía para transformar los procesos educativos. *Universitarios Potosinos* 10(178), 24–27.

Romero-Contreras, S., Garcia-Cedillo, I., Forlin, C., & Lomelí-Hernández, K. A. (2013). Preparing teachers for inclusion in Mexico: how effective is this process? *Journal of Education for Teaching*, 39(5), 509–522. https://doi.org/10.1080/02607476.2013.836340

Samaniego de García, P. (2009). *Personas con discapacidad y acceso a servicios educativos en Latinoamérica. Breve análisis de situación.* CERMI. http://repositoriocdpd.net:8080/handle/123456789/426

Schmidt, D. A., Baran, E., Thompson, A. D., Mishra, P., Koehler, M. J., & Shin, T. S. (2009). Technological pedagogical content knowledge (TPACK) the development and validation of an assessment instrument for pre-service teachers. *Journal of Research on Technology in Education*, 42(2), 123–149. https://doi.org/10.1080/15391523.2009.10782544

Serrato-Almendáez, L. T., & García-Cedillo, I. (2014). Evaluación de un programa de intervención para promover prácticas docentes inclusivas. *Revista Electrónica Actualidades Investigativas en Educación*, 14(3), 1–25. https://www.redalyc.org/articulo.oa?id=44732048015

Sharma, U., Loreman T., & Forlin C. (2012). Measuring teacher efficacy to implement inclusive practices. *Journal of Research in Special Educational Needs*, 12(1), 12–21. https://doi.org/10.1111/j.1471-3802.2011.01200.x

Spratt, J., & Florian, L. (2013). Aplicar los principios de la pedagogía inclusiva en la formación inicial del profesorado: de una asignatura en la universidad a la acción en el aula. *Revista de Investigación en Educación, 11*(3), 141–149. http://reined.webs.uvigo.es/index.php/reined/article/view/292

Tomé Fernández, M., & Manzano García, B. (2016). La educación inclusiva intercultural en Latinoamericana. Análisis legislativo. *Revista de Educación Inclusiva, 9*(2-bis), 1–17. https://revistaeducacioninclusiva.es/index.php/REI/article/view/279

Tomlinson, C. A. (2017). *How to differentiate instruction in academically diverse classrooms* (3rd. Ed.). ASCD.

UNESCO. (2005). *Guidelines for Inclusion: Ensuring Access to Education for All*. UNESCO: Paris. https://unesdoc.unesco.org/ark:/48223/pf0000140224

UNICEF. (2020). *Education on Hold. A generation of Children in Latin America and the Caribbean are Missing out on Schooling Because of COVID-19*. Panamá: https://www.unicef.org/lac/informes/educacion-en-pausa

van Dijk, J. A. G. M. (2006). Digital divide research, achievements and shortcomings. *Poetics, 34*(4–5), 221–235. http://dx.doi.org/10.1016/j.poetic.2006.05.004

Vélez-Calvo, X., Tárraga-Mínguez, R., Fernández-Andrés, M. A. I., & Sanz-Cervera, P. (2016). Formación inicial de maestros en Educación Inclusiva: una comparación entre Ecuador y España. *Revista de Educación Inclusiva, 9*(3), 75–94. https://revistaeducacioninclusiva.es/index.php/REI/article/view/254

Verdún, N. (2016). Educación virtual y sus configuraciones emergentes: Notas acerca del e-learning, b-learning y m-learning. In M. A. Casillas & A. Ramírez Martinell. (Coords.), *Educación virtual y recursos educativos* (1st ed., Vol. 3, pp. 67–88). Editorial Brujas. https://www.uv.mx/personal/mcasillas/files/2016/05/libro3.pdf

15
INTO THE MESA
A case study of Jordanian inclusion policy

Sarah K. Benson

Jordan, a small country located in the heart of the Middle East, has a long history of inclusive policies for students with disabilities. Its history and geographic location at the crossroads of numerous regional conflicts provides a unique opportunity to study the mesa-level policy transfer and adoption of inclusion. Owing to its strategic geographic location and economic needs, Jordan has historically partnered with international agencies to fund and develop its education system, and this has resulted in multiple reforms intended to include children with disabilities (Benson, 2020). However, current literature about Jordan demonstrates that despite the history of inclusive education policies, students with physical, learning and intellectual disabilities remain marginalized in schools and communities (Abu-Hamour & Al-Hmouz, 2014; Alkhateeb, Hadidi, & Alkhateeb, 2016; Benson, 2020). Researchers often use the term 'policy-to-practice gap' to describe this phenomenon. Innovative comparative case study methodology encourages researchers to look inside this gap and to understand how the flow among international, national and local contexts influences practice, while practice also influences policy (Schuelka, 2018). Developing inclusive education theory suggests broad and vague policy documents are a barrier to successful implementation, so generating insight into how policy is created and implemented is necessary to create change in the field (Bines & Lei, 2011; Eleweke & Rodda, 2002; Winzer & Mazurek, 2009).

Previous comparative work has contextualized Jordanian policy within international agreements and local practices. This research demonstrates the need to further understand how national-level policy decisions are being constructed (Benson, 2020). This chapter reveals the importance of mesa-level research that engages policy stakeholders in conversation with the policies they are enacting.

DOI: 10.4324/9781003091950-18

Jordanian inclusion at the macro and mesa levels

Jordan is a stable kingdom but bears significant social and economic burdens as a result of many regional conflicts throughout the Middle East. The country has limited natural resources, and while it rates as a middle-income country on economic measurement indices, it relies heavily on development aid, especially within the education sector (Saif & Choucair, 2010; US Department of State, 2018; World Bank, 2017). The influx of refugees from surrounding countries has taxed the government's ability to provide basic services and, as a result, international governing bodies and non-governmental organizations (NGO) have stepped in to provide technical and financial resources to the social sector (Abugattas-Majluf, 2012; Fishman, 2014). The volatility in Jordanian politics, the refugee crisis and an unstable economy have strengthened the technical and political influence of donor governments in education policy and created an optimal environment to study the policy transfer, adoption and implementation of inclusion (Benson, 2020). Thus, research focused on the politics of the country must address all policy-level institutions, including foreign donor governments and international governing bodies.

Macro view of Jordanian inclusion policy

Winzer and Mazurek (2009) describe the general global policyscape of inclusion, following the Salamanca Statement and Convention on the Rights of Persons with Disabilities (CRPD) (UN General Assembly, 2007), as having a 'rhetoric-to-reality gap.' This description is echoed in other comparative education research and often cited as the 'policy-to-practice gap.' Recognizing there is a difference between written policy and school-level practices is certainly an important contribution, and this gap should be flagged for further exploration. Unfortunately, the problems occurring between policy adoption and implementation have yet to be sufficiently explored. Building on the work done by previous scholars to analyze policy documents, this research adds the voice of the policy stakeholders who have crafted and implemented the legislation.

The migration of inclusion across the globe has been traced throughout inclusive education research. As a result, the aim is not to retrace the path again, except to put Jordanian law in context. Most major education legislation in Jordan pertaining to inclusion comes within a year of international milestones such as the Salamanca Statement and the CRPD (Benson, 2020). Despite passing laws related to inclusion beginning in the 1950s – and being a signatory on major human rights and inclusion declarations – the education system in Jordan remains exclusionary to many (Abu-Hamour & Al-Hmouz, 2014; Alkhateeb, Hadidi, & Alkhateeb, 2016; Benson, 2020). Understanding why, despite this history of inclusive legislation, students with disabilities remain marginalized requires recognizing policy is not a static entity but shaped by the stakeholders.

Mesa policyscape contexts

Global inclusive policy has been extensively analyzed by scholars throughout its growth (Artiles et al., 2011; Peters, 2007; Winzer & Mazurek, 2012). However, literature investigating the role of policy makers in this process is limited. While some have tackled the broadest terms of best practices of adoption (see Eleweke & Rodda, 2002; or Winzer & Mazurek, 2009), others have undertaken specific policy reviews (see Ahsan & Mullick, 2013; or Schuelka, 2012). There remains a major gap in the literature when it comes to in-depth research to understand how policymakers create meaning and develop inclusive education policies.

Previous policy analyses have developed frameworks and identified common barriers in policy documents, yet few interrogate those writing the legislation themselves. For example, Engsig and Johnstone (2015) demonstrate challenges in the Danish inclusive education policy through analysis of documents and historical comparisons. They identify competing views of inclusion that complicate implementation within the Danish system. I suggest that to further this analysis, questions should be asked as to whether the stakeholders who crafted these laws understand the difference between the two competing models; and whether the law is a result of compromise and negotiation, or if it lacks nuance of understanding. Similarly, Schuelka (2012) provides valuable insight into the Bhutanese inclusive education policy, using systematic, historical analysis to understand the current inclusive education law. Again, I suggest that the analysis can go further in demonstrating how policy makers were engaged, which would provide clarity for future policy development.

By not involving the motivations of stakeholders in policy research, and how they create the meaning of inclusive education, discourse continues to be stalled around the policy-to-practice gap. Ainscow and Miles (2008) identify policy as a performance indicator in their inclusive education framework for success. As a part of this indicator, three of the four measures identify policy-level leaders as key to making an inclusive school system; yet there is no model of how to engage these policy-level leaders in research. Alborz, Slee and Miles (2013) and Kalyanpur (2014) identify concerns and beliefs of stakeholders prior to legislation being passed, but they do not expose the ongoing negotiations after the finalized law. Duke et al. (2016) moves in this direction in Samoa by engaging in direct observation of policy-level meetings and model schools, but more empirical evidence can be gained through direct stakeholder interviews. Thus, the cultural clashes that are identified through these observations, researcher reflexivity and policy analysis remain a part of a black box, with no clear point of origin.

The importance of analyzing the intentions of policy stakeholders directly is emphasized by Liasidou (2012), who recognizes the complex and multidirectional nature of writing and enacting policy. Her supposition that policies are documents devoid of context but crafted by humans means we must interrogate the influences, ideologies and assumptions of those writing the law. Steiner-Khamsi (2014, 2016) and Anderson-Levitt (2001; 2004) present multiple research studies over their long careers demonstrating how international education policy is reinterpreted and negotiated as part of larger power structures, yet the inclusive education field has not similarly engaged the policy stakeholders in these conversations.

By analyzing the ongoing, dynamic discourse of stakeholders and the way they negotiate meaning to align with international pressures and cultural, historical realities, this research engaged policy stakeholders in dialogue with the policies. The goal is to answer how Jordanian legislative stakeholders, including foreign governments and development organizations, understand and interpret Jordanian inclusive policy and how it has been transferred from an international context to national-level government.

While globally inclusion has been adopted into law by a majority of countries, these laws are often written as direct translations of the international conventions, without consideration of country contexts, creating what Winzer and Mazurek (2009) term the "rhetoric-to-reality gap." Research on the macro level – rhetoric used by international organizations – and the mesa level – country-specific realities – can illuminate that gap, demonstrating that instead of a gap it is a complex flow of knowledge between differing contexts. Several established theories, policy-transfer theory and cultural-historical activity theory (CHAT) have limited but emerging application in the field of inclusive education research and are well-suited to this work.

Policy transfer

Policy-transfer theory posits that, while global commitments often appear to be uniform at the international level, on a country-by-country basis practices are negotiated, redefined and adapted for particular contexts (Anderson-Levitt, 2004; Steiner-Khamsi, 2008, 2014). The adoption, subsequent redefinition and influence of multiple stakeholder perspectives provide the basis for understanding how inclusion has developed in Jordan. The strong presence of both governmental and non-governmental donor agencies, government reform and global education discourse leads to policy borrowing and lending (Anderson-Levitt, 2004; Steiner-Khamsi, 2004, 2016). This is particularly relevant in the Jordanian context because of an influx of international organizations over the past ten years due to regional instability. Donor agencies have redoubled efforts to supply experts and finances to support an educational system taxed by a growing refugee population, lack of funding and other systemic issues (Benson, 2020). While these international organizations purport to be working side by side with the ministry and local implementing agencies, there are often competing visions of reform efforts based on the perspective of the stakeholder (Anderson-Levitt & Alimasi, 2001; Burde, 2004).

Education researchers have explored the borrowing process in depth, demonstrating how national governments translate, redefine and negotiate external influences. Anderson-Levitt and Alimasi's (2001) study into reading policy and textbook adoption in the Republic of Guinea utilized stakeholder interviews to document the process of negotiating external policies. By interrogating the policy stakeholders, the underlying motivations and in some cases, subversive actions, are exposed (Anderson-Levitt & Alimasi, 2001). Utilizing this more complete analysis of policymakers who are involved in borrowing and lending illuminates how and by whom the renegotiations take place. Within inclusive education, this is a missing area of study, despite clear conditions of policy borrowing.

In 2017, Jordan received $3.65 billion in aid, a portion of which was funneled directly to the Syrian refugee crisis, but a larger amount went directly to social development and reform efforts (Petra News Agency, 2018). The Ministry of Education (MoE) receives a large amount of donor funds – approximately $208.4 million in 2016 from just six donor countries – in order to undertake reforms and provide education for the Syrian refugees (Human Rights Watch, 2016). The World Bank underwrote both Education Reform for Knowledge Economy projects, major reform efforts spanning over ten years, and the concept of inclusive education can be found throughout the second iteration (World Bank, 2017). World Bank loans are often more than simple funding structures and also act as policy-change instruments, pushing the World Banks' view of education on the loan holders (Jones, 2004). These historic and ongoing relationships with international monetary and governance organizations, as well as the close relationship with outside governments eager to maintain a stable country in the region, have contributed to the adoption of inclusion laws in Jordan.

Policy-transfer theories help explain the mechanisms by which inclusion is spreading and the potential impact on not only policy but practices. As an internationally transferred policy, inclusion has spread widely over the past 20 years and is considered the mark of a progressive school system (Artiles & Dyson, 2005; Winzer & Mazurek, 2009). Many countries adopt educational policies with little commitment to adhere to the underlying principles, changing language to reflect the new policy but rarely changing practices or redefining the policy to fit existing practice (Burde, 2004). Inclusion is not immune to this occurrence, and several scholars note that adoption of inclusion tends to be hollow (Hettiarachchi & Das, 2014). Policy borrowing rarely results in an exact replica of international policy, as nations negotiate and redefine policies to meet their contextual needs (Steiner-Khamsi, 2004). Study at the mesa level exposes these negotiations and nuances relevant in a country with multiple national and international stakeholders.

Cultural-historical activity theory (CHAT)

In addition to using policy transfer theory to understand the implications of how inclusion is being legislated in Jordan, CHAT brings many aspects of this context into focus and highlights the impacts of culture and historicity in the mesa-level activity system.

An activity system comprises the rules, mediating artifacts, community and division of labor that are governing subjects and objects. Inclusive policy for the purposes of this chapter represents the object and policy stakeholder discourse is the

260 Sarah K. Benson

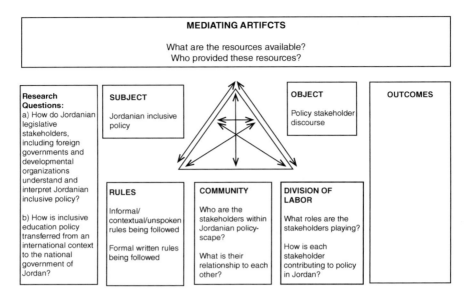

FIGURE 15.1 CHAT Matrix (adapted from Yagamata-Lynch, 2010)

subject. Rules include the informal and contextual rules that are followed in addition to the written laws and policies. Community refers to the actors present in a particular activity system. The community is connected to the division of labor in order to understand not only who the stakeholders are but what their role in the activity system is and how they are contributing to the outcomes. Mediating artifacts are defined as any resources available to and utilized in an activity system. These can include material and nonmaterial goods.

The interactions, represented by arrows (Figure 15.1), can expose the sociocultural and historical issues that might be creating what on the surface appears to be a rhetoric-to-reality gap, but is actually more nuanced and driven by factors beyond traditional challenges.

Results: Exposing tensions in Jordan's mesa level

Engaging policy stakeholders in direct discourse with the policy and analyzing the results using CHAT provides significant insight into the black box of the policy-to-practice gap. Previous research on inclusion in Jordan has identified many globally common challenges that contribute to the gap: lack of resources, ill-equipped schools and teachers, and cultural bias towards people with disabilities. The results of this research do not dismiss these challenges, but it unveils how the mesa-level politics creates and magnifies these issues within Jordan. To understand how stakeholders developed and interact with the policy of inclusion 18 interviews with Jordanian and non-Jordanian government level stakeholders, ethnographic field notes and policy documents were collected, see Table 15.1.

TABLE 15.1 Summary of interview participants

Date	Interviewee	Nationality	Organization	Funding Structure
21/1/19	Education Specialist	North American	Government	Donor
4/2/19 (a)	Head of Department	Jordanian	University	n/a
4/2/19 (b)	Professor	Jordanian	University	n/a
5/2/19	Director of Department	Jordanian	Ministry	Recipient
10/2/19	Program Manager	Australian	Government	Donor
14/2/19	Program Manager	European	Government	Donor
17/2/19 (a)	Communications Director	Jordanian	Quasi-governmental	Recipient
17/2/19 (b)	Education Coordinator	Jordanian	International Government Agency	Donor
19/2/19	Program Officer	European	International Government Agency	Donor
19/2/19	Program Officer	Jordanian	International Government Agency	Donor
20/2/19	Deputy of Department	Jordanian	Ministry	Recipient
21/2/19 (a)	Program Manager	Asian	Non-governmental Organization	Recipient
21/2/19 (b)	Director of Department	Jordanian	Ministry	Recipient
24/2/19	Program Manager	Jordanian	Non-governmental Organization	Recipient
24/2/19	Program Manager	Jordanian	Non-governmental Organization	Recipient
25/2/19	Head of School	Jordanian	Private School	n/a
27/2/19	Head of Mission	European	Government	Donor
6/3/19	Teacher Trainer	Jordanian	Non-governmental Organization	Recipient
19/3/19	Professor	Jordanian	University	n/a
1/4/19	Director	Jordanian	Quasi-governmental	Recipient

Note. Interviews that had two participants are listed separately, but not differentiated in citations.

Mediating artifacts

From Jordanian nationals to international donors, two resource issues were at the heart of policy and implementation challenges: personnel resources and funding. These resource challenges were also echoed in the various policy documents and have significant impact on the other connected parts of the activity system. The community and division of labor between members has significantly increased tensions as a result of donor funding. Resulting siloed labor practices will be discussed in subsequent sections, but first it is important to understand the initial impact of financial and personnel resources on inclusion.

Funding sources impact all areas of the activity system and are discussed first because they lead to inadequacies of other resources as well. Inconsistent or uneven funding has created tension in the community, and as a result, building an inclusive education system is stymied by uncoordinated efforts. Government-level stakeholders were all heavily focused on budgeting concerns as an impediment to inclusion. However, based on interviews with a large range of stakeholders, it is clear this is not necessarily the result of a lack of funds, but the faulty distribution and management of available funding.

The Ministry of Education (MoE) is the main recipient of millions of dollars, and to protect its status, it has siloed its work efforts, neglecting other government stakeholders and slowing progress toward a sustainable inclusive education system. For example, the Higher Council for Persons with Disabilities (HCRPD) was not allocated a budget in the 2019 fiscal year, disregarding the directives to focus on inclusive education (27/2/19; 17/2/19a; 17/2/19b). HCRPD is not the only Jordanian governmental organization being left out of the funding frenzy. The Ministry of Social Development (MoSD) receives limited funding from international donors and so they are often left out of planning meetings and sidelined in implementation, despite being the entity responsible for all 'special' or segregated placement schools and group homes. One interviewee was blunt in recognizing this slight,

> Why they exclude the Ministry of Social Development? Because maybe now it's not their table, there is no fund to include them. Once they decide there is a fund, you will find they will interfere in this process.
>
> (24/2/19)

The lack of cohesive vision between agencies means financial resources are often put toward small, unsustainable projects or model schools that cannot be replicated on a larger scale. As cited by this interviewee, the policy is not the only consideration driving inclusion efforts:

> What is pushing them to work on it [inclusion]? Number one, the new law …, number two because of the donor interest, you know if this fund or project will be supported the ministry, they will accept it.
>
> (24/2/19)

For these agencies that are left out of the funding, their exclusion becomes cyclical –they do not have funds to make progress so they are not seen as a good investment, and because they do not have funding they are left out of the planning and implementation projects.

The lack of collaboration is also apparent in developing personnel capacity. Schools and universities in Jordan are struggling to develop modern, accessible programs to produce capable personnel, which takes money and coordinated efforts. The public universities are at the mercy of the MoE, but teacher-training programs do not benefit from funding for inclusion projects because monetary efforts are more often put into small unsustainable professional development that shows only short-term outcomes. Like the cyclical nature of inadequate funding, the overly bureaucratic nature of working with higher education institutes puts off many funders, and so many international donor agencies have chosen to spend their millions with a single private teacher-training institution. The lack of resources means the public universities continue to struggle and look like poor investments, while private institutions benefit. Unfortunately, private institutions will not be able to generate enough teachers to make significant change. Funding sources are only one component of personnel resource scarcity; other systemic issues in higher education also contribute.

The higher education system was regularly blamed by stakeholders for creating subpar teachers, yet how students enter the teaching profession is not due to passion or desire to teach, but a result of low scores on their *Towjihi* [high school exit exam]. Frustrated by ongoing complaints about funding, one donor criticized ministry officials for these selection criteria:

> And I mean we just met him yesterday and we talked about the teacher reform, not only because of special needs teachers, the whole thing is a messed up, you know they are taking the worst.... I said you must take your clever students to be teachers. And I mean like Finland that or also South Korea, it's not only the funds, the salary, if you can also change other things it is possible.
> (27/2/19)

The impact of taking students who have not voluntarily chosen their field of study results in students who are unmotivated and less academically inclined, which was noted repeatedly by a former education major:

> The problem with the Ministry of Education teachers, they were not motivated ....You know, rather than we are stuck with education, and actually I changed my major from education to psychology, because people there they had have better grades and they were more motivated because I really was demotivated with the people that I have in education.
> (25/2/19)

It is a common criticism of inclusion scholars to point to untrained teachers creating a gap between policy and practice, but these examples in Jordan show how the policies and their funding choices are directly impacting the quality of teacher training, and thus the impact on practice is directly tied to policy and legislative failures. Mediating artifacts or resources plays an outsized role in defining the other areas of the activity system. As has already been evidenced, the competition for funding impacts the relationships in the community.

Community

The value judgments made about community members revealed cultural issues surrounding the royal family and government; interviews with both international actors and Jordanians revealed these judgments as a challenge to cohesive inclusion. The international community often displayed negative attitudes about the ministries, and this negativity influenced not only their funding direction but the way they viewed their partnerships. The policy-level stakeholder community in Jordan is characterized by silos; as one interviewee said, "You feel that each one of them is his own separate entity that's working its own projects, uh, no organization, no lines in between them whatsoever" (4/2/19a).

There was a pervasive negative attitude when speaking about the MoE or MoSD, especially when compared with value statements made about the HCRPD or other bodies closely associated with the royal family. Distrust of the appointed government and faith in the royal family is a cultural trait in Jordan that was emphasized throughout interviews with both Jordanians and international stakeholders. Sponsorship by the royal family demonstrated reliability, trust and program success, while the government was derided as incompetent or difficult to deal with. Jordanian stakeholders were direct about the distrust and their negative attitudes about the ministries were clear.

> But when it comes to their understanding, knowledge, mind-set of the staff, board of the Ministry is still under expectation, they need more forward, more awareness, more capital, more competence. They need to increase their competence. Unfortunately, the Department of Special Education, at the Ministry is a bit, uh crap. I'm sorry.
>
> (24/2/19)

> Now we have this issue in Jordan, people do not trust the government and that is an issue we are trying to work on, especially with the changing identity from a service provider to a policy maker.
>
> (17/2/19a)

The negative values associated with the MoE and the MoSD contributed to the inability to develop and implement successful inclusive education because stakeholders are less willing to engage with the ministries to create sustainable and systemic change. External agencies working with the government said many of their initiatives were motivated by the availability of funding from international donors, and not by a commitment to sustainable improvements.

> Sometimes the Minister of Education signs an agreement with an NGO, for instance, to train teachers, to train students for so much, and after the same Ministry might also sign a contract to make a training for the same teachers, the same students with a different institution—you see I know

many things in the universe of the minister of education that's awful, it's unbelievable, it's truly ridiculous.

(19/2/19)

Interviewees expressed these concerns several times, indicating how funding is impacting community relationships, as funding is given and accepted without coordination efforts. This is compounded by high turnover, inconsistency in implementation, and general bureaucracy within the ministries (4/2/19a).

The lack of confidence in government ministries to provide a consistent vision and capable staffing was echoed by several international stakeholders. One program director complained she had seen three ministers of education in her first two years; another struggled to locate ministry employees still working in the department just six months after participating in extensive technical trainings (27/2/19; 21/2/19a). The turnover in the departments creates a vacuum of technical expertise that frustrates all parties working with the ministries.

In contrast to these negative perceptions and distrust of the government, when speaking about the HCRPD and royal family most stakeholders spoke with positivity and hope for change. The HCRPD has been able to make significant progress as both an advocacy agency and policy body because it is headed by Prince Mired Raad Zeid Al-Hussein. Stakeholders credited his involvement with making Jordanian citizens "more comfortable turning to the HCRPD for assistance because it is headed by the prince" and believe that he is more "proactive" than the government (19/2/19; 17/2/19b). In addition, the prince is seen to have *wasta*, or 'influence,' within the government to accomplish the goals laid out in the Inclusive Education Strategy (HCRPD, 2017).

Two of the largest international donors to education initiatives have decided to work with the Queen Rania Teaching Academy, citing the endorsement of the queen to bring consistency and power the ministry does not. To justify this decision, one program director cited the inefficiency of the government and comparative effectiveness of working with the royal family:

> It's like they're slow. They're very bureaucratic. So I don't get a quick fix with a university; but I totally agree, this is what we need for sustainability, but Queen Rania Teaching Academy, they are doing it now. They're doing it now, and they're the ones most closely also now regarding teacher education for the ministry.... I mean I have to say it's because you have the Queen behind it, usually that's something which has the power to be sustainable.

(27/2/19)

This cultural mistrust of the government has impacted the international stakeholders, and as a result, inclusion policies developed and implemented by the government have little chance of success, while those endorsed by the ruling family have a higher chance of being accepted. The community is fractured due to conflicts over money, distrust and little cohesion, so as inclusion moves forward the divisions create unsustainable practices.

Division of labor

The conflict between community members directly ties to the way labor is divided between agencies in the policyscape. The data revealed many different concepts of responsibility for inclusive policy and practices: sharing, divided and shifting. Sharing responsibility occurs when multiple agencies work collaboratively toward their goal; this was rarely the reality but is outlined in policy documents. Divided responsibilities were identified when multiple agencies are working on the same or similar goals but doing so in isolation or even competition. Finally, shifting responsibilities happened when NGOs expressed interest in handing over responsibility to ministries or ministries distributed the work efforts to the point that no one held responsibility.

A striking example of policy documents outlining clear labor responsibilities that are then thwarted is in the Public Law n. 20 (2017), which clearly labels the HCRPD as the coordinating body for inclusive education. This is stated in Article 8, which outlines the specific roles of the HCRPD, and in the subsequent articles laying out the responsibilities of the Ministry of Health, MoE and MoSD. Unfortunately, in conversations with stakeholders, it became apparent there is significant tension between the HCRPD and the MoE.

> The Higher Council also supported the Minister of Education with four inclusive schools.
>
> (17/2/19a)

> But it is very hard to control the Ministry of Education, very, very hard because as I told you most of the international organizations, they go directly to them [MoE] which makes it difficult.
>
> (1/4/19)

> There's like a fight, a war, indirectly between the Higher Council and the Ministry of Education, miscommunication is the professional way, put more confusion, more responsibility on [Organization Name] and the other NGOs that provide services.
>
> (24/2/19)

Interview data repeatedly provided examples of the lack of shared responsibility between MoE and HCRPD; instead responsibility for implementing inclusive policy was regularly shifted to the other party.

Conflict also exists between the MoE and the MoSD, which again results in dividing and shifting responsibilities as a result of distrust and lack of clarity. Funding and differing rules about what constitutes disability fuel this conflict. Unspoken rules define physical and mild learning disabilities as eligible for inclusion but students with intellectual disabilities were deemed as too difficult to resource for and include in schools. This is in direct contradiction to the written policy but neatly divides the labor between the two agencies, leaving the MoSD in charge of segregated centers for children and adults with intellectual disabilities (20/2/19). Meanwhile, the MoE regulates the education of students with 'mild' learning and physical disabilities. The communication between the ministries is so low, when being questioned about collaboration one interviewee replied, after a significant pause and uncomfortable silence:

> Listen at the policy level it's easy, but at the cultural level it's difficult. Interviewer: So what is the conversation, how do the ministries talk to each other about those children? Policies by writing policies.
>
> (20/2/19)

Ironically, the official policy documents offer little guidance or support to help bridge this gap. According to Public Law n. 20 (2017), the responsibility for educating all students is that of the MoE, and the MoSD is only responsible for administering and reforming residential and institutional day-care facilities. In 2007 there was an effort to move students from these segregated facilities into schools, but because the divisions between ministries were too great nothing has moved forward in ten years:

> They [MoSD] mentioned we have the MOU with the Ministry of Education, but they did not take on the responsibility of transitioning the students and said we don't know how to do it. So I ask OK, you have this MOU, do you have an operational plan for it? They said no. Did you agree on timelines with the MoE? No. So it is just signed, and it's sitting there. That is it. So the MoSD is happy because they remove this load and they throw it on the MoE and then the MoE suffers or complains from the lack of effort or services.
>
> (24/2/19)

NGOs and international donors all noted the absence of the MoSD during Education Strategy and Inclusive Education Plan meetings. Again funding seems to play a dividing role, as several interviewees noted the MoSD's lack of participation was because of the lack of external funding to support them (24/2/19). So the conflict between ministries remains, and students remain segregated.

External agencies claim to support shifting responsibilities back to the ministries, however funding directives and siloed work creates little room for meaningful changes, as described here:

> Despite the numerous challenges facing the Jordanian educational system, the Ministry welcomes the contributions of national and international partners in supporting the management and implementation of joint programs ...
>
> (Ministry of Education [MoE], 2017)

> So we were successful in bringing school children to schools, and to private schools in particular. And we supported their transportation fees so some

students could go to the government schools. But at the same time, if you look at it from the other side, this gives the Ministry of Education the opportunity to rest and do nothing and do very little effort towards improving inclusive education.

(17/2/19a)

It was common to encounter donor agencies and NGOs that wanted to hand the reins of policymaking and implementation projects over, yet they continued to assume financial and technical responsibility, making external donors the primary support for successful inclusive education. As the country moves forward, coordination between all parties, external funding agencies, ministries and non-governmental organizations must create more shared, collaborative efforts.

Rules

The rules in written policy that state what a disability is and who must be accepted into schools shifted regularly in conversations with both Jordanian government officials and international implementing partners. If discussing the Educational Strategic Plan (ESP) (MoE, 2017), Public Law n. 20, or international agreements, all parties cited similar definitions that were closely aligned with the UN vision. However, when those stakeholders were pressed on implementation, a different standard of inclusion that actually excluded students who had intellectual disabilities, emotional and behavioral disorders, or autism was revealed. The exclusion was driven by not only cultural and historical values that emphasize shame and stigma but also the technical and financial resources of the education system.

During interviews with both Jordanians and foreign nationals, negative attitudes were referenced as barriers to implementing inclusion:

> We have so many barriers like physical, communication, attitude and all.... I think the attitudinal barrier is very, very strong, you know, and it is not only in terms of teachers and schoolchildren but also in terms of families, because there's social stigma that is attached to disability that is still a very strong factor.
>
> (19/2/19)

These attitudes are tied to parents' concerns about marriage opportunities for their children and stigma within the family (17/2/19a). Many parents keep their children with disabilities in the home to avoid the social repercussions. According to the ESP (MoE, 2017), only an estimated 138 total students with intellectual disabilities were enrolled in public schools in the entire kingdom. This does not include the segregated centers run by the MoSD or private centers that provide opportunities for students with intellectual disabilities.

While some interviewees reflected on recent changes, the sentiment that social stigma was still a significant factor in creating inclusive schools was pervasive.

> We worked really hard with their parents not to feel ashamed because one more time, in our culture, if you have you know a child with a disability, most of the time they are ashamed ….
>
> (25/2/19)

A direct result of this shame and stigma is a lack of acceptance in the community, school and government for persons with disabilities. Embodied in this participant's answer, '*There is a law that accepts them, but the people don't.*' (6/3/19) Inclusion policies have been in effect for more than 50 years in Jordan, but because schools at large have not accepted, nor been equipped to adhere to the formal written rules, students with disabilities continue to be marginalized by cultural shame and stigma.

While it is apparent that shame and stigma towards persons with disabilities contributes to exclusionary practices, the number of successful NGO-funded programs demonstrate these cultural attitudes are not insurmountable (Benson, 2020). However, practices at the government level seem to perpetuate a lack of acceptance for inclusion. Ministerial employees and supporting external agencies express adherence to the current inclusion law but define disability as physical impairments or mild learning disabilities. The single small department within the MoE for special education lacks technical expertise or strong leadership and experiences high turnover. Overall, this demonstrates there is not strong support or acceptance of inclusion policy within the ministry (19/2/19; Fieldnotes, April 11, 2019). This in turn leads to no enforcement for principals and schools that do not accept students with disabilities, allowing exclusion to continue as illustrated by this interviewee:

> According to the ministry's rules and regulations, children with learning disabilities should be accepted, but they are not being accepted, so many are referred to [organization name] for support because they have not been accepted by the school. The principal simply says we are not ready or equipped to deal with disability.
>
> (21/2/19b)

Using the defense that schools are not physically equipped, and teachers not technically capable, unspoken rules are revealed. Cultural shame and stigma drive a lack of resourcing for inclusion at the mesa level and so it is redefined to only encompass students who need few accommodations; more significant adaptations to schools and teaching practices are considered too resource intensive, giving an implicit message about the worth of students with significant impairments in society. As mentioned by some interviewees the attitudes are changing, but those examples are as the result of direct resource interventions and coordination between agencies, which, as noted in previous sections, is not widespread.

Discussion

CHAT has provided multiple means of understanding the complex flow created in this policyscape. How Jordanian legislative stakeholders, including foreign governments and development organizations, work together within the legislative activity system provides insight into how they are interpreting and transferring inclusion policy. Each interaction in the activity system underscores tensions that have developed between a wide variety of stakeholders. Jordanian education policy and surrounding discourse is creating a hollow inclusive policy, driven by the needs of the policy-level stakeholders, not an intrinsic commitment to education as a human right.

Focusing on interactions between each level of the activity system highlights problematic tensions; limited government spending and outsized donor investments that exploit historical and cultural divisions in the system and drive an uncoordinated effort towards inclusive education. Both international actors and Jordanians revealed these tense community relationships and divisions as a challenge to cohesive inclusion. These are exacerbated not only by historic cultural concerns about the acceptance of persons with disabilities, but other more prevalent attitudes and beliefs embedded in the working culture at Jordanian ministries and important education institutions. The one-dimensional format of traditional policy-to-practice gap challenges have not recognized the nuance and wider cultural factors at the mesa level. Studying the flow between levels of implementation and relationships in the mesa-level activity system bring new understanding to the perceived gap.

As demonstrated in the mediating artifacts section, it is clear the race for funding is driving inequities in the system that exacerbate existing tensions. Funding is often identified as a barrier to inclusive education; however, in the case of Jordan, there is ample money from donors to make significant impact. As donors choose which ministries and organizations will receive project funding, they are increasing a competitive, un-collaborative policyscape that creates the illusion of a funding shortage. Policy transfer studies have shown the renegotiation that occurs by stakeholders in order to secure funding (Anderson-Levitt & Alimasi, 2001), and this phenomenon is clearly present in Jordan. The competition between key government agencies results in exclusion from planning and budget, produces unsustainable projects and overall generates distrust in the community. Practically, this competition for funding creates issues for schools and institutes of higher education, who are caught in the fray, to develop inclusive educators.

Global inclusive education research commonly concludes that a lack of teacher training is a significant barrier; yet, as with funding, the contributing factors are not necessarily simple. The results here trace the issue to historical-cultural factors and funding issues between stakeholders that impede successful teacher training programs. The conflicts between agencies outlined earlier focus primarily on government institutions competing for international donor money. However, Royal Family sponsored organizations also compete for international grants and these organizations often win because, as discussed, the Jordanian public and subsequently international donors distrust government ministries. When funding is moved from public institutions of higher education that have a wide reach to a single private institution, a cycle of underfunded and dysfunctional teacher education programs is created. The less money invested in public institutes drives down quality and increases distrust of the government's ability to create programs while the private institutions flourish at a smaller and less-effective scale. Thus, while Jordan does suffer from a lack of well-trained teachers prepared to create inclusive classrooms, a view of the full activity system demonstrates it is not a gap between policy and practice, but the tensions within the mesa-level activity system that are creating problems of practice.

Another commonly referenced barrier to inclusive education is the attitudes and beliefs of teachers. Again, by studying the flow between levels it is possible to see how the issue is more complex and nuanced than poor attitudes towards disabilities. As noted, there is significant change being made in communities making it clear these attitudes and beliefs are not immutable. As we open the black box of a policy-to-practice gap, CHAT reveals how stereotyped ideas about disability and unspoken definitions are still prevalent in the government agencies charged with developing and implementing policy. As several respondents cited, the law respects disabilities, but the people do not. Research into inclusion finds that all school-based personnel must imbue a positive attitude towards inclusion for it to work (Lyons, Thompson, & Timmons, 2016); this can and should also apply to the stakeholders who are tasked with writing, implementing and enforcing the policies.

Interviewees also revealed that within the policy level, the driving beliefs and attitudes impeding inclusion are actually about honor and adherence to *wasta*. So while there are some shifting definitions of inclusion, in line with what is seen in other policy-transfers, it is deeper workplace cultures that are contributing to stalled practice. The system of *wasta* creates high turnover, competition and lack of sustainable professional development among government-level stakeholders. Many Jordanian interview respondents noted these challenges lead to a lack of continuity in projects or funding. Other respondents note the system of *wasta* can create corruption and a lack of expertise in government agencies. This, coupled with high turnover and each employee needing to distinguish themselves, has created challenges in knowledge, skill and capacity in key departments that diminishes overall inclusive efforts.

Conclusion: How do we move forward?

Despite a long history of legislative education for persons with disabilities, research into practices demonstrates these policy actions are not producing results, and students continue to be marginalized despite the documented right to an education. Several cultural and historical challenges have been exposed that go beyond the often-used shame and stigma towards persons with disabilities. Instead, this study reveals the complexity of the relationships among government institutions, donor organizations, school-based personnel, and the underlying sociocultural reasons that inclusion remains elusive.

Current inclusive education is being driven by a myriad of international donors that push inclusion in their social projects with little understanding of the underlying cultural and historical issues, from distrust of the government to competition between government agencies. Jordanian stakeholders are renegotiating the meaning of inclusion to fit current capabilities and maximize monetary benefit. While most Jordanian and international stakeholders acknowledge the official UN definition, in practice it is reimagined. This negotiation is made possible through vague policy language that permits the ministries and schools to claim inability to provide adequate care. It is also driven by multiple implementing partners that each filter inclusion through their particular lens and shift responsibilities accordingly.

Recent policy documents do little to alleviate the confusion and, in many cases, encourage shifting responsibilities to other agencies, despite efforts to develop systematic implementation. The conflicts among the MoSD, HCRPD and MoE over responsibility have been created by funding, cultural norms and unclear policies. These conflicts have stymied efforts to create a coordinated or systematic effort towards inclusion. It is unclear if the international donors truly understand the root of these conflicts and the way their funding programs are deepening the divides.

The lack of collaboration between ministries in a struggle for financial aid and prestige has created competition and siloed efforts within inclusion policy, thwarting the whole-systems approach recommended by the UN. The lack of coordination between governmental agencies has left donors seeking NGOs and royal family member projects to support inclusive efforts, but as a result these are not sustainable by public entities. The patchwork of inclusive schools, capable teachers and administrators, and budgetary neglect creates limited systems of support for inclusion.

While this analysis of barriers might seem bleak, by identifying the underlying causes of a failing policy – instead of glossing over these issues with the general, policy-to-practice gap explanation – systematic changes can begin. This research demonstrates the importance of conducting in-depth studies with the policymakers, not only of the policies. From this study alone it is possible to reimagine how government bodies, external funders and NGOs might begin to change their own discourse. The tensions in the mesa-level activity system reveal the need for more coordinated work, even funding distribution to public entities, less turnover, and more expertise within the institutions. Moving forward in Jordan and throughout the globe, it is imperative that researchers dig into what challenges in the different systems might underlay traditional barriers. Focus on more teacher training and resources, and passing policy, has not produced significant change in Jordan, possibly because root causes had not been identified. Neither policy nor practice can be looked at in isolation. Using a cultural-historic lens to study the full activity system, the tensions and relationships between stakeholders fill what previously has appeared to be a gap between 50 years of policy and little advancement in practice. Future inclusion research must push beyond looking at the same challenges, and instead begin inspecting the underlying reasons for these challenges at all levels of inclusive policy. This means engaging those within government, international organizations partnered with Ministries, and others engaged at the mesa level of policy.

References

Abugattas-Majluf, L. (2012). Jordan: Model reformer without upgrading?. *Studies in Comparative International Development*, *47*(2), 231–253. http://dx.doi.org/10.1007/s12116-012-9112-9

Abu-Hamour, B., & Al-Hmouz, H. (2014). Special education in Jordan. *European Journal of Special Needs Education*, *29*(1), 105–115. http://dx.doi.org/10.1080/08856257.2013.859820

Ahsan, M. T., & Mullick, J. (2013). The journey towards inclusive education in Bangladesh: Lessons learned. *Prospects*, *43*(2), 151–164. http://dx.doi.org/10.1007/s11125-013-9270-1

Ainscow, M., & Miles, S. (2008). Making education for all inclusive: Where next? *Prospects*, *38*(1), 15–34. http://dx.doi.org/10.1007/s11125-008-9055-0

Alborz, A., Slee, R., & Miles, S. (2013) Establishing the foundations for an inclusive education system in Iraq: Reflection on findings from a nationwide survey. *International Journal of Inclusive Education*, *17*(9), 965–987. http://dx.doi.org/10.1080/13603116.2012.725776

Alkhateeb, J. M., Hadidi, M. S., & Alkhateeb, A. J. (2016). Inclusion of children with developmental disabilities in Arab countries: A review of the research literature from 1990 to 2014. *Research in Developmental Disabilities Review*, *50*, 60–75. http://dx.doi.org/10.1016/j.ridd.2015.11.005

Anderson-Levitt, K. M. (2004). Reading lessons in Guinea, France, and the United States: Local meanings or global culture? *Comparative Education Review*, *48*(3), 229–252. http://dx.doi.org/10.1086/421178

Anderson-Levitt, K. M., & Alimasi, N. I. (2001). Are pedagogical ideals embraced or imposed? The case of reading instruction in the Republic of Guinea. In M. Sutton & B.A.U. Levinson (Eds.), *Policy as practice: Toward a comparative sociocultural analysis of educational policy* (pp. 25–58). Westport, CT: Greenwood.

Artiles, A. J., & Dyson, A. (2005). Inclusive education in the globalization age. In D. R. Mitchell (Ed.), *Contextualizing inclusive education: Evaluating old and new international perspectives* (pp. 37–62). London: Routledge.

Artiles, A. J., Kozleski, E. B., & Waitoller, F. R. (Eds.) (2011). *Inclusive education: Examining equity on five continents*. Cambridge, MA: Harvard Education Press.

Benson, S. K. (2020). The evolution of Jordanian inclusive education policy and practice. *Forum for International Research in Education*, 6 (1), 102–121.

Bines, H., & Lei, P. (2011). Disability and education: The longest road to inclusion. *International Journal of Educational Development*, *31*(5), 419–424. http://dx.doi.org/10.1016/j.ijedudev.2011.04.009

Burde, D. (2004). International NGOs and best practices: The art of educational lending. In G. Steiner-Khamsi (Ed.), *The global politics of educational borrowing and lending* (pp. 173–187). New York, NY: Teachers College Press.

Duke, J., Pillay, H., Tones, M., Nickerson, J., Carrington, S., & Ioelu, A. (2016). A case for rethinking inclusive education policy creation in developing countries. *Compare: A Journal of Comparative and International Education*, *46*(6), 906–928. http://dx.doi.org/10.1080/03057925.2016.1204226

Eleweke, C. J., & Rodda, M. (2002). The challenge of enhancing inclusive education in developing countries. *International Journal of Inclusive Education*, *6*(2), 113–126. http://dx.doi.org/10.1080/13603110110067190

Engsig, T. T., & Johnstone, C. J. (2015). Is there something rotten in the state of Denmark? The paradoxical policies of inclusive education—Lessons from Denmark. *International Journal of Inclusive Education*, 19(5), 469–486. http://dx.doi.org/10.1080/13603116.2014.940068

Fishman, B. (2014). Jordan: Caught in the middle again. *Adelphi Papers*, *54*(447–448), 123–134. http://dx.doi.org/10.1080/19445571.2014.995941

Hettiarachchi, S., & Das, A. (2014). Perceptions of 'inclusion'and perceived preparedness among school teachers in Sri Lanka. *Teaching and Teacher Education, 43*, 143–153. http://dx.doi.org/10.1016/j.tate.2014.07.003

Higher Council for the Rights of Persons with Disabilities [HCRPD] (2017). *10 year inclusive education strategic plan*. Unpublished report.

Human Rights Watch (Organization). (2016). *Barriers to education for Syrian refugee children in Jordan*. New York, NY: Human Rights Watch.

Jones, P. W. (2004). Taking the credit: Financing and policy linkages in the education portfolio of the World Bank. In G. Steiner-Khamsi (Ed.), *The global politics of educational borrowing and lending* (pp. 173–187). New York, NY: Teachers College Press.

Kalyanpur, M. (2014). Distortions and dichotomies in inclusive education for children with disabilities in Cambodia in the context of globalisation and international development. *International Journal of Disability, Development and Education, 61*(1), 80–94. http://dx.doi.org/10.1080/1034912X.2014.878546

Liasidou, A. (2012). *Inclusive education, politics and policymaking*. London: Continuum.

Lyons, W. E., Thompson, S. A., & Timmons, V. (2016). 'We are inclusive. We are a team. Let's just do it': Commitment, collective efficacy, and agency in four inclusive schools. *International Journal of Inclusive Education, 20*(8), 889–907. https://doi.org/10.1080/13603116.2015.1122841

Ministry of Education [MoE]. (2017). Education Strategic Plan 2018–2022. Retrieved from https://planipolis.iiep.unesco.org/en/2018/education-strategic-plan-2018-2022-6461

Peters, S. J. (2007). "Education for All?": A historical analysis of international inclusive education policy and individuals with disabilities. *Journal of Disability Policy Studies, 18*, 98–108. http://dx.doi.org/10.1177/10442073070180020601

Petra News Agency. (2018, December 12). Foreign aid to Jordan stands at $3.3 billion in 2018. Retrieved from http://petra.gov.jo/Include/InnerPage.jsp?ID=12127&lang=en&name=en_news

Public Law no. 20 The Rights of Persons with Disabilities of 2017. Retrieved from https://data2.unhcr.org/en/documents/download/66679

Saif, I., & Choucair, F. (2010). Status quo camouflaged: Economic and social transformation of Egypt and Jordan. *Middle East Law and Governance, 2*(2), 124–151. http://dx.doi.org/10.1163/187633710X500720

Schuelka, M.J. (2012). Inclusive education in Bhutan: A small state with alternative priorities. *Current Issues in Comparative Education, 15*(1), 145–156.

Schuelka, M.J. (2018). Advancing a comparative case study approach towards education and disability research: An example from Bhutan. In N. Singal, P. Lynch, & S. Johansson (Eds.), *Education and disability in the Global South: New perspectives from Asia and Africa* (pp. 89–106). London: Bloomsbury.

Steiner-Khamsi, G. (Ed.). (2004). *The global politics of educational borrowing and lending*. New York, NY: Teachers College Press.

Steiner-Khamsi, G. (2008). Donor logic in the era of Gates, Buffett, and Soros. *Current Issues in Comparative Education, 10*, 10–15.

Steiner-Khamsi, G. (2014). Cross-national policy borrowing: Understanding reception and translation. *Asia Pacific Journal of Education, 34*(2), 153–167. http://dx.doi.org/10.1080/02188791.2013.875649

Steiner-Khamsi, G. (2016). New directions in policy borrowing research. *Asia Pacific Education Review, 17*(3), 381–390. http://dx.doi.org/10.1007/s12564-016-9442-9

UN General Assembly. (2007, January 24). *Convention on the Rights of Persons with Disabilities: Resolution, A/RES/61/106*. Retrieved April 30, 2018, from http://www.refworld.org/docid/45f973632.html

US Department of State. (2018). *Foreign assistance—Jordan*. Retrieved from https://www.foreignassistance.gov/explore/country/Jordan

Winzer, M., & Mazurek, K. (2009). Inclusive schooling: Global ideals and national realities. *Journal of International Special Needs Education, 12*, 1–9.

Winzer, M., & Mazurek, K. (2012). Analyzing inclusive schooling for students with disabilities in international contexts: Outline of a model. *Journal of the International Special Needs Education, 15*(1), 12–23. http://dx.doi.org/10.9782/2159-4341-15.1.12

World Bank. (2017). *Implementation completion report: Jordan—ErfKE II* (Report No. P105036). Retrieved from http://projects.worldbank.org/P075829/education-reform knowledge-economy-program

Yamagata-Lynch, L. C. (2010). Understanding cultural historical activity theory. In *Activity systems analysis methods* (pp. 13–26). Boston, MA: Springer.

16
BECOMING AN ACTIVIST

A story of parental advocacy for inclusive education

Glenys Mann and The Queensland Collective for Inclusive Education

Introduction

I want to share with you the story of the Queensland Collective for Inclusive Education (QCIE). Through telling you their story, the parents I spoke with want to "pass forward" the lessons they have learned about advocating for inclusive education. They want to "fix the system." They want to "inspire others" and "shed a light" on their work and experiences as parent activists. They "want people to know what it takes."

QCIE is a group of parents from Queensland, Australia. Their children have disability, but it is not this that binds them. What unites these parents is "a belief that all children deserve to be genuinely included" and a drive "to move forward the rights of people with disability, and children in particular, and their rights to an inclusive education." They became part of QCIE because they want to connect with "like-minded people", "people who were like [them], who were experiencing the same stuff." They want to be "part of something"; "part of a movement, knowing that change wouldn't be possible without a strong parent voice." They know "how long and hard [parents have] been fighting and could see that there was a need for a group like this to exist."

The QCIE members that contributed to this narrative come from many different backgrounds and have different perspectives on the group, but together, and with other parents, they make up QCIE. This is their story. It is the story of each of them and the story of all. It is my story too as the researcher involved in the narrative process, but to foreground the voice of QCIE rather than my own, exact quotes from QCIE members are used as much as possible to tell the tale. The words of individual members are interwoven so that many voices, together, tell the shared story of QCIE. To distinguish my voice from theirs, my words will be written in italics.

DOI: 10.4324/9781003091950-19

Gathering the story: The process

Through 2020, and with ethical clearance from the Queensland University of Technology [#2000000064], I worked with members of the Queensland Collective for Inclusive Education (QCIE) to gather and tell the organisation's story. I met with ten QCIE members several times over the course of approximately six months. First we met as a whole group to talk about and record the story of QCIE, then I met with individuals to record their own personal perspectives of the organisation's history. We also met on subsequent occasions to re-present our conversations in written form and check that the story that was unfolding resonated with the storytellers. Although my role was to collaborate with the group and facilitate the telling and recording of the story, this was my story too. I had been active in parent advocacy collectives myself, and as an insider, knew firsthand of the concerns and experiences that the group described (Freedman & Combs, 2009, p. 349).

Storytelling has a pivotal place in parent movements for inclusive education (Runswick-Cole & Ryan, 2019). Has this been an effective approach for creating change in schools? Perhaps not, according to Runswick-Cole and Ryan (2019); however, storytelling can play an important role for people experiencing hardship and injustice (Denborough, 2011), and the literature is clear this is often the case for those parents who seek inclusive education for their children (e.g., Carey et al., 2019; Mann, 2016). Parents' stories also play an important role in bringing to light the reality of what it is like to advocate for inclusive education. Parent advocacy has been key in progressing inclusion and knowing what this takes is a critical piece in the inclusive education puzzle. Stories are a powerful way for parents to make meaning of their experiences (Freedman & Combs, 2009), and feel connected and acknowledged; both comforted and emboldened by the telling of their lives and the joining with others in a shared experience (Denborough et al., 2006). The telling of stories strengthens people's experiences of mutual support and solidarity (Freedman & Combs, 2009).

Storytelling, or narrative research, also has an important place in academia. Narratives are a well-recognised research method for investigating and explaining the complexity of human experience (Connelly & Clandinin, 1990) and, in this way, narrative methodology is a potent means for understanding the multifaceted nature of parental roles and experiences in inclusive education contexts. Typically, this methodology involves individual narratives (e.g., Fisher & Goodley, 2007; Knight, 2013); yet what was needed in this project was a way to collect the individual stories of parents and at the same time, their shared story of the organisation. We needed a collective narrative process.

Collective narrative

Collective narrative is relatively unknown in the literature, although recently, in contexts other than education, Dakich et al. (2016) proposed a community narrative whereby knowledge is organised and shaped through group participation;

Denborough (2011) described collective narrative as a connectedness that preserves individual distinctness; and Stapleton and Wilson (2017) wrote of shared narratives as a "collective remembering" (p. 61). We draw here on these understandings of collective narratives – and particularly on the writing of Denborough and others who have used collective narrative extensively in their community work (Denborough, 2005, 2011, 2012; Denborough et al., 2006; Freedman & Combs, 2009). The following principles from the community context guided the purpose and process of QCIE's collective narrative.

First, in community work, collective narrative is a positive way for individuals to respond to social injustice (Denborough, 2011). The "concept of narrative provides a bridge between the stories told by specific persons and the dominant discourses and narratives within which we all collectively live our lives" (Denborough, 2012, p. 48). Just so, the story told by QCIE members sits within a larger Queensland story of inclusive education and on a timeline of inclusive reform. It adds to an existing story of parental advocacy for inclusive education in Queensland and provides a means for current parents to respond to the continued exclusion of children with disability in this state. QCIE's experiences must be understood within a systemic context and as bureaucratic rather than just personal circumstances.

Second, a foundational principle of community narrative work is that in times of hardship, communities will be responding to the difficulties they experience in highly significant ways. By identifying the initiatives that community members take, future actions can be strengthened (Denborough et al., 2006). The gathering and recording of QCIE's story valorise the group's work and can strengthen this work going forward.

Third, critical to narrative work is a "profound belief in people's understanding about their life and abilities in managing their lives" (Freedman & Combs, 2009, p. 353). The QCIE narrative draws out the strengths that are to be found in the group and tells not just of struggle but of resistance to the status quo; of knowledge, skills, hopes, and dreams.

Fourth, an important feature of collective narrative is the participation of all members in deciding how the final account will speak for and represent them (Denborough, 2011). In this way, QCIE's narrative involved members in all stages of the narrative process – in decisions about what would be told; the gathering of the story; the identification of themes; and the preparation of the final account.

Fifth, collective narratives interweave individual stories to tell the story of the whole (Denborough et al., 2006). The words of each member "temporarily take centre stage before dissolving back into a collective ethos" (Denborough, 2011, p. 34). In the narrative told here, individual QCIE members have contributed what has been resonant to them regarding the organisation, and the final story brings together these diverse experiences into one collective retelling. Great care has been taken regarding how words are "rescued and re-presented" – ensuring that it is the words of individuals that make up the story, either quoted directly or paraphrased, storylines constantly intersecting with one another to tell a shared tale (Denborough, 2011, p. 35). The use of exact words has been a priority because of their power and significance for the final narrative (Denborough et al., 2006).

Telling the story: The setting

The story of QCIE is set in a time in Queensland, Australia, when parents are entitled to enrol their children with disability in their local regular school and expect that they will be welcome and included. In 2021, Australia provides legal protection to prevent discrimination and has ratified the Convention on the Rights of Persons with Disabilities (CRPD), an international convention that outlines the right of students with disability to an inclusive education. Queensland, specifically, has recently developed an inclusive education policy (Queensland Government, 2020a) explicitly grounded in the expectations of the CRPD and Australia's antidiscrimination laws (Disability Standards for Education, Australian Government, 2005). These protections have been a long time coming; QCIE's story is but the most recent chapter in a lengthy history of parental advocacy for these changes (see for example, Queensland Parents for People with a Disability, 2001, 2003, 2011).

Despite encouraging progress regarding inclusive education in Queensland, it is not surprising that the need for parent advocacy remains strong. Inclusive education change is slow, and in the face of ongoing bureaucratic barriers, parents must become fierce advocates in order to obtain the education they want for their children (Bacon & Causton-Theoharis, 2013). Systemic resistance to the voices of parents is still evident in Queensland. Students with disability continue to be denied or discouraged from enrolment in mainstream education (Poed et al., 2020) and the building of new special schools (Queensland Government, September 2020b) indicates that the drive to segregate remains strong. The ongoing need for parental advocacy in Queensland reflects experiences elsewhere. Lalvani and Hale (2015), for example, describe the continuing uncertainty, confusion, and frustration of parents over implementation of IE, and the subsequent adversarial relationships that some parents can have with educators. True inclusion in schools remains an elusive goal, according to Lalvani and Hale, and parents find themselves "still fighting the system" (ibid, Section 2). New laws and policies have done little to reduce the need for advocacy and without vigilance children with disability would still not be educated inclusively (ibid, "Implications" para. 1). In spite of parent campaigning across the past decades, there is still more to be done to challenge the "persistent poverty of aspiration for children with disability" (Runswick-Cole & Ryan, 2019, p. 1130).

While advocacy remains a necessity, and for some parents a moral obligation, (Lalvani & Hale 2015, "The battle for inclusion," para. 3), it can be exhausting, draining, and emotional work, and parents' individual efforts can be disregarded or foiled (Trainor, 2010). Consequently, parents can be drawn to other parents who have similar experiences and ambitions (Carey et al., 2019), and to join in collective activism where "the focus shifts to campaigning for change outside the family" (p. 51). Ryan and Runswick-Cole (2009) suggest that "activism ... may be a mechanism for expressing, in a 'selfless' way, ... mothers' aspirations and needs" (p. 48). Parent activism – collective campaigning for change beyond the concerns of individual sons and daughters – has always played a critical part in inclusive education reform (Carey et al., 2019) and the need for this work is not over yet. How do such parent collectives form? Are there key factors? What are the circumstances that lead to group rather than individual advocacy? What are the benefits and costs of activism to the individuals involved? The recent formation of QCIE provides a unique moment in time to learn about and capture the critical dynamics involved in parents' drive to act collectively. QCIE's narrative reveals those learnings and weaves individual accounts into a shared tale of the Collective. The group's story is told in four distinct chapters:

1] "The stars had to align" – the group emerges
2] "Our sudden birth" – the group forms
3] "How do you keep moving?" – the group looks to the future
4] "Something bigger than just ourselves" – the group reflects

The story of QCIE

Chapter 1 "The stars had to align" – The group emerges

We didn't come together by chance; "the stars had to align." "Enough people had to come together [and] be at the same place at the same time." "People had to not only think about the fact they wanted their child to be included in a regular school; they had to think about the fact that it was their right to be included and that every child deserves that right. They needed to understand that it was a social movement to end the segregation of people with disability. And I believe they had to be at a place that they wanted to be part of something bigger than just their own child's inclusion, wanting to be part of something that would move this issue forward for the greater good of our society."

Just prior to the formation of QCIE, a long-term advocacy group Queensland Parents for People with a Disability (QPPD) folded. The gap left by the closure of QPPD was a factor in the decision to form the new group, QCIE. "There's no group around here [to] talk about inclusive education." "I had seen QPPD come to an end." "We said a toast at the QPPD [celebration] dinner in August 2016, and there were a number of us then that were talking about [needing] to continue this." "We knew that something needed to follow on." "It's necessary for there to be a parent collective." "I remember being at that dinner and thinking just what positive relationships there were in the room. That was my first meeting with other people in the group."

"I suppose it was a bit before QCIE began, there was work being done by CRU [Community Resource Unit, https://cru.org.au/]. I think it was quite an intentional piece of work they were doing on family leadership and inclusive education. The work of QPPD was so important and was now missing. CRU seemed to work on restoring that parent voice in some form." *One specific individual from CRU, Lisa, is integral to this work and is mentioned throughout people's individual recollections.* "Lisa was setting up the relationships." "[She] was starting to plant seeds." "Lisa definitely was instrumental in bringing people together to create something." *Everyone speaks of the CRU events that were organised by Lisa as crucial to the emergence of the group. What* was also important to people was the content of the CRU events. "I just went for the CRU workshops, to learn more about inclusive education ... I was eager to gain knowledge and skills to support my son." *And then, finally there was a specific event that seemed to crystallise the intention to form a group.* "At that masterclass, things started to gain momentum. I think everyone needed a push to think that it could be done. Even though everyone was keen to get in and do it, we didn't have any direction." "It was that workshop in March 2017 that brought us all into the one location." "I remember us saying we would like to be part of more than just advocating for our own children. 'I want to come together and work collectively to try and create change.' We really didn't know what that would look like, or what that meant, we just knew we wanted to try and work on this together." "Yes, let's do it!"

"A number of us agreed to try and make it happen" and "things started to gain momentum." "Sue was the driving force behind that." "Sue, I remember, took the lead. She was quick to plant the seeds that CRU had provided and nurtured the group as it grew." "For QCIE to exist beyond the loose commitments made in the workshops, I think Sue became the driver that helped ignite those ideas and who kept them alight for some time. There were other committed individuals around her with a shared passion for the cause ... but she did an awful lot of the heavy lifting." "While many were still working out whether they had the time or not, Sue did things like creating a ... Facebook group, collating the messages as they were created and building a bank of resources, so nothing was lost along the way."

"It was all very tricky to begin with. Very tricky. And there were probably some points where it could have all just fallen apart." "But we just kept coming together, we kept having the conversations, over and over and over." "It's still a work in progress. But we really have come so far since those initial conversations."

Chapter 2 "Our very sudden birth" – The group forms

QCIE organised as a group at a critical time in Queensland. The Queensland government had commissioned a review into education for students with disability and a state election was looming. These two events galvanised the group. "I think the March 2017 [masterclass] is where we all came together thinking we needed to do something, but we didn't necessarily formalise anything until October." "Everyone knew there was the review happening with the department, and it just felt like good timing to do something. There were also some really ordinary things that had happened to children in Queensland, and I think that they'd been really public. You can't turn your back on that when you know about it." "Both with the department and the election looming ... I think that was the formal, 'Let's do something as a group, and call ourselves a group, and what does that look like?'" "We'd maintained that relationship and then [we] were ready for planning." "We had all these ideas bubbling away."

A number of key activities were foundational for the newly blossoming group. "We probably started out with a core group of about 15, and then the goal was to build supporters and members." "There was a need to develop and identify that QCIE was an independent group of parent advocates/activists." "The collaboration of the working group of QCIE members to develop the group's first brochure was helpful. It was a time to establish answers to questions such as, 'Who is QCIE? What do we do?'" "Pulling that brochure together, I think was a really formative experience for all of us, because it was nailing down the message." We also "developed a pack of resources" and "pulled together the first membership form." We started to "show a formal presence and I think at about the same time we talked about organising ourselves across the three groups." "We developed streams of engagement; these included community engagement, professional engagement, and political engagement." This was a "key piece of work as it helped the group to create a framework to build upon."

We "worked through the tone of the group's messages" and gathered "positive examples of principals and students and families, a suite of promotional messages." We developed our "visual imagery. We've been able to pull beautiful faces of our children together with some awesome statements, like #dreambigstandstrong. That was absolutely, that just knocked things over the line. That's how we really drove the campaign, and the state education week. It's developing that brand. That was extremely critical in that first year." "We used to talk about smoke and mirrors, where that professionalism, and the message, and the clarity of that message portrayed us as a much bigger group than we were. So the smoke and mirrors in that first year was really important to build our credibility."

"We had families that had children in all sorts of places, you know, kindy, primary school, high school, public school, private school, Catholic system. Having that variety in the group was an important theme from the beginning." *Bringing families together is clearly critical to the group. Peer support was one of the first of QCIE's activities.* "My passion has always been in peer support. I just think this is what is so important; that's the thing that doesn't change. Families really do have the best in mind for their kids. It's that love that we have for our kids – and I think that's shared by everyone, no matter where they're at – that drives us." "One of the most critical things is making sure those peer support networks grow. I think that's been the main push, and I can see how that's so important, to be able to get out into the neighbourhoods and the communities and have those coffee mornings", and "dinners once a term as well." "If you've got someone there who's just stepping out into the education arena, it's a real turning point. It's just such a crucial time [deciding] which path they're going to take. If there's a group here to support you, that change is, it's unbelievable what [difference] that change can make." "It's just having that parent voice; being able to support all the parents going through. It can be quite intimidating, going to [larger] organisations. Coming to a coffee morning might be less confronting. It's making sure people get included."

"The development of communication platforms was essential." "Social media, particularly Facebook has been the place where we've gathered numbers and interest." "Having a certain number of followers [is] a measure of credibility with politicians so there was a drive to use some of those positive messages to gather people across the page." "We've got a Facebook page and a closed group, making sure the closed group was the place to assist people, and to share our experiences in a positive way." "The online space is a really terrific way to keep people connected. Just to connect and not feel so alone is really important."

In the beginning, activities felt "safe", but the group continued to grow and soon branched out. "The November 2017 election was a much more public event as a group. We were waiting to see who would come, and what would be the reception ... and looking at what [we wanted] to share with people." *The group was starting to build credibility.* "The movement was really starting to get a roll ahead." "I could see that that was quite an important time, because the group had been together for quite a few months, and it was around that time that the inclusive education policy was just about to be released. Some of the Ed Qld people that were involved with inclusive education policy wanted to run a few things by the group, which was a real critical point. It had gotten to the stage where Ed Qld wanted to tap into their thoughts, and so I thought that was probably where they got to another level where they were considered a group that had information and knowledge that would be really helpful for policy." "One of the critical points was we were actually asked to give feedback on that."

"I think one of the other big moments was the second time that the department awarded the inclusive education award to a special school. I don't know that we were that organised the first time they did it, but the second time they did, it was an absolute shocker." "You guys all sitting down to draft a response." "It sparked a sense of, you know, we've been clear with our message. We've been positive. We've asked for meetings with the Minister. We've put in lots of work around constructive relationships and then the indignation about, you know, it was the QUT Inclusive Education Award!" "May 2018 was when the [*inclusive education*] policy came out, and then this was October 2018!" "It's those activities where we appear as a group, that's pretty critical."

Another example is "the QUT Inclusive Education Conference." "We've definitely made an intentional effort to become known." "The clarity and consistency of our message over time means that we've built credibility." Another example is "the Down Syndrome Conference last year. We designed the sessions. We delivered the sessions. Our flyers looked awesome! All that confidence-building, credibility building. We've always been clear, calm and consistent in our message." "Again, in 2019, we had another gathering with new members and old members, and to see the size grow yet again, and that was another big step forward; just seeing that growth from each stage."

Chapter 3 "How do you keep moving?" – The group looks to the future

At the time of the storytelling, QCIE is facing another evolution. "For the first couple of years, we were just people in a collective, passionate about this, and over time we realised, 'Well, we need some sort of structure and formality. We need to keep things moving, we need some sort of governance structure.' So that's still really evolving now. Not only just responding to things that are happening politically, but also actually getting some real direction ourselves; starting to create what we want, rather than being constantly reactive." *The group has come a long way.* "I think the Minister definitely knows who we are." "We have a reputation." "We've made a name for ourselves, definitely." "There is a definite clarity. We've moved people's understanding." *But there is also still a lot to be done and questions to be answered.* "It's been really difficult to figure this all out – [it's] not smooth. We are all individuals, dedicating our own personal time and energy into the collective, and figuring out how we each want to contribute and what we have time to contribute. It's not been easy figuring all of that out." "Knowing how to get more traction at the systems level has been really hard to nail down. We've done all the things to get established – peer support groups, FB page, social media, resources to share with people, website – so I feel like we're organised, but we can't really see how we can get the system to change. How much do we want to put ourselves and our children at risk? How do you keep moving when they're not interested in listening to us, no matter how organised?"

QCIE members are clear about the threats to the group's future. Exhaustion and strain are at the top of the list. "We are all time poor." "We're tired. It's a difficult situation at times, putting time and energy into QCIE voluntarily while also experiencing stress and pressure in our own personal lives." *A common theme in people's stories is the competition for their time and energy between their personal advocacy and their work with QCIE.* "This is the struggle. We are parents to children that require a lot of our time and energy." "How do you keep the clarity of the big picture when you're having conversations at your own school about how your child's going to go through the next day?" "When you're just fighting fires every single day, and just holding on, it is just so hard." *It is not difficult to see the irony in QCIE's situation – the fuel that drives them is the same fuel that threatens to burn them out. Adding to the pressure is the issue of continuity and having enough members to share the load.* "QCIE is still a young group and still developing its structure and leadership. It is still early days and I think a lot of those questions will be developed over time but until they are developed it will stop quite a few people from wanting to be involved because people want to understand what they're getting themselves in for." "We struggle through the schooling system, and then when we're out. 'Yay, I'm done! I can't go back there and keep fighting' So then you lose people, and it's up to the ones coming up to just keep on going, and they have the same struggle." *Another risk recognised by the group is feeling like they are not getting anywhere and that they are in the minority.* "There are just so many more parents of children with disability that are asking for something very different," "for more special, separate attention, and having their child removed from the class." "We're a very, very small minority." When we feel like there's not a whole lot of reward it can be deflating. We'd like to see a resolution before our children finish school, and feeling like we're not making much ground, it's difficult to keep positive and motivated."

QCIE's story is not just a story of struggle, however, and there are many things that keep the group vibrant and strong. "There is a shared passion for the work, and knowing you are a small part of that collective voice helps to sustain the movement." "I stay connected because the cause is so important" and so is "being able to link with like-minded people. It's not easy to always find them in your circle, or in your own neighbourhood." *Good times together are important:* "There has to be laughs. You have to have humour" *and so are the skills, agency and abilities that the group generates for individuals.* "After a couple of years of being surrounded by people like this all the time, you become just so much clearer." "Being part of a collective has definitely given me strength and confidence to insist for [my son's] inclusion. Having the support from others that share this belief has definitely given me a lot of confidence in advocating for what I know to be right." "It's just made me a lot stronger." "It gives me confidence to address things that aren't right and have conversations that I may otherwise have been reluctant to engage in." "You get a better understanding of what discrimination looks like in practice – gatekeeping. You become more aware of things." "For me it's really the first big kind of community action that I've been involved in."

Looking to the future, the group aims to bring more people along with them. "Several members of the group met with Queensland's Minister for Education in recent weeks and this meeting has fired everyone up again ready to charge ahead into [this year's] election and beyond. Funny … as prior to this meeting I saw signs that most were really weary, and I was worried we may run out of steam well short of the election. Sometimes a challenge can 'reignite the fire' even when you thought you were out of puff!" "If this is ever going to have an end, it'll be because we have that many people speaking about the value of this, there's just no push for segregation anymore, that it just dies." "The system has to change, and the parents have to be more informed." "Our next agenda is to go hard in a campaign-style approach" "for which we need more members," "more in the governance group, more energy, more time. Exactly! That's it!"

Chapter 4 "Something bigger than just ourselves" – The group reflects

Members of QCIE do not necessarily think of themselves as activists, although some have family histories of fighting for social justice. The step from advocating for one's own child to working together for systemic change is a big one, but most agree that there is more power in collective action than in working alone. "Our strength is greater as a group. It allows us to work towards very deliberate strategies and actions, which would be impossible individually." "I don't think that individual advocacy [has] anywhere near the power or strength of collective advocacy." "When you work in a group, there's more opportunity to use different people's skills, and have a stronger voice." "Collective lobbying is essential to driving change within schools." "Collective action [reminds] the system that students with disability and families are still here and will always be here."

Working collectively fosters a consistent, clear message. "It's a very considered voice when we're speaking on behalf of QCIE." "Our aim is to help people understand what inclusive education is and why it is in the best interest of all children, as well as society as a whole. We want to bring as many people along as we possibly can, gaining numbers and momentum; giving us a loud enough voice to influence change." "There's more weight behind a group of people saying the same thing." *Having a group makes it easier to hold systems accountable.* "It has to be shining a light on the continuing inequities;" "drawing attention [to systemic issues]. You need collective advocacy to discuss those issues, or to highlight them, bring them to the front, to make people aware." "So I guess that's the role of the collective – to take a step back and go, 'What are all the issues? And what are the most important? What will make the most difference?'"

Collective and individual work go hand in hand. "Grassroots support is essential to driving change within schools." "The real power is in that individual child in that classroom, and what they're doing, but without QCIE to drive that, it wouldn't happen." "I don't think I would be on this path with my son without the Collective. They are so key to ensuring parents feel supported and are knowledgeable. Without a group like the Collective, I think there'd be far fewer families doing the hard yards." "Change happens when a group of people, just ordinary people, get together." *And for those families not in QCIE?* "I'd like to think it will make the path for the next person a little easier." "Collective advocacy has to work for those families. It has to be on behalf of those families. Not in their place, and not to take over their voice, but to have some impact for them, so that their individual advocacy isn't so hard." "You're advocating for everyone, not just my kids, my own children, but to recognise and support everyone's rights."

QCIE members reflect on how advocacy has and hasn't changed. "With social media you can reach more people," and "you have a wealth of information at your disposal." "The way people communicate has changed. Social media is having a big influence on activism." "There's a lot of power in that space." "It's easier to get a bigger audience." "Being able to share your message with thousands and thousands of people at any given time is a positive; being able to ask a question, share information." "Things happen so, so fast, and we have the ability to make things happen very, very fast" "but there's issues with that as well;" "less consideration is put into our messaging." "Messages can be misconstrued; the meaning [can be] misinterpreted."

"What hasn't changed is the fact that parents still have to be strategic, still have to nurture relationships, still have to stay informed." "The system isn't any more open. The Department is just as insular. There's certainly no greater transparency." *Although the new Queensland Inclusive Education Policy is a positive development* – "schools tread a bit more carefully these days and personal advocacy is a bit easier" – "it's also a way of shushing you." "Before, discrimination was more blunt and clear, and now I guess, it's probably a bit more subtle and deceiving." "The legislation's there. It looks beautiful, but then you go and get the premier saying things like, 'Oh, we're opening all these special schools', and you're just like, 'What?!' So I think there's all this conflicting information that's difficult to navigate." "It's so confusing."

Conclusions: Making meaning of the story

The impact of parents in educational reform cannot be overestimated (Lalvani & Hale, 2015). Parents have been, and continue to be, major contributors to the shaping of legislation and policy regarding education for children with disability

(Trainor, 2010; Lalvani & Hale, 2015). Parents bring to the inclusive education revolution a "passionate interest, deep needs, symbolic authority and persuasive power" (Carey et al., 2019, "fields, alliances, and frames", par. 5), and their advocacy has "long provided the impetus and served as a driving force" for inclusive educational change (Lalvani & Hale, 2015, "historical struggles", para. 2).

While the parents of QCIE are passionate about inclusive education, they did not initially seek collective advocacy or to be activists. QCIE was formed through necessity and vision; shared values and experiences drew members to each other, and the drive to activism was powered by ongoing systemic resistance to authentic inclusive education reform. A lack of formal parent advocacy in Queensland was the final catalyst for intentional efforts to fill that gap. QCIE's story paints a picture of a committed group of parents that seeks to drive change and to benefit not only their own children but all children with disability. Critically, they are prepared to pay a personal cost in order to do that; while the group is collaborative, strategic and persistent, it is also under considerable pressure. Here are some key lessons that can be learned from the rise of this parent collective:

1. Parents will continue to come together to fight for inclusion and to advocate for their children as long as discrimination and injustice in education exist. Parents not only have natural authority in their children's lives (Kendrick, 1996) but are also natural sources of accountability regarding the implementation of inclusive practice. They will demand more than just rhetoric when it comes to the inclusion of their children. While they may not start out as advocates, parents can reach a "breaking point" when policy is not implemented (Bacon & Causton-Theoharis, 2013, p. 693). Advocacy is an important tool parents utilise to claim their children's rights to an inclusive education (ibid, p. 683). In contrast to the disempowerment typically described by parents of students with disability, activism can be an empowering and positive experience (Trainor, 2010; Ryan & Runswick-Cole, 2009).

2. Strong leadership is critical to driving group formation and the collective process going forward. In QCIE's case, the group was intentionally 'seeded' and energised by a community organisation through deliberate and planned work that brought parents together for this purpose. Key parents then kept things moving, especially in the start-up phase. One of the worries of the group – and for parent advocacy in general (Runswick-Cole & Ryan, 2019) – is who will be the parent and community leaders driving collective activism for inclusive education in the future.

3. Personal growth is an important benefit of the Collective that sustains QCIE members. Parents speak of skills and competencies they have developed, and of the knowledge and understanding they have gained through their membership of QCIE. The literature suggests that these are benefits of activism that are experienced more widely (Ryan & Runswick-Cole, 2009; Carey et al., 2019; Trainor, 2010). So, too, is the power of being exposed to parents' more optimistic understandings of disability than are typically experienced in dealings with professionals (Ryan & Runswick-Cole, 2009).

4. Relationships are a crucial factor in the Collective's health and longevity. It is through participation in networks that people redefine themselves as activist (Ryan & Runswick-Cole, 2009). Shared values and experiences connect individuals; this connection is a source of support and confidence and was a key reason for membership of the Collective. Relationships can also be a risk to the group's stability when there are different views and approaches.
5. Participating in formative shared experiences is discussed as a key factor in QCIE's development – members working collectively on the group's identity, messaging, resources, activities, and future plans. Individual stories highlight that shared values, vision, and purpose are critical to the group's stability.
6. Finally, a key insight from QCIE's story is the question of sustainability. It is clear that most of the parents driving QCIE are tired and stressed by their complicated and overlapping responsibilities. They are compelled (and even energised) to fight for the rights of all children but at the same time they are advocating for their own child on sometimes a daily basis. The efforts required to do both (and in some cases work and look after other family members) are not sustainable. Parents spoke of moving in and out of QCIE activities depending on their circumstances, and some reflected on the guilt they feel at not being able to do more. They worry about the issue of increasing the QCIE membership to share the load, and about who will follow in their footsteps and keep the organisation alive.

While the power of parents in inclusive education reform is undisputed, the story of QCIE leaves me wondering why the responsibility for change continues to rest so heavily on the shoulders of parents. Certainly, others work for inclusive reforms, but it is parents who have historically been most invested in the fight for inclusive education, perhaps because it is they (and their children) who bear the consequences of educational inertia in this space. However, parents, even when working collectively, cannot and should not be driving inclusive education reform alone. Activism is difficult to sustain when those at the forefront are tired and stressed. Sustainability is made even more problematic by the cyclic nature of parents' involvement. Once a child leaves school, parents' thoughts turn to different matters, and a new wave of parent advocates must emerge if activism is to continue. As Runswick-Cole and Ryan powerfully argue (2019), the obligation for change lies not solely with parents but is the responsibility of all. Inclusive education is everybody's business and if we are to see real transformation in the system, we must all be accountable for that change. In an era of inclusive education policy and legislation, instead of seeking to resist or drown out the voices of parents, we must all join loudly in support.

The last word

I asked QCIE members to have the final say and to share the essence of what the Collective means for them as individuals. Here is what they want you to carry forward from this chapter.

I guess the **feeling for me, of not being alone**, is what I take from the group. Even if progress is slow, the feeling of knowing that other people are experiencing and feeling the same way and wanting the same changes. That's really invaluable.

~

It's meant a lot to me that there are **other people that are advocating the same thing** as what I am and feel as passionate about the inclusion of all children with disability. That force for parents is important to me so that young parents can connect with us from the very earliest point in time and know that there's many, many other people that believe just as strongly as they do about their child being included.

~

The relief to find other **people that are just as passionate about their child** having the same experience and the same rights as all other children. No matter how difficult it is, we can't accept anything less than that. It's strengthening to know that I have a group of families that understand how it feels to need to be able to provide that for your child. Can't ignore it. Can't deny it. Have to keep working towards it.

~

Hopes for your kids. Knowing that we're all going to come out on the right side of history at some point in time. Seeing through the Facebook posts, and peer support network, people celebrating little wins here and there ... that stuff is really empowering for me, especially when I am talking to families who, you know, they're struggling, they've given up and admitted defeat. They're just tired of fighting the fight every day. It's very empowering when I can say, **"Well let's connect with this network, and connect with these people"** and you'll hear stories of hardship, and you'll hear stories of difficulty, but you'll also hear stories of success and in the end that's what we all want for our kids.

~

Value of validation; feeling that there are other people out there who have the same values, beliefs, ideas, that you're not a crazy person out there on your own, asking for things, pie in the sky. It makes you feel stronger. That makes **you feel more bold and courageous** that you would otherwise be. And to see the older kids that are now adults and [feel] that you are carrying on the fight; that you're the voice for your child. You've got no choice; you have to do it.

~~

"I was at a crossroads; I had friends and family, I even had the HOSES [Head of Special Education Services] at his old school, all directing me in to the special ed arena again. We were being pulled down another, that old hole that I didn't want to go back into. I wasn't hearing too much positive from anybody. But I went back to QCIE. Many of them had been in a very similar situation. They came out of that devastation and gave it another go. They encouraged me to do the same. I think that sort of sums it up, just having the backup is so important; **that real sense of community and understanding** is so vital for families in our situation."

~

This is not a selective sport; E does not have to prove anything. She's spent a lot of her life being told by educated people what she can and can't do. E may never have a play at the Sydney opera House; she may never be an Olympic athlete, but she will have an inclusive education. She will go to her local school, she will have that experience, and do all the things that other kids do. That, to me, is a success. I want people to know that **there is no measure of success greater than going to your local school and having some mates.**

~

When I think about the power of QCIE, it's less about pushing your rights, and the law, even though that's really important, and more about our children, and how we all love them so much, and that this **[inclusive education] has been really life changing for our children**. This is what we want to achieve and why, always sharing that vision we have for our child, and why it is so important to us. Most people want that for their child, they want them to have a great adult life as well as an inclusive childhood, and they can see that what happens now does make a difference. The power of QCIE really is that connection with other families.

~

I will never get tired of hearing like people over the phone, or people at coffee, or often young parents, they've been battling along in the mainstream school with no support and no connection and come along and say "I am so glad. **I was supposed to come here today. I've just been at my wits end**. It's all been going very badly." Even if this is a fight that we just keep fighting and don't actually win, it's way worse to be questioning your own sanity, from loving your child, than to just be going along with the status quo and abandoning those dreams.

~

References

Bacon, J. K., & Causton-Theoharis, J. (2013). 'It should be teamwork': A critical investigation of school practices and parent advocacy in special education. *International Journal of Inclusive Education*, 17(7), 682–699. doi: 10.1080/13603116.2012.708060

Carey, A., Block, P., & Scotch, R. (2019). Sometimes allies: Parent-led disability organizations and social movements. *Disability Studies Quarterly*, 39(1). doi: http://dx.doi.org/10.18061/dsq.v39i1.6281

Connelly, F. M., & Clandinin, D. J. (1990). Stories of experience and narrative inquiry. *Educational Researcher*, 19(5), 2–14. doi: 10.3102/0013189x019005002

Dakich, E., Watt, T., & Hooley, N. (2016). Reconciling mixed methods approaches with a community narrative model for educational research involving Aboriginal and Torres Strait Islander families. *Review of Education, Pedagogy, and Cultural Studies*, 38(4), 360–380.

Denborough, D. (2005). A framework for receiving and documenting testimonies of trauma. *International Journal of Narrative Therapy & Community Work*, 3 & 4, 34–42.

Denborough, D. (2011). Resonance, rich description and social-historical healing: The use of collective narrative practice in Srebrenica. *International Journal of Narrative Therapy & Community Work*, 3, 27–42.

Denborough, D. (2012). A storyline of collective narrative practice: A history of ideas, social projects and partnerships. *International Journal of Narrative Therapy & Community Work*, 1, 40–65.

Denborough, D., Koolmatrie, C., Mununggirritj, D., Marika, D., Dhurrkay, W., & Yunupingu, M. (2006). Linking stories and initiatives: A narrative approach to working with the skills and knowledge of communities. *International Journal of Narrative Therapy & Community Work*, 2, 19–51.

Disability Standards for Education 2005 (Cth) (Austl.), www.comlaw.gov.au/Details/F2005L00767

Fisher, P., & Goodley, D. (2007). The linear medical model of disability: Mothers of disabled babies resist with counter-narratives. *Sociology of Health & Illness*, 29(1), 66–81. doi: 10.1111/j.1467-9566.2007.00518.x

Freedman, J., & Combs, G. (2009). Narrative ideas for consulting with communities and organizations: Ripples from the gatherings. *Family Process*, 48(3), 347–362.

Kendrick, M. (1996, July). The natural authority of families. *CRUcial Times*, 6, 6. https://static1.squarespace.com/static/59ff91890100276a4ea3efe7/t/5a1380a1e4966b29cf745edd/1517378657259/4.+The+Natural+Authority+of+Families+MKendrick+CT06.pdf

Knight, K. (2013). The changing face of the 'good mother': Trends in research into families with a child with intellectual disability, and some concerns. *Disability & Society*, 28(5), 660–673. doi: 10.1080/09687599.2012.732540

Lalvani, P., & Hale, C. (2015). Squeaky wheels, mothers from hell, and CEOs of the IEP: Parents, privilege, and the "fight" for inclusive education. *Understanding and Dismantling Privilege*, 5(2), 21–41.

Mann, G. (2016). From here to there and back again: The story of a mother, her son, disability, and school choice. *International Journal of Inclusive Education*, 20(9), 909–920. doi: 10.1080/13603116.2015.1122842

Poed, S., Cologon, K., & Jackson, R. (2020). Gatekeeping and restrictive practices by Australian mainstream schools: Results of a national survey. *International Journal of Inclusive Education*. https://doi.org/10.1080/13603116.2020.1726512

Queensland Collective for Inclusive Education (QCIE). (2021). https://www.qcie.org/

Queensland Government (2020a). *Inclusive education policy*. Department of Education, Queensland. https://ppr.qed.qld.gov.au/pif/policies/Documents/Inclusive-education-policy.pdf

Queensland Government (2020b, September). New schools for 2021. https://qed.qld.gov.au/programs-initiatives/det/building-education/new-schools-for-2021

Queensland Parents for People with a Disability. (2001). *Education Queensland's Placement Policy and Process: A report by Queensland Parents of People with Disability Inc*. Retrieved from http://www.aph.gov.au/~/media/wopapub/senate/committee/eet_ctte/completed_inquiries/2002_04/ed_students_withdisabilities/submissions/sub151a_zip.ashx

Queensland Parents for People with a Disability. (2003). *There's small choice in rotten apples: An exploration of the process of parental decision-making around educational choice for parents of children with disabilities*. Retrieved from https://www.family-advocacy.com/our-resources/there-and-39s-small-choice-in-rotten-apples/

Queensland Parents for People with a Disability. (2011). *Diving for pearls: An account of parents' quest for an inclusive education in Queensland*. Retrieved from http://cru.org.au/wp-content/uploads/2016/09/QPPD-Diving-for-pearls-March-2011.pdf

Runswick-Cole, K., & Ryan, S. (2019). Liminal still? Unmothering disabled children. *Disability & Society*, 34(7–8), 1125–1139.

Ryan, S., & Runswick-Cole, K. (2009). From advocate to activist? Mapping the experiences of mothers of children on the autism spectrum. *Journal of Applied Research in Intellectual Disabilities*, 22(1), 43–53.

Stapleton, K., & Wilson, J. (2017). Telling the story: Meaning making in a community narrative. *Journal of Pragmatics*, 108, 60–80.

Trainor, A. A. (2010). Diverse approaches to parent advocacy during special education home-school interactions: Identification and use of cultural and social capital. *Remedial and Special Education*, 31(1), 34–47.

17
EXPLORING THE CONGRUENCE BETWEEN BHUTANESE TEACHERS' VIEWS ABOUT INCLUSION, GROSS NATIONAL HAPPINESS, AND BUDDHISM

Dawa Dukpa, Suzanne Carrington, Sofia Mavropoulou, and Matthew J. Schuelka

Introduction

Bhutan is a small country in the Himalayas with a 2020 population of about 750,000 (National Statistics Bureau, 2020). Bhutan was a monarchy before transitioning to parliamentary democracy in 2008 when the king handed down democracy to the people. With happiness mandated in the Constitution of Bhutan as an explicit societal goal, Bhutan prioritizes and measures people's happiness and wellbeing through a Gross National Happiness (GNH) approach (Dema, 2018; Karma Ura, 2016).

Before the evolvement of secular education in the later part of the twentieth century, Buddhist monastic education was the main form of schooling in Bhutan. Even though modern secular education in Bhutan is not based on monastic education, the two education systems exist simultaneously and the influence of monastic education on the cultural and religious context of Bhutan is significant (Dukpa, 2016). It is important to note that the development of secular education in Bhutan has been influenced by the British Colonial education system in India in terms of curriculum content and teaching approaches, as well as provision of supports in schools (Gyamtsho & Dukpa, 1998). Since then, over the last six decades, education has become more contextualized with changes in the curriculum reflecting the needs of the Bhutanese society and with Bhutanese teachers replacing foreign teachers (Singye Namgyel & Phup Rinchhen, 2016).

Bhutan implemented the inclusion of students with disabilities in general schools in 2002 when the government introduced a Special Educational Needs (SEN) programme in Changangkha Middle Secondary School in the capital city of Thimphu. As of 2020, there are 24 'SEN Schools' (inclusive schools) – out of 535 public schools and 38 private schools – and two special schools catering to students with specific sensory and alternative communication needs (Ministry of Education, 2020).

DOI: 10.4324/9781003091950-20

There are also several non-governmental organisations that fulfill a daily educational role for children with significant physical and cognitive difficulties.

Bhutan has ratified several international instruments and conventions, including the United Nation Convention on the Rights of Child (1989), the Salamanca Statement (1994), the Education for All (EFA) conference in Jomtien, and it is signatory to the United Nations Convention on the Rights of Persons with Disabilities (CRPD) (Rinchen Dorji & Schuelka, 2016; UNESCO, 1994; United Nations, 2006). As a consequence, Bhutan has developed key policy documents that support and enhance inclusion including the National Education Policy (draft) and the Standards for Inclusive Education (Ministry of Education, 2017, 2019b). Reflecting the key points of an equitable and participatory learning experience for all students from the CRPD General Comment No. 4, The Standards for Inclusive Education in Bhutan define inclusive education as 'the process of valuing, accepting and supporting diversity in schools and ensuring that every child has an equal opportunity to learn' (MoE, 2017, 4). Table 17.1 presents the significant milestones in the development of the education system in Bhutan.

In this chapter, we will explore how the GNH framework informs the Bhutanese school system and how the GNH approach and its Buddhist origins are compatible with the notion of inclusion in Bhutanese teachers' views. This argument is informed by an analysis of interviews conducted with Bhutanese teachers. In this chapter, we are referring specifically to the inclusion of children with autism spectrum disorder that are socio-culturally constructed as 'having' a 'disability' in Bhutan.

The concept of Gross National Happiness in Bhutan

The Fourth King of Bhutan in 1972 declared GNH as more important than Gross Domestic Product (Karma Ura, 2016). Since then, the concept of GNH has been adopted as the country's guiding philosophy for the foundation of any government policies and all policies must first be approved by the GNH Commission to ensure that they promote the happiness and well-being of Bhutanese citizens. GNH in its simplest form means development with values (Karma Ura, 2016). Long (2021) aptly defined GNH as a multidimensional approach to development that pursues balanced progress among the material, spiritual, emotional, cultural and environmental needs of the society. It is a holistic approach to well-being that pursues development in tandem with Bhutan's Buddhist values and culture (Long, 2021). In the GNH framework, there are four pillars (economic development, environmental preservation, cultural promotion and good governance) and nine domains (psychological wellbeing, balanced time use, community vitality, cultural diversity and resilience, ecological diversity and resilience, good governance, living standards, health and education) that are used to measure progress and reflect on GNH values across the four pillars. These domains represent a wide array of human needs associated with holistic or collective happiness, which is prioritized over happiness at a personal or individual level (Karma Ura, 2016). Ura (2009) suggested that values related to the nine domains should be specified and practised as part of the school curriculum.

TABLE 17.1 *Timeline* with the key historical events in the education context of Bhutan

Date	Key event
1913	The first modern school in Bhutan started in Haa.
1962	Language of instruction in the schools was changed to English from Hindi.
1968	The first higher education school with Sherubtse School in Kanglung.
1968	The first teacher training institute was established in Samtse, Bhutan.
1972	Development of the philosophy underpinning the GNH was first pronounced by the Fourth King of Bhutan.
1973	Muenselling Institute was established in Khaling, Trashigang was established as the first special school in the country for visually impaired.
1975	The Teacher Training Centre was established in Paro.
1976	The first National Education Policy in which Dzongkha, the national language, received increased importance in schools was developed.
1983	Samtse's Teacher Training Institute was upgraded to National Education Institute.
1985	The New Approach to Primary Education (NAPE) was launched to promote a child-centric approach to instruction as opposed to a teacher-centric. Curriculum reform incorporated learning material based on the Bhutanese context.
1990	Bhutan ratified the Convention on the Rights of the Child.
1994	UNESCO's Salamanca Statement and Framework for Action on Special Needs Education.
1994	Teacher Training Centre at Paro was upgraded to a National Education Institute.
2002	Introduced a Special Educational Needs programme in Changangkha Middle Secondary School to integrate children with disabilities into mainstream schooling.
2003	Established the Royal University of Bhutan (RUB) with twelve institutes (including the two teacher training institutes in Paro and Samtse) forming the constituent colleges under the university.
2010	Bhutan became a signatory to the Convention on the Rights of Persons with Disabilities.
2010	The Ministry of Education launched Education for GNH (EGNH) initiative.
2017	The government developed and endorsed the Standards for Inclusive Education.
2020	Paro College of Education introduced a Masters in Inclusive Education course.

We suggest that there is alignment between specific domains of GNH and values of inclusive education. In particular, as Karma Ura (2009) suggests, attributes such as compassion, generosity, empathy and calmness should be incorporated under the domain of psychological well-being (i.e., the subjective or spiritual/inner wellbeing of an individual) to nurture and facilitate the development of positive behaviour and character among students. Compassion and empathy are important attributes that nurture behaviours and attitudes of individuals acknowledging human differences and promoting inclusive approaches in schools and in society.

Other domains of GNH that align with the values of inclusive education are the education domain and the community vitality domain. The education domain considers educational attainments in a holistic manner and acknowledges that knowledge, skills, competency and values can be learned beyond school and emphasis is given on developing creativity, openness, diligence, insight, perseverance and patience (Karma Ura, 2009). We argue that teaching values on diligence, insight, perseverance and patience align with the fundamental values required for an inclusive society (Carrington et al., 2012). Similarly, the community vitality domain aligns with the values that underpin inclusion. Karma Ura (2009) recommends that schools need to instil values such as altruism, trust, fairness, equality, unity, sociability and cohesion by encouraging activities like volunteering, family closeness, friendship, social support and community participation and socialisation. These values and corresponding practices directly support inclusive practices and can contribute to inclusive schools and society.

Another domain of GNH that also reflects inclusive values and practices is the cultural domain. Karma Ura (2009) proposes that the cultural domain should promote values such as identity, diversity, dignity and non-alienation. Practices related to diversity foster acknowledgement of human differences and prevent alienation of others and therefore align with inclusive values and practices. Furthermore, Karma Ura (2009) emphasises a holistic approach highlighting the interrelationships of values and practices among the GNH domains.

Among many initiatives taken by the government to implement GNH–based policies and reforms, the Education domain has developed considerably over the last 50 years (Drupka & Brien, 2013; Karma Ura, 2016). Inspired by the need to embed GNH values into everyday learning in schools, the Bhutan Ministry of Education launched an education reform initiative in 2009 called Educating for GNH, which brought changes into the Bhutanese education system through the infusion of GNH values and principles in the curriculum. A GNH–inspired school curriculum focuses on imparting knowledge of the nine GNH domains by specifying the relationships among those domains as constituents or contributors to happiness (Karma Ura, 2016). As part of the Educating for GNH initiatives, values such as critical and creative thinking, ecological literacy, reverence and respect for culture, care for nature and others, and civic engagement were attempted to be infused in daily lessons, although some confusion remains by teachers and much of the Educating for GNH initiatives occurred in extra-curricular activities (Kezang Sherab, Maxwell & Cooksey, 2016). According to Schuelka (2012), infusing GNH values in the school curriculum attempts to make education contextual and relevant for Bhutanese students by instilling Bhutanese culture and values.

Another important aspect of the Educating for GNH initiative is the promotion of inclusive education as an approach to provide equitable educational opportunities and promote the capabilities of all children in the community (Pema Tshomo, 2016). An inclusive approach to education is expected to serve the needs of all children including those with disabilities and create an atmosphere of care, respect and warmth in schools. The foundation of all these values lies in the Buddhist approach to moral development that emphasizes collective happiness and embraces inclusiveness and an individual's relationship with the community (Karma Ura, 2016). This principle of GNH is rooted in the Buddhist belief of cause and effect [*karma*], interdependence [*pratītyasamutpāda*], and the commitment to others in the form of merit-making through giving or helping others [in Dzongkha, *Jimba*]. Buddhism in Bhutan informs the country's worldview and influences the Bhutanese way of living in all aspects of social, economic and political spheres (Karma Phuntsho, 2013). As Jagar Dorji (2003) and Singye Namgyel (2011) have suggested, the Bhutanese education system with its deep roots in Buddhist culture and Buddhist belief in the interconnectedness and interdependence of all beings supports an inclusive approach to education. In addition, the Standards for Inclusive Education, as guidelines for implementing inclusive education (MoE, 2017), are informed by the Index for Inclusion's focus on culture, policy and practice (Booth & Ainscow, 2002) and promote the values of embracing cultural diversity, community vitality, cooperation and interdependence.

The importance of culture

Ideas about how the understanding of gender, race, class, or ability and disability have evolved and changed over time are good examples of socially and culturally constructed knowledge (Carrington, et al., 2012). The socio-cultural model views disability as a social construct asserting historical and culturally specific construction of knowledge and views that aligns with the assumption of social constructionism (Burr, 1995; Crotty, 2010). While we acknowledge that cultural and social factors inform contemporary socio-cultural models, we consider that a cultural model of disability goes further in saying that disability can be structured and lived through cultures (Waldschmidt, 2017). Therefore rather than focusing only on a socio-cultural model, we want to also highlight the cultural assumptions about disability in Bhutan. A cultural model considers disability as a discourse about experience and recognises how disability may be understood within cultural contexts. We suggest that a cultural model of disability focuses our attention on how identities of people with disability are framed within a broader social-cultural pattern of experience. Therefore we suggest that culture could influence how dis/ability is embodied and constructed.

According to Mitchell (2005), disability is a concept that people understand and interpret in different ways depending on their cultural values, beliefs and socio-historical context. The cultural model of disability considers disability as a concept constructed through discourse or as a process, experience, situation or event specific to a society and historical period (Waldschmidt, 2017). In the context of Bhutan, even though many people still associate disability with the Buddhist concept of *karma* or the effects of past misdeed from other lifecycles (Kamenopoulou & Dawa Dukpa, 2017), other explanations for the cause of disability are becoming more prevalent. Schuelka (2015) noted that the discourse on disability has shifted to a more complex and, in some ways, cognitive dissonant construction of disability as older, local beliefs intermingle with newer, global discourses of disability conceptualisation. For example, many Bhutanese people are increasingly pointing towards heavy consumption of alcohol, the practice of cross-cousin marriages (now rare in Bhutanese society), and medical causes as contributing factors for the occurrence of disability while they also continue to hold beliefs in *karma* and the Buddhist conceptualisation of disability as being an 'impure' form of humanity.

In Bhutan, considering its history as predominantly an agrarian society, people with specific learning difficulties were not considered as having a disability, or the meaning of their difficulty was not relational, because the most important skill required for social participation was the ability to work on a farm rather than read. Once all children were expected to attend school, it became apparent that some children struggled with academic learning and so the concept of learning difficulty emerged in Bhutan. Schuelka (2018) argued that with the introduction of modern secular schooling in Bhutanese society, 'disability' was constructed as a category of difference and an attribute for societal marginalization. The cultural and religious belief in the *karmic* cause of disability has been identified as a context-specific barrier to the inclusion of students with disabilities (Dawa Dukpa & Kamenopoulou, 2018; Schuelka, 2015). However, it is important to note that Bhutanese teachers appear to be generally supportive of including children with disability in mainstream schools (Dorji et al., 2021).

Our intent was to explore how Bhutanese teachers' views about inclusive education can be influenced by concepts of GNH and Buddhist beliefs. The research questions were focused on teachers' views about the inclusion of a particular group, that is students with autism spectrum disorder. The current study was guided by the neurodiversity perspective of autism which recognizes autism as part of human diversity through a socio-cultural lens (Jaarsma & Welin 2012; Robertson 2010). The neurodiversity perspective of autism aligns with the social constructionist approach because its proponents claim that an individual becomes disabled by the barriers in the environment such as inaccessible infrastructures, negative attitudes and other social and political aspects of society (Jaarsma & Welin, 2012; Robertson, 2010). This notion is based on the social model of disability, which considers disability as a social construction resulting from physical, organizational and attitudinal barriers. The social model recognizes that people may have impairments but they become disabled through the social and environmental barriers (Waldschmidt, 2017). The current study aimed to extend understanding of these barriers by considering how Bhutanese teachers' views about disability can be culturally constructed.

Research has demonstrated that teachers hold a pivotal role in the successful inclusion of students with autism spectrum disorder (Garrad et al., 2019; Graetz, 2009; Humphrey & Symes, 2013; Sansosti & Sansosti, 2012) and teachers' commitment to inclusive practice is largely dependent on their views about inclusion (Avramidis & Norwich, 2002; Garrad et al., 2019). Furthermore, it has been noted that teachers face challenges in including students with autism spectrum disorder due to attitudinal (such as lack of knowledge and understanding of the autism spectrum disorder) and systemic barriers as well as lack of training and resources (Lindsay et al., 2013). It appears that considerations of how cultural understandings of disability such as autism spectrum disorder have not been covered in previous research, particularly in a country like Bhutan.

The present study

This chapter reports on the qualitative component of a larger study that adopted an exploratory sequential mixed-method design (Creswell & Creswell, 2017). The qualitative approach enabled the lead researcher (Dawa Dukpa) to gather in-depth information through interviews. The reflexive thematic analysis (Braun & Clarke, 2020) of qualitative interviews generated themes that informed an understanding of Bhutanese teachers' views about the inclusion of learners with autism spectrum disorder and the influence of the cultural context on their perspectives. The current study was framed to consider teachers' crucial role in the implementation of inclusive practices within the socio-cultural context of Bhutan. The findings presented in this chapter aimed to address the following research question: *What are the influences of culture on the Bhutanese teachers' views about inclusion and the congruence with GNH domains and Buddhist beliefs?*

Research setting and participants

Eighteen primary and secondary schools across Bhutan listed as 'SEN Schools' (inclusive schools) in the 2019 Annual Education Statistics report were chosen as research sites (Ministry of Education, 2019a). Sixteen (n=16) teachers from seven schools self-nominated as participants in on-site semi-structured individual interviews (Table 17.2). Interviews were conducted in English (the official language of

TABLE 17.2 Demographic characteristics of interviewed participants (n=16)

Participant Code	Gender	School location	Highest qualification attained	Teaching experience in inclusive schools (in years)	Overall teaching experience (in years)
1	F	Paro	B.Ed	6	7
2	F	Paro	B.Ed	5	14
3	M	Paro	B.Ed	7	14
4	M	Gelephu	B.Ed	5	31
5	F	Gelephu	B.Ed	7	18
6	F	Thimphu	B.Ed	5	10
7	F	Thimphu	M.Ed	13	29
8	F	Thimphu	PTC	17	33
9	M	Pemagatshel	B.Ed	3	9
10	M	Pemagatshel	B.Ed	3	9
11	F	Mongar	B.Ed	3	9
12	F	Mongar	B.Ed	3	9
13	M	Chukha	M.A	2.5	15
14	M	Chukha	M.A	5	17
15	M	Samtse	B.Ed	4	11
16	M	Samtse	B.Ed	5	3

Note. M.Ed (Masters in Education), M.A (Master of Arts), B.Ed (Bachelor in Education), PTC (Certificate in Primary Teaching).

instruction in schools) and the seven schools were chosen based on the criterion that they catered for students with autism spectrum disorder.

A guide comprising six open-ended questions was developed for the semi-structured interviews. The interview guide aimed to elicit teachers' views on the inclusion of students with autism spectrum disorder ("What is your opinion on inclusion of students with autism spectrum disorder in the mainstream classroom?") and their responses to context-specific questions ("What is your opinion about inclusion in the Bhutanese context?"; In terms of values, cultures and religious beliefs do you see any challenges or opportunities?"). The interview guide was informed by literature on the conceptualization of disability and inclusion in the context of Bhutan (Kamenopoulou & Dawa Dukpa, 2017; Schuelka, 2012, 2015, 2018).

Research procedure

The current study met the requirements of the National Statement on Ethical Conduct in Human Research (2007) in Australia (QUT Ethics Reference number: 1900000803) and approval was also obtained from the Ministry of Education, Bhutan. Participants were interviewed individually (8–31 October 2019). Interview questions were piloted with six teachers and a few questions were removed and some changes were made to the wording according to feedback from participants. Interviews lasted approximately 20–40 minutes, were audio recorded and transcribed in full verbatim by Dawa Dukpa. All participants were given the opportunity to review the interview transcripts via email. Two participants responded with comments indicating their agreement with the transcripts of their recorded interviews.

Data analysis

An inductive and deeply reflective method (Braun & Clarke, 2020) informed by the theoretical framework of social constructionism and the cultural model of disability was adopted to analyse the qualitative data. Interview transcripts were imported into NVivo 12 (QSR International, 2018), and following repeated readings of the transcripts by the research team, codes were generated and organised into themes and sub-themes under two topics. The thematic analysis of the interview data was guided by the six-phase process of analysis outlined by Braun & Clarke (2020): 1) data familiarisation; 2) systematic data coding; 3) generating initial themes; 4) developing and reviewing themes; 5) refining, defining and naming themes; and 6) writing the report. Themes were generated through active engagement of all researchers with consideration to the relevance of information to the broad research area, prevalence across some of the participant responses and richness in the narratives (Braun & Clarke, 2012). For example, the theme *cultural influences on teachers' views* was generated to include views on GNH, Buddhism and beliefs, because understanding the influence of the cultural and social context on teachers' views about inclusion is relevant to the current research. The analytical process was grounded in the data and involved active immersion of all the researchers in the data, reading, reflection, questioning, imagining and retreating from the data (Braun & Clarke, 2020). Therefore, the subjective and analytical skills that the researchers brought to the process were considered as valued aspects of the analysis. We contend that the use of Reflexive Theme Analysis (Braun & Clarke, 2020) was underpinned by the theoretical assumption of social constructionism; so the social, cultural and ideological positioning of the researchers was an important element of generating narrative evidence from the interview transcripts.

Findings

A summary of the topics, themes and subthemes is presented in Table 17.3.

Topic 1: Benefits of inclusion

This topic is used to organise data on teachers' views on the benefits of including students with autism spectrum disorder in the general classroom under two themes: *Social and academic gains for students* with autism spectrum disorder and *learning gains for peers and teachers*.

1.1 Social and academic gains for students with autism spectrum disorder

All participants emphasized *learning social skills* as an important benefit for students with autism spectrum disorder who are included in the mainstream classroom. For example, participant 3 shared that when students with autism spectrum disorder are included 'they can socialize with the general students so they can learn social skills'. In support of inclusion, one of the participants expressed their opposition to the isolation of students with autism spectrum disorder and stated, 'these are a group of children who have difficulty in interaction, building social relationship,

TABLE 17.3 Organization of themes/subthemes for each topic

Topics	Themes and subthemes
1. Benefits of inclusion	1.1. Social and academic gains for students with autism spectrum
	1.2. Learning gains for peers and teachers
2. Cultural influences on teachers' views	2.1 Alignment between GNH and inclusive values
	2.2 Alignment between Buddhism and inclusive values
	2.3 Religious beliefs as barriers to inclusion
	2.3.1 Karmic beliefs as barriers for inclusion
	2.3.2 Superstitious beliefs as barriers for inclusion

[and] if we isolate them then we might be depriving them of the natural environment' (T1). In addition to the evidence on social gains and the engagement for students with autism spectrum disorder from inclusion (see: Lindsay, Proulx, Scott, & Thomson, 2014; Marks et al., 2003), our findings show that teachers' views about the inclusion of students on the autism spectrum disorder reflect the socio-cultural context of Bhutan that prioritizes cultural values such as interconnectedness and collective wellbeing over segregation and individual wellbeing, which are all values that support inclusion and are influenced by Buddhism and the GNH framework.

In addition to the social gains, two participants highlighted that inclusion offers academic benefits to students with autism spectrum disorder. For instance, participant 6 stated, 'in terms of learning, [academic] there are benefits, from friends they observe and learn and also they try to seek help'. Similarly, participant 5 stated 'they interact and they try to, if the child is not writing they try to come up with the writing and they tend to copy others'.

1.2 Learning gains for peers and teachers

Three teachers shared that other students benefit from having peers with autism spectrum disorder in their class. Participant 1 stated, 'when these children are put together, they learn to embrace the differences and they do not see these children [students with autism spectrum] as something very different'. Participant 8 shared that other students learn values such as caring for others from being with students with autism spectrum disorder in their classrooms and stated 'other children are learning how to take care'. Further, participant 12 stated; 'yes, they [typically developing student] are also learning from them [students on the spectrum], because the skills that they have he does not have, the skills that he has, they don't have. So, they learn from each other' (T12). Interestingly, one participant noted that the inclusion of students with autism spectrum disorder can also have benefits for the teachers. He stated, 'even the general teacher is also learning how to deal with that kind of child, probably they don't have expertise in autism but somehow the child is teaching them' (T8). It is clear that these participants believe that inclusion supports the development of close relationships, friendships, social support and community participation as suggested by Karma Ura (2009).

Our participants' acknowledgement of the academic and social gains for students without disabilities from the inclusion of students with autism spectrum disorder could be associated with the Buddhist belief that all living beings are interconnected and dependent on each other as well as the existence of strong community bond. These beliefs and values are not only embedded in the Bhutanese culture but are also promoted as an integral part of both Buddhist and GNH values. This is congruent with the cultural model of disability that perceives persons with disabilities and those without disabilities as being interdependent (Waldschmidt, 2017).

Topic 2: Cultural influences on teachers' views

This topic is used to organise data related with cultural influences on teachers' views. Three themes were generated through the reflexive thematic analysis: Alignment between GNH and inclusive values; Alignment between Buddhism and inclusive values; and Religious beliefs as barriers to inclusion. The final theme has two sub-themes: *Karmic beliefs as barriers*; and *superstitious beliefs as barriers*.

2.1 Alignment between GNH and inclusive values

Considering that GNH is a guiding philosophy of development in Bhutan, it was not surprising that three participants made specific references to GNH when asked about inclusion in the context of Bhutan. Participant 1 stated, 'I feel this inclusiveness and GNH policy would complement each other … because gross means it should include everyone which is inclusiveness'. Participants also mentioned other terms such as acceptance, helping, compassion, community and diversity, which are all key indicators of the values promoted through the Educating for the GNH initiative. Other supporting quotes from participants include

> school community is one thing … acceptance is another and … helping them [those on the spectrum].
>
> (T2)

> from the religious point of view … from a compassionate point of view, I think inclusion might help [students on the spectrum].
>
> (T4)

> Bhutanese are like that in general when they see a particular child or person suffering they come together and help.
>
> (T6)

> in our context because of our compassion they help
>
> (T6)

These responses indicate that the participants understand the connection between the values of inclusive education and GNH values that have been embedded into everyday learning in Bhutanese schools.

2.2 Alignment between Buddhism and inclusive values

Five participants shared that the cultural and spiritual values of Bhutan, largely influenced by Buddhist values, align well with inclusive values and provide a conducive environment for inclusive education to develop. Participant 1 stated, 'because we belong to a religious country [referring to Buddhism as a religion], inclusiveness or accepting children has been always easy for us'. Other participants also mentioned the compatibility between the Buddhist value of compassion and inclusion. Participants offered the following sentiments:

> as a Bhutanese, we have compassion, so when we have children with disability … they [other students] are accepting them … when we ask students to come forward as a buddy we could see many students coming forward to help.
>
> (T2)

> our context I think it will support inclusion because Bhutanese are religious minded and when they see people suffering they have that feeling that we should help.
>
> (T6)

Participant 12 also mentioned the positive response from the community and the involvement of parents in the school committees. 'community as far as we know they have positive feelings and they are supportive … we have parents in the committee in our school and they are always supportive'. Considering that community vitality is a key component of GNH, community support and involvement is vital in the success of inclusion. Moreover, Bhutan being a close-knit society that promotes collective happiness, community support and involvement have always been vibrant features of Bhutanese society.

Interestingly, participant 15 referred to religious and cultural beliefs such as *karma* as a positive influence in terms of supporting those with autism spectrum and stated, 'when it comes to religious belief such as *karmic* effect sometimes there is positive effect because people say that we have to be supportive and helpful since they are born like this because of their karmic effect'. This idea has been raised in research conducted in Myanmar which is also a Buddhist society (Ware & Schuelka, 2019). However, most sentiment on *karma* pertains to a negative conceptualization of disability.

2.3 Religious beliefs as barriers to inclusive education

This theme reports on teachers' perceptions of context-specific barriers to the inclusion of students with autism spectrum disorder in Bhutan and will be discussed under two sub-themes: *Karmic beliefs as barriers for inclusion* and *superstitious beliefs as barriers for inclusion*.

On the first sub-theme of *karmic* beliefs, it is worth highlighting that three teachers identified *karmic* beliefs among Bhutanese people as a barrier to inclusion. For example, participant 1 shared:

> in our culture and again I talked about grandparents having some exclusive notion, they do not exclude to the extent of criticizing but they do pity them, thinking that it must be because of some karmic deed in the past, so in this sense, I mean about exclusion.

The cultural perspective of treating people with disability with pity is evident in this comment and may be more prevalent in older people in Bhutan. It is important for school staff to be mindful of these assumptions which can create a cultural barrier for progressing inclusive education.

Pertaining to the second sub-theme of *superstition*, one participant (T13) stated that some parents and community members believe that those with autism spectrum disorder are captured by spirits and therefore spiritual performance by shamans [*pam/pow*] and traditional medicine healers [*drungtsho*] could relieve them of their condition. He stated: 'people still are with the belief that a child has been cursed'. The same participant shared that these superstitious beliefs can hinder the inclusion process for those children, whose parents refuse to send them to school because they think that their child is being possessed by spirits and thus education will not offer any relief or healing from their spiritual deeds.

Discussion

Our findings show that there is a connection between the concept of GNH, Buddhism and inclusive education. Consistent with evidence from existing research (Lindsay, Proulx, Scott, & Thomson, 2014), our study reports that social gains for students with autism spectrum disorder are described by teachers as a key benefit from inclusion along with the development of values such as acknowledging individual difference, empathy, acceptance and care for all students. These attributes reflect integral values promoted by GNH as well as Buddhism. Our focus on interpreting teachers' responses through the cultural model of disability indicates that disability in Bhutan is culturally constructed. For example, participants discuss values such as interconnectedness and collective well-being over segregation and individual well-being which are Buddhist values that support inclusion.

Another significant finding that emerged from our analysis and reflects the congruence between the concept and values of inclusive education, the GNH domains and Buddhist beliefs, is related with the value of 'acceptance'. Terms such as acceptance, helping, and compassion were common terms used by participants in their responses about inclusion. The use of terms such as 'acceptance' by teachers reflects Buddhist values rooted in the belief of karma or cause and effect (Karma Ura, 2016). We argue that considering acceptance of any condition in both self and others could be influenced by the Buddhist cultural context in which the Bhutanese education system is enmeshed. Values such as acceptance, sympathy, empathy and harmony are not only important values in Buddhism but are also important elements of the Educating for GNH approach (Karma Ura, 2016). We argue that teachers' beliefs are a reflection of societal and cultural values influenced both by the Buddhist values and values promoted by the GNH approach. The Bhutanese culture emphasizes harmony and collective well-being, which is evidence of the Buddhist influence. Similar findings on Bhutanese teachers' views were reported by Rinchen Dorji et al., (2021) and Dawa Dukpa and Kamenopoulou (2018). For instance, Rinchen Dorji et al. (2021) found that compassion and altruism were major elements of teachers' attitudes towards inclusive education. The congruence between GNH and the concept and values of inclusive education has been previously documented by Schuelka (2012). We argue that GNH-influenced policies based on Buddhist beliefs promote compassion, empathy and harmony, which contribute to inclusive education.

We consider our findings on GNH as important because the concept of GNH is integral to any policy development in Bhutan. We argue that the commonalities and similarities in the value framework for inclusion, GNH and Buddhist beliefs provide a sound foundation for reinforcing inclusive education in Bhutan. It is also important to note that some teachers seemed to understand that inclusion is not a concept that is imported and borrowed from other education systems, but an approach inherent in the local socio-cultural GNH framework and Buddhist values and beliefs.

In agreement with previous research conducted with teachers in Bhutan (Rinchen Dorji et al., 2021; Kamenopoulou & Dawa Dukpa, 2017), our findings also showed that teachers' perceived prevalence of the *karmic* association of disability and superstitious beliefs can be a barrier to the inclusion of students with autism spectrum disorder. Those who believe their current state as being predetermined by the deeds in their past life can have very low expectations for individuals with disabilities. This belief tends to focus more on charity and pity instead of empowering them through education (Ware & Schuelka, 2019). Considering that the majority of the Bhutanese population is Buddhist, their belief system is deeply rooted in the Buddhist cultural values and principles such as the belief in the *karmic* connection and fate. The Bhutanese way of living, including the education system, is deeply influenced by Buddhist cultural values and principles (Karma Phuntsho, 2013). It should be noted that the finding on the majority of the teachers being able to recognize and acknowledge that the prevalence of *karmic* association of disability can be a barrier to inclusion is another positive step in the inclusion process. This is because the first step towards addressing barriers such as belief in *karma* is to identify and acknowledge that such beliefs can hinder the process of inclusion. However, it is important to note that a few teachers also had the perception that a person might be born with a disability because of their past *karma*. Once again this is not surprising considering that teachers, despite their education, are members of the larger community and are influenced by the socio-cultural context.

Viewing persons with autism spectrum disorder as victims of their *karma* represents the charity model of disability that sees persons with disabilities as victims of their impairment and requiring special treatment (Retief, & Letšosa, 2018). This view is not congruent with the neurodiversity perspective of autism spectrum disorder as it views persons with disabilities as requiring special treatment and as dependent on other people. However, as affirmed by Miles (2013), the belief in *karma* does not necessarily have to be perceived as contradictory to inclusion. Moreover, Rinchen Dorji et al. (2021) argue that the Buddhist belief in *karma* generates unconditional feelings of compassion and empathy for others, which support inclusion and are congruent with the GNH values.

We would like to note that the generalizability of the findings from the present study is impacted by the fact that only a sample of Bhutanese teachers teaching in inclusive schools were interviewed in our study. Therefore, the findings cannot be generalised to all teachers in Bhutan.

Conclusion: Implications and recommendations for future research, policy, and practice

The findings from the current study contribute to the limited research on the influence of culture on teachers' views about the inclusion of students with autism spectrum disorder. The new knowledge is contextually relevant to Bhutan and it will be of interest to other countries in South Asia. Our findings indicate that teachers described social gains for students with autism spectrum disorder and development of values such as acknowledging individual difference, empathy, acceptance and care for all students as key benefits from inclusion. Therefore, to enhance an inclusive approach to education, the Bhutanese Government should support the integration of inclusive education principles into all teacher training modules – rather than as one stand-alone module – and consider the meaning/value/purpose of inclusive education as a vehicle for enacting the GNH framework in the social and cultural context of Bhutan. Our findings on the connections between the concept of GNH, Buddhism and inclusive education reveal that GNH-informed policies and initiatives are supportive of inclusive education and therefore the government should continue prioritizing GNH education in schools with emphasis on the conceptual links between the GNH approach and inclusive values. Following Karma Ura (2016), we argue that GNH values should be embedded into teacher preparation and professional learning programs that focus on inclusive education and highlight the connection between GNH, Buddhism and inclusive values. Further, as Samadi (2020) suggests, the cultural knowledge and competencies of teachers should be more strongly considered in professional learning and professional practice for teachers.

We contend that this study challenges the copious amounts of research conducted on 'teacher attitudes towards inclusion' in the field of inclusive education research. Avramidis and Norwich (2002) themselves conceded that teacher attitude surveys are plentiful in research because they are easy to do. In our qualitative research in Bhutan, we found that teachers do not hold 'attitudes' that are divorced of social and cultural context. Rather, the Bhutanese teachers expressed their views as influenced by their views on GNH, Buddhism and within the context of their professional role, expectations, resources, training, professional incentives and role identity. In other words, 'atittudes' towards inclusion are not within the purview of teachers alone, but rather as a result of the socio-cultural context in which teachers are situated, and particularly in the case of Bhutan, strongly influenced by a cultural model of disability. This argument has been made by others to a certain degree (e.g., Schuelka, Kezang Sherab & Tsering Y. Nidup, 2019; Singal, 2009), but this study further reinforces the importance of conducting qualitative research with teachers to understand how their cultural perspectives influence their 'attitudes'. We also recommend future studies to include teachers from schools that are not currently identified as inclusive schools to get a broader perspective of teachers' views about inclusion and include important stakeholders such as students, parents and policymakers.

Our findings revealed that concepts that are specific to the Bhutanese context such as GNH and Buddhism not only influenced teachers' views about inclusion but the underlying principles are congruent and supportive of inclusive education. Our findings contribute to the scarce literature about the influence of social and cultural factors on teachers' views about inclusion in South Asia. More specifically, our collective work extends previous research by supporting a better understanding about how disability is culturally constructed.

References

Avramidis, E. & Norwich, B. (2002) 'Teachers' attitudes towards integration/inclusion: a review of the literature.' *European Journal of Special Needs Education*, 17(2), 129–147. https://doi.org/10.1080/08856250210129056.

Booth, T. & Ainscow, M. (2002). *Index for inclusion: Developing learning and participation in schools*. ERIC.

Braun, V. & Clarke, V. (2012). Thematic analysis. In *APA handbook of research methods in psychology, Vol 2: Research designs: Quantitative, qualitative, neuropsychological, and biological*. (pp. 57–71). American Psychological Association. https://doi.org/10.1037/13620-004

Braun, V. & Clarke, V. (2020). One size fits all? What counts as quality practice in (reflexive) thematic analysis? *Qualitative Research in Psychology*. 1–25. https://doi.org/10.1080/14780887.2020.1769238

Burr, V. (1995). *An introduction to social constructionism*: Routledge.

Carrington, S.B., MacArthur, J., Kearney, A., Kimber, M., Mercer, L., Morton, M., & Rutherford, G. (2012). Towards an inclusive education for all. In S. Carrington & J. MacArthur (Eds.), *Teaching in inclusive school communities* (pp. 3–38): John Wiley & Sons Inc.

Creswell, J. W. & Creswell, J. D. (2017). *Research design: Qualitative, quantitative, and mixed methods approaches*. Sage.

Crotty, M. (2010). *The foundations of social research: Meaning and perspective in the research process*: Sage.

Dema, S. (2018). *Educating for Gross National Happiness*. [Master of Education dissertation, University of Victoria]. UVicSpace. https://dspace.library.uvic.ca//handle/1828/9913

Dorji, J. (2003). *Quality of education in Bhutan: A personal perspective on the development and changes in Bhutanese education system since 1961*. KMT Publisher.

Dorji, R., Bailey, J., Paterson, D., Graham, L., & Miller, J. (2021). Bhutanese teachers' attitudes towards inclusive education. *International Journal of Inclusive Education*, 25(5), 545–564. https://doi.org/10.1080/13603116.2018.1563645

Drupka, K. & Brien, K. (2013). Educating for gross national happiness: A new paradigm for education in Bhutan. *Antistasis*, 3(2), 11–15.

Dukpa, Z. (2016). The history and development of monastic education in Bhutan. In M.J. Schuelka & T.W. Maxwell (Eds.), *Education in Bhutan: Culture, schooling, and gross national happiness* (pp. 39–56). Singapore: Springer.

Dukpa, D. & Kamenopoulou, L. (2018). The conceptualisation of inclusion and disability in Bhutan. In L. Kamenopoulou (Ed.), *Inclusive Education and Disability in the Global South* (pp. 53–79). Springer.

Garrad, T. A., Rayner, C., & Pedersen, S. (2019). Attitudes of Australian primary school teachers towards the inclusion of students with autism spectrum disorders. *Journal of Research in Special Educational Needs*, *19*(1), 58–67. https://doi.org/10.1111/1471-3802.12424

Graetz, J. (2009). Effective academic instruction for students with high functioning autism or Asperger's syndrome. *Teaching children with autism in the general classroom*, 45–74.

Gyamtsho, D. C. & Dukpa, N. (1998). *Bhutan: Curriculum development for primary and secondary education*. http://www.ibe.unesco.org/curriculum/Asia%20Networkpdf/ndrepbt.pdf

Humphrey, N. & Symes, W. (2013). Inclusive education for pupils with autistic spectrum disorders in secondary mainstream schools: Teachers' attitudes, experience and knowledge. *International Journal of Inclusive Education*, *17*(1), 32–46. https://doi.org/10.1080/13603116.2011.580462

Jaarsma, P. & Welin, S. (2012). Autism as a natural human variation: Reflections on the claims of the neurodiversity movement. *Health care analysis*, *20*(1), 20–30. https://dor.org/10.1007/s10728-011-0169-9

Kamenopoulou, L. & Dawa Dukpa (2017). Karma and human rights: Bhutanese teachers' perspectives on inclusion and disability. *International Journal of Inclusive Education*, *22*(3), 323–338. https://doi.org/10.1080/13603116.2017.1365274

Lindsay, S., Proulx, M., Scott, H., & Thomson, N. (2014). Exploring teachers' strategies for including children with autism spectrum disorder in mainstream classrooms. *International Journal of Inclusive Education*, *18*(2), 101–122. https://doi.org/10.1080/13603116.2012.758320

Lindsay, S., Proulx, M., Thomson, N., & Scott, H. (2013). Educators' challenges of including children with autism spectrum disorder in mainstream classrooms. *International Journal of Disability, Development and Education*, *60*(4), 347–362. https://doi.org/10.1080/1034912X.2013.846470

Long, W. J. (2021). Modern Bhutan's Buddhist Statecraft. In W.J. Long (Ed.), *A Buddhist approach to international relations: Radical interdependence*. (pp. 71–86). Palgrave Macmillan. https://doi.org/10.1007/978-3-030-68042-8_5

Marks, S. U., Shaw-Hegwer, J., Schrader, C., Longaker, T., Peters, I., Powers, F., & Levine, M. (2003). Instructional management tips for teachers of students with autism spectrum disorder (ASD). *Teaching exceptional children*, *35*(4), 50–54.

Miles, M. (2013). *Buddhism and responses to disability, mental disorders and deafness in Asia*. West Midlands, UK. http://www.independentliving.org/miles2014a

Ministry of Education. (2017). *Standards for inclusive education*. Ministry of Education.

Ministry of Education. (2019a). *Annual education statistics*. Policy and Planning Division, Ministry of Education, Royal Government of Bhutan.

Ministry of Education. (2019b). *National education policy (draft)*. Policy and Planning Division, Ministry of Education, Royal Government of Bhutan.

Ministry of Education. (2020). *Annual education statistics*. Policy and Planning Division, Ministry of Education, Royal Government of Bhutan.

Mitchell, D. (2005). Introduction: sixteen propositions on the contexts of inclusive education. In D. Mitchell (Ed.), *Contextualizing inclusive education* (pp. 1–21): Routledge.

Namgyel, S. (2011). *Quality of education in Bhutan: Historical and theoretical understanding matters*. DSB Publications.

Namgyel, S. & Rinchhen, P. (2016). History and transition of secular education in Bhutan from the twentieth century into the twenty-first century. In M.J. Schuelka & T.W. Maxwell (Eds.), *Education in Bhutan: Culture, schooling, and gross national happiness* (pp. 57–72). Singapore: Springer.

National Statistics Bureau. (2020). *Statistical Yearbook of Bhutan 2020*. National Statistics Bureau, Royal Government of Bhutan. http://www.nsb.gov.bt/publication/files/SYB_2020.pdf

Phuntsho, K. (2013). *The history of Bhutan*. Random House India.
QSR International. (2018). *NVivo 12 for Windows*. Melbourne QSR International Pty Ltd.
Retief, M., & Letšosa, R. (2018). Models of disability: A brief overview. *HTS Teologiese Studies/Theological Studies, 74*(1). https://doi.org/10.4102/hts.v74i1.4738
Rinchen Dorji & Schuelka, M. J. (2016). Children with disabilities in Bhutan: Transitioning from special educational needs to inclusive education. In M.J. Schuelka & T.W. Maxwell (Eds.), *Education in Bhutan: Culture, Schooling, and Gross National Happiness* (pp. 181–198). Singapore: Springer.
Robertson, S.M. (2010). Neurodiversity, quality of life, and autistic adults: Shifting research and professional focuses onto real-life challenges. *Disability Studies Quarterly, 30*(1). https://doi.org/10.18061/dsq.v30i1.1069
Samadi, S.A. (2020). Parental beliefs and feelings about autism spectrum disorder in Iran. *International Journal of Environmental Research and Public Health, 17*(3), 828. https://doi.org/10.3390/ijerph17030828
Sansosti, J.M., & Sansosti, F.J. (2012). Inclusion for students with high-functioning autism spectrum disorders: Definitions and decision making. *Psychology in the Schools, 49*(10), 917–931. https://doi.org/10.1002/pits.21652
Schuelka, M.J. (2012). Inclusive education in Bhutan: A small state with alternative priorities. *Current Issues in Comparative Education, 15*(1), 145–156. https://files.eric.ed.gov/fulltext/EJ1000220.pdf
Schuelka, M.J. (2015). The evolving construction and conceptualisation of 'disability' in Bhutan. *Disability & Society, 30*(6), 820–833 https://doi.org/10.1080/09687599.2015.1052043
Schuelka, M.J. (2018). The cultural production of the 'disabled' person: Constructing difference in Bhutanese schools. *Anthropology and Education Quarterly, 49*(2), 183–200. https://doi.org/10.1111/aeq.12244
Schuelka, M. J., Kezang Sherab, & Tsering Y. Nidup (2019). Gross national happiness, British values, and non-cognitive skills: The role and perspective of teachers in Bhutan and Englsand. *Educational Review, 71*(6), 748–766. https://doi.org/10.1080/00131911.2018.1474175
Sherab, K., Maxwell, T. T., & Cooksey, R. W. (2016). Teacher understanding of the educating for gross national happiness initiative. In M.J. Schuelka & T.W. Maxwell (Eds.), *Education in Bhutan: Culture, schooling, and gross national happiness* (pp. 153–168). Springer.
Singal, N. (2009). Inclusion in the real world: Practitioners making sense of inclusion education in Indian classrooms. In M. Alur & V. Timmons (Eds.), *Inclusive education across cultures: Crossing boundaries, sharing ideas* (pp. 210–219). New Delhi: SAGE.
Tshomo, P. (2016). Conditions of happiness: Bhutan's Education for Gross National Happiness initiative and the capability approach. In M.J. Schuelka & T.W. Maxwell (Eds.), *Education in Bhutan: Culture, schooling, and gross national happiness* (pp. 139–152). Singapore: Springer.
UNESCO (1994). *Salamanca statement and framework for action*.
United Nations. (2006). *Convention on the Rights of Persons with Disabilities*. https://www.un.org/development/desa/disabilities/convention-on-the-rights-of-persons-with-disabilities.html
Ura, K. (2009). *A proposal for GNH value education in schools*. Gross National Happiness Commission, Royal Government of Bhutan.
Ura, K. (2016). Gross national happiness, values education and schooling for sustainability in Bhutan. In R. N. Gorana, and P.R. Kanaujia (Eds.), *Reorienting Educational Efforts for Sustainable Development* (pp. 71–88). Springer. https://doi.org/10.1007/978-94-017-7622-6_5
Waldschmidt, A. (2017). Disability goes cultural: The cultural model of disability as an analytical tool. *Culture–Theory–Disability: Encounters between Disability Studies and Cultural Studies*, 19–27.

Ware, H. & Schuelka, M.J. (2019). Constructing 'disability' in Myanmar: Teachers, community stakeholders, and the complexity of disability models. *Disability & Society*, 34(6), 863–884. DOI: 10.1080/09687599.2019.1580186

Editor's Note: Bhutanese names are not strucutred around a surname or family name. Rather, traditional Bhutanese naming convention is one or two given names that are non-gendered. Given this, all Bhutanese names are cited fully and alphabetised according to the first letter of their first given name.

INDEX

Page numbers in *Italics* refer to figures; **bold** refer to tables and page numbers followed by 'n' refer to notes numbers.

Aboriginal Education Team (AET) 107
academic achievement, visibly rewarding learners for 131; competitive learning environments 128–129; desire for recognition 127; excellence 132; exclusionary beliefs and attitudes 129–130; mixed methods study 125–126, **126**; motivation of 122–123, 131; negative interdependence model 130; overview of 119–120; South Africa, *see* South Africa; subjectivity of awards 127–128
ADA, *see* Americans with Disabilities Act
AET, *see* Aboriginal Education Team
Agenda for Sustainable Development (2030) 6
Ahmed, S. 67
aid model 30
AIHW, *see* Australian Institute of Health and Welfare
Ainscow, M. 232, 257
Akbar, M. A. 51
Alborz, A. 257
Alimasi, N. I. 258–259
Alonso, F. 234, 235
American Sign Language (ASL) 53
Americans with Disabilities Act (ADA) 53
Amka 90
Anderson, B. 68
Anderson-Levitt, K. M. 258–259
Andries, C. 172

Annual Education Statistics report (2019) 299
apartheid 121, 123
Appadurai, A. 189
Archer, M. S. 188
Armenian Center for Democratic Education (Armenian-CIVITAS) 174
Arnold, M. L. 35
Artiles, A. J. 3, 19, 187
ASD, *see* autism spectrum disorder
ASGS, *see* Australian Statistical Geography Standard
ASL, *see* American Sign Language
Australian Aboriginal students: belonging education, stories of 104–109; colonisation 99–100; distrust and scepticism, of inclusive education 101; inclusive education 102–104, 110–111; policy of assimilation/absorption 100; research projects 101–102
Australian Education Review 109
Australian Institute of Health and Welfare (AIHW) 31
Australian Statistical Geography Standard (ASGS) 31
autism, neurodiversity perspective of 298
autism spectrum disorder (ASD) 300, 306; in Cambodia, *see* Cambodia, autism spectrum disorder in; social and academic gains, for students 301–302
Avagyan, A. 171
Avramidis, E. 18, 307

Bakthin, M. 188
Bamblett, M. 105
Barad, K. 202
Battiste, M. 100
Belonging, Being and Becoming: The Early Years Learning Framework for Australia (EYLF) 104, 106
belonging education 15, 104–109
Beresford, Q. 107
Berry, A. B. 40
Best, M. 82
Bhutan: cultural influences, on teachers' views 303–305; cultural model, importance of 297–298; data analysis 300–301; education context of 294, **295**; formal school system 4; Gross National Happiness in 294–297; implications and recommendations 307–309; inclusion benefits 301–302; qualitative approach 299; research procedure 300; research setting and participants **299**, 299–300; topics, themes and subthemes **301**
Bhutan Ministry of Education 296
Bigoni, M. 131
biographical life-history 190–192
Birch, S. H. 105–106
Blanco, R. 233
Blanks, B. 40
blended learning (b-learning): academic skills 250; characteristics, of participants 243, **244**; collaborative spirit 249; context 235; course design, phases of 236–240, **237**, *238*; course management system 249; COVID-19 pandemic 251; designing 233–235; face-to-face component 249; implementation of 250; inferential tests 247; knowledge and teaching strategies 244–247, **246**; pre- and posttest results 243–244, **245**; psychopedagogical principles 235–236; regression analyses 248; self-efficacy beliefs 248–249; self-report instruments 240–243, **241**; technological skills learning 247
Booth, T. 232
Boylan, C. 34
Braunsteiner, M. L. 128, 130
Brayboy, B. M. J. 106
British Colonial education system 293
Bronfenbrenner, U. 105–106
Brown, P. 124
Buddhist monastic education 293
Burris, M. A. 218, 219

Cambodia, autism spectrum disorder in 137–138; diagnosis 142–143, 147–148; disabilities in 136–137, **137**; families with 139, *140*; medical treatment/social education 143–145, *144*; multi-case study 138–139; national call, for inclusion 145–146; overview of 135–136; prognosis, of inclusive education 148–149; reconciling difference, identification in 141–142; Trifecta of Support *146*, 146–147
Canada, Universal Design for Learning in 171
Center for Applied Special Technologies (CAST) 170
Center for Disease Control 137
Center for Universal Design 169
Certificate in Teaching Students with Hearing Loss program 52
CESA, *see* Complex Educational Systems Analysis
CHAT, *see* cultural-historical activity theory
Chee, C. W. 52
Chen Pichler, D. 46
Chilean schools, affects and materiality in: at centre of inclusion, in education 67–69; inclusive public policies in 69; ordinary moments at 70–73, *71*, *73*; special classroom 73–77, *74*, *76*
"chronic child cognitive fatigue," 46
'city of education,' in Indonesia 85
City Primary School 155–156, 164
Clinic for Youth Mental Health (CYMH) 138, 142, 143
close-knit teaching community 40
Cluley, V. 221
COAG, *see* Council of Australia Governments
collaborative professional learning 153–155
collective activism 279
collective responsibility 212
Colley, A. 2
Collins, P. H. 47, 48
community-related factors 36–38
Community Resource Unit 280–281
community support, inclusive education 93–94
competitive learning environments 128–129
Complex Educational Systems Analysis (CESA) 9, *9*, 16, 19
complex learning profiles, children with 29–31
conceptual innovation 5–10, *9*

conceptualisation, of inclusive education 91–92
Connell, B. R. 169
Constitution of Bhutan 293
contextually sensitive approach 89
Convention on the Rights of Persons with Disabilities (CRPD) 45–47, 81, 82, 84, 86, 173, 256, 279
Convention on the Rights of the Child (CRC) 173
Corbett, M. 35
Corcoran, T. 82
Council of Australia Governments (COAG) 104
course management system 249
Covid-19 pandemic 15, 251
Crenshaw, Kimberlé 47
Critical Race Theory 102
critical reflexivity: awareness and human agency 192–193; biographical life-history 190–192; description of 183–186; and dialogical self 188–189; established rationale and justification 189–190; and human agency 187–188; relevant to inclusive education 186–187; into teacher education 189; teachers' reconstruction 194–195
CRPD, *see* Convention on the Rights of Persons with Disabilities
cultural competence 104–106
cultural-historical activity theory (CHAT) 258, 259–260, *260*, 269, 271
culturally diverse population 232–233
Culturally Responsive Pedagogies of Success 102
Culturally Responsive Schooling 106
cultural relativism 31
CYMH, *see* Clinic for Youth Mental Health

Dakich, E. 277
Dalton, E. M. 171
Dart, J. 174
Davies, B. 204, 205
Davies, R. 174
Day Diary 107
deaf and hard of hearing (DHH) 13, 45–46; advancing policy 57–58; CRPD 47; insights on 46; intersectionality theory 47–48; language-centered guidance 47; Rwanda 48–50; Singapore 51–52; training and technical capacities 58–59; United States 52–54; Viêt Nam language 55–57
Deklarasi Bandung (2004) 83

Deklarasi Bukit Tinggi (2005) 83
Deleuze, G. 68
De Meulder, M. 47
democratic community, theories dealing with 10–11
Denborough, D. 278
Department of Education (2009) 121
DHH, *see* deaf and hard of hearing
dialogical self 188–189
Directorate of Special Education 83, 86
Disability Law 84
Disability Service Unit 86, 92
Disability Studies in Education (DSE) 200
Dorji, J. 297
Dorji, R. 305–306
Duk, C. 233
Duke, J. 257
Dukpa, D. 8, 305
Dye, M. W. G. 46
Dyson, A. 19, 232

EASNIE, *see* European Agency for Special Needs and Inclusive Education
Educating for GNH initiative 296, 305
Educational Strategic Plan (ESP) 268
Education for All (EFA) 31, 45
Education Law (2015) 173
education leadership, for inclusive education 13–14
Education White Paper 6 (WP6): Special Needs Education: Building an Inclusive Education and Training System 120
EFA, *see* Education for All
electronic learning (e-learning) 234
Emmorey, K. 46
emotional reactions 67–69, 175–176
Engelbrecht, P. 131
Engsig, T. T. 17, 257
ESP, *see* Educational Strategic Plan
ESTRAT Self-Rating Scale 242, 245, 248
ethic of discomfort 208
ethnography 69
European Agency for Special Needs and Inclusive Education (EASNIE) 11
European Association of History Educators (EUROCLIO) 174
Evans, D. 93

Farman, J. 208, 209
Fataar, A. 125
Flanders and New Zealand, *see* New Zealand and Flanders
Flemish documentary 201–202
Florian, L. 152, 154, 155, 160

Index 315

Forlin, C. 131
Fort, M. 131
Foucault, M. 208
Framework for Action on Special Needs Education 1
Franck, B. 36

Gagné, F. 124
Giangreco, M. F. 5
Global Education 2030 Agenda, The 94
Global Education Monitoring Report 2, 6, 86
global inclusive education 18, 257
Global Monitoring Report (2020) 31
GNH approach, *see* Gross National Happiness (GNH) approach
government-level stakeholders 262
Graham, L. 103
Gravelle, M. 40
Graven, M. 164
Gray, J. 107
Green, N. 34, 37, 40
Griful-Freixenet, J. 172
Gross National Happiness (GNH) approach 294–297, 303, 307
grounded theory 139
group work 177
Guattari, F. 68
Gulson, K. N. 125

Hale, C. 279
Hardy, I. 151
Hayes, A. 171
Hayes, D. 107
Higher Council for Persons with Disabilities (HCRPD) 262, 264–266
Hitch, D. 172
Hồ Chí Minh Sign Language (HCMSL) 56
"How do you keep moving?" story, of QCIE 283–285
Howley, A. 36–38
human agency, critical reflexivity and 187–188, 192–193
human rights 29–30

ICESCR, *see* International Convention on Economic, Social and Cultural Rights
Identity as Narrative (Sfard and Prusak) 163
IEPs, *see* Individual Education Plans
Imray, P. 2
inclusion, definition of 81
Inclusion Is Dead, Long Live Inclusion (Imray and Colley) 2
inclusion students/teachers, definition of 82

Inclusive Education Action Plan (2015) 92
Inclusive Education Concept Paper 173
Inclusive Education for Children with Special Needs and Children with Talent and Giftedness 83–84
Inclusive Education Isn't Dead, It Just Smells Funny (Slee) 2
inclusive pedagogical approach in action (IPAA) 152, 154, **155**; principles of 158–163; teacher agency, aspects of 155, **156**
Inclusive Teaching Practices Assessment Protocol-Self-report (GEPIA) 242, 246, 247
Independent Public School (IPS) 109
Index for Inclusion 125, 131
Indigenous storying methods 101
Individual Education Plans (IEPs) 54
Individualized Education Plan 147
Indonesia, inclusive education in: community support 93–94; conceptualisation of 91–92; description of 81–83; disabilities 83–85, 94; parent's voice 89–91; strong policy 92; student's voice 87–88; teacher's voice 88–89; Yogyakarta Province 85–87
INOVASI (2019) 93
instructional model 236–237
instruments, b-learning: attitudes assessment 242; characteristics of 240–241, **241**; digital abilities 243; inclusive education concepts 243; teaching practices assessment 242
International Convention on Economic, Social and Cultural Rights (ICESCR) 30
intersectionality theory 47–48
IPAA, *see* inclusive pedagogical approach in action
IPS, *see* Independent Public School
ipsative assessment 131

Jankélévitch, V. 210
Johnson, D. W. 125, 177
Johnson, R. T. 125, 177
Johnston, K. 107
Johnstone, C. J. 3, 171, 257
Jordanian inclusion policy 255; community 264–265; cultural-historical activity theory 259–260, *260*; exposing tensions in 260, **261**; labor division 266–268; lack of collaboration 272; at macro and mesa levels 256; macro view of 256; mediating artifacts 261–263; mesa policyscape contexts 257–258; policy documents 272;

policy-transfer theory 258–259; rules 268–269
Joshi, D. K. 36

Kahonde, C. 171
Kalyanpur, M. 257
Kamenopoulou, L. 305
Kelompok Kerja Guru (KKG) 93
Kenway, J. 77
King, A. 107
Kohn, A. 122
Kunc, N. 21

Ladd, G. W. 105–106
Lalvani, P. 279
language-rich education, for DHH learners, *see* deaf and hard of hearing
Latin America: inclusive education in 232–233; virtual learning in 233–234
Lazarus, S. 132
learning communities 236
Le Maire, D. 47
Lester, Eileen 99
Lewis, I. 222
Lewis, P. 105
Li, L. 155
Liasidou, A. 257
Lieblein, V. S. D. 105
Lomofsky, L. 132
Long, W. J. 294

Mace, Ron 169
Macfarlane, S. 172
Maitenes School: architectural programme 70–71, 71; classroom setting 70–72, 71, 73; reception office of 75–76, 76
Majoko, T. 121
Māori principles and values 200
Mariano-Lapidus, S. 128, 130
Marutyan, M. 171
Master Plan on National Development of Inclusive Education 85
Mavrou, K. 172
Mazurek, K. 256, 258
McCrimmon, A. W. 11
McDermott, R. 3
McKenzie, J. A. 171
Mead, George Herbert 184–185
medical model 7, 33
mesa levels 256; policyscape contexts 257–258
Messiou, K. 20
methodological innovation 5, 16–20
Miles, M. 306

Miles, S. 35, 40, 222, 257
Millennium Development Goals 6
Mind, Self, and Society (Mead) 184–185
Minister of Basic Education 123
Ministry of Education (MoE) 87, 262, 264, 266, 267
Ministry of Education, Youth and Sport (MoEYS) 135, 137, 145, 146, 148
Ministry of Health (MoH) 142, 145, 146, 148
Ministry of National Education 83
Ministry of Social Affairs, Veterans and Youth Rehabilitation (MoSAVYR) 137, 145, 146
Ministry of Social Development (MoSD) 262, 264, 266, 267
Mitchell, D. 297
mixed-learning, *see* blended learning
mobile learning (m-learning) 234
MoE, *see* Ministry of Education
MoEYS, *see* Ministry of Education, Youth and Sport
MoH, *see* Ministry of Health
MoSAVYR, *see* Ministry of Social Affairs, Veterans and Youth Rehabilitation
MoSD, *see* Ministry of Social Development
Most Significant Change framework 174
Mueller, C. 222–223, 225
multiple-track model 233
multi-rhythmic analysis 204
multi-sensory groups 177
Murray, J. J. 47
Musyawarah Guru Mata Pelajaran (MGMP) 93

Namgyel, S. 297
Nardotto, M. 131
narrative methodology 277
Nash, T. 233
National Aboriginal and Torres Strait Islander Education Policy (NATSIEP) 105, 108
National Center for Education Statistics (NCES) 32
National Education Department 83
National Institute for Special Education 135, 148
National Institute of Education in Singapore 189, 195
National Statement on Ethical Conduct in Human Research 300
NATSIEP, *see* National Aboriginal and Torres Strait Islander Education Policy
NCES, *see* National Center for Education Statistics

negative interdependence model 130
neurodiversity perspective, of autism 298
New National Curriculum (NNC) 172
New Zealand and Flanders: collective responsibility 212; complexity and multi-layeredness 212; Disability Studies in Education 200, 201; re-turn belonging, film scenes in 202–211, *203*, *207*
Nguyen, X. T. 8
Nihill, C. 172
Northern Territory (NT) 102, 109; juvenile justice system 108
Norwich, B. 18, 233, 307

Ochs, K. 178
Oliver, M. 17–18
one-way model 233
Oswald, M. 131, 151
"Our sudden birth" story, of QCIE 281–283
Ovalle School 66, *78*, 78–79

Pantić, N. 155, 160
PAR, *see* participatory action research
PARD, *see* Psycho-Education and Applied Research Center for the Deaf
parent activism 279
parent advocacy 277
parent's voice, inclusive education 89–91
participatory action research (PAR) 218–219
pedagogical strategies 185
Peraturan Daerah 86
Peraturan Gubernur 86
Peraturan Pemerintah 84
Peraturan Walikota 86
Phasha, N. 121
Phillips, D. 178
photo novella 218
photovoice methodology: accessibility 220–221; aims and procedural overview of 219–220; collective power of 222–223; firsthand stories and 229; flexibility 221; hearing contributions of *223*, 223–225, *224*; historical origins and theoretical underpinnings of 218–219; "out of bounds" photo *217*, 217–218; power redistribution 221–222; research utility of 220; seeing contributions of 225–228, *226*, *227*
PIE policy, *see* Programa de Integración Escolar (PIE) policy
Pink, S. 69
PISA report 103

PLCs, *see* Professional Learning Communities
policy-level stakeholder community 264
policy of assimilation 100
policy stakeholders 257, 258
'policy-to-practice gap,' 255, 256
policy-transfer theory 258
poorly resourced communities 30
poor-quality education 231
power redistribution, photovoice methodology 221–222
pragmatic innovation 5, 10–11; education leadership 13–14; flexibility 15–16; school cultures 14–15; training and professional practice 11–13
pre-service and in-service programs 233
Professional Learning Communities (PLCs) 152–153, 157–160, 165; collaborative learning 153, 154; discussions 156–157; sessions and topics 156, **157**
professional learning programmes 152
Programa de Integración Escolar (PIE) policy 69, 77
Prusak, A. 153, 163
Psycho-Education and Applied Research Center for the Deaf (PARD) 56–57
psychopedagogical principles, blended learning 235–236
Public Law n. 20 (2017) 266
Puelche School, special classroom 73–74, *74*

QCIE, *see* Queensland Collective for Inclusive Education
qualitative survey methodology 139
Queen Rania Teaching Academy 265
Queensland Collective for Inclusive Education (QCIE) 20, 276; advocacy 287; collective narrative 277–278; personal growth 287; relationships 288; story of 279–286, 287, 288; storytelling 277; strong leadership 287; "The stars had to align," 280–281
Questionnaire on Inclusive Education (IE-CON) 243, 247

Rahman, K. 106
Redwood-Jones, Y. A. 220
reflexive thematic analysis 299, 301
reflexivity, *see* critical reflexivity
Reggiani, T. G. 131
"regionalism," 31
Regulation No 41/2013 86
religious beliefs, to inclusive education 304–305

remoteness 31–32
response-ability, for teachers 212, 213n6
'rhetoric-to-reality gap,' 256, 258
Richards, Z. 123
Roberts, P. 35
Royal Government of Cambodia 138, 145
RSL, *see* Rwandan Sign Language
Rumdul School 139, 143, 144, 146; developed grass roots approach 148; matrix of instruction *144*
Runswick-Cole, K. 277
Ruppar, A. 155
rural contexts: children with complex learning profiles 29–31; defining rurality 31–32; inclusivity in 32–33; notion of Place 34–35; strengths-based approach, *see* strengths-based approach; teaching in 33–34
rural-deficit models 33
rurality, definition of 31–32
Rusznyak, L. 12
Rwanda: classroom settings and practical innovations in 49–50; DHH education & inclusive education in 48–49
Rwandan Sign Language (RSL) 49, 50
Ryan, S. 277

Said, E. 104
Salamanca Statement 1, 2, 31, 256
Samadi, S. A. 307
Sands, A. 103
Sauer, J. S. 222
Scholte, B. 185
Schön, Donald 185
school communities 14–15, 37
School Integration Programme 69, 74, 77
school leadership, for inclusive education 13–14, 16
school-related factors 38–39
Schools Providing Inclusive Education (SPIE) 84, 85
Schuelka, M. J. 3, 10, 17, 19, 257, 296–298, 306
SEE, *see* Signing Exact English
Self-efficacy in Implementing Inclusive Practices Scale (TEIP) 242
SEN, *see* special educational needs
Sentiments, Attitudes and Concerns about Inclusive Education Scale (SACIE) 242
Sfard, A. 152, 163
SHOWeD technique 219, 228
Signing Exact English (SEE) 51
Singapore: classroom settings and practical innovations in 51–52; DHH education & inclusive education in 51

Slee, R. 2, 3, 41, 82, 187, 257
Snoddon, K. 47
social cohesion 121
social constructivist theories 186
social interdependence theory 130
social model: from strengths-based approach 33; of disability 8
socio-cultural model 297
socioecological theory 35
Socio-economic Survey 135
"Something bigger than just ourselves" story, of QCIE 285–286
Song, S. 179
South Africa: academic talent 123–124; inclusive education in 120–122; meritocracy 124–125; teacher's interactions in 13
special educational needs (SEN) 12, 31, 67, 68, 73, 77, 293
Special Needs and Inclusive Education Policy 49
SPIE, *see* Schools Providing Inclusive Education
Spinoza, B. 68
Spratt, J. 152, 154
Standards for Inclusive Education 297
The Standards for Inclusive Education in Bhutan 294
Stapleton, K. 278
Steiner-Khamsi, G. 257–258
strengths-based approach 35–36; community-related factors 36–38; school-related factors 38–39; social model from 33; teaching practices 39–41
strong policy, inclusive education 92
Struyven, K. 172
student's voice, inclusive education 87–88
Student *t* test 243
Supporting Effective Teaching (SET) project 18
Sustainable Development Goals (SDGs) 6
Swart, E. 151
Sweller, N. 103
Symeonidou, S. 172

Tannock, S. 124
teacher education/teacher talk: agency 160–163, 166; collaborative learning 153–154; identity 158–160, 166; inclusive pedagogy 154; overview of 151–152; productive dissonance 163–166; professional learning, for inclusion 152–153, 166
teachers training programs 84
teacher's voice, inclusive education 88–89

technicist approach 189
Tejaningrum, D. 90
Telfer, D. 36–38
"The stars had to align" story, of QCIE 280–281
Thomas, G. 3
Three Spheres of Support Model for School Re-entry 139
TPACK model 243
Trifecta of Support *146*, 146–147
Tschumi, B. 78
21st century, inclusive education in 6, 10, 16
two-track model 233

Ubumwe Community Center (UCC) 49, 50
UDHR, *see* Universal Declaration of Human Rights
UDL, *see* universal design for learning
UN Convention on the Rights of Persons with Disabilities 7, 31
UNCRC, *see* United Nations Convention on the Rights of the Child
Underwood, K. 47
UNESCO 31, 232
UN General Assembly 31
UNICEF 30, 148
United Nations Convention on the Rights of the Child (UNCRC) 31
United States: classroom settings and practical innovations in 53–54; DHH education & inclusive education in 52–53; socio-cultural norms 147
Universal Declaration of Human Rights (UDHR) 30
universal design for learning (UDL) 15–16, 79, 89, 170, 242; color of victory 175–176; global literature review 171–172; guidelines for 170; key informant 174; methodology 173; multi-sensory groups 177; policy context 173; procedures 174; quizzes 176–177; revolution 170; secondary qualitative analysis 174; Van kingdom 175
Universal Design Principles 169–170

"universal usability," 178
Ura, K. 294, 295, 296, 302, 307
U.S. Census Bureau 32

value diversity 231
Van Bergen, P. 103
Van kingdom 175
Verdún, N. 234
Verstichele, M. 172
Việt Nam language : classroom settings and practical innovations in 56–57; DHH education & inclusive education in 55–56
virtual learning, in Latin America 233–234
visual methodologies, importance of 70
Volmink, J. 121

Waitoller, F. R. 187
Wallace, A. 34
Walqui, Á. 47
Walton, E. 12, 121–122, 125
Wang, C. C. 218–220
Warnock, M. 2
Watson, C. 103–104
Wenger, E.: conceptualisation of identity 165; imagination, alignment and engagement 165; "learning as social practice," 153; modes of belonging 154, **155**; modes of identity 159; theory of learning 152
WHO Cambodia Representative Office 147
Wilson, J. 278
Winzer, M. 256, 258
Woodcock, S. 151
World Conference on Special Needs Education 1
World Federation of the Deaf 45
World Health Organization 137, 147

Yogyakarta Province, inclusive education in 85–87
Yosso, T. J. 109
Youdell, D. 77

Taylor & Francis eBooks

www.taylorfrancis.com

A single destination for eBooks from Taylor & Francis with increased functionality and an improved user experience to meet the needs of our customers.

90,000+ eBooks of award-winning academic content in Humanities, Social Science, Science, Technology, Engineering, and Medical written by a global network of editors and authors.

TAYLOR & FRANCIS EBOOKS OFFERS:

- A streamlined experience for our library customers
- A single point of discovery for all of our eBook content
- Improved search and discovery of content at both book and chapter level

REQUEST A FREE TRIAL
support@taylorfrancis.com

Printed in the United States
by Baker & Taylor Publisher Services